THE
NATURAL HOUSE
BOOK

THE NATURAL HOUSE BOOK

David Pearson

A GAIA ORIGINAL

CONRAN OCTOPUS

A GAIA ORIGINAL
From an idea by David and Joss Pearson

The author gratefully acknowledges the help of the Consultants below and the contribution of natural architects, ecologists, and home-builders from many places and many times, whose achievements are represented here.

Project editor
Jonathan Hilton

Art editor
Bridget Morley

Editor
Lizzie Boyd

Assistant editor
Eva Webster

Research
Anna Kruger

Design assistance
Helen Spencer

Production
Susan Walby

Copy management
Lesley Gilbert

Special photography
Philip Dowell

Special artwork
Keith Banks

Photographic stylist
Jean Banks

Picture research
Shona Wood
assisted by
Penny Cowdry

Artists
Dick Bonson
Chris Forsey
Sally Launder
Sheilagh Noble
Ann Savage

Direction Patrick Nugent   Joss Pearson

First published in 1989 by
Conran Octopus Limited
37 Shelton Street
London WC2H 9HN

This edition published in 1991 by Conran Octopus Limited

Reprinted in 1995

British Library Cataloguing in Publication Data

The natural house book.
  1. Household management – Manuals
  I. Pearson, David
  640
  ISBN 1-85029-326-0

10 9 8 7 6 5 4 3

Filmset by Marlin Graphics Ltd, Sidcup, Kent
Reproduced by Adroit Photo Litho Ltd, Birmingham
Printed and bound in Spain by Artes Graficas Toledo, S.A.

About the author and consultants

David Pearson is an architect and planner with wide experience of inner city housing and new communities in both Britain and the US, a Harkness Fellow of the Commonwealth Fund of New York, and a post-graduate of the Universities of London and California. Now actively involved with the Gaia movement (inspired by the view of the Earth as a living planet), he is Director of the eco and health consultancy Gaia Environments, a founder member of the Institute of Building Biology, England, and in touch with ecological architects worldwide.

Debra Lynn Dadd, US consultant, is a well known and dedicated consumer researcher in nontoxic environments and wholistic planetary living, and author of *Non-Toxic and Natural* and *The Non-toxic Home*.

Dr Sydney A Baggs, Australian consultant, is a chartered architect/landscape architect/environmental impact consultant and an honorary research fellow in the Graduate School of the Built Environment at the University of New South Wales, and a recognized leader and pioneer in ecological housing, especially in the subject of his book, *Australian Earth-Covered Building*.

Dr Jean Monro, Consultant on Chapter Two, is Director of the Allergy and Environmental Medicine departments at two British hospitals and author, with Dr Peter Mansfield, of *Chemical Children*.

Hartwin Busch, Baubiologie consultant, is an architect and builder and Director of the Institute of Building Biology, England.

Richard Freudenberger, US consultant, is a Senior Editor at *Mother Earth News* magazine, specializing in home construction and improvement, conservation, and alternative energy. He also manages the magazine's in-house research and testing facility.

Foreword

From birth to death, each one of the 5 billion (and counting) inhabitants of this planet presses hard on the environment. If the Earth were a human being admitted to hospital, the prognosis would not be good and the patient would probably go on the critical list. Among the more alarming symptoms: an ulcerated atmosphere and a temperature rising steadily out of control.

Indeed, if any single problem has convinced governments around the world that environmental issues need to be at the heart of the political agenda for the 1990s, it has been the alarming trend of global warming caused by the accumulation of greenhouse gases in the atmosphere. At the same time, the discovery of the hole in the ozone layer above the Antarctic (and, more recently, the Arctic), and of the role of CFC aerosol propellants in ozone destruction, have vividly demonstrated that the finger of the ordinary consumer is often, quite literally, on the button of environmental destruction.

Many of us now realize that the decisions we take and the consumer choices we make throughout the day have an important, cumulative effect on the quality of our environment – both inside the home and outside. As a result, a new type of consumer is emerging: one who is prepared to make choices based on what is best for the planet and who demands that products and services don't "cost the earth".

The commercial impact of the new consumer awareness has been extraordinary, with major supermarket groups beginning to see the virtue of turning into "Green Purchasers" and insisting that manufacturers provide "environmentally friendly", natural products for use in and around the home.

To have any real hope of safeguarding the wellbeing of the planet, we all need to fight the environmental battle on the home front. From designing, restoring, maintaining, and cleaning to adapting and furnishing, as David Pearson makes clear, our homes draw on natural resources, expose us to potentially dangerous indoor pollution, and even contribute to global problems such as the greenhouse and ozone effects.

So how do we turn sick homes into healthy ones? The answer, as this book forcefully points out, is firmly in your hands. Whether you live in a flat, a terraced house in an inner-city suburb, or a detached country cottage, you will find that **The Natural House Book** pulls together a wealth of innovative ideas and hard-to-find factual reference to ensure that, instead of being part of the problem, your home starts to become part of the solution.

JOHN ELKINGTON

CONTENTS

Introduction

This book has been written at a time when global environmental concerns have become urgent. No longer are they minority interests discussed only by academics, campaigned for by environmentalist groups, or merely the subject of occasional wildlife documentaries. It is also written in the context of growing public anxiety about polluted water supplies, contaminated food, and the level of chemical exposure we are all subjected to in our ordinary lives. The tendency is to see these areas as separate and as being too large for us to cope with, and almost always as being for others to deal with. But the truth is that these problems are interlinked and often have the same roots in our daily lives. And they *are* too big for individuals or separate governments to solve alone. The only way is for all of us to tackle them together.

"Well body, well earth" was a phrase coined in the US not long ago. It communicates the vital message that our health and that of the planet are inextricably linked. For, just as we need good health to stay alive, so, too, does the planet in order to be able to support us and all the other life forms.

At present we are making the planetary systems ill and, as a result, becoming ill ourselves. What we must do is reverse this trend – heal ourselves and, in the process, heal the planet. Unless we find ways to make ourselves better, we may never be in a situation to remedy the wider damage we are doing. It is unfortunately true that the environmental sickness has already spread to our homes, creating the modern phenomenon of the "sick building syndrome". Our homes are so much a part of the planetary sickness and we should really be saying: "well body, *well home*, well earth."

We all care about our homes and spend time, effort, and money trying to make them more comfortable. For most of us, our homes represent the biggest investment we ever make; they are, lifelong, a centre of our concern and our wellbeing. So it probably comes as something of a shock when you realize that the home today can be a very uncaring place – uncaring of us, and uncaring of the environment. Our homes can damage our health, the air we breathe, and the water we drink without our even being aware of it. But "home" doesn't stop at the front door: it affects, and is affected by, its surroundings. If we were as conscious of the needs of the environment as we are of the needs of our homes, it would indeed be the first step in changing the world.

The global crisis

Everyday, it seems, we hear of new and worrying developments in the approaching ecological disaster – virgin Brazilian rainforest the size of Belgium devastated in a single year; global warming from greenhouse gases, with the real danger of worldwide flooding as the polar caps melt; the disappearing ozone layer and the increasing risks of skin cancer; pollution causing acid rain that is killing forests, rivers, and lakes; polluted air, water, and food. The list is growing, and what seemed like isolated events in distant places a few years ago, are now reaching across our very doorsteps.

Nobody knows just how much punishment the planet will take before it reacts – or how strong the reaction might be. What is certain, though, is that the reaction has already started, and it started some years ago, with increasing desertification, crop failures, and starvation. And the combined effect of individual disasters may set in train a complex series of unpredictable events – global warming, currently thought to be the key danger, could bring dramatic climate changes everywhere, and threaten life in all its forms. A continuing increase in global temperatures would lead to more deserts, both in the developed and developing worlds, and cause dramatic changes in plant life, from tree cover to agriculture; it would bring increasing food shortages and, worse, massive flooding of lowlands, devastating many countries, and reducing global land area. But well before these changes could take full effect, the pressures they would bring would cause worldwide instability and, perhaps, a new type of conflict as the main powers defended and extended their command over increasingly scarce resources.

It may seem a big jump to be talking of global conflicts in the same breath as how we design our homes – the central subject of this book. But the two are intimately linked through our consumption patterns – and it is only by changing our own lives and homes that we can begin to save the environment. Time is too short and the issues too urgent for them to be solely national preoccupations, let alone party political wrangles. The problems must be managed on a global scale with the open-handed participation of every individual. But how is this co-operation to be achieved? Many people feel that the chances of this happening in time, or at all, are very slim. Like a massive supertanker that takes miles to reach full speed and miles to stop, the damage to the environment takes a long time to be perceived, and even longer to be reversed. Even if concerted action were to be taken now, it could take centuries in order for the damage to be repaired – to replace, for example, devastated tropical rainforests and ecosystems.

But we can't wait. If governments and industry are going to drag their feet, it falls to individuals to take action – and many people are. It is at last being realized, even by the most cynical, that "green" concerns are not just another fashionable vogue; they are here to stay. We are entering a new age when these concerns will increasingly become accepted parts of our everyday lives. Countries and regions, such as West Germany, Denmark, and Scandinavia, have long recognized the importance of these issues and have a highly developed awareness at all levels of society. Not only is there this awareness, there is also an impressive record of preventative and remedial action.

Although by no means ecologically perfect, these societies today are already living the future way of life, in which the things you buy, the way you travel, dispose of your waste, educate your children, and build your offices and houses all demonstrate this new respect for the environment and care for personal health. In North America and Australia the change is more localized, and although public awareness is growing and beginning to demand action, industry and government are farther behind. Britain, until recently, was thought to be almost ecologically blind. But, surprisingly to many, public opinion polls show that environmental issues are now thought to be the greatest threat to the future – greater even than the risk of nuclear war. The polls also show that most people would be happy to help in simple ways by pre-sorting

houshold rubbish and recycling more waste if the facilities existed – and this attitude is the same in many parts of the world.

"Green" issues are suddenly everywhere in the media, and there are encouraging signs that the message is finally getting through to governments and industry, who will eventually be obliged to respond positively to this new public demand. Consumer power and the vote are strengths we are beginning to wield to effect.

We are also beginning to realize that there are two sides to every coin, and that the consumer choices we make can have far-reaching effects and do harm to people and places far away – people we have never met and places we have never seen. The Communication Age has brought about an increased awareness of the global links in human affairs and the inequity, especially in the developing world, of which we are a part. How should we feel about buying a healthy, nonpolluting product for our home knowing that it may possibly have caused ill health, suffering, or damage at source – where it was made or processed?

The developed world – North America, Europe, Australia, the USSR, and Japan – may comprise only one-quarter of world population but it consumes up to three-quarters of world resources, and is thus responsible for the bulk of global environmental impact. Meat consumption in richer countries leads to rainforest clearance for cattle ranchers (the famous "hamburger connection"); pesticides that are banned at home are exported to developing countries. The public is increasingly demanding the right to know how and under what conditions products are made. We are now more conscious, too, that we waste resources that others may need and, in particular, that those who have the luxury of being able to consider conservation,

Contents page: House at Stavanger, Norway, by Cobolt Architects.

Overleaf: For thousands of years, the nomadic peoples of the vast territory stretching from Iran to Mongolia have lived in portable, willow-framed houses, or yurta, *covered with felt and canvas.*

rather than survival, have the greater responsibility for the survival of us all.

Personal health

The risk to our personal health from the home and environmental causes is a more recent concern. The chemical pollution that is harming the planet also means that indoor air is often more polluted than that outdoors. We are exposed in our homes to the hidden effects of gases and vapours from synthetic materials made from petrochemicals, to heavy metals and pesticides in water and food, and to the same combustion pollutants that cause acid rain.

Bad health from this complex mix of causes is increasing. Allergies and undiagnosed illness are affecting more and more people, who have to go to specialists in environmental medicine or to alternative therapists for the help they cannot obtain from conventional medicine. Understanding of healthy products and design in the home has lagged behind other fields of consumer interest, such as food and medicine. Whereas health foods and natural health are now well established and accepted by large numbers of people, the concept of the "healthy home" is novel to most people. Ironically, the same people who select "natural" personal care products and organic foods are still likely to choose furnishings, paints, and DIY items made of materials containing the very burden of chemical additives that they have rejected for food and body care.

Understanding the need to extend healthy living directly into the home, its materials, and its services has come first in West Germany and is now growing in the rest of Europe, while in the US and Australia the demand for a "nontoxic home" is beginning. Consumer power has yet to make itself really felt in the field – labelling of product contents is almost non-existent and many manufacturers seem unaware that there is even any problem.

The spirit of home

Home is more than the total of its parts. It is our spiritual centre, our place to be. A house can be healthy, yet still lack the spirit of home we need. In fact, many people are put off ecology and health concerns by the feeling of restriction, worthiness, even self-righteousness they sometimes convey. We seem constantly to be having to give up things we like, whereas a home should be a place of comfort and healing, a place where we feel in harmony with ourselves and all of life. This sense of belonging and being part of the natural world, which is the source of true wellbeing, is fundamental to the new vision of ecology with its concept of our planet as "Gaia" – a living entity seeking, like the original Earth goddess of the Greeks, always to create and sustain life. Far from being masters of nature, we are an integral part of Gaia. Real ecology is not about giving up; it is about joining in – co-operating with nature and actively seeking a balance between health, conservation, and the spirit in our lives.

It is these three interwoven strands of the Gaian approach that form the subject matter of this book. It brings to bear the wisdom and practical knowledge of many cultures to show you how to balance the demands of ecology, health, and spirit and create a natural house integrated with the natural systems around it. Natural homes are not new. Quite the reverse. They are the way people have always built instinctively until the modern age divorced us from this understanding.

To support personal and planetary health, we need healthy and conserving homes; homes that help us to lead a new lifestyle; homes that are designed not to damage the environment but to bring positive regeneration to it; homes, in fact, that are not sick, but are healing places for body, mind, spirit, and planet.

How to use this book

This book is divided into three parts. The first describes how your home interacts with the environment and with you. The second deals with all the components of a home, showing you how to build, service, and furnish it for health and ecology. And the third applies all the principles introduced in the book to the design of spaces in the home. It is not necessary to read these parts, or indeed chapters, in any particular order, but you will find the charts in Chapter Two and in the Appendices a helpful cross-reference source for the rest of the book.

PART ONE
THE WHOLE HOUSE

Chapter One
THE NATURAL HOUSE

"There is one timeless way of building. It is thousands of years old, and the same today as it always has been." Christopher Alexander, *The Timeless Way of Building*

Health for the body, peace for the spirit, harmony with the environment – these are the criteria of the natural house. All three have deep roots in the human experience and in the ethnic traditions of home building in cultures across the world – the "timeless way". But in the last two centuries the Western tradition has turned aside from such understanding, and respect for the criteria of the natural home has moved to the fringes – to the alternative health, environment, and wholistic "New Age" groups. The pioneers of natural architecture have been many – from Frank Lloyd Wright to the Japanese, from Baubiologie in Germany, appropriate technology in Wales, and earth-sheltered homes in Australia to biospheres in the USA. More and more, the strands of health, ecology, and spirit are coming together – the new architecture is alive and well. Ideas and technologies that seemed revolutionary a few years ago are more widespread and natural products more available.

Great areas of the planet were once covered by forests rich with a profusion of plants, birds, and animals. Our ancestors, few in number, roamed at will living from anything to hand and moving on as the seasons changed and animals migrated. From archeological evidence, and from contact with surviving remote peoples, it is becoming evident that these cultures were far from primitive. They were (and, where they still survive, are) as sophisticated in many ways as modern urban society. They accumulated over generations a very detailed and intimate knowledge of everything around them – climate, seasons, animals, and plants. Their lives may have been more insecure, but they enjoyed more freedom and an intimate relationship with a world still untouched and beautiful.

Home to these first peoples was their whole territory and spiritual landscape. Caves, trees, grass shelters, and hide tents provided natural and traditional temporary campsites for different seasons. By the millennial clock of our existence, it is only in the last minute of the eleventh hour that we have changed our primordial living patterns and started to build permanent homes and settlements. Indeed some archeologists now think that the life of the

Early human settlements took maximum advantage of local topography for security and to give shelter from both cold winds and heat from the sun. The remains of a Moki Indian cliff dwelling (left), high up on the face of Lake Canyon, overlooking Lake Powell, Utah, is typical of many such natural shelters.

Standing in the middle of fir trees and moss-covered boulders, a modern Scandinavian house (right), continues an ancient tradition. Sited carefully to retain the forest trees, and slightly raised to leave the ground untouched, the house respects the locality and minimizes its impact. Architect: Kai Lohman

early hunter-gatherers was not willingly exchanged for the relative security of settled agriculturalism, but only under pressure of increasing population and decreasing wild resources. The change meant the gradual loss of that deep spiritual contact with all their fellow species, the earth, and the heavens. In their dreamtime walkabouts, Australian Aborigines still seek this today as they follow ancestral spirit paths to sacred sites.

The earliest settlements and much of indigenous architecture throughout history since, nonetheless, continued to express a close link with nature. Everywhere across the world there are diverse and ingenious types of ethnic housing, built of local materials that sit comfortably in the landscape, and respond well to local climate. They follow generic vernacular types that have taken thousands of years of trial and error to perfect.

There is a danger that when we look at houses of primitive or unfamiliar cultures we misinterpret what we see. As Enrico Guidoni stresses in his book *Primitive Architecture*, there is a tendency to over-emphasize the influence of local climate and materials and to underestimate the importance of the social, cultural and spiritual context. Not all ethnic houses are appropriate to their climate nor do local people, even when given sufficient natural resources and space, automatically make the best use of their materials. The Masai house (see p. 144), for example, is too low to stand upright in and smoke from cooking fires fills the inside. Nevertheless, most ethnic homes around the world manage both

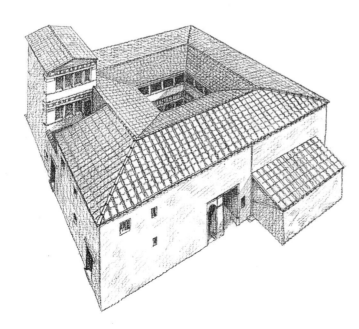

The climate of the Mediterranean and North Africa gave birth to the enclosed courtyard house with its massive earth walls and cool interior plantings (left). The hot and wet areas of the tropics and Far East produced open, raised platform houses, typified by the Malays and Japanese (above far left). Cold dry regions and mountain areas led to the earth- or turf-covered home of the Norse lands and the North American Indians (above left), while temperate and damp lowland countries turned to the brick and timber frame of the cottage (above).

The city of Pueblo Bonito, Chaco Canyon, New Mexico, was built by Anasazi Indians in the 12th century AD, and it once housed 1200 people in its semi-circular and tiered structure. Oriented according to the sun's winter and summer solstices, it maintained a balanced temperature, day and night, summer and winter, and gave protection from the cold mountain winds. Within its stone and adobe terraces were sacred kivas, *underground ceremonial chambers, for the observance of seasonal fertility rituals.*

to integrate spiritual and physical needs and to be in harmony with the local environment.

Early city builders may have understood better than we do the principles of natural ecology. The Greeks appreciated the benefits of the sun and even treated equal access to sunlight as a legal right. They planned the city of Olynthus in the 5th century BC with streets oriented so they all received equal sun. In the New World, Pueblo Bonito showed as great a sophistication (see above). The terraced "sky city" of the Acoma Indians near Albuquerque constructed on a sheltered mesa also ensured the "sun rights" of all houses, even when the sun was at its lowest in winter. Thick adobe walls absorbed the heat of the day and released it at night while straw and adobe roofs gave insulation against the hot summer sun.

Concern for healthy housing has a long history, too. Evidence from ancient cities, such as those built by the Sumerians, or in the Indus Valley, and by the Egyptians, Greeks, and Romans, indicates a developed and sometimes sophisticated understanding of health and comfort. Piped water and cisterns, hypocaust underfloor heating, hot baths, and steam rooms, toilets and sewers, courtyards cooled with pools and fountains, and gardens of medicinal herbs all existed. Most of this earlier knowledge was lost in Europe in the Dark Ages after the fall of the Roman Empire. But in many other cultures it remained a continuing tradition, from thermal baths in Japan to the sweat lodges of the North American Indian.

Today, many agencies in developing countries are seeking to draw on the rich heritage of ethnic building and combine it with modern appropriate technology to provide self-build housing. And it is often to the ethnic tradition that modern natural architecture turns for its inspiration in seeking new solutions to old problems – of climate, health, and the sense of home.

The Western tradition

In the 18th century, the vernacular, craft-based traditions in Europe were first disturbed by the Agrarian Revolution. Large land enclosures and rich landlords displaced self-built communities and imported foreign styles and materials were introduced for manor houses and merchant city homes. Homes and towns still, however, retained much of their former grace and integrity to the landscape and the local climate.

The American settlers developed new ecological traditions in response to their adopted land. New England "saltbox" houses were built with their high side to catch the sun and the low, sloping roof at the back turned to the prevailing winter winds. The ovens and fireplaces formed a central core to heat the surrounding rooms efficiently and some rooms were closed off in winter, too. In summer, a pergola hung with vines shaded the sunny side from excessive heat. In the hot and humid Southern states, great ingenuity was used to

In a Dogon village in Mali
(left), earth-built houses,
animal stalls, and thatched
granaries are all symbolic of
their ancient myths. The thick-
roofed toguna, meeting place,
is upper right.

Desert settlements, such as the one in Algeria
(above), are densely packed to expose little to
the sun except the barrel-vaulted roofs and
domes of the houses.

A mother and her young child sit outside
their grass-thatched, circular earth home in
India (below).

cool homes with cross-ventilation. Open as well as shuttered verandahs and passages cooled the classic plantation mansions while a straight-through corridor served to ventilate the humble "dogtrot" house. In the drier Southwest and Mexico, the Spanish adapted their mediterranean heritage to the hacienda, ranch, and adobe house and the city square, or *zocala*.

It was the Industrial Revolution that finally ended the thousands of years of the "timeless way". More than the mechanization it brought, it was the new world view that was to change our direction so completely. The Industrial Age ushered in a belief in mastery of nature by science and machines, and a change to a mass society. In terms of the home, the consequences were a move away from the individually craft-built houses in villages or small towns to uniform and anonymous urban terraces close-packed around the factory, mill, or mine and, later, radiating outward from the city centre in great bands of suburbs. People were no longer involved in shaping or understanding their own role in the wider environment.

Not only was the ecology of housing lost but health, long neglected in the home, became a major problem. It was not until mid 19th century reformers, such as William Cobbett, decried the appalling rural social conditions and Sir Edwin Chadwick surveyed those of the urban poor that large landowners and the British government were forced to realize that improvements must be made. Overcrowding, disease, lack of sanitation, and dark and airless conditions roused humanitarian feeling. Much of the impetus of the modern age has been a progressive struggle to remedy these ills – a struggle only just beginning in many developing countries.

By the end of the 19th century, the evils of the machine age were being attacked by John Ruskin, William Morris, and others in the Arts and Crafts Movement. Its emphasis on craft revival, appropriate use of materials, and simple functional designs, although influential, looked back toward a medieval dream world and only catered for an aesthetic élite. But the domestic revival of older English styles, as at The Red House, Kent, built by architect Philip Webb for Morris, inspired many informal and comfortable country houses, later to be emulated by the inventive and picturesque mansions of Sir Edwin Lutyens. Interest in America's historic vernacular buildings was revived by the New England "Shingle Style" and in California by the Greene brothers with their love of crafted woods, such as the redwood Gamble House.

The romantic domestic style that flourished in England from the 1890s to 1914 was also the style adopted by the early garden cities and suburbs. Popularized by Ebernezer Howard's book *Garden Cities of Tomorrow*, the concept of building town-housing in green environments was adopted in the US by Clarence Stein for such remarkable projects as Radburn, New Jersey. Health was one motivation behind the Garden City Movement, with its vision of families living in well-designed housing far away from city smoke. From Reston and Columbia in America to Welwyn Garden City and Milton Keynes in England, the vision has become a successful reality; but it takes more than a generation for a mature community to emerge, with a sense of home and locality.

Far from being hostile to the Industrial Age, the pioneer architects of the Modern Movement of the early 20th century were passionately inspired by it. They sought to destroy "dead styles" and find a new honesty, advocating an International Style. Walter Gropius, Le Corbusier, and Mies van der Rohe were the new "gods" and their influence redirected mainstream architecture into radically opposite paths from those of the past. The new vocabulary – flat roofs, plain surfaces, white cubist forms – and such new materials as reinforced concrete, steel, and plate glass and glass blocks were used boldly and with deliberate disregard for local conditions. Rather than the house being part of the natural surroundings, it stood out or even "floated" above the ground on steel *pilotis* (columns) like some sort of machine.

Ecologically philistine, the Modern Movement expressed a new health awareness in its clean, light, and airy spaces, sunny terraces resembling the decks of ocean liners, and its solaria, gymnasiums, and clean, minimally furnished interiors. Since World War II, the International Style has come to dominate our cities. But the high towering blocks replacing streets of small terrace houses and gardens have been extremely unpopular in many countries, and some have already been demolished. And architects are fighting new style battles again – Post-Modern, Neo-Classical, or Neo-Vernacular – while many of the general public are reverting to the familiar and nostalgic styles of the past.

One outstanding architect remained a strongly dissenting voice in the modern age. The houses of American architect Frank Lloyd Wright embodied the deeper ecological principles of natural building. He intended them to be at home in nature and grow "out of the ground and into the light". His concept of organic architecture not only meant design that worked with natural conditions but design that was an organic whole, like a living organism. Because it was "living", it was a dynamic process and for this reason he believed that "no organic building can ever be 'finished'" – it continues to respond to its environment and its occupants. In his own book *The Natural House* he also emphasized the importance of integrity – that a house should be "integral to site, integral to environment and integral to the life of the inhabitants".

Modern architecture, in losing connection with its roots in traditional building, has lost much – the craft of materials, the understanding of climate and adaption to site, the sense of place and locality, the spiritual links of home and family and community. Had it been Frank Lloyd Wright, rather than Le Corbusier, who became the model for our age, our cities and homes would have developed in a very different direction over the past 50 years. Today, at last, there are signs of a reawakening to the needs of communities and natural environment.

Ecological houses

While mainstream architecture and building turned a blind eye to ecology, new directions were being explored in other fields. The twin roots of modern eco-housing were the conservation movement and alternative, or "appropriate", technologies.

Concern for the protection of nature is very old, but until the 19th century it was usually the prerogative of princes. Then came the great American concern for "wilderness", voiced by John Muir, with the founding of Yellowstone Park in 1872, the Sierra Club in 1892, and Britain's National Trust in the following year. The movement continued to grow and spread. In the 1960s, Rachel Carson's *Silent Spring* alerted the world to the dangers of pollution; The World Wildlife Fund, Friends of the Earth, and Greenpeace began. The household consumer was increasingly targeted in campaigns to save energy and water, recycle, and stop using harmful products. In the mid 1980s, planetary awareness awakened and the Gaia movement emerged, inspired by James Lovelock's *Gaia: A New Look at Life on Earth*. This book describes the Earth and all its life systems as an entity, Gaia (the ancient Greek Earth goddess), which is self-sustaining and has the characteristics of a living organism. The 1980s also saw "deep ecology", and its concerns with a change of personal direction. In deep ecology, the house is seen as an micro-ecosystem, interacting with the wider ecosystem of Gaia.

Thinking of the house as an ecosystem seems to strike many people as something new and strange. But it is only a current way of expressing what people once knew instinctively and did not need to put into words. The very word ecology is derived from the Greek *oikos*, meaning house. In the study of ecology, animals and birds are all said to live in their own "habitats" and their lives, food, and

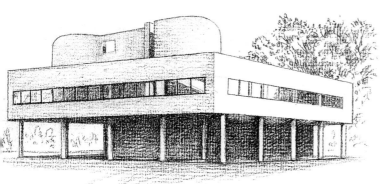

Villa Savoie at Poissy, France, by Le Corbusier, 1928-30.

The traditional American "dogtrot" house of the hot and humid southern states is an excellent cooling design (left). The straight passage funnels air through the middle of the house, drawing the hot air out and the cooler air in. New homes are now using older, passive cooling methods.

Built as a semicircle, this house (right) is designed for passive solar gain, with a suntrap in the front, an earth mound to deflect cold winds at the back, and massive stone walls. The Jacobs' House, Wisconsin by Frank Lloyd Wright, 1949.

The fine antebellum mansion "The Shadows" on the Bayou Teche, Louisiana (below) was built in 1830. Its verandahs, shuttered sitting areas, and open corridors were designed so that every room had at least two sides exposed to the cooling breezes of cross-ventilation.

nests are part of chains, or flows, of material and energy, each dependent on the other. An ecological balance exists, since all these interactions contribute to maintaining a dynamic equilibrium. In the past, our houses used to be more closely part of the local ecosystem – built of local materials, dependent on local energy, food, and water, and recycling wastes locally. But today, in suburbs and cities, we need to relearn this and apply it in the urban setting: making the most of the shelter from surrounding buildings, planting vegetation for more, and adapting for solar heating and cooling, and recycling systems.

The search for alternative, ecologically based technologies is also old. Many attempts have, for example, been made to harness the sun's energy using scientific principles. In the 1880s, the printing press of *Le Journal Soleil* was powered by a solar steam engine and in 1908 Frank Schuman, an American scientist-inventor, devised a prototype "flat plate" collector – the basis of solar panels used today. For the 1933 Chicago World's Fair, the Keck brothers designed the "Crystal House" – a show house with walls of glass and heat-absorbing masonry. In France, the architect Felix Trombe devised a glass and masonry solar wall (see p. 72),

while from 1939 to 1961 the Massachusetts Institute of Technology systematically researched and developed solar design in their four experimental campus houses. At this time, too, the unique inventor-philosopher Buckminster Fuller pioneered startling house technologies, from the factory-made Dymaxion House to geodesic domes or "space frames" – fertile ideas for eco-design.

In the 1960s, it was only the solar pioneers such as Dr George Löf who actually lived in solar houses – the others were used as laboratories. Then, as he said, "there were nine solar buildings in the world, including my own house". But the 1973 oil crisis triggered the growth of hundreds of solar homes, especially in the USA, as well as renewing interest in conserving and alternative technologies generally. These were then adopted by owner-builders such as Ken Kern and the emerging communal groups. Steve Baer built his dome cluster New Mexico house with its water-drum walls and insulating rooflight "skylids"; the Farallones Institute, Berkeley with the eco-architect Sim van der Ryn created the "integral urban house". In 1974 E F Schumacher's book *Small is Beautiful* was published, providing a philosophy for self-sufficiency. In

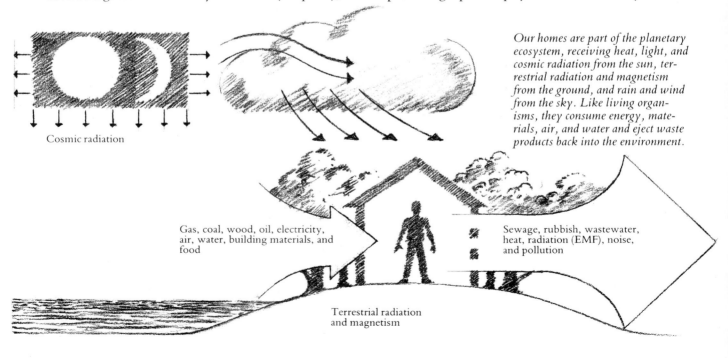

Cosmic radiation

Our homes are part of the planetary ecosystem, receiving heat, light, and cosmic radiation from the sun, terrestrial radiation and magnetism from the ground, and rain and wind from the sky. Like living organisms, they consume energy, materials, air, and water and eject waste products back into the environment.

Gas, coal, wood, oil, electricity, air, water, building materials, and food

Sewage, rubbish, wastewater, heat, radiation (EMF), noise, and pollution

Terrestrial radiation and magnetism

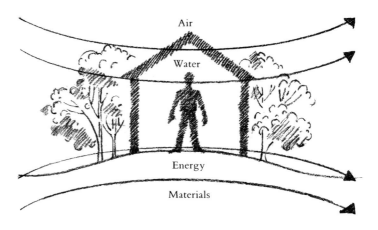

Wales, The Centre for Alternative Technology became a show centre and self-sufficient community to popularize "soft" energy and recycling systems. And among people concerned for the developing world, the movement for Intermediate Technology began to develop locally appropriate building techniques and energy systems based on wind, water, biomass, and solar designs. Many research groups on eco-housing were set up in the 1970s and 80s and many experimental projects begun. The Ecology House in Toronto and the Rocky Mountain Institute with its beautiful Visitor Center are good examples.

Alongside these developments comes a renewed interest in traditional building materials – timber, reed, stone, earth, and brick – and in building with waste materials, from bottles to paper and board. There has been a revival, too, of earth-covered homes. Architects Sydney Baggs in Australia, Arthur Quarmby in England, and Malcolm Wells in the US, plus the Underground Space Center, Minnesota, have all built attractive and extremely energy-efficient homes.

The most ambitious project in modern ecodesign is Biosphere 11. It is to be completed in 1990 and replicates seven of the planet's "biomes", from rainforest to savannah, in an airtight, sealed glass spaceframe, built in the Arizona desert. The ecological systems inside will recycle the air, water, and nutrients to maintain the life of the 3800 plant and animal species and eight human researchers who will be isolated within it.

Modern houses (above) are wasteful in their consumption and pollute the environment. The basic resources of air, water, energy, and materials have all become part of a throughput system that takes but does not give in return. Air and water are polluted, energy and materials are wasted. The damage is far reaching and the effects long term. By making the whole house into a recycling system (below), all the resources are used with care and economy, so the house becomes, as it once was, a part of the local ecosystem and supports its health and sustainability.

The healthy house

Concern over personal health and the effect of toxins *inside* the home, as opposed to those exported from it as pollutants, has been largely ignored by the ecology movement. Until recently, most people in the West felt their homes were healthy – much healthier than in the past – and that this had been achieved by modern technology.

But we are now facing new problems caused by the very technology that was designed to improve our lives – the puzzling "Sick Building Syndrome", badly polluted air and drinking water, chemical vapours, and synthetic building materials,

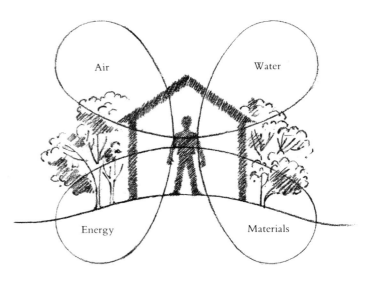

and fields from electrical supply and appliances all make us worried about just how healthy our houses really are. The flourishing alternative health movement has begun to spill over into housing and lifestyle. Western consumers are turning to new diets, fitness regimes, and self-care health and they are increasingly aware of chemical triggers in the environment as the source of disease or allergy.

The new disciplines of clinical ecology and environmental medicine reflect growing research evidence, especially from America, that illness is often as attributable to environmental factors as it is to infection or organic disease. In 1980, Dr Alfred V Zamm alerted the American public to hazards in their homes with his book *Why Your House May Endanger Your Health*. In England, Dr Jean Monro has set up a specialist allergy hospital designed as a toxin-free environment. Allergy sufferers and concerned consumers in the US and Canada are taking matters into their own hands, seeking out safer alternatives, and campaigning for them. Debra Lynn Dadd's *The Non-toxic Home* offers choices to the new consumer, and architects in various parts of the US are designing toxin-free housing.

The most advanced movement at present is that developed in German-speaking countries. Born of disenchantment with much post-war building, and of the prevalent green awareness and concern about chemical pollution from synthetic building materials, *Baubiologie* (building biology) is a wholly new concept in architecture. It combines a scientific approach with a wholistic view of the relationship between people and their buildings. The house is compared with an organism and its fabric to skin – a third skin, which, like our own skin (and our clothes, the second skin), fulfils essential living functions: protecting, insulating, breathing, absorbing, evaporating, regulating, and communicating. Baubiologie aims to design buildings that meet our physical, biological, and spiritual needs. Their fabric, services, colour, and scent must interact harmoniously with us and the environment. This constant exchange between inside and outside depends on a transfusive skin to maintain a healthy, "living" indoor climate.

But many of our modern homes are now sealed units and have thus become sick. Plastic vapour barriers, concrete floors, airtight windows and

The earth used for the walls of this house in West Germany (left) was dug from the site and extruded into long sausage shapes. They were then stacked to form the walls and the shrinkage joints filled later to give a smooth finish. Architect: G Minke

The "dome a barreau" at Agen, France, (above right) designed by Francis Séguinel captures solar heat through the glass wall and stores it in a central heat core at the top of the dome.

The architect Floyd Stein (right) relaxes in a solar balcony he designed for this Copenhagen apartment block.

Fire, water, and earth were the themes for this house (far right) at Linzenbach, Germany. Water surrounds the living space, the roof is covered with earth, and there is fire in the central core. Architect: Horst Schmitges

doors, insulation foam, and impermeable layers of plastic paints and adhesives, all wrap-up the building so tightly that it cannot breathe. Being a sealed system, it traps stale air and chemical vapours inside until they reach concentrations that can cause disease. The natural materials we used in the past have largely been replaced by or treated with synthetics. Not only do these emit potentially harmful vapours, you usually cannot recycle them, and so add to the burden of pollution on the environment.

Baubiologie has reintroduced traditional, natural materials and building methods, such as solid-timber frames, clay blocks with lime mortar and plaster, and earth building and grass roofs, often improved by recent research. The materials are handled with great sensitivity, all the paints, treatments, and finishes are organic, and colour and light are consciously used for health. It employs techniques from eco-architecture for heating and ventilation by natural systems, together with older traditions, such as the German tile oven. And it seeks to site the house and design the interior in recognition of our links with nature and our spiritual wellbeing.

Siting and design are also influenced by the potential dangers of electromagnetic fields (EMFs) and static, both from high-voltage power lines and from domestic electricity, appliances, and synthetic materials. EMF radiation emanates from the ground, too, and when disturbed by underground faults and streams it can be a source of a disease known as geopathic stress. By contrast, homes with steel frames, reinforced concrete, and pipes and ducts, may act like a cage to block out or disturb energy fields beneficial to us. Indeed, Baubiologie sees our health as dependent on our contact with the normal ambient energy levels of the Earth. Ground surveys, which may include dowsing and examining plants and trees, are used to map energy zones.

Divining and dowsing have been studied by German scientists since the 1920s, when some illnesses were first linked with ground radiation. Since then Dr Manfred Curry and Dr Ernst Hartmann have proposed that EM from the ground runs in a grid or net, and sites where two grids cross are the most hazardous to personal health.

Our skin is vital to our health and comfort. Via its unique capacity to breathe, and in conjunction with nerve endings, blood vessels, and glands, our body temperature, moisture, and bioelectrical balance are maintained. Our second skin – our clothes – must also be able to "breathe", as must our third skin – our homes – if they are to provide a healthy indoor environment for us all.

Reaching back to Goethe's humanitarian philosophy and romantic love of the natural world, and to the wholistic health approach of Rudolf Steiner, *Baubiologie* has affinities with deep ecology. A major pioneer is Professor Anton Schneider who set up his Institute for Building Biology and Ecology in 1976 in West Germany; branches now exist in England and the US. Today, there are many biological architects, builders, and specialist suppliers in German-speaking countries and biological homes are being built by Peter Schmid in the Netherlands, Floyd Stein in Denmark, the Gaia group in Norway, and many more.

Baubiologie combines many old traditions with a fresh, new approach. It teaches a gentle art of building that brings balance and harmony to people, buildings, and nature. Health and ecology are increasingly interwoven in natural architecture of all kinds and the newest generation of pioneers often draws on the new spiritual awareness, too. Many have been inspired by the vision of Gaia and already there are Gaia architectural groups springing up around the world.

The spiritual house

Apart from the obvious need to live in homes that are healthy for the body, there is the much older and deeper desire to dwell in a place that is healthy for the mind and spirit. The spiritual aspects are the most important for indigenous peoples. There are many accounts of how they fall ill or even die if forced to leave their ancestral homes. The modern break up of a community and its dispersal into disconnected "domestic islands" and anonymous housing produces similar alienation, stress, family breakdown, and illness and again can even be fatal. Our links with the earth, the spiritual community, and natural places are being lost and forgotten throughout the world today. In the increasingly rootless Western society, these links must be recreated if we are to be truly well.

To indigenous peoples, the whole land is home. As Sir Laurens van der Post has recorded so vividly in his accounts of the Bushmen of the Kalahari, the understanding of the land and how it is used is based on fundamental spiritual beliefs

A house needs to be integrated into the natural processes around it. In Norway, Cobolt Architects are developing this concept in their new houses. The walls, floors, and ceilings, seen in cross-section above, are "air and moisture transfusive". Rather than lining the house with plastic vapour barriers, the house "breathes" and allows air and moisture to pass gradually through. The exterior timber (below) protects the structure from rain and snow and the wide cavity insulates the inner porous wall.

1 Timber boarding (soaked with sulphate of iron)
2 Bituminous paper
3 Wood fibre boards 12mm (1/2in)
4 Wood wool cement board 150mm (6in)
5 Linseed oil varnish
6 Timber boarding 28mm (1 1/8in)
7 Non-bituminous paper
8 Light clay aggregate 200mm (8in)
9 Timber ceiling 19mm (3/4in)
10 Timber tongue and groove boards 28mm (1 1/8in)
11 Perlite 200mm (8in)
12 Timber tongue and groove boards 19mm (3/4in)
13 Bentonite 15mm (5/8in)
14 Light aggregate blocks 250mm (10in)
15 Wood wool cement boards 100mm (4in)
16 Panel 19mm (3/4in)
17 Timber boarding 19mm (3/4in)
18 Lime-cement plaster
19 Wood wool cement board 250mm (10in)

This extremely attractive, modern earth-covered home in Australia relies on the modifying effects of the soil to keep it cool in summer and warm in winter. The natural landscape, restored after construction was complete, now spreads over the roof of the house and integrates it into the local terrain. Over a 50-year period, better energy conservation and less maintenance make the running costs between 40 and 70% less than an above-ground home. Architect: Sydney Baggs

The central staircase in this house at Stavanger, Norway (above) is silhouetted against the wintergarden in an innovative design by the Gaia Architects' Group. Built of timber and other organic materials, it has "air transfusive walls" that allow the house to breathe (see also pp. 6-7 and 171).

Built over an old mill and next to a waterfall, the Charles Coughlan House at Meath, Ireland, benefits from a stunning setting (right). A multilevel sunspace opens on to cantilevered terraces that step down to the mill pond. Passive solar heat, stored by the massive stone core, supplements energy from a water turbine driven by the old mill race. Architect: Paul Leech, Gaia Associates, Ireland

reaching far back to their creation myths. The land is not merely property to be owned, but a spiritual landscape to be honoured in the image of the ancestors and heroes. For first peoples, this spiritual world can operate on many different levels: from the cosmic heavens and depths of the earth to the tribal village and family house. The symbolism may take the form of fashioning the land and the home after the primordial house built by the first couple, for example, or it may represent the shapes of the human body or spiritual beasts.

These *anthropomorphic* or *zoomorphic* models are also used to divide the home into male and female parts. The complementary forces of opposites are combined – sky and earth, sun and moon, dark and light, fire and water, and so on. At the centre is the place of power and worship – the altar or sacred tree – and in the home – the shrine, hearth or granary. Every part of the home can extend these symbols: the roof as sky or heavens; the door as mouth to another world; the window as eyes of perception; and water as female procreation. Careful choice of propitious site, orientation, and timing (of building), earth spirit offerings, and cleansing or blessing ceremonies before occupation all help to protect the home from malign forces and to integrate it into the community's spirit world.

In Hinduism, the primal energy flowing in the universe, earth and body, is known as *prana*. It is channelled along the energy network of the body –

In feng shui, mountains are symbolic "protective dragons" and mountain streams are veins channelling ch'i, or "dragon's breath". The ideal country site is an armchair formation. A high mountain at the rear is flanked to the west by Yin – a (fierce white tiger) hill and to the east by Yang – a slightly higher (azure dragon) hill and in front, a low foothill. Ideally, the house should be at the point of most ch'i – the symbolic sexual union of female and male (Yin and Yang). The best site is half way up the mountain with a commanding view over the foothill. Water, symbolizing wealth, is crucial and a pond, lake, or river in front of the house is very beneficial – as long as the water is "alive", clean and gently moving.

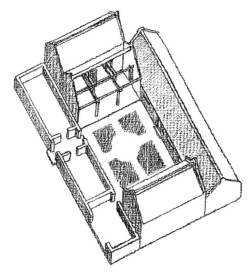

"From the ground up, the traditional Chinese house was a universe in itself. Timbers rose from the foundation of stamped soil, symbolically linking heaven and earth. Behind high surrounding walls, a garden court presented all nature in microcosm. All around it, the building itself mimicked the most auspicious feng shui arrangement: the U-shaped, dragon-tortoise-tiger armchair hill, protecting the center and ideally facing south. The ideal garden was both central and simple. No matter how far the house lay from a truly pastoral countryside, its residents must never lose touch with the elemental universe. . . . Rocks were mountains, fish ponds were oceans, and bonsai, of course, were old gnarled trees." Sarah Rossbach, Feng Shui. The Chinese Art of Placement, E.P. Dutton, NY, 1983

the *meridians* – and focused on energy centres, or *chakras*. The third chakra up the spinal chord is the *hara*, which corresponds with the solar plexus – the main storage centre for prana. These energy centres also occur in the Earth and cosmos and are recognized in the Hindu system of sacred siting and building placement, known as *Vastuvidya*.

Another ancient system is *feng shui*, the Taoist art and science of auspicious siting and layout. Literally meaning "wind and water", it states that these forces help to determine health, prosperity, and good luck. Taoism seeks harmony via the natural "way" and feng shui finds harmonious places that have good *ch'i*, the vital life force or breath, and avoid *sha*, or "noxious vapours". This Earth ch'i influences the body's own ch'i to promote health and vitality. Feng shui is still much used in the city of Hong Kong, for new buildings and adaptions. Planting and water are used to reduce the modern "noxious vapours" of pollution and noise. Inside, furniture, mirrors, lighting, wind chimes, and plants all help beneficial ch'i.

North European paganism and ancient American Indian beliefs also sought accord with the natural order. The movement of the sun, moon, and stars and the building of complex observatories to record and predict the solstices and equinoxes underlay the division of time and determined the annual festivals. Solar geometry was the basis of the orientation of religious buildings and homes. In many cultures, locations with a great focus of energy are known to be "places of power" and reserved as holy sites; but they are also mirrored in the home. To the Greeks, the sacred centre of Earth energy, equivalent to the body's *hara*, was known as the *omphalos* or navel of the world. The foundation-stone represented the omphalos, and the birth of the building. Foundation rituals formally asked the Earth Mother to allow the building on the soil, to guard it, and to bring the occupants good fortune. In old Norse sagas, they built around a living tree making this a symbolic foundation with its roots anchored in the earth.

The contemporary spiritual revival is reflected in many aspects of natural building. One of the first visionaries to bring sacred ecology into architecture was Paolo Soleri, who proposed his "arcology" in the 1960s. His city in the Arizona desert, Arcosanti, is a growing community today. British architect Keith Critchlow is a proponent of sacred geometry and the creation of a spiritual symbolism for the home. In his Lindisfarne Chapel in Crestone, Colorado, a millstone is placed at the centre to symbolize the fertility of the earth and the turning of the heavens. At Findhorn in Scotland, long a centre of wholistic spirituality, a planetary village is being built. A similarly inspired centre in America is the New Alchemy Institute with its Cape Cod Ark – a solar greenhouse and gardens – and its ecology house now under construction designed by the architect Donald Watson.

Geomancy, in many respects the Western equivalent of feng shui, is undergoing a revival and

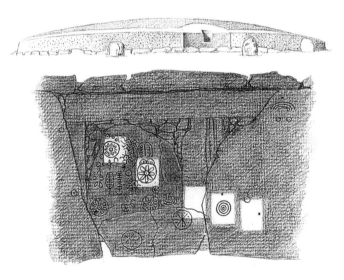

The reconstructed neolithic stone mound of Newgrange in the Boyne Valley, Ireland (above), was built with its central passage aligned to record the rising sun of the winter solstice on 21 December. As the sun rises, the rays shine through the rectangular entrance and the beam of light moves from left to right, illuminating the carved solar symbols.

Rising out of the huge boulders of the Sonoran desert (overleaf), the house designed by architect Charles Johnson, reinterprets, in completely modern style, the old traditions of adobe building (see also p. 147).

the older astrological traditions, with orientation to solstice and equinox, are being adapted to modern sacred architecture. The new eco-feminist groups too are often deeply spiritual, drawing on links with the Earth goddess image of Gaia. Personal healing is another spiritual aspect of housing, as described by Carol Venolia in her book *Healing Environments*.

At a simpler, personal level, many people are turning to Eastern traditions of meditation and are creating spaces in the home for quiet and spiritual retreat. Most practising religious people of all faiths have always done this – and cherished some sacred icon, cross, shrine, statue, or lighted lamp in the home. Even the most secular of homes may have its quiet garden or corner, its object of beauty, honouring this fundamental need.

Choosing a place to live

Moving to another home or a new apartment or looking for a site to build a house obviously involves all the usual criteria of value for money and position in relation to work, schools, stores, and leisure facilities. But extra priorities will help you make your natural home healthy, conserving, and happy. On a practical level, this will usually mean minimizing the problems rather than finding the ideal place. Certain houses and locations may already have many of the essential ingredients and will, therefore, require less effort.

Whereas a country location may be best for health, it may be much less conserving than living in an urban location close to most of your needs. "Instead of thinking of *going* places, think in terms of *being* places" is the advice of Richard Register in his book *Ecocity Berkeley*.

Proximity reduces travel, commuting stress, and the need for a car. Moreover, the countryside is under increasing pressure from development. It is much more ecologically sensitive, therefore, to improve the environment of the cities we have and live better in them, rather than lose more countryside to yet more development.

Wherever you decide to live, before moving be sure to investigate the area thoroughly to find out what is there now and what plans there are for the future. Note sources of pollution and noise, such as nuclear/other power stations, factories, incineration plants, airports and flight paths, large highways, railways and parking lots, high-voltage power lines, and telecommunication transmitters (and the direction of prevailing winds that may transport pollution). Check if there is a radon problem and ask planning departments, environmental and consumer organizations and local people about the plans and policies for the area. Look for the positive natural living advantages, too – neighbourhood recycling schemes, open space and public transport and cycle paths, pedestrianized roads, alternative therapy and arts centres, and sources of organic food and bulk supplies.

At the spiritual level, the most important thing is to spend a lot of time in the new location getting to know how it feels. Look at vegetation, orientation, and views and assess if you respond positively to what you see. In bioregionalism, which sees areas (including cities) as ecological habitats rather than administrative units, getting to know your home involves knowing the soil, the water sources, the air, the earth history, the flora and fauna, and even the stars. Some wholistic architects now also spend much time assessing your personal profile before designing either a conversion or a new home. You may be asked to give a detailed picture of your life – your preferences, aspirations, and beliefs. Seen as "healing architecture", the design and building process are therapies, too.

Whatever else you do, before starting on the road of choosing a particular site or adapting an older house try to look at the following factors. Taking care now can give you a homesite closer to your ideal and amenable to local ecology, and so reduce the need for expensive compensatory work and an overconsuming lifestyle.
○ Orientation to the sun and any obstructions (especially to winter sun). A city plot that is sun-facing at the back away from the street is preferable to allow for a solar greenhouse or sunspace addition, large solar windows, and solar panels, which local planning regulations may not permit at the front of a building. Find out if local regulations include "sun rights" that prevent you from being overshadowed by later neighbouring buildings or additions.

○ Direction of the prevailing winds and seasonal temperature, or shielding by trees and landform in cold climates, which allow design for shelter, natural ventilation, and summer cooling features. To avoid city pollution and still be cool in summer, it is best to live on the sheltered, sun-facing slopes above valleys, or near the sea, or in apartments high above street level. For energy conservation in cold climates, choose a central apartment with others above and below, or a central house in a terrace. If you are building a new house, make it as compact as possible (a dome or cube shape is most conserving) and shelter it from prevailing winds. You should also consider an earth-sheltered construction.
○ Ecology of the site, including vegetation, topography, wildlife habitats, soil type, and groundwater, which must be considered if the house and garden are to be integrated with the natural ecosystem and landscape of the location. Choose a site with as much ground as possible to allow for tree planting, which acts as a buffer against noise and pollution, and for creating an organic garden. Alternatively, consider a roof garden or a large balcony if you are in an apartment.
○ Geobiology of site, including radon, high-voltage power lines, ground electromagnetic (EM) radiation, underground watercourses, and geological and subsoil formation. Have a specialist survey carried out to avoid a site with excess EM radiation and geopathic zones (see p. 201), but also to determine the presence of beneficial energy areas. If anybody living there has had cancer, a professional dowser may be able to locate hazardous spots.
○ Air and water (rainwater and drinking) quality and levels, and types and sources of pollutants. Assess if you think filtration and purification treatments are necessary, and/or water conservation and rainwater collection.
○ Local traditional building forms and styles and techniques. The home should harmonize both with neighbouring buildings as well as with its setting. If you are contemplating a new or extended construction take your lead from traditional local styles, skills, and experience.

Choosing a house or apartment

The construction and materials of the building itself are as important as its location. Most of us will be buying an existing house or apartment, and this can be a definite advantage – particularly if the building is old, since it is more conserving of natural resources and of the countryside. Also, houses built before the 1950s were made largely of stone, brick, or timber. Thus, an older structure often circumvents the problems associated with chipboard floors and cupboards and plywood all containing formaldehyde, timbers impregnated with pesticides, and vinyl flooring and plastic finishes, all of which are almost impossible to eradicate. Even an old building may have since been treated with chemicals or had asbestos installed – but unless this happened recently it should not be a problem (and asbestos can be dealt with by experts). Damp and timber decay can be cured with nontoxic methods now. But avoid cavity wall homes with urea-formaldehyde foam insulation (UFFI).

Other bonuses with older homes are that they are more solidly built, with heavier materials, and so noise is usually less of a problem; spaces, too, are more generous and may still include larders; and the quality of materials is superior.

To find a building that you can convert easily to a natural home, look out for the following:
○ Chemical history – find out about the types of treatments to timbers, insulation in walls, and damp injection. Avoid UFFI in cavity walls.
○ Fuels – avoid fixed oil storage tanks close to or within the house structure or integral garage. Find out annual fuel and electricity consumption.
○ Materials, exterior, and interior – look for thick walls and solid-wood floors, wallboarding and cupboards and doors; for floors, ceramic tile, cork, terrazzo, stone, or brick. Avoid composite boards, hollow-core doors, and thin stud walls. Avoid asbestos, vinyl tiles, plastic surfaces, and foam-backed synthetic carpets.
○ Spaces – look for extra spaces, such as larders, attics, basements, or outbuildings, to allow natural kitchen and health areas to be developed. Look for a garden, even if small, at the front as well as back, as a buffer against street noise and pollution, and for potential sunspace locations.

Personal space

Our homes are reflections of ourselves – or should be. But the whole conformity of the modern consumer society acts against this. We are bombarded with advertising images of "successful" lifestyles and fashionable surroundings, and encouraged to buy this image for ourselves in mass-produced goods and luxuries. When we are then disappointed and ill at ease with our homes, we frequently remodel their interiors and this dissatisfaction fuels our overconsuming society. Instead, the home should grow and reflect the increased richness of our experience, reminding us of our history and friends, our loves and interests, our own unique identity. Any room that has grown like this through a lifetime will show the richness of the owner's personality.

Cultures of the past, with less, or no, access to marketed design, created almost everything for themselves – and every object (from patchwork quilts handed down through generations to hand-painted or carved furniture and interiors) reminded somebody of its making and its maker. Today, this individuality is returning as people try to rediscover the sense of self and place that has been lost. There is now more of an aspiration for a handbuilt home, personally designed and full of unusual and innovative ideas that blend old and modern technology and forms. A new respect for the planet and its diversity of life, and for the skills and labour of people, is reflected in a preference for objects whose individual history we know (and know not to be harmful) rather than factory-made items about which there is nothing to know.

You can create a personal natural space in the smallest rented room or city apartment. Look for the right basic ingredients – a room with sun and good daylight, solid materials, and a view of some greenery, away from a noisy and polluted street. Ask permission to remove anything toxic or synthetic, and then start introducing natural colour, scent, and sound – with indoor plants, a window box with herbs and scented flowers, natural fabric wall hangings, and personal items.

This highly ornate 18th-century Norwegian birthing bed (left) features a painted tree hanging heavy with ripe fruit.

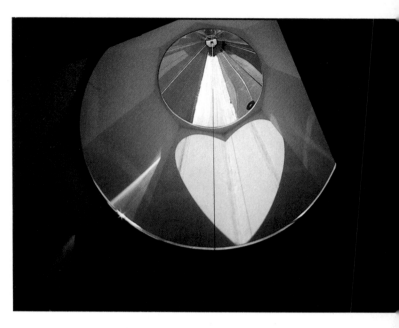

At noon, on 21 June – the midsummer soltice – the sun reaches its maximum altitude in the northern sky. To celebrate this, architect Peter Ayley's rooflight and mirror (above) catch the sun's rays and reflect them vertically into his house in Bristol, England.

Handcrafts are still very much part of the way of life in India. This interior, with its intricately decorated screen, small inset mirrors, and hand-printed cloth, is a fine example of individual and personal design.

The Gaia house

Many people have had visions of the house of the future. Modern ones are often of a complex technological world. Built of the latest plastic and synthetic materials, the house is controlled by computers that monitor all its systems and are programmed to cater to our every whim. Robots do all the work and shop by remote control. More akin to a space capsule designed to cope with a hostile environment than an earthly home, this house ignores people's emotional needs as well as the harsher realities of the coming world. We need the ground beneath our feet; and we are approaching not a brave new world but one of energy shortages, pollution, insecurity, crime, and a crisis of poverty and debt in the developing world.

Far from expensive technological dreams, we need a "down-to-earth" vision – a future home integrated with a sustainable lifestyle for us all. Whether old or new, future housing will need to employ life-support systems, materials, and spatial designs that meet the health, conservation, and spiritual criteria below. More and more people are turning to such lifestyles and we need homes that support, rather than hinder, these new aims and priorities for living.

Adapting your home will be challenging – it may cut across your habits, as well as surprise some of the conventions. But you should never consider it a restrictive chore. It should be fun, liberating, and stimulating and a process that allows your personal ideas to come to the fore. Only do what you are ready for and can carry through. Let your imagination go to work on the house that you would love to live in. Then you can experiment, sketch, or build models, test colours, lights, and fabrics and talk to local builders and craftspeople, before you commit yourself. Don't be talked out of your ideas by professionals unless you are certain the alternative is better. Once you have begun, like the Zen masters, take delight in every step.

The Gaia house charter

Design for harmony with the planet
○ Site, orient, and shelter the home to make best and conserving use of renewable resources. Use the sun, wind, and water for all or most of your energy needs and rely less on supplementary, nonrenewable energy.
○ Use "green" materials and products – nontoxic, nonpolluting, sustainable, and renewable, produced with low energy and low environmental and social costs, and biodegradable or easily reused and recycled.
○ Design the house to be "intelligent" in its use of resources and complement natural mechanisms, if necessary with efficient control systems to regulate energy, heating, cooling, water, airflow, and lighting.
○ Integrate the house with the local ecosystem, by planting indigenous tree and flower species. Compost organic wastes, garden organically, and use natural pest control – no pesticides. Recycle "greywater" and use low-flush or waterless toilets. Collect, store, and use rainwater.
○ Design systems to prevent export of pollution to the air, water, and soil.

Design for peace for the spirit
○ Make the home harmonious with its environment – blending in with the community, the building styles, scale, and materials around it.
○ Participate with others at every stage, using the personal ideas and skills of all in order to seek a wholistic, living design.
○ Use proportions, forms, and shapes that are harmonious, creating beauty and tranquillity.
○ Use colours and textures of natural materials and natural dyes, paints, and stains to create a personal and therapeutic colour environment.
○ Site and design the house to be life enhancing, and increase the wellbeing or the vital life force, *ch'i*, of its occupants.
○ Connect the home with Gaia and the natural world and the rhythms and cycles of the Earth, its seasons, and its days.
○ Make the home a healing environment in which the mind and spirit can be free and flourish.

Design for health of the body
○ Create a healthy indoor climate by allowing the house to "breathe", and use natural materials and processes to regulate temperature, humidity, and air flow and quality.
○ Site the home away from harmful EM radiation from power lines and also away from negative ground radiation. Design to prevent the build-up of static and EMF from domestic equipment, and to avoid interference with beneficial cosmic and terrestrial radiation.
○ Provide safe and healthy air and water, free from pollutants (radon especially), with good humidity, negative ion balance, and pleasant fragrance from herbs, materials, and polishes. Use natural air flow and ventilation.
○ Create a quiet home, protected and insulated from external and internal noise, and a pleasant, sound-healthy environment.
○ Design to allow sunlight and daylight to penetrate, and thus rely less on artificial lighting.

Design copyright © David Pearson, 1989

This design is a prototype for the concept of the Gaian house, incorporating the new criteria that will have to be increasingly part of future housing. It could be a detached house in the country or, as here, an urban terrace; it could, of course, be a new house but, perhaps more important for most people, it could easily be a gradual adaptation of an older one.

On the street-side of the building, trees, shrubs, grass mounds, and dense wall creepers (and perhaps a grass roof) all offer protection from cold winds, traffic noise, and pollution. On the rear, sun-facing side, a two-storey sunspace is a pleasant place in which to sit and relax.

The house is free of toxins, built, furnished, and insulated with natural materials. The walls, roof, floors, and the inner surfaces and finishes are all porous and allow the house to breathe. The heating (and cooling) relies as much as possible on natural mechanisms, with solar gain from the large sunspace and solar collectors on the roof. Back-up heat is provided by a high-efficiency boiler sited in the basement, with a central heat and services core running up the whole house. The core also venti-lates and cools the house in summer. All excess heat is circulated and stored in deep rock beds under the house.

Human and kitchen organic wastes are collected and processed in a com-poster in the basement for use in the garden and greenspaces. Other wastes are presorted into bins and recycled, as is the "greywater". A larder or pantry is a cool store for fresh vegetables and bulk dry goods. The bathroom has a deep tub for soaking and a greenhouse window. In the loft, a quiet meditation space extends on to a balcony overlooking the tranquil garden.

Chapter Two
THE DANGEROUS HOUSE

The home has always been a symbol of a safe and protective environment; somewhere that shields us against harsh climates and outside dangers; a place that provides security, privacy, and comfort for healthy growth – "safe as houses".

Great efforts have been made over the years to eradicate the worst and most basic dangers in the home – fire, structural collapse, damp, inadequate sanitation, cold, accidents, and electric shock. In the richer developed countries much of today's housing is built to very high standards and is safe in most conventional respects. In developing countries, however, this is far from the case and the struggle to achieve a decent level of housing continues. Meanwhile, a new generation of problems has arisen, one that is causing unforeseen and wider dangers to our health and to the environment.

Our health is under threat from the constant and insidious pollution pervading the home, caused by the massive increase of chemicals and synthetics used everywhere. Many of the new chemicals, synthetic materials, and plastics that have been so successful and become so widespread in the home environment are only now making us aware of the "hidden costs" we have been paying. We are daily spending more of our lives in artificial, possibly hazardous, and certainly stressful, surroundings, removed and alienated from the more natural habitat the environment offers.

But the environment is also in danger from pollution by these same chemicals and synthetics, and we are responsible for increasing this load every day by our actions and decisions at home. Every time we use an aerosol, wash the dishes or our clothes, bathe ourselves, paint a room, buy over-packaged goods, or choose crease-resistant fabrics we are increasing the pressure on ourselves and the environment. On top of this, our homes are high consumers of valuable resources – energy, materials, and water – and are extremely wasteful of all of these. They also generate unmanageable amounts of waste, much of which is toxic and eventually enters the environmental systems.

There have to be limits to how much individuals and the planet can stand, and many people are beginning to recognize them. As consumers we can do a lot, both personally and through group pressure expressed as consumer choice, to steer a route out of the chemical jungle and back toward a healthy and sustainable lifestyle. It *is* possible to strike a balance between living in good health and comfort while conserving the natural environment.

Indoor pollution is not a modern phenomenon – only the causes have changed – as this 19th-century engraving reveals.

The recently fashionable hi-tech interiors express more than most others our present mechanistic values. Divorced from natural settings, we have begun to design for ourselves a spaceship world where everything is synthetically provided – and we *even see ourselves as machines for living in it. The glossy exterior, however, may conceal many hazards – toxic materials and offgassing, electromagnetic pollution, and generally poor conditions for both the mind and body (right).*

The chemical revolution

Since the human species evolved on this planet we have lived a relatively stable existence, eating the same type of food, drinking the same water, and breathing the same air. Until recently, a delicate balance existed between ourselves and the rest of the natural world, and as changes occurred in the environment or climate, this balance adjusted in a continuous, evolutionary process.

But because of our intelligence and manual dexterity, the human species has developed a special capacity to intervene in the natural balance and to alter the environment. The making of tools, the discovery of fire, the domestication of animals, planned agriculture, and the building of settlements were the first steps in our innovative progress.

In the early stages, human intervention was on a relatively minor scale. Populations were small and scattered and their impact temporary and local, thus allowing the environment to recoup and our bodies gradually to adapt. But as the world population grew and became concentrated in cities, human interference became more intense and permanent. During the last half century our ability to quicken the pace of change has developed dramatically, and after millions of years of gradual evolution we are rapidly endangering ourselves, other living species, and the planetary environment.

Our world is composed of chemicals, some of which are beneficial to us, others harmful. Their concentrations and our exposure to them are crucial. Oxygen, for example, is vital to life, part of the air we breathe, yet pure oxygen can kill. During the Earth's long evolution, millions of chemicals, organic (carbon based) and inorganic, have been formed. All species must use, adapt to, or avoid them to survive. These are the "natural" chemicals of our environment and we are the product – and producers – of them. The whole system of life's chemical interaction is self-regulating provided that the natural chemicals remain basically in the same concentrations, as well as in the same pathways through the cycles of air, water, soil, and food chains as have evolved within the planetary ecosystem.

But since the discovery of fire our understanding of chemistry has progressed – from the simple smelting and working of metals we have now moved on to the synthesis of wholly new sub-stances, derived mainly from oil, coal, and gas. The Chemical Revolution that started tentatively a century ago has, since World War II, become an avalanche affecting every aspect of our lives. We are now bombarded daily with substances that were not present during our evolution and which our bodies have never before encountered. Increasingly, we are surrounding ourselves with a synthetic, alien world.

The danger of artificial substances is that we do not know their precise, long-term effects. Laboratory tests are usually restricted to a single new chemical in isolation. They consider neither the synergistic effect of mixing it with the cocktail of many other chemicals to which we are exposed, nor the local concentrations experienced in the real world (see pp. 96-9). Moreover, laboratory tests often involve experiments on animals. Not only is there growing opposition to this practice on humane grounds, but also we cannot be sure of the validity of transferring results gained to humans. What we *do* know is that harmful effects may not show for many years: asbestos-related diseases, for example, may not occur until 10 to 20 years after exposure.

Freedom of information

Concern is growing about the level of secrecy surrounding product information, ingredients, and labelling. While many countries require details to be published for food, medicines, and clothes, it is very difficult, if not impossible, to find out the exact ingredients of household cleaners, detergents, plastics, paints, adhesives, and most of the synthetic building materials, which are guarded as "trade secrets". Even though the US has the most statutory freedom of information, this is still mainly restricted to foods, drugs, and cosmetics. Most other countries lag behind and, in many, a cloak of secrecy hangs over product information and the decision-making processes.

Pollutants and toxins

Although there are many pollutants, not all are toxins. Pollutant is a general term for any material released into the environment as a byproduct of human activity. Some are excess loads of naturally occurring substances, such as ozone, carbon dioxide, or radon gas; others are chemical synthetics. Many pollutants are absorbed or broken down harmlessly by our bodies or the environment; but many do not exist in natural background concentrations and are, therefore, persistent once introduced into life chains. And some, such as dioxin, are lethal toxins, even in minute concentrations.

The most serious pollutants are those that cause changes in the fundamental building blocks of the body, the cells. They include the carcinogens (cancer-producing substances), the mutagens (causing changes in genetic structure), and the teratogens (resulting in birth defects). Next on the list are the toxins and subtoxins; then come the aeropathogens (airborne, infectious agents such as some viruses and bacteria) and the allergens (a diverse group of pollutants that may cause allergic reactions).

Very little is yet known about acceptable concentrations and exposure levels of any of the new pollutants, or about what may constitute an "unreasonable risk" (see right). A manufacturer's evaluation should be subject to checks and final approval by independent government bodies, which should also monitor the substances' uses and concentrations. Most governments, however, cannot keep pace with the deluge of new chemicals and controls are weakening despite efforts by consumer and pressure groups.

Even when a substance is banned in one country it may be exported to another, especially to one in the developing world, and reimported unknowingly as a treatment or produce ingredient. Certain pesticides on cotton and wool are banned in Europe and the US but are imported in clothes and furnishings from developing countries. Others return via imported coffee and chocolate.

Tragically, it often takes a disaster, such as Bhopal, before the dangers are fully comprehended. Nobody should assume that because a product is on sale it is automatically safe. As concerned consumers we must be on our guard and treat new substances with suspicion until independent tests show them to be acceptable. The consumer is at the centre of the production system with all its implications for our health and the environment.

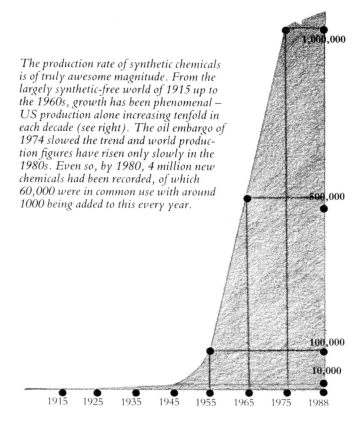

The production rate of synthetic chemicals is of truly awesome magnitude. From the largely synthetic-free world of 1915 up to the 1960s, growth has been phenomenal – US production alone increasing tenfold in each decade (see right). The oil embargo of 1974 slowed the trend and world production figures have risen only slowly in the 1980s. Even so, by 1980, 4 million new chemicals had been recorded, of which 60,000 were in common use with around 1000 being added to this every year.

1,000,000
500,000
100,000
10,000

1915 1925 1935 1945 1955 1965 1975 1988

Assessing the risks

The potential risks of a new substance are usually evaluated in laboratory tests by the manufacturer (subject to checks by government bodies); but the same company gains by marketing the product. Ideally, risks should be assessed both for toxicity to humans and for dangers to the environment, including persistence. But even rigorous laboratory analysis leaves many questions unanswered on real-world and long-term effects. Inherent in the assessment, too, is the sociological question of who takes the risks and who benefits. Smokers, for example, risk their health voluntarily, while nonsmokers are subject to an involuntary risk by passively inhaling the smoke. The tobacco company benefits, but puts both parties at risk. In the end, the manufacturer's decision about risk has to be a value judgement, open to all kinds of influence, bias, and interpretation.

The sick home

Most people are now familiar with the growing worldwide threat of atmospheric pollution; far fewer, however, are aware that they are surrounded by this danger inside their own homes.

Take a tour around your home and you will be surprised to find sources of pollution everywhere. Starting at the top, roofing timbers may have been treated with toxic fluids or be insulated with potentially unhealthy materials, and the roofs of older buildings may contain asbestos-cement products. Cavity walls could have been injected with insulating foam emitting formaldehyde vapour, while interior decoration will consist of petrochemical-based paints or vinyl wallpapers, which emit more dangerous vapours, especially when new. Older paint may contain lead. Timber floors and stairs may, too, have been treated; synthetic carpets may cover them (emitting formaldehyde and creating dust) or else plastic tiles may have been used that can emit chemicals.

Furnishings are often filled with highly flammable polyurethane foam and upholstered with synthetic fabrics. Kitchen units and living room or bedroom furniture may be constructed of processed boards containing yet more formaldehyde, glued with vaporous adhesives, and finished with plastic. The characteristic "new house" smell, like a new car interior, warns of this chemical cocktail.

As if this were not enough, homes still suffer from the older generation of pollutants – fumes and gases produced by poor combustion in open fires, stoves, cookers, and heating appliances; lead in water pipes; mould, bacteria, and airborne organisms. And then there are the modern consumer products – household cleaners, polishes, bathroom cosmetics, medicines, processed and sprayed foods, garden pesticides, and DIY, car maintenance, and hobby materials.

The services supplied to the home – water, gas, and electricity – are now increasingly seen to offer their own hazards. Water may be polluted; electricity, apart from the dangers of shock, may generate fields that interfere with the body's natural rhythms; and gas is not only explosive but it may be an allergy trigger. Even the ground on which the house stands may not be good for our health. Ground rock may be releasing radioactive radon gas into the home, while homes sited over zones of negative earth energies may impair our mood and wellbeing (see p. 201).

Of course, no one home is going to contain all these pollutants, and both concentrations and individual susceptibility vary widely. But caution is always advisable where health is concerned. Try using the checklist on page 271 to judge your own exposure. Once you become aware of a problem, there is a lot you can do. The next few pages examine the pollutants in more detail, and the chart on pages 54-5 then summarizes the most common problems, their sites in the house, and the solutions covered by this book.

There are three main categories of indoor pollutants: gases and vapours, particles, and radiation. And of the gases and vapours there are three types: combustion byproducts of domestic fuels, vapours given off by household products, and unusual concentrations of natural gases.

Combustion gases

The fuels we use for cooking and heating are among the most serious sources of pollution. Natural and utility gas, paraffin (kerosene), oil, coal, and wood, all release harmful byproducts, more so if combustion is inefficient. These can build up to dangerous levels indoors, especially if windows are sealed in cold weather or for insulation (see pp. 100-1). They also pollute the environment. In particular, all combustion fuels produce carbon dioxide, one of the main constituents of the "greenhouse" gases that are raising global temperatures.

Gas cookers and boilers produce large amounts of carbon monoxide, carbon dioxide, nitric oxide, and nitrogen dioxide as well as smaller amounts of formaldehyde, sulphur dioxide, and other byproducts. Old models with pilot lights or faulty burners (burning orange rather than blue) make matters worse. Gas appliances can be deadly: they must be regularly checked and serviced, and properly vented.

Portable paraffin (kerosene) and gas heaters, being unvented, are particularly hazardous. They release noxious gases as well as high humidity, with subsequent condensation. They are a serious health

Timber treatment

Petrochemical paint

Formaldehyde

Polyurethane foam

Polyvinyl floor tiles

Electromagnetic radiation

Combustion hydrocarbons

Household chemicals

Radon

Insulation materials

Sources of pollution

The modern home is not the safe haven we think. The newer or more recently renovated it is, the higher the likely pollution level. From roof to ground, potential hazards may occur in every room – in the garden and the garage, too (which should not be built on to the home). Basements can collect stale vapours, boiler fumes, or locally occurring radon, which can seep up through the house. Timber treatments, insulation, formaldehyde impregnated materials, paints and vinyl floor coverings, cleaners, polishes and pesticides, water supplies, fuels, and wiring circuits all add to the health burden, as we breathe in chemicals, ingest them, or absorb them via our skin. And foam-filled furniture poses a serious fire hazard. If you have an older house, you may be free of many of the problems. And radon is a local problem. But you will probably still be surprised at your "toxic burden".

and fire risk and should never be used in closed rooms where gases can build up. Keep a window fully open and avoid long-term use.

Oil furnaces also emit pollution, while leaks or spillages around storage tanks yield vapours that are difficult to eradicate and which, if the tank is in a basement, will rise into the house. Car exhausts emit potentially lethal amounts of carbon monoxide, lead, and other pollutants, so never run an engine in a closed garage. Ideally, garages should be separate from the house.

Wood and coal smoke both contain many pollutants, the most deadly being carbon monoxide. Most should go up the chimney (polluting outside air), but inefficient, poorly designed flues, unswept or cracked, can prevent complete combustion and allow toxic gases to re-enter rooms. Wood smoke also contains some carcinogens, and smoke from bonfires where plastic or rubber is burned is suspected of containing lethal dioxin. Coal smoke contains high levels of sulphur dioxide – once responsible for city smogs and now for acid rain. Sealed primary and secondary combustion stoves are becoming popular; efficient, and safer, they are also environmentally cleaner.

Tobacco smoke is one of the commonest dangers. Of over 2000 chemical constituents, at least 40 are known carcinogens. "Sidestream" smoke pollutes the air with more harmful compounds than "mainstream" smoke entering the smoker's lungs. Passive smoking is a significant health risk to nonsmokers.

Vapours from household products

Modern homes contain many organic chemicals in their structure and furnishings, and householders use a wide range in cleaning, pest control, and decoration. Most are extracted or synthesized from petrochemicals; usually combustible and insoluble in water, they are either liquids or solids with a low melting point. The problem is that so many of them belong to the large class of volatile organic compounds (VOCs) – that is, they readily release vapours at room temperature or below, both by evaporation from the volatile liquids and by off-gassing from many synthetic solids. Accumulated

vapours are often toxic and nearly all are irritants. Our exposure to a cocktail of these vapours can be high – in a new car interior, for example, over a hundred may be present. The worst hazards are formaldehyde, organochlorines, and phenolic compounds; worst exposure comes from decorating, housework, pest control, and the use of plastics.

Formaldehyde, much valued in industry as a binder and preservative, is used in hundreds of household products and building materials – pressed wood sheets, paper products, furnishing fabrics, rugs and carpets, cosmetics, and deodorants. Although its presence in each product is small, the cumulative effect of many items together in an enclosed space can be hazardous. It is known as an irritant to the skin, eyes, nose, and throat; it is associated with breathing difficulties, nosebleeds, headaches, fatigue and nausea; and it is now suspected of being carcinogenic. Moreover, it acts as a sensitizer, both to itself and to other chemicals, lowering the threshold of allergy reactions. Widely used in the 1970s for cavity wall foam insulation, urea-formaldehyde (UFFI) has now been banned in some countries. It is a serious health risk and should never be used. Heat and humidity can increase the problem, while time may gradually reduce it.

Organochlorines, compounds of hydrocarbons and chlorine, are potent and persistent health and environmental hazards. They are mostly toxic and potential carcinogens, and react with living fatty tissues where they accumulate to pass up lifechains. Many pesticides, solvents, and cleaning fluids that emit harmful vapours are organochlorines, as are PVC (polyvinyl chloride) and the very carcinogenic PCBs (polychlorinated biphenyls).

Phenols include pure phenol or carbolic acid, a common disinfectant that is strongly irritant, plus many compounds found in cleaners, air fresheners, polishes, and hygiene products. Phenolic synthetic resins, containing formaldehyde, are used in hard plastics, paints, fabric coatings, and varnish. Phenols cause many unpleasant symptoms from skin rashes to nausea and breathing difficulties, and should be avoided as strenuously as formaldehyde.

Home decoration involves the use of paints, varnishes, stainers, removers, and adhesives, all containing dangerous VOCs that release large concentrations of vapours in use, and some even afterward when dry. Metals in paints are also a hazard. Paint removers are a worse danger, since they may contain highly flammable and carcinogenic chemicals, though one of these, benzene, is now banned in many countries.

Housework with polishes, detergents, fabric and carpet cleaners, oven cleaners, air fresheners, and so on brings exposure to potentially harmful VOCs such as ammonia, turpentine, naphthalene, sodium hydroxide, acetone, chlorine, and many others. Aerosols dispense large volumes of harmful propellants in a fine mist that can easily be absorbed via the lungs and skin. They also emit chlorinated fluorocarbons (CFCs) that persist in the atmosphere and are damaging the Earth's ozone layer. In 1987, more than 40 countries signed the UNEP Montreal Treaty limiting all CFC use.

Pest control involves chemicals designed to kill small organisms, but these can also harm humans! Many are mixed with volatile organic solvents that slowly pollute the air, while garden chemicals may persist in lifechains and enter groundwater. Timber treatments for rot and pests may contain lethal substances, such as lindane or dieldrin insecticide, and pentachlorophenol (PCP) to kill fungi.

Plastics, in hundreds of types and forms – hard, soft, liquid, and dry, and in sheets, films, and threads (see p. 168) – are used for almost everything in the home. Soft plastics are potentially more harmful, since they may offgas into stored foods. PVCs are the worst; they can cause birth defects, cancer, chronic bronchitis, and skin diseases. Acrylics contain acrylonitrile, a suspected carcinogen, as is polyethylene. Polystyrene can irritate eyes, nose, and throat and cause dizziness. Polyurethane foam in furniture can cause bronchitis, coughs, and skin problems. More lethal, though, is the fire hazard. Once alight, many plastics produce deadly toxic smoke and gases. Plastics burn twice as fast and hot and with up to 500 times as much toxic fumes as more conventional materials. Sometimes they ignite with a "flashover" effect from the build-up of gases, and allow little time for escape. In the UK the use of flammable polyurethane foam in new furniture was banned from March 1989.

Hazardous gas concentrations

This type of problem is less universal and arises from locally high exposure. Ozone is a cause of immediate discomfort; radon, however, a more serious, long-term hazard.

Ozone is an unstable poisonous gas present in small amounts in the air, and it is responsible for the protective atmospheric layer that shields the Earth from ultraviolet (UV) radiation. Ozone is also generated when the UV in sunlight acts on hydrocarbons and nitric oxides in polluted air, as well as by electrical discharges from appliances with brush-type motors and photocopiers. High ozone concentrations cause smog conditions and can be hazardous to people with chest problems.

Radon, an odourless, colourless, radioactive gas produced mainly by the decay of uranium-238, is found naturally in rocks, groundwater, and soil. It may enter the home through building materials, such as stone (especially granite and pumice), bricks, plaster, and concrete made from radon-rich sources; it can also enter via tap water and domestic gas. But the worst source is the ground itself, where radon occurrence is localized to certain regions. The gas seeps up into the house through cracks, drains, and even solid concrete. In tightly sealed, insulated homes in radon areas, concentrations can be hundreds, even thousands, of times higher than that found outside. Radon decays into radioactive substances, the most harmful being polonium isotopes, which, when inhaled, emit alpha radiation into the body, affecting the respiratory system, and are carcinogenic with long exposure. Radon is a serious problem; overall, it contributes about half the average background radiation dose people experience from all natural sources. Locally, indoor levels may be hazardous, but the problem can be dealt with effectively (see p. 101).

Particles in house dust, air, and water

A six-room house in the city may accumulate as much as 40 pounds of dust in a year. This dust is not just dirt, but a highly complex mixture of remnants from occupants, pets, clothes, furnishings, building materials, and food, plus airborne soot and microorganisms. Fine dust is the worst hazard, since this escapes the body's respiratory filters and can enter the lungs. Water, too, carries many organic and inorganic particles. Few of these invaders are life threatening but many bring disease or allergies as we inhale or absorb them.

Organisms carried in dust include viruses and bacteria that bring illnesses ranging from influenza to TB. Badly maintained air-conditioning systems can harbour the organisms and spread infection – fatally in the case of Legionnaires' disease from large cooling towers. Condensation in bathrooms and kitchens provides breeding grounds for moulds (fungi); their spores drift with the dust to cause unpleasant musty smells and can trigger allergic reactions, as can pollen, mites and animal dander.

Toxic particles also occur in dust. Asbestos fibres (from older building materials) if inhaled over long periods may result in cancers years later; glass fibres (from insulation) are less of a hazard, but they do irritate the lungs. Pesticide and plastic dusts and smoke particles are both irritants and toxins. Sensitivity to dust is very variable but it is often found to be the reason for such breathing and chest problems as asthma.

Metals enter the body through inhaled dust, water, and food. Lead from water pipes, traffic fumes, or old paint is particularly harmful to children; its modern equivalent in paint, titanium oxide, is only slightly less so. Aluminium in cookware reacts with many foods, and its absorption may be linked to Alzheimer's disease. Cadmium, mercury, and copper are also toxic.

Radiation and EMFs

As living beings, we function via minute electrochemical charges and our whole body is surrounded by natural bioelectrical fields. Our metabolism is geared to the background levels of radiation and electromagnetic energies from the Earth, sun, and planets. We depend on these for our health of mind and body and we are sensitive to any unusual exposure, whether artificial or natural. Too much radiation is our usual worry, but we can equally suffer from deprivation – as has been found in scientific tests of subjects in Faraday cages, which exclude all radiation. Whether similar shielding by modern building materials harms us is not fully understood, but sunlight- and daylight-deprivation responses (see p. 112) indicate that we are indeed much affected by this factor.

Radioactivity exposure is mainly (nearly 90 per cent) due to natural sources, with medical use causing most of the rest. Of natural radiation, most is terrestrial (from the ground). Local levels can vary widely – either from proximity to nuclear power stations or, more often, from radioactive-rich (especially radon-bearing) rocks.

EMF pollution is a more recently recognized problem. Today, we are surrounded with electrical equipment and circuits, TVs and VDUs, and high- and low-frequency electromagnetic waves from micro and radio to gamma. The risks of living close to high-voltage cables is now recognized, following the New York State Power Lines Project's report that children so exposed were twice as likely to develop cancers, especially leukemia and brain tumours. There is growing, but not conclusive, evidence that long-term exposure to low-level EMFs in domestic electrical circuits and equipment can be harmful – at least as an allergy trigger in the hypersensitive and generally upsetting to our metabolism and raising stress levels.

Microwave ovens can leak radiation from badly fitting doors. It is, therefore advisable to have them checked regularly. If operating properly, the level of exposure should be well below government safety limits, though these vary from country to country. Health risks from microwave radiation are not proven.

Ultraviolet (UV) radiation is causing more concern as damage to the ozone layer increases our natural exposure. In this context, UV generation by artificial lights (see p. 120) needs to be treated with a measure of caution.

Earth energies have been studied in West Germany for 50 years and by dowsers for hundreds of years. The natural electromagnetic radiation from the Earth varies in intensity and type from place to place, particularly over groundwater, fissures, and faults. Some German scientists believe that sleeping or working for long periods over areas of more intense radiation can cause "geopathic stress" leading to a higher risk of disease and cancer.

Indoor pollutants and toxins

Substance	Biological effects
GASES	
Ozone (O_3) Unstable, poisonous gas with penetrating odour; protects the earth from dangerous UV radiation. Also generated by photocopiers; exposure of polluted air to UV radiation; appliances with brush-type motors.	**O_3** Decays rapidly into oxygen, but even small amounts are serious irritants to eyes, nose, throat, and respiratory tract.
Radon (Rn) Colourless, odourless, practically inert gas, present in certain geological areas. A serious contaminant which is carried into the home via dust, water, natural gas, and some building materials.	**Radon** inhalation damages lung tissues and long-term exposure is linked with cancer.
COMBUSTION GASES	
Carbon monoxide (CO) Colourless, odourless, poisonous gas from incomplete combustion in gas flames, wood, coal and tobacco smoke, vehicle exhausts.	**CO** reduces absorption levels of oxygen, causing headaches, dizziness, nausea and loss of appetite. Those with heart, lung, and circulation disorders are most susceptible.
Nitric oxide (NO) and Nitrogen dioxide (NO_2) Strong-smelling toxic gases from incomplete combustion of gas flames via cookers and boilers.	**NO_2** is the most toxic of the nitrogen oxides, affecting the respiratory system.
Sulphur dioxide (SO_2) Pungent gas present in coal and wood smoke, and emitted by paraffin (kerosene) heaters. SO_2 was once responsible for urban smogs: now it produces acid rain.	**SO_2** rarely occurs at dangerous levels but it can exacerbate breathing difficulties.
Carbon dioxide (CO_2) Colourless, odourless gas. A combustion product of bottled gas heaters. It is responsible for stale and stuffy air in poorly ventilated rooms.	**CO_2** Continuous exposure may affect the central nervous system and slow down reactions.
VOLATILE ORGANIC COMPOUNDS (VOCs)	
Formaldehyde (HCHO) Binder and preservative with a pungent odour. At room temperatures, toxic vapours are released that contaminate the air. Widely used as a bonding agent and adhesive in timber and plastic products; a preservative in paper products, carpeting, furnishings; a finish for clothing and bed linen. Occurs in combustion byproducts from cooking and heating appliances, as well as in tobacco smoke. Urea-formaldehyde foam insulation (UFFI) foam used prior to mid 1970s is particularly hazardous.	**Formaldehyde** is a potent irritant to skin, eyes, nose, and throat with accompanying headache, dizziness, nausea, and breathing difficulties. It may cause nosebleeds. Suspected carcinogen. Chronic exposure to UFFI vapours causes depression and triggers chemical sensitivity.
Organochlorines Compounds of hydrocarbons and chlorine, which form the basis of many synthetic chemicals. Found in vaporous cleaners, air fresheners, polishes. Organochlorines are the most toxic and persistent of VOCs. They include **polychlorinated biphenyls (PCBs)**, known carcinogens; **polyvinyl chloride (PVC)**, a plastic that can offgas into stored food; **chloroform** and **chloramines**, both toxic gases. **Chloramines** are released when household bleach and ammonia-based cleaners are mixed together. Other hazardous VOCs include ammonia, turpentine, and acetone in cleaners and solvents; naphthalene in moth balls; chlorine in bleach.	Pungent vapours from **volatile organic compounds** are serious irritants to skin, eyes and lungs; they cause headaches and nausea and damage the central nervous system. All are potentially carcinogenic. **Organochlorine** vapours in solvents, pesticides, and cleaning fluids irritate skin, cause depression and headaches, and may damage liver and kidneys. **Chloramine** can be deadly.
Phenols or carbolic acids are caustic contaminants found in disinfectants, resins, plastics, and tobacco smoke. Phenolic synthetic resins in hard plastic, paints, coatings, and varnish contain formaldehyde. Never inhale **pentachlorophenol** found in wood preservatives and fungicides.	**Phenols** are corrosive to the skin and damage the respiratory system.
PARTICLES	
Asbestos Naturally occurring hazardous fibre mined from calcium magnesium silicate, used in insulation and fire-proofing. Banned in many countries.	Airborne **asbestos** fibres are a serious health risk causing asbestosis and cancers.
Microorganisms present in dust include disease-carrying bacteria and viruses, plus moulds, spores, and pollen.	**Microorganisms** spread infections and diseases. They also cause allergies.
Metals Trace elements from lead, cadmium, mercury, aluminium, and copper can be absorbed and accumulate to toxic levels in the body. Lead is present in old water pipes, exhaust fumes; lead and cadmium in paint; mercury in tinned tuna; aluminium is absorbed into food from cookware.	**Lead** and **cadmium** can damage brain and nerve tissues. **Cadmium** can also affect vision. Toxic levels of metals in the body give rise to headaches and breathing troubles.

The "sick building syndrome"

Recently, workers in modern offices, public buildings, and schools have complained of recurrent symptoms, including headaches, fatigue and sleepiness, irritation to eyes and nose, dry throat, general loss of concentration, and nausea. Studies monitoring the indoor air of these environments have found a complex mix of pollutants – formaldehyde, radon, carbon monoxide, sulphur dioxide, ozone, and particulates such as tobacco smoke. But the symptoms are also thought to derive from factors such as fluorescent lighting, air that is too hot or dry, a build-up of positive ions, and a lack of individual control of the environment. This problem has been defined as environmental and is known as the "sick building syndrome".

Increasingly, Western medicine is having to relate illness not to viruses and microbes but to environmental phenomena. These can be chemical (organic and inorganic substances); biological (bacteria, moulds, dust, and pollen); and physical (electromagnetic, light, temperature, and noise).

With the massive increase of toxic chemicals in the environment, "chemical sensitivity" has become a major concern of environmental medicine (or clinical ecology). It is defined as an adverse reaction to toxic chemicals at levels generally considered not to be harmful in the environment.

Sensitivity will depend on such factors as the types and concentrations of chemicals, the parts of the body involved, and the susceptibility of the individual. A chemically sensitive person may experience a gradual increase in vulnerability, so that much smaller quantities of chemicals and exposures trigger a reaction. A spreading effect can also result whereby toxic chemicals, other than the original sensitizer, can cause reactions.

There are four principal mechanisms that tend to influence health when chemical sensitivity occurs. These are described by numerous specialists, notably the American consultant Dr William J Rea and British allergy physician Dr Jean Monro:

Total load Each person has an individual threshold to the load of contaminants he or she can bear. This threshold is variable and can be lowered by stress, infections, lack of sleep, and poor exercise.

Adaption A person will often have a physiological response to a contaminant but become so used to it as to no longer be aware of it. This adaption, or "masking", will continue with repeated exposures as the body strains to adjust. Eventually, an exhaustion phase is reached and disease may result.

Bipolarity The body's natural response to a contaminant is to activate its defensive immune and non-immune (enzyme) systems. First, the metabolic rate increases in an attempt to eject the pollutant. Next, after prolonged periods, comes the depressive stage when the response systems can no longer cope. This "high-low", or bipolar, response over many years will deplete the immune system's essential nutrients and illness will follow.

Biochemical individuality Everybody's immune system is different, hence individual susceptibilities vary. There are known to be over 1500 inborn metabolic defects and these will affect the body's defensive capacities.

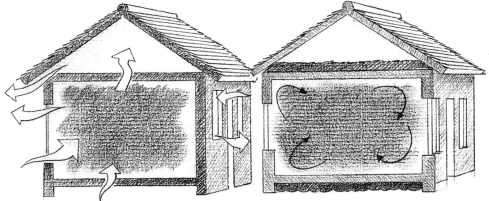

Energy-conservation measures and newer, synthetic materials are both partly to blame for the adverse health effects of the modern sick house. The "sealed" house of today is like a closed box of impermeable materials: ventilation is dramatically reduced so that pollutants build up and recirculate around the home and through air-conditioning systems (near left). In the older, "leaky" house (far left), fresh air from outside penetrates more readily, and the chemical load, which is lower in the first place, dissipates through cracks and porous, "breathing" materials.

How to respond

Faced with this complex and worrying situation that so many of us find ourselves in, how should we react? There are three main schools of thought.

Trust the system This says that all we can do is trust the professionals, scientists, companies, and government to see that safe limits and controls are placed on anything harmful to us or to our environment.

Total avoidance This approach says that there are so many unknowns, possibilities for error, misjudgements, professional and corporate vested interests, and lack of any real control that it is best to avoid all new synthetic chemicals and materials. This may be the approach that chemically sensitive and allergic people will have to take anyway.

Lessen the load This says that it is not realistic for most people to avoid totally all synthetic chemicals. Instead, you should try to avoid them as much as possible and to reduce the load on yourself and the environment by using safe, natural alternatives whenever practicable (see below).

It is the premise of this book that, except for the hypersensitive, we should all adopt the third alternative as the guiding principle for living in the present world.

Lessening the load

The following sections of this book will help you to adapt your home to be freer from harmful chemicals and other pollutants. The chart on pages 54-5 is a guide to finding the relevant sections. But as a general approach to this transformation, you will need to bear in mind some overall principles.

○ If you find a substance that is very hazardous, do not attempt to remove it yourself – seek professional advice immediately. Although asbestos, for example, represents a serious threat to health, it does not usually cause harm while it remains intact. The real danger occurs when it is disturbed and the tiny fibres are released into the air and can be inhaled. In some situations, professional advice may be to leave it in place but seal it off completely to contain the fibres. As with many hazardous and toxic substances, asbestos removal is illegal in many countries unless undertaken by special contractors.

○ Remember that unless you take proper precautions, all decorating and building work may be hazardous to health. Too often, the householder is unaware of or minimizes these potential dangers. For example, the accumulated dust you find in roof spaces and that caused by demolition of walls or stripping old plaster can be harmful if you inhale it and you must do everything possible to protect yourself in situations such as these.

○ Paint stripping is another danger area. Whether you use volatile paint removers, heat, or abrasion, large quantities of harmful vapours or fine dust will be produced. Much old paint contains lead and this is released into the air by all these methods. In the desire to remove hazards in the home, make sure you are not subjecting yourself and others to more (or even worse) hazards by the method you use.

○ Adapt your home gradually rather than trying to do it all at once. Start simply and easily with items such as better cleaning materials, cosmetics, and clothes; move on to curtains, fabrics, and decoration; and then later to the larger and more expensive items, such as furniture, carpets, and fittings. This is a process that may take several years – the actual time span will depend on the level and type of pollution and individual reactions to it. If the problem is sensitivity to, for example, formaldehyde, then you should remove items containing this substance first.

○ Take adequate preventative measures. If it is not possible to remove the sources of the pollution, the next best thing is to dilute the pollutant to more tolerable levels. Increasing the ventilation of the home where necessary is extremely important as a first step (see pp. 100-1).

Follow your nose

If you are a chemically sensitive person you need to be as sure as you can be that materials in your home, or any new item you may want to introduce, will not trigger an adverse response. An effective way of testing in many cases is to place a small sample in a clean glass jar with an airtight lid. Place the jar somewhere at least as warm as the highest temperature in the home for a minimum of two days. Then open the jar and sample the vapours. You can check further on certain materials, such as fabrics for clothes, bedding, and furnishing, that pass the "nose test" by placing a small sample on your pillow or under your clothing directly against the skin. If you react to the material after a few hours, you will know for certain that it is unsuitable for use. In extreme cases of sensitivity, you may have to create a "sanctuary" (see p. 241) and introduce there only personally safe materials and products.

Responding to pollutants

Source	Hazards	Action
Heating systems Paraffin (kerosene) and bottled gas heaters.	Carbon monoxide, nitrogen dioxide, carbon dioxide, sulphur dioxide. Condensation.	**Do not use.** If unavoidable, use for short periods only. Ventilate well.
Gas ranges, furnaces, and water heaters.	Carbon monoxide, nitrogen dioxide, carbon dioxide, sulphur dioxide. Leaks from pilot lights.	Vent all gas appliances to the outside. Replace with electrical models, or choose gas furnaces with sealed combustion chambers. Buy pilotless gas appliances. Have burners regularly serviced.
Oil furnaces.	Combustion byproducts; vapours from spillage.	Ventilate to the outside. Replace with electrical heating system, or seal boiler room from house.
Wood stoves and fireplaces; coal fires and furnaces.	Carbon monoxide, smoke, benzopyrene.	Have flues regularly swept and checked. Seal chimney cracks. Install air supply direct to fireplace. See pp. 184, 192. See also p. 78.
Electricity Electrical wiring and appliances (TVs, VDUs, food processors, blenders, mixers, power tools, hair driers, photocopiers).	Low-level electromagnetic radiation. Ozone.	Use less electrical equipment and keep it away from sleeping spaces. Ensure protective wiring and devices are fitted. See pp. 80–1, 188, 192, 201.
Refrigerators.	CFCs released from coolant system.	New CFC-free models being developed. Meanwhile use a larder. See p. 212.
Microwave ovens.	Radiation through ill-fitting doors.	Use other fast cooking methods (e.g. pressure cookers). Have ovens checked regularly.
Fluorescent lighting (old fittings).	PCBs from rapid start ballasts.	Replace old fittings. See p. 120. Use incandescent or halogen lamps instead.
Water supply	Lead and other heavy metals from pipes. Nitrates and other trace pollutants and chemicals. Bacteria and radon in showers.	Remove lead pipes and those with lead-soldered joints. Have water tested. See p. 90. Use filtration systems pp. 90–1. See radon p. 229.
Air Air-conditioning and ventilation systems; humidifiers, heating ducts.	Airborne microorganisms, fungi, bacteria, moulds. CFCs released from some systems.	Maintain comfortable indoor humidity; ventilate to the outside. Have mechanical systems regularly checked. See pp. 102–3, 224–5, 266–7.
Construction materials Earth, stone, granite, pumice; concrete, cement, fired bricks, aggregate blocks and tiles made from alum shale, calcium silicate slag, and uranium mine trailings.	Radium, radon. Concentration varies according to locality of source.	Contact local health and safety authorities for information on radon concentrations. Where necessary, seal cracks in building foundations. Increase ventilation to the outside. See radon pp. 101, 226, 229.
Plaster, cement, and plasterboard made from phosphogypsum.	Formaldehyde. May contain high levels of radon.	Use natural gypsum plasterboard or lime plaster. See formaldehyde pp. 100, 153.
Asbestos, insulation, and fire-proofing materials around pipes, boilers, and tanks; roof and floor tiles and boards.	Minute mineral fibres; blue and brown asbestos is more dangerous than white.	Asbestos is now banned in many countries, but is still found in older houses. **Do not disturb or remove flaking asbestos; seek expert advice.**
Urea-formaldehyde foam insulation (UFFI) for cavity walls.	Formaldehyde.	Banned in the US. Have indoor air tested. If found, seek specialist advice. See p. 100.
Timber and timber products Pinewood, spruce, and other conifer wood.	Resin vapours.	Use older, recycled wood or other solid timber. Seal with nontoxic finish. See pp. 166, 264–5.
Chipboard, fibreboard, hardboard, particle board, plywood: used in furniture, units, shelving, floor decking, and wall finishes.	Formaldehyde vapours from resin binder, especially when product is new, and in hot, humid climates.	Use solid timber or "low-emission" formaldehyde boards pp. 148, 153. Buy solid wood or rattan, bamboo, and wicker furniture. See pp. 156–9, 262–3. See also sealants pp. 166, 264–5.

Source	Hazards	Action
Timber treatments.	Lindane, pentachlorophenol (PCP), tributyl tin oxide (TBTO).	Avoid these toxic insecticides and fungicides. Use safe preservatives p. 153.
Fabrics and fibres Synthetics (e.g. polypropylene and polyester used in carpeting, underlays, upholstery, bedding, clothes).	Formaldehyde vapours. Also insecticides, soft plastics, flame retardants, crease and stain repellants.	Avoid synthetic products, especially wall-to-wall carpeting. Use natural, untreated materials such as cotton, linen, wool, hessian. Wash before use. See natural fibres pp. 160–1, 201, 262–3.
Feathers, down, hair.	Allergies in sensitive people.	Use natural latex pillows, mattresses, and cushions. Protect with close-woven, natural cotton.
Paints, varnishes, stainers, removers Used throughout the home on walls, floors, ceilings, woodwork, furniture.	Volatile organic compounds (VOCs). Toxic vapours and odours in drying: paint removers are the most toxic. Added fungicides and insecticides. Metals.	Avoid petrochemical paints: if you must use them, keep windows fully open and allow plenty of time for the paint to dry before reusing the room. See paints and varnishes, pp. 165–6, 264–5.
Adhesives Adhesives, glues, and mastics: used for wall and floor tiles, furniture assembly, weather sealing, wallpaper paste.	VOCs, notably formaldehyde. Toxic vapours during application and drying.	Use traditional nonchemical glues or water-based acrylics with low solvent content. See adhesives p. 152.
Metal products Cookware, paints, pipes, structural uses, furniture.	Leaching of trace elements into water – lead, cadmium, mercury, aluminium, iron, magnesium, copper. Lead and cadmium are ingredients of paints. Aluminium and cookware can leach into food. Metal furniture springs can distort electromagnetic fields.	See water supply p. 54. Use natural paints pp. 165, 264–5. Change to stainless steel, glass, or enamel cookware. See electricity p. 54.
Plastics Foam filling in chairs, mattresses, cushions, and pillows.	Polyurethane: serious fire hazard.	Banned in UK and other countries. Use safe alternatives. See natural fibres pp. 160–1, 262–3.
Vinyl plastics in floor and wall tiles, electrical equipment, imitation wood panelling, wallpapers.	Formaldehyde and other toxic vapours. Vinyl chloride.	Use natural alternatives. See pp. 152 and 160–1.
Acrylics used in imitation glass sheets, wrappings.	Toxic vapours. Suspected carcinogens.	Avoid: even small amounts can be dangerous. Use safe alternatives. See pp. 152 and 160–1.
Soft plastics (thermoplastics) used in numerous household products (e.g. food packaging and storage).	Vapours, especially in hot conditions. Food contaminants.	Use natural alternatives such as cellophane or greaseproof paper. Store food in glass, earthenware, or china containers. See p. 220.
Household maintenance Cleaners for ovens and carpets, polishes, bleaches, disinfectants, detergents, air fresheners, personal hygiene products.	Formaldehyde. Phenols, vinyl chloride, aldehydes, benzene, toluene, ketones, ammonia, chlorine, lye. All are highly irritant and toxic if swallowed. Aerosol sprays with CFCs.	Use natural alternatives and home remedies. See pp. 192, 266–7. If you must use chemical cleaners, wear gloves and protect skin from splashes. Store in a safe place away from children. Ventilate to the outside.
Pesticides and fungicides	Toxic – irritants and possible carcinogens.	Practise biological pest control. See p. 257.

The polluting home

Pollutants and waste exported from our homes, and from industries producing the goods we consume and use there, enter the air, water, and soil, ultimately entering food chains. Eventually, the damage rebounds on us, like a toxic boomerang; we drink polluted water; we buy polluted food; we breathe polluted air; and global climatic changes affect us all.

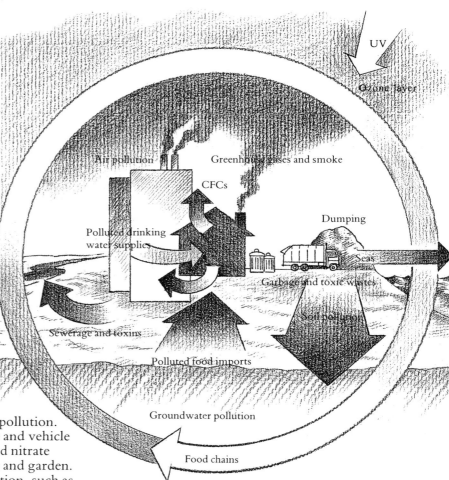

The house is a considerable exporter of pollution. Polluted wastewater, indoor air, smoke and vehicle exhausts, rubbish, garden pesticides, and nitrate fertilizers are all emitted from the house and garden. But what starts as a simple, everyday action, such as washing the dishes or clothes, lighting a fire, starting the car, killing garden pests or using an aerosol air freshener, finishes up causing complex problems locally as well as generally for the environment. Pollution will not go away until we stop creating it in the first place.

Smoke and exhaust gases, together with industrial emissions, result in local smogs, but they will also be blown far by prevailing winds, perhaps across continents and seas, where they react with moisture in the atmosphere to produce acid rain. The result: dead trees and sterile lakes anywhere downwind of the source of the pollution. Aerosols containing chlorofluorocarbons (CFCs) in their propellant gas are contributing (along with methane) to the destruction of the ozone layer, while carbon dioxide is gradually warming the atmosphere. Carbon dioxide is one of the greenhouse gases and the resultant climate changes will alter the globe as the polar caps recede.

We are also subject to a "boomerang" effect – for what we export we also import in kind. Most home-generated pollution gradually and inevitably finds its way into the larger planetary systems and contributes to the growing contamination of the land, air, and water. Chemicals we add to our water and the pesticides and nitrates that are leached from gardens and farmland into rivers and groundwater ultimately enter our drinking supplies. But they also pollute the seas, entering animal lifecycles via small organisms. These can be eaten in turn by migratory species, which then travel the globe carrying the poisons with them. Pollutants, whether they are in the air, soil, or water, that enter the food chains will work their damage at all levels and eventually come back to us via the food we eat – no matter where in the world it is produced.

As consumers, there is much we can do by our ordinary, everyday actions to lessen this burden of pollution (see p. 129).

The wasteful home

The Western world is geared to consumption on a massive scale. Powerful and seductive advertising campaigns attempt to generate the need to possess the latest products and styles. We continue to consume valuable and irreplaceable resources at an ever-increasing rate, with seemingly no real regard for the inevitable future when those resources will be unable to meet demand. And high consumption on the part of those in the richer countries of the world leaves poorer nations still poorer. We are locking ourselves into a future crisis.

Our homes are part of this system and they reflect these values in the way we build and live in them. They are wasteful and inefficient not only in their design but also in the way in which we maintain them.

Processed and scarce materials

The procurement of any material uses at least some energy, but the production of processed ones consumes the most. On the energy balance sheet, manufactured materials such as metals and plastics draw heavily on reserves, while basic materials such as timber and stone can more easily be accommodated, especially if derived from local sources and not transported from other regions or countries.

A glaring example of waste is the production of plastics from oil, itself a limited resource, in an energy-intensive process that uses yet more scarce resources. More than 30 per cent of plastics in the UK are devoted to packaging, used once, and then discarded. Plastic should be regarded as one of our most valuable processed materials; instead, it has become the symbol of the throw-away society.

Part of the built-in obsolescence of many of the modern products is undoubtedly driven by changes in fashion. But whereas in the past it was possible to mend defects with minimum effort, the modern trend is to build equipment of such sophistication that replacement rather than repair is the cheaper and easier option.

Water consumption

Another indicator of basic attitudes is the wasteful way in which the developed world takes for granted clean, piped drinking water, while well over half those living in developing countries do not have access to safe supplies. But now in the West, overconsumption of water and water pollution are making clean and safe tap water a scarcer and more expensive resource, especially in dry, hot regions. Many public supplies of drinking water are becoming polluted and are below the standards laid down by the World Health Organization and regional bodies, such as the European Economic Community. The more water we use, the more energy is needed to collect and process it, pipe it to our homes, and then treat it again afterward. Many public water treatment facilities are now not able to cope with the increasing load and there is a real danger of polluted water contaminating the environment and our drinking water supplies.

In the developed world, an average family of four uses between 10,000 and 40,000 gallons of water per year – creating a huge demand on piped supplies. But at the same time, most of us waste all the rainwater that falls on our homes (instead of storing it). As well, we also waste all the resusable "greywater" (see pp.92-5) from baths, basins, and so on. The American eco-architect Malcolm Wells has calculated that the city of Philadelphia receives as much rain annually as its total piped water demand, but uses none of it.

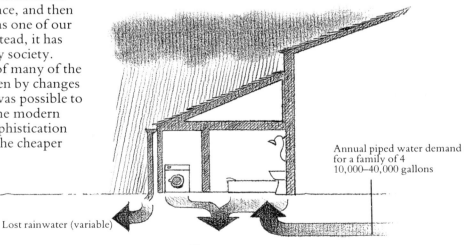

Annual piped water demand for a family of 4
10,000–40,000 gallons

Lost rainwater (variable)

Waste greywater
35-40% of supply

Energy consumption

We use far too much energy and, worst of all, we waste most of what we draw from main supplies anyway. Since it costs only one-tenth as much to save energy through conservation measures as it does to produce more of it, this is obviously the place to make a start.

An average-sized, older-style house uses 20,000 to 30,000kWh of energy each year. Of the total amount spent on energy, between 40 and 60 per cent (depending on climate and the level of insulation) goes on space heating, 20 per cent on hot water, and 15 to 30 per cent on cooking, lighting, and electrical appliances. The remainder goes on maintenance and standing charges. By improving insulation and draughtproofing and by using better controls, it is possible to save at least half the money now spent on heating and hot water.

Two factors that often work against us becoming more energy efficient are the siting and orientation of our homes (see pp. 68-9). In cold climates we lose the natural heating benefits of the sun but fail to shelter buildings from cold prevailing winds. In hot climates we fail to shade the house from the sun or to use the cooling effects of prevailing winds. Added to these fundamental problems, poor insulation, gaps around doors and windows, open chimneys, and old, inefficient boilers all contribute to making the home energy hungry.

The modern home is becoming inundated with energy-consuming electrical appliances and gadgets. Not only should we begin to question just how necessary these are in the first place, we should certainly be more careful to use them as economically as possible.

Household waste

It is almost impossible to buy anything today that is not packaged in one way or another. Stores will also usually want to place purchases in paper or plastic bags emblazoned with their name. Every household in the US and UK produces on average a minimum of a tonne of rubbish every year, which has to be disposed of as bulk waste of no value. Yet virtually all of it has a potential reuse value, provided that it is sorted for recycling (see pp. 268-9).

Energy waste

Energy leaks out everywhere from a house. About 30-40% of an average home's heat is lost due to leaky construction and the "bellows effect" – cold air infiltrating and hot air escaping. Windows and doors lose a further 20%, walls 15-25%, roof and ceilings 12%, and 10% is even lost via ground floors or basements. In an average older house, indoor air will be changed with outdoor air at the rate of about once every hour or faster; in a newer, well-constructed house this will be about once every two hours; but in an extremely tightly sealed house this rate can be reduced to once every three hours or more (but this may pose health hazards – see pp. 100-1).

Waste or rubbish?

An analysis of the contents of your own garbage will be illuminating. It could include paper/cardboard, glass, cans, plastics, textiles, vegetable matter, and toxic items (such as household cleaners, medicines, and pesticides) all mixed together and impossible to sort. But most, such as glass, metals, plastic, and paper, are expensive, processed materials, which are far cheaper to recycle than to produce from raw materials. Plastics are a problem, since only a few can be recycled if sorted and the rest are not biodegradable and thus will not decay after disposal. Toxic substances also cause pollution unless they are specially treated or disposed of.

Glass

10%   10%

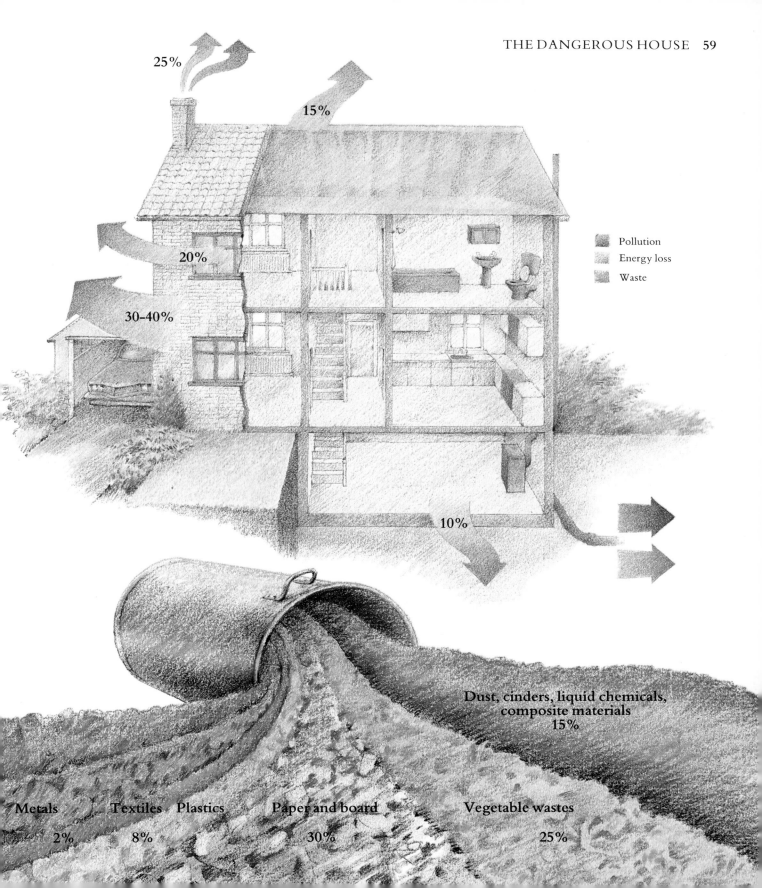

25%

15%

20%

30–40%

10%

Pollution
Energy loss
Waste

Dust, cinders, liquid chemicals,
composite materials
15%

Metals   Textiles Plastics   Paper and board   Vegetable wastes

2%   8%   30%   25%

The alienating home

Much of Western lifestyle is bound up with the rejection and distancing of nature from everyday life. The once intimate relationship with the land, the seasons, and the local climate that formed our past is disappearing as more and more people settle into urban or semi-urban environments. The partnership that existed formerly between people and the natural habitat is being replaced with a mastering of nature. This process is worldwide, and while it can be seen in its most advanced stages in affluent Europe and North America, it is also spreading to the developing world where vast areas of tropical rainforests are being destroyed.

The gradual dislocation from traditional backgrounds and roots and the estrangement from the family and familiar places are compounded by a loss of identity and of spiritual values. The urban ills of anonymity, isolation, and stress have come in their place. With no real sense of roots or belonging, people can feel divorced from control of their own lives and environments.

Ownership and materialism

For many people a growth-orientated and materialistic view is the new order. The one certain way of achieving identity and status is through material wealth. This preoccupation conditions us to a world view where "having" rather than "being" is the prevailing theme. Status becomes synonymous with consumption and possessions.

Insensitivity to the character of a locality, its climate, land, indigenous materials, and traditions creates alienating homes. Poor orientation to the sun and the natural shelter of hills and trees increases the need to compensate with sophisticated heating, cooling, and lighting systems. Sealed buildings lack the ability to interact with the local environment. Excessive amounts of waste and pollution damage the landscape and further weaken any harmony that might exist between the home and its habitat.

The home can become a microcosm of this new society, displaying all its alienating tendencies. At the extreme, it can become merely a repository, a place of status: a place where the kitchen becomes the end processor of convenience foods; the living room a furniture showroom with TV and stereo. And a garden can come to represent a ritual weekend tidying of nature with noisy, polluting machines and the destruction of wildlife with a barrage of pesticides and herbicides.

Loss of individuality

Each room in an alienating home is a sterile space filled with mass-produced furniture and standardized objects that lack a personal history, and, increasingly, are made of "dead" synthetic materials. Of the origins of these objects and of the people who made them, we know less and less. The influence of media advertising and current trends and fashions are so strong that our own needs and preferences are suppressed. We have little time or inclination to create anything for ourselves, and loss of confidence in our own abilities to make and do things is also a loss of individual power. Relinquishing creativity in designing and furnishing our homes to "experts" diminishes and weakens us to the extent that our homes are no longer expressions of ourselves – no longer homes at all.

PART TWO
ELEMENTS

Chapter Three
LIFE SYSTEMS

"The more you know, the less you need." Old Australian Aborigine proverb

Animals, birds, and insects respond to a far greater range of natural stimuli than do people. Dolphins, whales, birds, butterflies, and many other creatures can all detect electromagnetic energy and use this "supersense" to navigate and guide them in their migratory routes. Beyond our visible spectrum, insects use ultraviolet to see food-bearing plants and snakes use infrared to detect their prey. Although our sensory awareness is not as acute as this, our own senses were once far sharper.

Our move indoors, out of the wild and into cities, coupled with the effects of pollution, have dulled our senses, as well as altered the emphasis we place on them. In a world beset with noise, unpleasant air, and bad smells, amid the dominance of visual information, TV, and advertising, we have come to rely heavily on sight and have pushed into the background sensory input from our ears or nose (let alone the subtler messages of electromagnetism to which we may also be sensitive). These "sensory blind spots" have had their effect on our homes.

While we plan and decorate them with meticulous care, we often then proceed to fill them with unnoticed chemical vapours and electrical pollution, leaving our senses disorientated, confused, and frustrated.

In the past, when our labours each day made us aware of our reliance on the life systems of air, water, sun, and soil, we treated them as the domain of the gods. In some cultures this is still the case, and there the natural systems are honoured and cherished – not in an abstract or ritualized way, but simply by working with them, respecting and nurturing them. Most importantly, we all (as individuals and societies) must learn to steer a path that does not further upset the intricate global cycles upon which all life depends.

Our cities and our homes are an integral part of these vital systems. We have to find ways of designing and adapting them to use air, water, and energy more efficiently while generating less pollution. A few years ago, this might have seemed a rather marginal concern; but today it is paramount and must be a top priority for all of us.

Except for electric light, the Nature House, Sweden (right and far right) runs entirely on natural systems. The timber house, built within a glass outer shell, is light, bright, and spacious. The perimeter spaces are filled with green conservatories of exotic plants and sunspaces, while fruit, flowers, and vegetables flourish in the glass roof garden. The sun's rays trapped by the glass shell give immediate warmth; a

thick layer of pebbles under the house stores the heat, which is circulated by a fan. A wood-burning stove in the living room supplies back-up heating, if required. A waterless toilet composts all human and other organic wastes, and a large tank set into the indoor terrace stores rainwater. Fresh air, drawn in through the rooftop garden fills the house with the sweet scent of flowers and plants. Architect: Bengt Warne

The senses

When we experience the world, we do so with all our senses acting in unison. With food, for example, we see, touch, smell, and taste (and even hear it as it cooks). Our skin combines a multitude of senses and reactions – awareness of touch and air movement, heat, and moisture – and has mechanisms to protect us from harmful extremes. These bodily systems and our brain are all designed to allow us to interpret the environment around us, and to maintain by feedback responses a dynamic balance, or *homeostasis*, which permits us to survive.

All our senses are more acute than we realize, capable of detecting minute changes and variations. Today, most of us live almost exclusively in artificial environments – at home, in cars and trains, and in the office or factory – and may suffer long-term sensory deprivation, from, for example, inadequate natural or artificial light, from living and breathing in stale air, and drinking dull, lifeless, and often polluted water.

Sensory deprivation can arise too from environments that are too uniform. A home where all the rooms are the same temperature, for example, can induce boredom and lethargy, as well as eventually making us less tolerant of minor variations. We may equally suffer from overstimulation and stress – from electromagnetic fields, from the strong glare of artificial lights, or ill-designed windows, from continual noise and disturbance, dry and overheated rooms, and artificial scents.

All of these potential problems are the result of poorly conceived indoor environments and their associated indoor climates. Most architects and designers have traditionally spoken a mainly visual language – a vocabulary of aesthetic considerations of space, form, scale, and style. Who, if anybody, specifies that the house must also smell, feel, and sound healthy and pleasing? Or that it should have a healthy electromagnetic environment or provide for our closer contact with nature?

Healing environments

Our public buildings and homes need to be reconceived as total environments. As a basic priority, they need to be free of any toxic or harmful elements. This will allow the body to detoxify itself and lessen its chemical and pollutant load. But they need to go beyond this, to become places that are positively designed to heal and rejuvenate and be supportive and enhancing of all aspects of life and spirit. The Baubiologie concept of a "living climate" (see pp. 26 and 66) is an attempt to do this. Realizing that the creation of a pleasant indoor climate is linked to its interaction with that outdoors, the whole house – its form, siting, materials used, and services – is designed to bring all the contributing forces into dynamic balance.

Another approach holds that environments should be therapeutic and that light, colour, scent, sound, and water can all be used as therapies when incorporated into home design and decoration. Aromatherapy, colour therapy, hydrotherapy, sound and light health all bring their deep and personal healing qualities into the home. In Eastern philosophy, air, light, earth, and water all carry *ch'i*, or vital energy, which can increase our personal ch'i, and it is this energy flow that many therapies seek to release. Even in a Western view, the air, food, water, light, and heat we need all are in fact different forms of energy, which, together with Earth radiations, form part of the energy system of the whole planet.

We live in, and by, this energy system, sharing it with all other life forms. Our senses are tuned to its many manifestations, and we can be healed through them.

Integrated environments

In many ways, our homes act as extensions of our senses and, like a "third skin" (see p. 66), also serve to protect us from the world around us. Internally, the home can be likened to the human organism, with organs to process energy, water, food, and wastes. The house can be made "intelligent", too – not by expensive and complicated high-technology computers, electronic monitors, and control devices, but much more simply – by using the natural mechanisms of air, sun, water, and materials. These, together with the best computer available – your own brain – and the most sensitive monitors yet devised – your own senses – complete the process. As American architect Malcolm Wells has said: "the only water-saving shower head worth having is the one between your ears. That's where all the real savings begin."

With a greater understanding of the basic mechanisms that control the natural world – solar heating and cooling, the water cycle, recycling – we can introduce more "passive", self-regulatory controls and mechanisms into our homes. Such appropriate and organic design relieves pressure on the world's scarce resources. Energy is the fundamental building block of civilization. High energy consumption based on burning fossil and other fuels is responsible for global climatic changes that now threaten all our futures. The developed world, with already high energy use, must seek an energy-efficient and low-polluting path if the poorer countries are to catch up without the total load on the environment reaching breaking point.

Divergent strategies

New ideas on how to design your home to use the life systems efficiently come from several quite different groups. The ecology movement has produced ideas for energy-saving homes, from heat exchangers to earth-sheltered buildings or solar panels. Ecohouses may be exciting concepts but they are often rather extreme and demanding on the user, and they are seldom concerned with either personal health or beauty. Many ecodesigners are engineers, and see the challenge as technological in nature. They risk being accused of having a "technofix" approach to problems that are essentially human – those of lifestyle and habit. The health movement, concerned with allergies and illnesses due to toxic materials and pollutants, is more human-centred, but also more self-indulgent and seldom concerned with eco questions, such as energy and water conservation. Homes designed to be allergy free are not necessarily ecological or concerned with creating an attractive environment. Yet this aspect is important. Meantime, by way of contrast, architects put beauty, or rather "style", first and both health and ecology last!

For the individual, these divergent approaches can pose a real problem. Where do you turn for reliable literature or to find experts to advise you on home design? It is very difficult to find in one organization or individual a balanced view of the three elements of health, ecology, and beauty. And consultants on home design concerned with spiritual and personal wellbeing and for creating healing environments are few and far between. The newer Baubiologie, just beginning to spread beyond its home in West Germany, began more with healthy housing but now, increasingly, combines ecology and spiritual elements, too.

It is ironic that most people want the very thing that is usually missing: not a high-tech solar house, not a rigorous allergy-free one, not a designer status symbol, but a simple home that provides reasonably for health, ecology, and spirit and is attractive and comfortable to live in. To achieve this, help and advice are needed, because it is often necessary to trade one element off against another when making practical design decisions. More window area for daylight, or less to save heat loss? A hot tub for health, or a water-conserving shower? An open fire for comfort, radiators only to avoid producing greenhouse gases, or a compromise with a high-performance stove? Healthy lighting, or less-healthy fluorescent tubes to save energy? You can extend this list endlessly but, in the end, it largely comes down to what you consider most important – for you, your family, and the environment. This chapter is concerned with providing some of the basic facts and introducing many of the options that are available.

Even if you introduce only one of the many ideas here, you will have helped. Small changes, when multiplied by millions, make a significant difference. Above all, you may learn to think of your home in terms of its "impact". A low-impact home is the opposite of dangerous – it does least harm to your own health and that of the environment. It is more a part of its local bioregion, more conserving and healthy, and using the life systems with care and respect.

Comfort and climate

Although human populations can survive in all but the most impossibly harsh climatic conditions, the human body is "comfortable" in only a relatively narrow range of thermal conditions. There have been many attempts to define what precisely these conditions are but it is more complex than it first seems. First, there are age-difference variations in perceived comfort as well as racial and cultural differences. Temperature and humidity are certainly critical factors, too, but there are others. A movement of the air, for example, is needed to avoid feelings of stuffiness and, together with air freshness, stimulate the skin and assist correct breathing (see p. 97). The air quality will also affect thermal comfort, and such related factors as the presence of a higher ratio of negative to positive ions, electromagnetic radiation, and air pollutants have not yet been given sufficient attention. As studies of the "sick building syndrome" indicate (see pp. 52-3), our perceptions of our internal environment are a mixture of many stimuli.

If your body is to function properly it needs to maintain an average temperature of 37°C (98.4°F). Heat is produced by metabolic processes and it must be dissipated if you are to stay at this temperature. The body normally loses about 45 per cent of its heat by radiation, 30 per cent by convection, and 25 per cent by evaporation. But if you are to remain comfortable thermally then these three factors must be in balance. Although you can regulate thermal losses or gains by, for example, changing your body's activity, location, and clothing, these controls are limited and cannot by themselves keep your body comfortable in severe weather conditions. This, in fact, is the function of the building fabric of our homes – what has been termed our "third skin".

But what is the best balance of the climatic factors that allow your body's thermal-regulating systems to work properly and keep you feeling comfortable? Although you must allow for a lot of variation depending on local climate and your personal adaptation to it, there is a range of temperature and humidity levels – known as the comfort zone (see below) – that most people regard as pleasant. This is usually between about 18°C (65°F) and 24°C (75°F), but varies depending on the relative humidity, which should remain between 30 and 65 per cent. Relative humidity is a measure of the amount of water vapour in the air – 100 per cent being saturated air. Within the above general limits, the higher the relative humidity becomes the lower the air temperature needs to be in order for you to feel comfortable.

The comfort zone

A pleasant environment has been described as one needing to fulfil six main requirements, and can also be expressed in graph form (see right):

○ Rooms should be as cool as is compatible with comfort.
○ The velocity of air movement should be about at least 10m (33ft) per minute in winter – less than 6m (20ft) per minute may cause stuffiness.
○ Air movement should be variable.
○ The relative humidity should not exceed an upper maximum of 70% and should preferably be substantially lower than this.
○ The average temperature of internal surfaces should be above, or at least equal to, the air temperature.
○ The air temperature should not be appreciably higher at head level than it is at floor level, and excessive radiant heat should not fall on the heads of occupants.

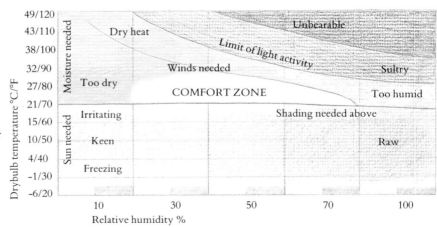

This timber-frame house near Horte, in Telemark, Norway (above) incorporates many of the best features of environment-friendly housing. As well as providing living accommodation, it also has a guitar workshop and weaving studio. All the new timber for the house was bought and sawn locally, but the owners ensured that as much recycled material as possible was used from other houses nearby. To improve insulation during the long winter, snow is left on the roof and piled up against the walls.

The verandah on a New Mexico house has a slatted roof to provide shade without inhibiting ventilation. You will also find this tradition throughout the Mediterranean, where roof timbers are hung with fruiting and flowering vines, making them ideal living spaces in all but the most extreme winter or summer weather.

The energy-efficient home

The home and its setting in the landscape symbolize our relationship with nature. A building can be constructed in such a way that it supports the natural ecology of the area – the vegetation, water, and wildlife – or it can be disruptive and damaging. Most buildings have a major impact on the local environment and unless the degree of disturbance is carefully controlled and the land restored afterward, the delicate ecological balance could be destroyed.

For your home to be comfortable (see pp. 66-7) yet use as little energy as possible, working with nature rather than against it is the fundamental principle. The location, siting, and orientation are all vitally important if you are to gain the maximum benefit of winter sun but also make the most of shelter given by hills and trees against any prevailing winter winds and summer overheating. A well-sited, energy-efficient home will use the natural features of the locality and, therefore, will never have to draw on as much supplementary energy as one built without any regard for its surroundings.

Whatever climate prevails – cool, temperate, hot and humid, or hot and dry – the natural home will need to be located, built, or adapted for it to be receptive to its unique local conditions.

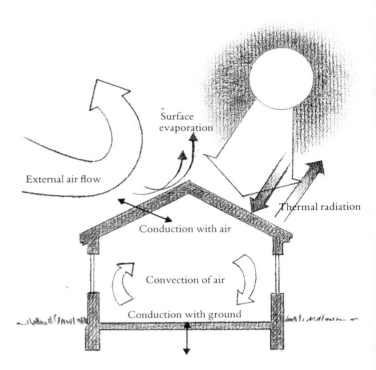

Surface evaporation

External air flow

Thermal radiation

Conduction with air

Convection of air

Conduction with ground

Heat movement

Our perception of temperature is affected by the way heat moves. Heat moves naturally from warmer to cooler areas always seeking to balance air temperature.

Heat, such as that received from the sun or an electric radiator, is *radiant heat* and, like light, is a form of electromagnetic energy. Heat waves are transferred from their source directly through the air and they are absorbed by the surfaces on which they fall. Surfaces and materials have different capacities to absorb (or reflect) this heat – a dark surface absorbing most and a light one reflecting most. All objects radiate heat in all directions; the warmer ones having more heat to exchange with the cooler ones until they reach the same average temperature.

Uncontrolled radiant heat can be the

cause of discomfort in the home. Even though the measured indoor air temperature is comfortable, radiant heat can make you feel overhot during the day. At night, however, if windows are not properly insulated, your body will lose potentially uncomfortable (or, in the case of the elderly, potentially dangerous) amounts of radiant heat in cold environments.

When air is heated it expands, becomes lighter, and rises. As it passes over less-hot objects it gives off some of its heat, cools, contracts, and then falls. This process is known as *convection* and the faster the movement of the air the faster heat is transferred. If, however, air is trapped in the spaces of porous material, such as clothing or in the cavity between two brick walls, you have the basics of insulation.

Heat is also transferred from molecule to molecule in a solid material and from one material to an adjacent one. This is a process known as *conduction*, and the rate of transfer depends on, among other things, the densities of the materials involved. Metals are highly conductive, wood is less so, and gases even lower.

Heat is lost or gained by a building via all three methods of movement (radiation, convection, and conduction), and the cumulative rate of thermal resistance is known as the R-value, while the amount of heat transference is known by its coefficient, the U-value. The higher the R-value or the lower the U-value, the less heat is gained or lost.

The ideal site
The best place to site a house will vary from one climate region to another. The main aim (right) is to make the best possible use of natural features – trees, land forms, and local winds and water – for warmth and shelter and thereby lessen the need for artificial forms of heating, cooling, and insulation.

Shelter from prevailing winds
In cold and temperate climates, a house sited to take maximum advantage of local shelter will be protected from cold winter winds and will be warmer, quieter, and more energy-conserving (above).

Hot humid
Shade the house as much as possible with a high canopy of deciduous trees planted nearby. You can increase air movement by facing the house into cool prevailing winds and siting it high up slopes. In the same way as this Malay house, elevate the structure and make rooms and verandahs open to the wind. Light-toned walls and roof help.

Hot arid
Have most shade in the late morning and all afternoon and allow trees to overhang the roof. Site the house to catch the summer winds and moisten the air with water and vegetation. With hot/cold extremes – day and night, summer and winter – a courtyard house of heavy materials to store heat and protect against the cold is ideal. Use light colours.

Temperate
Warm the house with winter sun and use trees and bushes to shelter it from cold prevailing winds. In summer, use deciduous trees and creepers to prevent overheating. Water in ponds reflects the winter sun into the house and also cools it in summer. Pitched roofs throw off rain and medium-toned colours absorb the sun's heat.

Cool
Maximize the warmth from winter sun and shelter from cold winds. Avoid a site in a cold-air pocket. One option is a house built into the ground with an earth-covered grass roof. Plant dense screens of evergreen trees on exposed sides. Shallower, pitched roofs retain snow for extra insulation. Use thick insulating walls with dark tones.

Siting and climate
Most early peoples showed a great sensitivity to local conditions. Cultures in every climate region around the world have developed their own distinctive ways of coping with the climate. Whether it is living high up in tree houses in humid areas or dug down in cave houses in hot or cold locations, they all demonstrate the most efficient means of staying comfortable. With central heating and air conditioning, siting the house in relation to its locality no longer seems to be so important. But with the increasing pressure on world energy resources, these commonsense considerations are again becoming basic requirements.

The solar home

The way the sun heats the planet is the basic model for the solar home. Heat radiates from the sun and warms the planet's surface. Heat is retained near the surface by the layers of the atmosphere and it is also stored in the land and water masses. Winds and water currents, themselves produced by the sun's energy, then circulate the heat around the planet.

In a solar home, these four principles (radiation, retention, storage, and circulation) are at work. A structure heated by the sun absorbs and collects the sun's energy. The fabric of the building retains the heat because of its insulating properties and also because any openings are covered with glass, curtains, or thermal shutters. The interior stores the heat in solid partitions and floors and thermal movement then circulates it. In this respect, you achieve the ultimate in energy efficiency in the well-designed, earth-covered home (see pp. 74-5).

Solar methods of heating the home can be either *passive* or *active*. With a passive solar system, the sun warms the interior directly through windows or a "sunspace" (see p. 73). The building structure is designed to store the heat and release it at night or on cloudy days. Often, natural thermal movement – convection, conduction, and radiation – is all that is needed to circulate heat, but ceiling fans can help. (A word of warning: you will need some method of shading structures such as sunspaces during the summer months in hot climates.)

An active solar system relies more on mechanical components such as solar panels, which absorb the sun's heat and store it in water tanks, rock beds, or similar. Pipes and ducts are required to distribute the heat with the aid of fans, pumps, and valves.

There are a number of advantages with passive solar systems. They require little or no maintenance, for example, since there are no mechanical parts. The initial installation cost and running costs are also low and so they repay the investment in a relatively short time. Very often, if you are building a new home, or even remodelling an existing one, it is possible to incorporate basic passive solar heating at virtually no additional cost and thus reduce both the size and cost of the conventional system. However, depending on the climate, it may be necessary to combine passive and active systems in order to achieve effective and flexible heating and cooling.

The Everett Barber house, Connecticut (above), built in 1975 uses passive and active systems. Inside, solar heat, plus that from kitchen, fireplace, and people, cycles through a rock heat store under the floor and back into the house. Architects: Charles Moore & Associates

This sunspace (left) is also a passive solar collector. It absorbs sunlight in the day, stores it in a thick concrete slab under the floor, and releases it at night.
Architect: T Whitcomb Iglehart

Liquids store heat better than solids. These vertical Kalwall translucent columns, filled with water store the sun's heat, admit daylight, and make attractive and practical features. Architects: C/S Architects

The main systems

Solar windows

This is the simplest solar system since it is designed to allow the direct radiation from the sun to penetrate the interior through sun-facing windows. The windows, either in a house or apartment, act as collectors and the internal building materials become the heat store, radiating the accumulated heat at night or on cloudy days. To be effective, the sun-facing windows have to be larger than normal and you can add skylights or clerestories to allow light penetration into otherwise sunless rooms. All glass surfaces should be double or triple glazed in severe climates with, ideally, low-emissivity glass.

It is important that the internal sun-absorbing surfaces are effective as thermal-storage features. Materials such as heavy masonry walls and concrete floors are excellent, but you can give existing lightweight walls and floors more mass by covering them with additional plaster or thick ceramic tiles. You can also use water drums if the floor will support the weight. Although heat can be distributed around the home by normal thermal movement, fan-assisted circulation can help to reduce the amount of thermal mass required.

Adequate shading in summer is vital to prevent overheating, and insulating curtains, insulating blinds or shutters, and even plants can be both effective as shading devices as well as attractive features in their own right.

Solar walls

Rather than allowing the sun to heat the internal partitions and floor, you can build a special glass-covered thermal-storage wall on the sun-facing side of the structure. As the sun's rays shine on the wall, generated heat is stored and circulated passively through wall vents into the living areas.

There are two types of solar wall: Trombe walls, named after Dr Felix Trombe, and water-container walls. The former are built of heavy masonry material, such as brick, stone, block, or earth, with a dark-coloured surface toward the sun. The wall can have window openings, with double or triple glazing fixed close in front forming a cavity between the two surfaces. It is possible to adapt most existing sun-facing masonry walls by painting the surface dark, covering it with glazing, and installing vents. However, in hot climates, such as in Australia and large areas of the US, you must provide summer shading.

Water-container walls use water drums or columns as heat stores instead of masonry. Water is more efficient than masonry as a thermal store but it is extremely heavy and needs regular maintenance to combat leaks and the growth of algae.

With both types, you either need to close vents or insulate the glazing at night and shade it in summer.

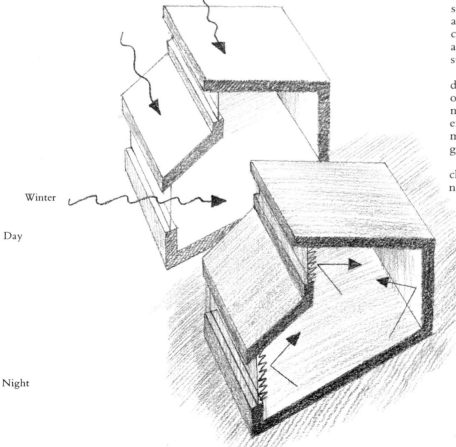

Summer

Winter

Day

Night

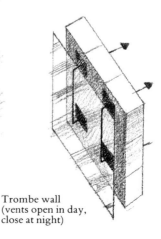

Trombe wall
(vents open in day,
close at night)

Sunspaces

Adding a sunspace to your home has become one of the most popular conservation features in recent years. Known also as a conservatory, solar greenhouse, solarium, or sunroom, a sunspace is an ideal area for a family room, growing plants, or to use as a solar heat collector. It is important, however, to decide what the primary use of the sunspace will be. It is really only successful when it is designed to fulfil one main purpose.

Working in much the same way as a solar window, the sunspace is basically an attached room built on the sun-facing side of a house with a large expanse of glazing. Also effective is a glassed-in balcony area in an upper-floor apartment. During the day the air warmed by the sun flows into the home by natural convection either through open windows or via special vents. At night, if the space is not being used as a living room or greenhouse for plants, you can close the area off and the temperature of the sunspace will then drop below that of the home.

If, however, you want to use it, either for recreation or as a contributor to night time heating, you will need to provide thermal storage and insulation to the glazing. Heat can be stored either in the heavy materials surrounding the sunspace or it can be transferred by fan during the day to a heat store.

To prevent overheating, especially in hot climates, you should incorporate roof vents or windows and, in summer, deciduous trees and vines can provide additional shade.

Sunspaces can contribute significantly to reducing heating bills, but in temperate climates recent UK research has revealed that the expense of installation is too high to be justified on energy-saving grounds alone. Less-expensive measures, such as solar windows, insulation, and draughtproofing, are much more cost effective. The popularity of sunspaces has more to do with their use as versatile, sun-filled living spaces, with a reduction in heating bills coming as a welcome extra bonus.

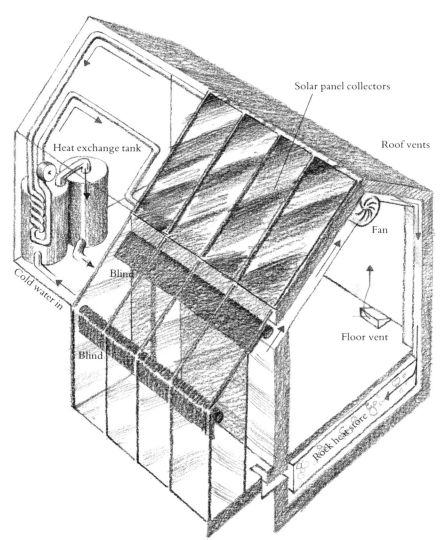

Heat exchange tank

Solar panel collectors

Roof vents

Fan

Blind

Cold water in

Floor vent

Blind

Rock heat store

Active systems

In this system the sun heats glass- or plastic-covered metal collector panels housed in shallow boxes fixed in rows on a sun-facing roof. The absorbed heat is taken from these by passing liquid or air through or around the panels and is then fed into a thermal store under the ground floor. This store is either a rock bed for air systems (but you need to check for radon – see p. 101) or a water tank for water systems in hot climates. When you need the heat in the home it is distributed by water pipes or air ducts, assisted by fans or pumps. Alternatively, you can use a sunspace as the solar collector (see left).

Depending on the climate, solar hot water systems can provide between half and three-quarters of a household's requirements. In hot climates, the solar-heated water is stored directly in hot water tanks, but in cooler climates it is more usual to use it as preheated water for a conventional boiler.

The earth-covered home

The most ancient dwellings we have evidence of were in natural caves and later, when houses were built, these were often dug into the ground or covered with earth. The pit houses of the North American Indians, Eskimo (Inuit) houses with sturdy timber roofs to support earth and a deep covering of snow in winter, and the early Scandinavian farms are just a few of the many examples of this once widespread building principle. Today there is a growing interest in this technique and there are successful examples in Europe, North America, and Australia.

The advantage of integrating a building with the surrounding ground and covering the roof partially or entirely with grass is that the earth is a natural moderator of temperature. Below the frost line the temperature of the earth remains fairly constant and is usually close to the area's average annual air temperature. Nearer to the surface, although the temperature will follow the daily and seasonal changes, the earth will still act to moderate the larger variations. This means that an earth-covered or earth-sheltered home will have an extremely stable year-round temperature compared with a surface-built structure.

The soil, depending on its depth and thermal properties, slows the passage of heat gained or lost to such an extent that the heat gained in the summer will reach the house in early winter, and the cooling effects on the soil in winter will not flow through to the house until early summer. This time lag of months, known as the "thermal flywheel effect", means that the ground around the house becomes a heat source in winter and a cooling device in summer. Experience has proved that the little amounts of supplementary heating and cooling required can mostly be provided by passive solar systems (see pp. 70-3), thus reducing reliance on conventional energy sources to an absolute minimum.

As an indication of how effective this type of construction can be in practice, an earth-covered home in Australia used no conventional energy sources during a monitored period to heat or cool its interior, where temperatures varied only 12°C (22°F); during the same period, outside air temperatures varied between -2° and 42°C (28° and 108°F).

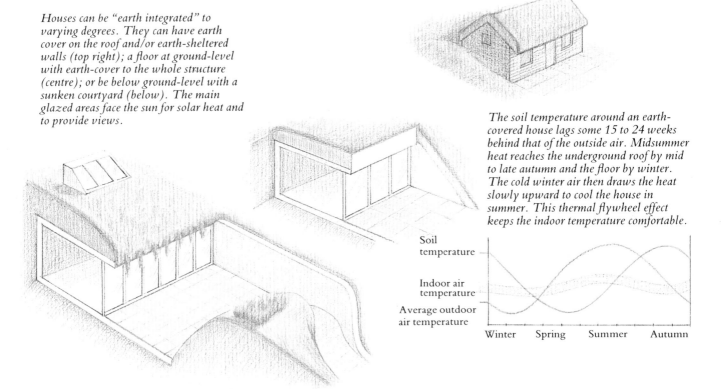

Houses can be "earth integrated" to varying degrees. They can have earth cover on the roof and/or earth-sheltered walls (top right); a floor at ground-level with earth-cover to the whole structure (centre); or be below ground-level with a sunken courtyard (below). The main glazed areas face the sun for solar heat and to provide views.

The soil temperature around an earth-covered house lags some 15 to 24 weeks behind that of the outside air. Midsummer heat reaches the underground roof by mid to late autumn and the floor by winter. The cold winter air then draws the heat slowly upward to cool the house in summer. This thermal flywheel effect keeps the indoor temperature comfortable.

Soil temperature

Indoor air temperature

Average outdoor air temperature

Winter   Spring   Summer   Autumn

In the old Scandinavian tradition, this timber house has its roof covered with a thick layer of turf.

Conceived in the late 1960s as architect Arthur Quarmby's own home, architectural delight rather than energy saving was the main aim of "Underhill". Set into the wild landscape of the Peak District National Park, Yorkshire, a large arched living space and circular swimming pool is lit by an overhead dome, which floods the house with sunlight and reflections.

Hundreds of tons of earth on the roof of this experimental Cape Cod house sustain natural wild gardens that require no watering or other maintenance. The house appears to have grown spontaneously rather than have been built. A long skylight brightens the interior. Architect Malcolm Wells

The cool home

Too many homes in hot or humid climates rely on air-conditioning systems as the chief means of cooling during the summer months. But there are alternatives, many of which have been used successfully in different countries for centuries. Of course, in the hottest and most humid climates it may be necessary to use some form of air conditioning when temperatures are at their most extreme, but by using traditional alternatives as well, the need will be much reduced.

To make the home comfortable in this type of climate there are a number of things you need to do. The first and most obvious of these is to lower the air temperature; then you should concentrate on speeding up the movement of the air, making surfaces cooler, and finally reducing the humidity.

Shading

Reducing the amount of the sun's energy falling on the home and entering through the windows is the initial step. The techniques are basically the same as those used for reducing light levels (see pp. 116–18) – wider roof eaves, awnings, shutters, screens, verandahs, blinds, and low-emissivity glass – but here you should place more emphasis on shading the whole structure with trees, shrubs, creepers, and earth-cover (see pp. 74–5). Where shading is difficult, the next-best alternative is to reflect as much light as possible by painting the roof and outside walls white or, as has proved successful in California, covering the roof area with shiny, reflective aluminium sheeting.

The form and layout of the home has a dramatic effect on the level of shading you can achieve, and courtyard houses have proved their worth since ancient times. The thick outer walls and roof protect the inner living spaces, and the sun reaches the floor of the courtyard for only a short period around midday.

The courtyard house is cooled naturally by convection currents. As the cool air from the inner rooms warms, it rises and is drawn into the courtyard. As the sun sets, the outside air temperature drops quickly, the flow reverses, and cool air is drawn into the rooms to cool them. The warm courtyard floor and flat roofs radiate their stored heat at night and are often used as sleeping areas. In winter, shutters retain the heat in the house interior. Trees, planting, pools, and fountains in the inner courtyard all serve to add humidity to dry air.

Ventilation

Increasing the air movement helps evaporation from the skin and makes you feel fresher and more active. Fortunately, in many hot areas there are prevailing winds that can cool the home by natural ventilation. Cross-ventilation, from one side of the home to the other, is the traditional method. Cool air enters, preferably at low level, and expels warm air through windows or vents at high level. If you live in a dry climate you can moisten the air blowing into the home by allowing it to pass over water in a pool, in earthenware containers and wide, shallow bowls, or through vegetation.

As an alternative, wind-scoop devices commonly used in the Middle East, such as the *malqaf* or *badgir* can be built to catch cool breezes at roof level and channel them down a shaft to lower-level living areas. High pressure on the windward side and low pressure on the leeward side of the building ensure that cool air is sucked downward. Window lattices and screens, such as the Egyptian ornamental wooden-peg *mashrabiya*, allow air to filter freely into the rooms while, additionally, reducing the strong glare of direct sunlight.

Where you do not have the benefit of prevailing winds, you can use the thermal-stack effect to induce ventilation. It works on the same principle as convection (see p. 68), and you can use it with passive solar heating systems – sunspaces and solar windows and walls (see pp. 70–3) – working in reverse. When used for heating, passive solar heaters deliver the warm and rising air into the interior. But if you vent the warm air at high level to the outside instead, you can use them for cooling by drawing in cool air at low level. The thermal mass of the materials helps to keep the cycle going at night. In order to exploit this method fully, passive thermal chimneys used solely for ventilation, and performing in the same way as a reverse wind scoop, are now being incorporated into many homes in countries such as the US and Australia.

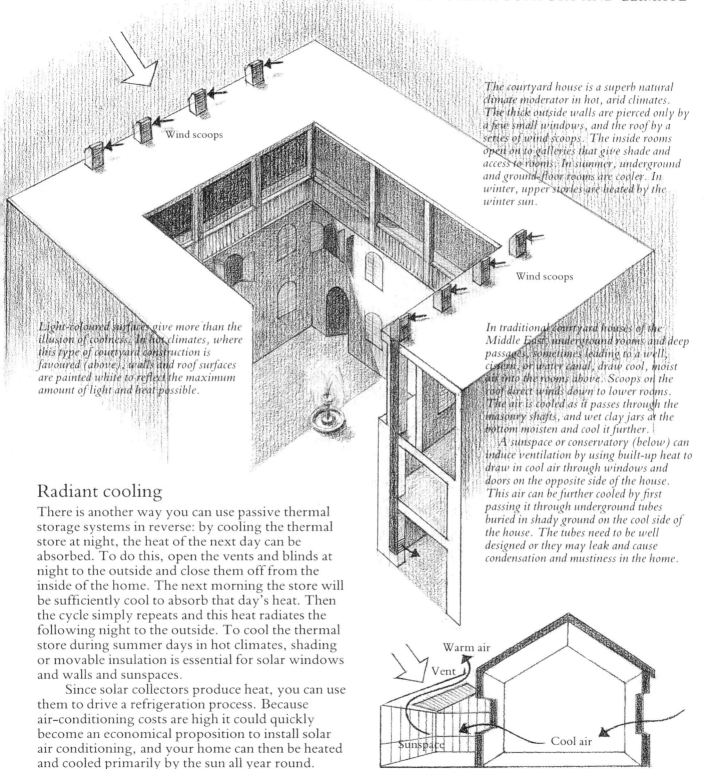

Wind scoops

Wind scoops

The courtyard house is a superb natural climate moderator in hot, arid climates. The thick outside walls are pierced only by a few small windows, and the roof by a series of wind scoops. The inside rooms open on to galleries that give shade and access to rooms. In summer, underground and ground-floor rooms are cooler. In winter, upper stories are heated by the winter sun.

Light-coloured surfaces give more than the illusion of coolness. In hot climates, where this type of courtyard construction is favoured (above), walls and roof surfaces are painted white to reflect the maximum amount of light and heat possible.

In traditional courtyard houses of the Middle East, underground rooms and deep passages, sometimes leading to a well, cistern, or water canal, draw cool, moist air into the rooms above. Scoops on the roof direct winds down to lower rooms. The air is cooled as it passes through the masonry shafts, and wet clay jars at the bottom moisten and cool it further.

A sunspace or conservatory (below) can induce ventilation by using built-up heat to draw in cool air through windows and doors on the opposite side of the house. This air can be further cooled by first passing it through underground tubes buried in shady ground on the cool side of the house. The tubes need to be well designed or they may leak and cause condensation and mustiness in the home.

Radiant cooling

There is another way you can use passive thermal storage systems in reverse: by cooling the thermal store at night, the heat of the next day can be absorbed. To do this, open the vents and blinds at night to the outside and close them off from the inside of the home. The next morning the store will be sufficiently cool to absorb that day's heat. Then the cycle simply repeats and this heat radiates the following night to the outside. To cool the thermal store during summer days in hot climates, shading or movable insulation is essential for solar windows and walls and sunspaces.

Since solar collectors produce heat, you can use them to drive a refrigeration process. Because air-conditioning costs are high it could quickly become an economical proposition to install solar air conditioning, and your home can then be heated and cooled primarily by the sun all year round.

Warm air

Vent

Sunspace

Cool air

Fuel and power

After the shock of the oil crisis in the 1970s, there was a surge of activity from governments and industry in the fields of conservation and the use of alternative energy sources. But the recent oil glut and the fall in oil prices have lulled many back into the old belief that cheap energy is here to stay.

At present, three-quarters of world energy consumption comes from nonrenewable "hard-energy" sources – a third of this amount is oil, a quarter coal, and the rest from natural gas. The other quarter of world usage is supplied by a mixture of nuclear power, hydropower, and biomass. In developing countries, however, there is heavy dependence on biomass, and the burning of fuelwood and animal dung is resulting in serious environmental destruction.

Our reliance on these nonrenewable, largely fossil-fuel sources is not only shortsighted (predictions show that unless we make drastic reductions in consumption they will become scarce, expensive, and soon depleted), but also environmentally dangerous (acid rain and the potentially disastrous climatic change caused by greenhouse gases).

The need for a new global energy strategy is urgent and the transition to a low-energy future, reliant on benign and sustainable renewable sources, is something each of us can influence locally, while still retaining acceptable standards of comfort. The goal is then to make the maximum use of natural, "soft-energy" sources – the sun, wind, and water – and to site or protect your home so that it requires a minimum of supplementary energy (see p. 69).

Supplementary fuel choices

To balance the energy deficit from alternative energy sources in the home you have, depending on your locality, a choice of gas, coal, oil, or wood, as well as electricity generated from central supplies or perhaps locally from sun, wind, and water. But for the reasons given above, you should start to think of fossil fuels – coal, oil and gas – more as back-up energy sources. If the rigorous standards recently introduced in Oregon become generally accepted, the only way that you will be able to enjoy a fire in the future will be in high-performance stoves with efficient emission controls on smoke and gases.

Like other combustion products, wood has the major disadvantage of being a source of pollution. But despite this, it is generally viewed as a good ecological fuel source, since it is both renewable and sustainable, provided that it comes from properly managed forests. But recent global developments may be changing this picture. In industrialized countries, although supplies can be increased, acid rain and forest fires have devastated large areas of woodland and this will have a significant impact on future availability.

Once the political will exists, waste heat from, for example, power stations or industrial plants can be used to heat large residential areas organized in district-heating projects. Battersea Power Station in London, before it was taken out of service, was one of the few to make use of some of its waste energy. Some of this heated large apartment blocks, housing 11,000 people, on the opposite side of the Thames river. In Iceland, the energy of the planet itself has been put to work and volcanic springs are used to heat whole towns. District-heating projects have had their problems in the past, but with improved and cleaner technology, such as the highly efficient and economic Combined Heat and Power (CHP) method, and the new ideas of "energy from waste" (where plastics are incinerated in low-emission furnaces to produce heat and electricity), these schemes are likely to become more generally applicable and widespread. Latest developments are heading in the direction of "Micro-CHP", which uses local, small-scale generators.

Electricity is often claimed to be the cleanest and most efficient form of energy. Whereas this may be true once it reaches the home, these claims depend on how and where the electricity is produced. Being mostly generated from coal and oil, there is a global problem of air and water pollution, made more serious by the presence of greenhouse gases. Hydroelectric projects are notorious worldwide for destroying the environments of rivers and lakes with huge dams and reservoirs. In general, power stations are only about 30 per cent efficient – the remaining 70 per cent of fossil-fuel input is wasted as heat. The nuclear alternative is unacceptable to many and radioactive wastes represent a menace too dangerous to sanction.

Wind and water have been used for centuries as a power source and they can also be used to generate electricity. But they both need expensive equipment, which is unlikely to be cost effective unless you live in a remote area without access to normal supplies. Wind farms may prove more viable but their visual impact, being sited as they must on hilltops, plus the disturbance to radio, TV, and microwave communications, are disadvantages.

Solar electricity produced from photovoltaic cells on site at home is an attractive alternative. It bypasses the problems mentioned above and is becoming increasingly competitive with other sources of energy. In North America, Australia, and many developing countries there is growing interest in domestic solar electricity systems, even though at present they may retain a link with mains power to provide a boost on cloudy days. It is now feasible to become self-sufficient and, in some situations, even to sell surplus power to a local utility.

With the support of both US state and federal incentives, farmers in California began harvesting the wind. But the visual intrusiveness and noise of the wind generators (above) provoked strong local dissent.

Used for 500 years in Russia, Scandinavia, and in German-speaking countries, where it is known as the kachelofen, the tile stove (left) is still popular. It can heat one or more rooms, and has hot water and cooking ovens as options. A pleasant and healthy radiant heat penetrates the house, warming the walls and giving a subtle aroma.

The electric home

We have become so dependent on electricity that we can hardly imagine the world without it. But electricity is still a relatively new technology and it is only recently that its potentially harmful effects on human health and wellbeing have been seriously considered (see opposite). As well, in common with other conventional energy sources, the consumption of electricity is increasing and its production continues to deplete the planet's dwindling reserves of nonrenewable fuel resources.

There is already a growing body of concern about the stress from "electronic smog" (see p. 201) and the associated risk of cancers, including leukemia, caused by high-tension power lines (see p. 50). Now, however, there is mounting evidence that there may also be problems associated with electricity within our homes. These problems may stem from the additional physical and psychological disturbances electricity causes to our natural biological systems. These effects are thought to result from the very nature of electricity and from the electric and magnetic fields present in all domestic circuits and appliances. However, bear in mind that research into this area is still in its infancy and as yet results, although giving cause for concern, are tentative and inconclusive.

What can we do to protect ourselves in our homes and workplaces from this imperceptible pollution? The most experience has been gained from the work carried out in German homes using the Baubiologie approach (see p. 26). Although electrical surveys are best, there are many simple and commonsense solutions that everybody can introduce into their own homes.

Certain commonly used domestic appliances also raise questions of safety. TVs and VDUs, for example, emit various forms of static electricity and radiation and also deplete negative ions in the air. Good ventilation and humidity levels are therefore important to prevent dry air and to remedy negative ion deficiency. As a precaution, always sit well back from the screen (and not to one side, where most leakage occurs). VDUs are of more concern since people tend to spend long periods using them, either at work or as recreation (computer games). You can have the amount of radiation coming from VDUs tested and protective screens, which are at least of some help, are readily available.

Like VDUs, microwave ovens need testing regularly since the door can become defective and release radiation. There is also argument regarding evidence of biological effects from microwaves, irrespective of thermal effects. Currently, however, safety standards in the West take account only of the thermal effects. In the USSR, however, safety requirements are about 1000 times more stringent.

Alternating/direct current

All domestic supplies that come from central grids are alternating current (ac) and the voltages in common use are 120v in North America, 220v in Europe, and 240v in the UK and Australia. Unlike direct current (dc), such as that produced by a battery where electrons flow in one direction only between positive and negative poles, ac reverses its flow continually in a cycle alternating in direction between the charged poles. Domestic main current is generally supplied in Europe at a frequency of 50 cycles per second (50 hertz, or hz) and in North America at 60hz. Alternating current is the preferred form of electricity supply for numerous reasons: it can be generated by large power stations more efficiently than dc; it can be transmitted over long distances at high voltages with little loss of power; and it can be converted easily from one voltage to another, or to dc, as required, by the end user.

The Earth's pulse

The Earth has its own electromagnetic field that pulses at the rate of only 7.83 beats a second (7.83hz). Our body's own bioelectrical system – alpha and beta waves – also pulses at about the same rate. The Earth's natural beat, also known as Schumann waves, are thought to be essential to our health and wellbeing. When individuals, such as astronauts in space or passengers on long-haul flights, are separated from this natural pulse there can be a loss of orientation. So well recognized is this now, that NASA installs 7.83hz electronic oscillators in its spacecraft in order to "ground" the crews. But what is a problem in everyday life in the home is the masking of the Earth's pulse by non-natural electronic smog.

Hazards	Actions

Electric fields

When an object is charged with electricity the region near it has an electric field. The field will move in different directions depending on whether the object is positively or negatively charged. When a particle is charged it is described as being ionized. Air is ionized most strongly in the upper atmosphere (the ionosphere), but since air is a poor conductor the electrons flow with difficulty to the ground. Solid objects, such as houses, are far better conductors in this respect.

Weak charges of electricity in the atmosphere that cannot be earthed due to the presence of insulating materials will accumulate as static electricity. Common materials around the home that cause static include plastics, synthetic fibres, rubber- or foam-backed carpets, rubber underlays, and rubber-soled shoes. Static is more likely to build up in poorly ventilated rooms.

You can prevent the accumulation of static electricity by avoiding materials with high electrical insulation properties. If acute, you can discharge static electricity by taking a bath or shower, going barefoot for a few hours (preferably on uncarpeted floors or in the garden), or by wearing leather-soled shoes. Natural materials and fabrics are more conductive and allow static to disperse. Adequate ventilation and humidity (see pp. 102-3) can also prevent static build-up.

Any metal object can cause problems. Being a good conductor of electricity it can act as an antenna and become charged. This may add to your own personal charge if the metal is sufficiently close – as it is in the metal springs of a mattress or a metal bed frame. Consider replacing metal-framed beds with wooden ones and using only fibre-filled mattresses and natural fabrics for bedding.

EMFs and ELFs

Of particular concern is our continual exposure to electromagnetic fields (EMFs) and, in particular, to extremely low frequency (ELF) electromagnetic fields in our homes and workplaces emitted by mains supply alternating current pulsating at 50 or 60 cycles a second. Although studies are still at an early stage, there is enough evidence to suggest that all living organisms react to even weak electromagnetic ELF stimuli. It is this continual exposure to these sources and the effects they may be having on us that are of present concern.

German research has shown that people vary considerably in their sensitivity to electricity and that reactions to ELFs take many forms, including high blood pressure, nervousness, and disturbed sleep. In the UK it has been estimated that as many as one-third of the entire population may be suffering adverse reactions to ELFs at one time or another. Research in the UK has also found that certain low frequencies act as a trigger to allergy patients and cause sickness, headaches, nausea, sweating, and other unpleasant reactions.

Be aware that metal pipes and radiators holding water are often the source of sizeable EMFs. Sleep away from these if possible.

EMFs and ELFs exist all the time an installation is "live". Even if you unplug appliances the wiring feeding the sockets is still live. A simple remedy for blocking those fields emanating from wiring inside the home is to use shielded cables or conduits. Better still, or when shielded cable is impracticable, simply switch off the main fuses at night, but you might have to run a spur for appliances, such as refrigerators, that need constant power. Also available are "demand switches" that isolate all or just some circuits once no more electricity is needed.

EMF sources from outside the home, such as those from overhead transmission lines, are another matter and you cannot shield them off since they travel straight through the fabric of the building. In the US there are at least six states that limit the intensity of electric fields around power lines. Beds, particularly those of children, should be located as far away as possible from power lines.

Energy conservation

The extra energy that could be made available from conservation measures is one of our most underused and invisible resources. Yet, it is cheap, safe, and available in abundance everywhere from our over-consuming ways. Most older homes were built with scant regard for the energy they used and although more care is taken now, many newer ones are still ill prepared for an era of scarce energy.

Fortunately, houses are extremely adaptable and making them more conserving is often a series of relatively inexpensive do-it-yourself jobs. You can carry these through as a gradual process, starting with simple and mundane tasks, such as draughtproofing and insulation, and then move on to more complex and exciting projects, such as "going solar".

In terms of priorities, making your home weatherproof is more important as a first step than installing solar panels. Obviously you can do a bit of both at the same time but if you want to see some immediate cost savings in colder climates, then draughtproof your doors and windows and insulate the loft and hot-water tank. Double glazing is effective but very expensive to install, and it will be many years before you realize any cost savings from energy conservation over initial costs. You may have other reasons, however, such as noise reduction, that make it a more attractive proposition.

The amount of work you need to carry out on your own particular home will depend on many things: the local climate and shelter; the type of structure it is (detached, terraced, or apartment, for example); its orientation; construction; the type of heating systems and fuel sources available; and, of course, your lifestyle and comfort needs. To assess these factors properly is a complex, technical task and you should seek the advice of a professional, especially before embarking on the more expensive projects. But you can work out your own strategy using standard tables for computing such things as "degree-days", "fuel heating index", and "R-" or "U-values" for materials, costs, and pay-back periods. If this is all too daunting, use the general list of priorities (see right) instead, which applies to most types of home. This, plus advice from conservation groups and local authorities, will bring benefits not only to you but also the environment.

1 In houses with central heating, set thermostats to a lower temperature in winter – 16-18°C (60-65°F) – and use hot-water tank and individual radiator thermostats. In summer set the air-conditioning controls a little higher – 21-24°C (70-75°F). Zone rooms so that some are warmer, some cooler. Use small room heaters or coolers to adjust the background temperature when the room is in use. Use portable and ceiling fans in summer. Adjust the temperature timer or programmer accurately to your daily and seasonal routines.

Improve the efficiency of your boiler and stove and install heat-recovery and heat-exchange devices to mechanical ventilation systems and to hot waste-water pipes.

2 Draughtproof doors and windows. Seal air leaks in the structure itself – skirtings, floorboards, unused fireplaces, ducts and electric switches, and power outlets in outside walls.

Heat exchangers, also known as heat-recovery ventilators (HRVs), ventilate the home and transfer some of the heat from the warm, stale air as it leaves the house to the fresh cooler air coming in, keeping the two airflows separate.

3 Place reflective foil behind radiators on outside walls.

4 Fit heavy, lined curtains or insulating blinds and shutters to all windows. Use pelmets at the top of window frames and fix curtain sides to seal them. Fit wide window sills over radiators to deflect the hot air.

5 Insulate the loft, hot- and cold-water tanks, and lag pipes. Insulate the ground and basement floors.

6 Insulate walls – cavity fill them if appropriate or apply internal or external insulation to solid walls.

7 Double or triple glaze windows. Add internal lobbies or enclosed porches to outside doors.

8 Increase solar gain – remove winter shading from trees and vegetation. Draw curtains well back and clear clutter from sun-facing windows. Add solar windows, solar walls, and sunspaces. Fit solar panels to heat or preheat water.

9 Increase shelter from cold prevailing winter winds by using planting, earth cover, and mounds. Add shelter from hot summer sun and catch cool breezes by using planting, earth cover, roof and window shades, verandahs, thermal chimneys, and wind scoops.

General conservation strategies

Save electricity by using an energy-efficient electric cooker and appliances. Many small savings together have a large impact: don't use unnecessary electric gadgets; dry washing outside; hand-wash dishes; use hand tools (not power tools) as much as possible.

Save water by reducing the flush from toilets and taking showers instead of baths. Other measures include: using full loads and economy cycles in washing machines; fitting and monitoring a water meter; and using rainwater and recycled greywater for the garden.

Save transport energy by walking, cycling, or using public transport. If you need a car, choose a low-pollution model.

Water

Water is the fundamental life giver and sustainer bringing the bounty of a fertile and productive planet. Our earliest settlements were built next to rivers, natural wells, or springs, and even today the major centres of human habitation depend on the great river basins, from the Rhine to the Nile. Water has always been a powerful spiritual source, and at Delphi and Olympia the oracles drew on the powers of the sacred springs for their prophecies and advice. In many religions, water signifies creation and regeneration. Immersion in the waters of the holy Ganges and the act of Christian baptism dissolve and cleanse the past and bring spiritual rebirth for the future. To the Chinese, running water carries the life force known as *ch'i*.

Water in and around the home

The health and healing properties of water have always been highly valued, and natural hot and cold springs, with their unique mineral contents, have become a focus of spas and resorts around the world. The Greek physician Hippocrates prescribed bathing and drinking spring waters and the Romans were firm believers in the therapeutic value of hot springs and *Thermae*, meaning communal baths. For the Japanese today, bathing, either at home or in mountain spas, is as much a meditation as a bodily pleasure, and hydrotherapy and bathing facilities, in the form of saunas to jacuzzis, are again increasingly in favour in the West.

   Water has long been used as an integral part of the home, not only for drinking and bathing but as an indispensible design element in itself, inducing feelings of wellbeing and harmony. In gardens, pools and ponds become aesthetic features – mirrors, reflecting trees, rocks, statuary, and the sky. In this type of setting, water really has impact when it is moving. Streams, waterfalls, cascades, and fountains all contribute life and soothing, stress-reducing sounds. The flowing forms of moving water have intrigued artists and scientists from Leonardo Da Vinci onward and they are the basis of new ecological building designs today. In hot climates, architecture may introduce water into the home interior or courtyard, as in Moorish and Spanish buildings. Even in temperate climates, proximity to

Water makes life possible. Over 97% of the water on Earth is salty. Less than 3% is fresh but most of this is locked away in the ice caps. Less than 1% is present in the atmosphere, rivers, lakes, and in the form of groundwater. Sun and wind cause water to evaporate from oceans and lakes and transpire from vegetation. This moisture is distilled and purified (barring pollution) and rises to form clouds. Precipitation as rain, snow, or dew seeps into the ground to replenish groundwater or runs off the surface into rivers that empty back into the lakes and sea, completing what is known as the "hydrologic cycle".

Evaporation

water gives a special quality – the classic example is the American architect Frank Lloyd Wright's design for "Falling Water" in Pennsylvania. So important to the Japanese is the idea of water in a garden that it will sometimes be represented by stone, gravel, or sand in a waterless version known as *kare sansui*. Water near the home also brings with it a different habitat and the delight of new species of wildlife, fish, frogs, and aquatic plants.

   Like the planetary hydrologic cycle (see above) in miniature, water in and around the home helps to regulate humidity, increases the percentage of beneficial ions, and purifies and cools the air. It is also the most efficient heat transporter and store and is used in solar design and many forms of home heating and

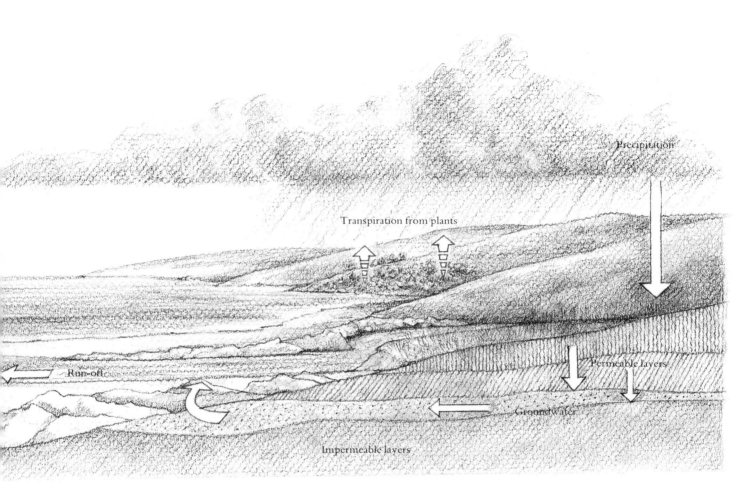

Precipitation

Transpiration from plants

Run-off

Permeable layers

Groundwater

Impermeable layers

cooling. The energy generated by the flow of water, from rivers to waves and tides, is an underused resource of renewable and nonpolluting power. Locally, water turbines in small streams can power homes, just as traditional wheels powered mills in the past.

Our bodies are more than two-thirds water. Like air, water is a vital component of life. We can survive for weeks without food but without water, for only a few days. Although the surface of the planet is mainly comprised of water, most of this is salt sea water or ice. Only 1 per cent is available fresh water and it is on this minute fraction that we and most other species depend. But today, this resource is in danger from the threats of increasing

pollution – from acid rain, toxic byproducts, and agricultural run-off – and overconsumption and waste, especially in affluent societies.

This situation is much worse in many parts of the developing world, particularly in arid countries, where according to the World Health Organization (WHO), "the number of water taps per thousand persons is a better indication of health than the number of hospital beds". But the danger is worldwide. We ignore it at our peril, for when water disappears from the Earth, so too does all life.

Designing with water

The hanging steps lead down from the living room to Bear Run, the shallow brook and beautiful waterfall over which Frank Lloyd Wright built "Falling Water", or the Kaufmann House, in 1936 (right). Wide terraces cantilever over the middle of the stream and project right over the waterfall. The westerly concrete terrace cantilevered so far into space that the worried client asked the builder to construct a low wall under it. On completion of the house, Wright confided: "When I was here last month, I ordered the top layers of stone removed. Now the terrace has shown no sign of failing. Shall we take down the extra four feet of the wall?"

Inspired by the natural, moving qualities and patterns of meandering rivers and flowing water, John Wilkes, artist and sculptor, started experimenting with water sculptures in 1970. His aim was to induce the rhythmically swinging motion of water streaming through his work, and create a pulsating and purifying flow. He developed "flowform vessels", sculptures that could be used singly or in series to reproduce the characteristic figure-of-eight meander pattern. The cascade at the Rudolf Steiner Seminariet, Järna, Sweden (below), is one of his many fascinating projects worldwide.

In the dry Arizona desert, where daytime temperatures can reach 50°C (122°F), the thick adobe walls and shaded rooms of this ingenious Pyramid House are essential to make life comfortable. Water, too, is cleverly integrated into the heart of the house to give life to the interior and also bring soothing sounds and welcome humidity to the air.

Pollution

Water in its natural state is not pure H_2O. It contains such things as minerals, salts, trace metals, nutrients, bacteria, and organic matter. At low levels of concentration these substances may be harmless and some, such as minerals, even beneficial. At higher levels, however, these same substances may be toxic.

The major threat to our water today is contamination, which is rapidly becoming worse on all fronts – industrial, agricultural, municipal, and household. Industrial waste dumping and landfilling, effluents and radioactive wastes, agricultural pesticides and fertilizers, municipal toxic wastes, sewage, leaks from underground tanks and pipes, and household toxic wastes and leaking septic tanks all percolate into rivers, lakes, and groundwater supplies and degrade them. Added to this already catastrophic catalogue of damage is the airborne pollution of the atmosphere, which mixes with moisture in the air to form smogs and acid rain.

The extent of the problem

In the US the Environmental Protection Agency (EPA) has identified more than 700 regular pollutants in drinking water. Of these, 20 are known carcinogens. But even this figure, disturbing as it is, is thought to represent only a small fraction of the untested pollutants actually present.

Synthetic organic chemicals Hundreds of these carbon-containing synthetic organic chemicals (SOCs) have been found in drinking water. Some of them are volatile organic chemicals (VOCs), which means that they form gases at normal room temperature and you can inhale them in baths, showers, or in the kitchen. Exposure through the skin is also likely. Chlorine in drinking water combines with natural organic matter (dead leaves, soil, and humus) to form trihalomethanes (THMs), the most common being chloroform (a carcinogen affecting the colon, rectum, and bladder). Benzene and trichloroethylene are other examples of suspected carcinogens in water. Pesticides such as chlordane – a mutagen and carcinogen – can also be present. The problem is that many SOCs have not been tested sufficiently for their full effects to be known.

Nitrates These originate in chemical fertilizers and leach into rivers producing high concentrations in drinking water in both country and city areas. Nitrates are particularly dangerous to babies and infants, reducing the oxygen in the blood and causing "blue baby syndrome". There is also a suspicion that nitrates cause stomach cancers in adults.

Metals Lead in old pipes and in the solder used on copper pipes is gradually absorbed as a cumulative poison with the most damage being done to fetuses and young children. This is a particular problem in soft-water areas where lead is more easily leached.

Aluminium can reach high levels in water due to water treatment processes and will cause discoloration. It is suspected that apart from being unsightly, water containing high concentrations of

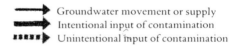

Groundwater movement or supply
Intentional input of contamination
Unintentional input of contamination

Freshwater supply

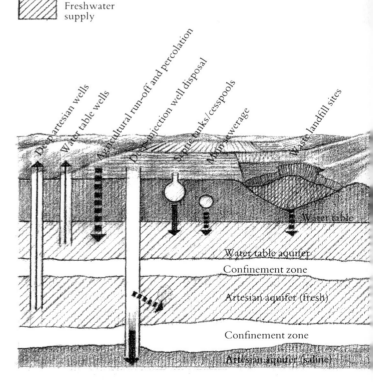

aluminium (and aluminium from other sources) can cause Alzheimer's disease (senile dementia).

Iron and magnesium, which occur naturally in some areas, corrode pipes and turn water brown and cloudy.

Sulphuric and nitric acids formed in the atmosphere as acid rain soak into the soil and groundwater and release toxic trace metals. This problem is compounded by the corrosive effect these acids have on metal pipes – cadmium, lead, aluminium, mercury, and copper are now reaching higher concentrations in drinking water.

Whether your water is hard or soft depends on the amounts of calcium and magnesium present – the more of these the harder the water. Studies have revealed that a greater number of people die of heart diseases in soft-water areas, and this may be due to the fact that here metals are more easily dissolved.

Another possible explanation is that there may be some, as yet unknown, beneficial effects of the water hardeners themselves.

Fluoride This is a controversial substance. On the one hand it is supposed to reduce dental decay and inhibit the loss of bone strength in the elderly; on the other, it has been linked to a spectrum of medical problems, including premature aging, cot deaths, and an increased incidence of cancer.

Radon This is a naturally occurring radioactive element in groundwater in some areas. It is made more hazardous, however, when it is released into the air and it can be inhaled when water is heated or sprayed from a shower (see p. 229). But it is also a danger to your health if you consume it in the form of drinking water.

Groundwater contamination

Underground water is a major source of drinking water supplies and, in some areas, the only one. This water can be contaminated by many sources: agriculture (pesticides, chemical fertilizers and soil run-off); industry (waste disposal, spills, and leaks); domestic (sewage, septic tanks, traffic pollution, and household chemicals and cleaners); mining (waste disposal of toxic byproducts and leakage of chemicals); and leakage from petroleum and natural gas wells and processing. Solid waste dumps are one of the worst sources. Often, not properly checked, toxic wastes and harmful pollutants are inadequately processed or contained before disposal and, when it rains, percolate through the soil into the groundwater. As well, septic tanks and sewer pipes are rarely fully maintained. Air pollution and acid rain also fall on and pollute vital supplies.

Household pollution

Most of us are unknowingly contributing to the pollution of water supplies by using toxic household wastes and garden products. Cleaners for ovens, metals, furniture, and carpets; bathroom products, pesticides and insecticides, paints, and paint removers; and vehicle products, such as oil, antifreeze, and petrol can all contaminate water if they are poured down drains or toilets or end up on refuse tips. Sewage treatment plants are not equipped to remove these substances and many will eventually be passed back into our drinking water supplies. Safe disposal is vitally important and is every individual's responsibility (see pp. 268-9).

Pipes

It is not only lead pipes and lead-soldered copper pipes that contaminate water. Tests in the United States have shown that plastic pipes can be dangerous, too. Underground plastic pipes (polybutylene and polyethylene) can be permeated by dangerous chemicals in the soil. And polyvinyl chloride (PVC) pipes and jointing solvents used inside the house can produce a wide variety of toxic and carcinogenic chemicals that accumulate in the water, especially if it is left standing even overnight. Asbestos-cement surfaces, too, release carcinogenic asbestos fibres into water supplies. This source of pollution is confined largely to areas where rainfall collection is the chief means of water supply, such as in some rural areas of Australia and New Zealand. Here, water runs off the once commonly used asbestos-cement roofs and pipework, picking up the dangerous fibres as it goes.

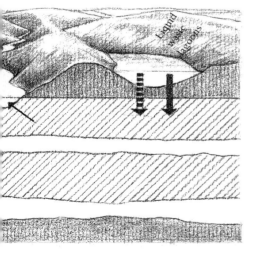

Water standards

There is now growing concern that drinking water is becoming substandard in most industrialized countries (let alone in developing ones) and that increasing water pollution is not being dealt with adequately by ageing municipal and private treatment works. At present much drinking water is still considered safe, but the evidence of US federal standards authorities, the EEC, and WHO indicate that contamination is mounting.

Once pollutants have entered the water supply they are much harder and more expensive to deal with. A cheaper, more efficient, and certainly a more positive approach is that of prevention – eliminating pollutants at source. This entails not only far tighter controls on industry, agriculture, and on the water treatment authorities, but on us, as individuals, as well. As users of pollutants we have a particularly important role to play in preventing them entering the water supply.

There is also concern about other ways we are exposed to pollutants in water – by absorption through the skin and by inhaling vapours. A paper published by *The American Journal of Public Health* in 1984 stated that many organic compounds are easily absorbed through the skin and suggested that exposure in baths, showers, swimming pools, and spas and hot tubs could in fact be greater than that from drinking water. The US Environmental Protection Agency (EPA) has reported that you can inhale chloroform (a byproduct of chlorinated water) from hot showers, as you also can radon gas (see p. 229).

Home water treatment

Widespread concern about poor-quality water is evident not only from the increasing growth in sales of bottled water but also from the popularity of simple water filter jugs and tap devices. These are a first step and remove some of the most common pollutants, such as chlorine, chalk, and some organic chemicals and bacteria. But if you want high-quality water with more pollutants removed you will have to invest in a more complex and expensive system.

Before deciding whether to take this step you must first have your tap water tested to assess if it is sufficiently polluted to justify the expense. But as with air testing (see p. 100), choose an independent, professional company that carries out tests only and does not sell devices, too. Bear in mind that a one-off test will show only what is happening at that time; not predict tomorrow's problems. To overcome this you should have your water tested on a regular basis, and even if you install a system, you should check at least annually that it is effective and not itself creating any pollution problems due to inadequate maintenance.

Providing purer water for drinking and cooking is usually the function of point-of-use systems (see right) installed in the kitchen. They are not designed to prevent health problems caused by bathing in water containing high levels of toxins. To deal with all the water in the house, you will need to install a point-of-entry system where the water supply enters your house or apartment.

Bottled water

With bottled spring water costing hundreds of times the price of tap water, it is worthwhile doing a little research before drinking a lot of it. Although the quality of bottled water is controlled in the UK, Australia and USA and, in general, conforms to the set standards, tests of some brands have found contaminants in excess of the limits. Under present standards, bottled water is not guaranteed to be a safe and wholesome product. It is treated by the producers as a non-alcoholic beverage and it is not intended to be a main source of drinking water. If you intend to use one particular brand, choose one that is controlled and ask the company for a water analysis report giving the source and treatments (or look for independent consumer reports). Bear in mind that plastic bottles can leach byproducts into the water.

Bottled water does not usually contain extra minerals, and unless you drink a lot you will receive more benefit from a varied diet. Nitrate levels of bottled water are usually lower than those of tap water, but take care since some well-known brands do contain quite high levels. They may also contain more bacteria than tap water, although these are generally not harmful.

Point-of-use systems

There are three basic point-of-use systems: activated carbon, reverse osmosis, and distillation. Each one uses a different principle and removes different pollutants. At present, home-treatment devices are not tested or regulated and advertising claims are often exaggerated and misleading. Some consumer organizations have carried out comparative tests on different systems, which you should try to get hold of, or you should take independent, professional advice.

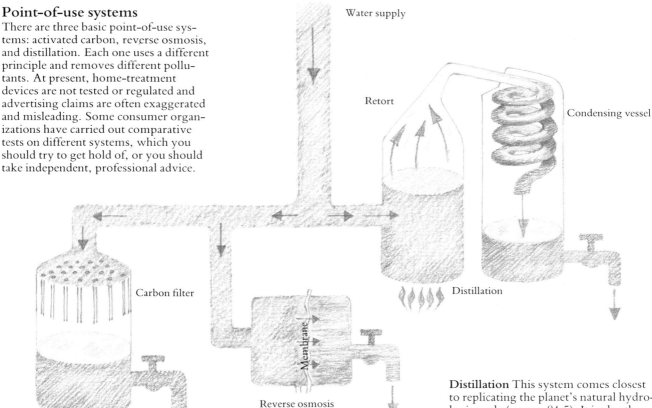

Water supply

Retort

Condensing vessel

Carbon filter

Membrane

Reverse osmosis

Activated carbon

Distillation

Activated carbon This system filters tap water through carbon granules or blocks that absorb or trap pollutants, including organic chemicals and chlorine and some of its byproducts. A major disadvantage with carbon is that as its pores fill up with absorbed pollutants it becomes less and less efficient, and it can then become the breeding ground for bacteria. Carbon filters (in the form of filter jugs or tap filters) are, however, readily available and inexpensive to buy, install, and maintain. Carbon-block, under-the-counter units with a pre-sediment filter are the most effective, and you can also use them as a prefilter at the point of entry for the whole water supply to your home.

Reverse osmosis Here, you use three canisters that fit under the sink. The first is a prefilter to remove dissolved solids. The next is a cellophane-like semipermeable membrane that lets water molecules through but not pollutants. The final canister is a carbon filter to remove organic chemicals. The system, although generally effective, does not cope with inorganics. It is also expensive to install and the canisters are usually made of plastic.

Distillation This system comes closest to replicating the planet's natural hydrologic cycle (see pp. 84-5). It is also the most reliable and the one traditionally used in laboratories needing the highest purity of water – but it is expensive. For it to work, water is boiled and the steam condensed to produce pure water. Boiling kills bacteria and extracts dissolved solids, trace metals, particulates, and radioactive particles. You require an extra carbon postfilter, however, to remove organics effectively, although the latest systems will deal with most inorganics. Glass distillers are the safest to use, since aluminium has been found in water distilled in stainless-steel models. Distilled water is certainly the purest, but some people find its taste flat and lacking in minerals, which are generally thought to be beneficial. If you find the taste of distilled water not to your liking, you can add the missing minerals or simply drink bottled spring water as a supplement.

Water conservation

Equally as important as the quality of our water is the quantity we consume. Most of us have become accustomed to using a lot of water everyday and take it for granted that supplies are limitless (or at least put to the back of our minds the fact that they are not). This attitude is particularly in evidence in North America where an average family of four can use on average up to 1000 litres (220 gallons) a day – between two and four times average consumption for a family in Europe.

Water leaks

Before water even reaches your home, huge amounts are often lost through old and corroded underground distribution pipes. This waste can be as high as 40 or 50 per cent of valuable, processed drinking water. On top of this, an additional 5 to 10 per cent can be lost through leaks in the home, mostly from faulty toilet cistern valves and worn tap washers – a steadily dripping tap can lose 90 litres (20 gallons) per day. Hot-water leaks increase your energy costs, too. As a first priority, run a regular check on all your tap washers and cistern valves. You can also fit a check valve to the incoming main water supply. This valve shuts off the flow if a predetermined rate is exceeded by either a sudden or slow, steady loss.

Water-saving devices

The current design of home plumbing systems actually encourages us to be extravagant with water usage, and it can be difficult to conserve water even if you try to modify your behaviour. In most cases, it really is necessary to go a step further and install water-conservation devices. Once in place, they are unobtrusive and permanently eliminate waste without your intervention. And since toilets use nearly half and baths and showers a third of household water (see opposite), you should concentrate your attention in these areas first.

Toilets Since the widespread introduction of the flushing water closet in the 19th century, little has changed in its basic design. An ordinary toilet uses anywhere between 9 litres (2 gallons) in the UK and Australia to 20 litres (4.5 gallons) in the US for every flush. This is excessive and you can achieve a 30 per cent saving in water consumption simply by displacing that amount of water in the cistern (see opposite).

New and more efficient toilets have now been developed that use only 6 litres (1.3 gallons) or even as little as 4 litres (less than 1 gallon) per flush.

In areas of constant water shortages or erratic supplies, however, or where there is no sewer system, it is not appropriate to install a flush toilet at all. Here, a more suitable solution is the waterless compost toilet (see p. 228). This device will cut household water consumption by nearly 50 per cent, it uses virtually no energy, and it treats wastes on site, thus dramatically reducing demand on centralized treatment plants. But this type of toilet is not acceptable to some local authorities in certain countries, such as Australia and the US.

Showers A standard shower delivers about 20 litres (4.5 gallons) of water per minute. If, instead, you use an inexpensive water-saving head, you can halve water consumption while still enjoying an invigorating shower. Various types are available – flow restrictors, aerators, and sprayers.

Taps Depending on the water pressure and the type of tap, flows vary between 10 and 20 litres (2 and 4.5 gallons) a minute. But for most uses, a flow of about 3 litres (about 0.5 gallons) is adequate. You can easily fit flow-control aerators giving these lower amounts to most taps.

Washing machines Washing machines use between 110 and 220 litres (24 and 48 gallons) of water per load. If you have a small amount of washing only, consider if you really need a machine. It will certainly be cheaper, and probably quicker, to do it by hand or in a laundromat once a week.

If you are buying a new machine, choose a front loader, since this type of machine uses 40 per cent less water than a top loader. Try to find one that allows you to adjust the water usage to match the size of the load and one that reuses the rinse water and has an economy cycle.

Dishwashers Hand-washing dishes for a family of four in a bowl without running water uses between 25 and 40 litres (5.5 and 9 gallons) a day. Automatic dishwashers use about 60 litres (13 gallons) per cycle. Part loads waste water, so unless you wash all the dishes, pots, and pans together once a day as a full load, a dishwasher will be a considerable water waster. Smaller-capacity machines make dishwashers less wasteful for smaller families.

Gardens Hoses and sprinklers use about 9 litres (2 gallons) every minute. For most outside activities – watering lawns and plants and washing the car – you do not need drinking water, and you should try to use alternative supplies, such as collected rainwater or recycled wastewater (if permitted by local authorities). If this is not possible, use watering cans and buckets instead of a hose. The design of your garden or yard – the types of plants, amount of lawn, shading from sun, and groundcover – can dramatically reduce your need for water.

It is extravagant to fill swimming pools or hot tubs with drinking water. You should consider using rainwater instead (but have it tested first).

Water meters

Metering is commonplace in many countries and its introduction is being looked at seriously in most others. In Europe, North America, and Australia, for example, experience has proved that water consumption drops by up to 40 per cent once meters are installed. Meters are also early-warning devices in case leaks develop.

If you can change your water-using habits by gradually adapting your plumbing fixtures and fittings you should be able to at least halve your current usage. If you install a water meter you should see even greater savings. But this assumes that most of the water you use in the home still comes from processed sources and will be of drinking-water standard.

Domestic water use

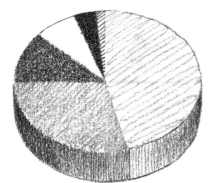

Toilets	35–45%
Showers/baths	20–30%
Drinking/cooking	5–10%
Laundry	8%
Dishwashing	5%
Garden/car★	2%

★ Can be 25% in dry climates with a swimming pool installed.

Adapting your cistern

If you place objects such as bricks, stones, or two or three bottles filled with water and weighted with stones in your toilet cistern, you will displace water and thus reduce the amount used. Make sure these objects are well clear of the internal mechanism.

Water-saving checklist
○ Fix all dripping taps and faulty toilet cisterns.
○ Flush the toilet less often, or use a low-flush cistern.
○ Take short showers rather than baths.
○ In the shower, turn the water off while lathering and shampooing.
○ Hand wash dishes in bowls, not under running water.
○ Use washing machines with full loads only and on economy cycle whenever possible.
○ Water gardens with a watering can rather than a hose. Cover soil with compost or bark chippings to reduce evaporation and so reduce the need for constant watering.
○ Wash the car with bucketfuls of water rather than a hose.

Integrated low-water systems

We use only about 5 to 10 per cent of our valuable processed drinking water for drinking and cooking and it is plainly extravagant to use it for flushing the toilet, bathing and showering, car washing, and watering the garden. Not only extravagant, it can also be unnecessary – if you are prepared to introduce into your home an integrated water-conserving system employing special rainwater collection, wastewater recycling, and landscaping techniques (see right).

In homes with these systems, reliance on municipal supplies is cut by two-thirds, with the added bonus of a 90 per cent reduction in waste-water going for sewage treatment. However, the systems are relatively experimental, complex, and expensive to install and they will probably be cost effective only in drier areas where water is a scarce and costly resource. Some of these systems may not be permitted by your local water or health author-ity, so check first and seek advice from those with local experience (see p. 275).

Rainwater collection You can liken this system to the gardener's rainwater butt or the ancient under-ground water cisterns of the Greeks and Romans, where all rain falling on the house and its immediate grounds is channelled into large-capacity storage tanks. Although not drinkable, it can be of adequate quality for greenhouses, gardens, toilets, washing machines, carwashing, and possibly hot tubs and swimming pools (although you will still have to disinfect the water as usual). Depending on the area in which you live, rainwater pollution may be a problem and you will need to investigate this before embarking on a harvesting project. Water from roofs with lead flashings or valleys is not suitable.

Wastewater recycling This is really still at the experimental stage and may not be permitted in your area. Unless the system is properly installed and maintained it may, itself, pose health risks. Wastewater (also known as greywater) is collected from the bath, shower, and bathroom basin, rather than from the kitchen sink, dishwasher, and washing machine (where the water is more heavily contaminated with food particles, grease, and deter-

gents). The water is then treated and filtered using sand, gravel, mechanical, and biological filters. It is absolutely vital that no toxic or harmful substances are used in the water that goes into the system or it will be impossible to filter and reuse it. The filtered wastewater is then piped from storage for use in the garden and greenhouse. With some systems it can also be used to flush toilets.

Recycled wastewater, as well as collected rainwater, can also be used in the garden. In fact, a water-conserving landscape is an integral part of the whole system. In areas of low rainfall, you will need to concentrate on hardy, drought-tolerant plants.

In this low-water system, drinking water supplies are used for bathing, cooking, and washing as usual, and toilet and kitchen blackwater goes to the sewer. But the less-polluted bath and washing greywater is recycled through hyacinth and sand filters and used to flush toilets and water the garden.

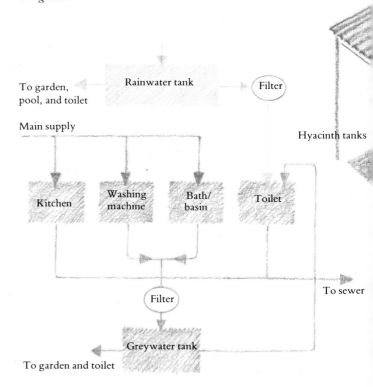

Landscape elements

Deciduous trees and creepers are an important part of the integrated natural home, providing shade in summer yet still allowing winter sunshine through once their leaves have dropped. For half-hardy plants, and perhaps a small lawn, build a mini-oasis next to the house or in a sheltered courtyard area.

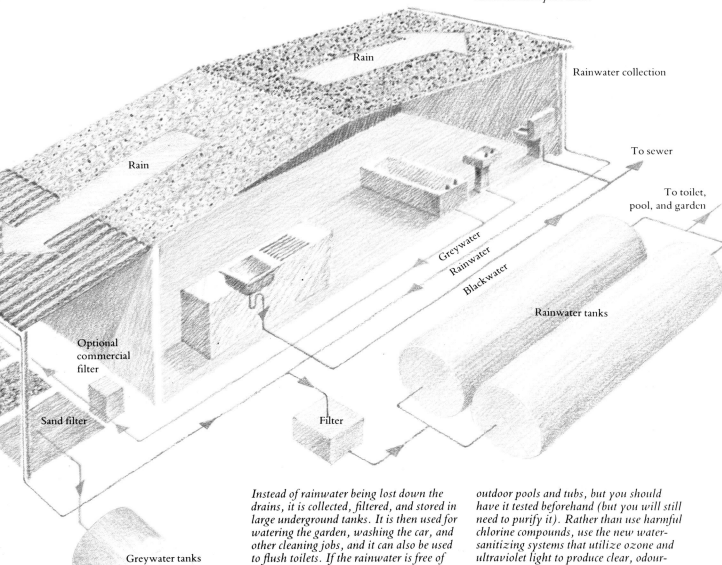

Rain

Rain

Rainwater collection

To sewer

To toilet, pool, and garden

Greywater

Rainwater

Blackwater

Rainwater tanks

Optional commercial filter

Sand filter

Filter

Greywater tanks

Instead of rainwater being lost down the drains, it is collected, filtered, and stored in large underground tanks. It is then used for watering the garden, washing the car, and other cleaning jobs, and it can also be used to flush toilets. If the rainwater is free of pollutants, it might also be used for outdoor pools and tubs, but you should have it tested beforehand (but you will still need to purify it). Rather than use harmful chlorine compounds, use the new water-sanitizing systems that utilize ozone and ultraviolet light to produce clear, odourless, and biologically safe water.

Air

It would seem that we have come full circle once again and we are now as concerned as the Victorians were with the subject of fresh air. Just as they were reacting against the smoke of the Industrial Revolution, today we are faced with the more pervading pollution of the Chemical Revolution. The Victorians, however, went too far and in the process almost forgot that there was a range of requirements for a pleasant and comfortable environment – adequate heating, an appropriate level of humidity, and freedom from draughts. Today, we are in the process of going too far in the other direction and concentrating all our efforts into sealed, energy-saving homes. What we are missing out on, though, is the potential for healthy, fresh air.

For many of us living in cities and the suburban sprawl surrounding them, the only time we have the opportunity to breathe healthy air may be on vacation or on trips to the coast or into the wilderness. But you would be wrong to think that simply because you live away from cities that you are somehow immune from the problem: you may be unknowingly polluting your own indoor air.

The composition of air
The air we breathe consists largely of nitrogen (78%) and oxygen (21%) plus very small amounts of other gases. This balance has remained remarkably stable for millions of years. But this composition of gases is not arbitrary – if the amount of oxygen or nitrogen increased by only a few per cent, all life on earth would be at risk. It is now thought, as part of the Gaia hypothesis, by an increasing number of scientists that this balance is maintained specifically by living things as the perfect medium for creating and sustaining life.

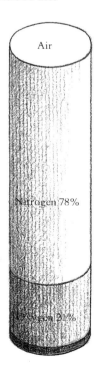

Air

Nitrogen 78%

Oxygen 21%

Other gases (including CO_2)

Breathing

Most of us take the air we breathe and how we breathe it for granted. The process is automatic and on average you take a breath between 20 and 40 times a minute – that could be as many as 56,000 breaths every day of your life. But how you breathe is more important to your wellbeing than you might think. The lungs are a sophisticated processing plant filtering the gases and particles in the air you inhale, absorbing oxygen into the bloodstream, and expelling carbon dioxide.

Most people, however, have forgotten how to breathe properly. You should avoid breathing shallowly through the mouth, and hardly using your diaphragm or muscles. In this way you take in only a small amount of oxygen and lose much life-giving energy and vitality and, at the same time, lay down the pattern for many respiratory problems and a lowered resistance to disease.

Correct breathing is fundamental to many natural and self-help therapies and ancient religions and teachings. In yoga, for example, the two main functions of breathing are to bring more oxygen to the blood and brain and to control the vital energy, or life force "prana", leading to the control of the mind. "Pranayama" is the science of breath control, designed to maintain the body in vibrant health.

Posture is part of the breathing process and how you stand, sit, and lie are affected by the types of furniture you use and how your home is designed for both work and leisure. Often, poorly designed chairs, beds, worktops, and storage cupboards are at least some of the sources of bad posture.

Air quality

But just as your breathing technique is important, so too is the quality of the air you breathe. The respiratory system is extremely sensitive and exposure to pollution can harm even normally healthy people, but an allergic or hypersensitive person can react to minute amounts of pollutants.

Until recently it was outdoor air pollution alone that was the main focus of attention. Coal smoke from factories and homes mixed with natural fogs to form poisonous smogs – one of the worst recorded was in London in 1952 when 4000 people

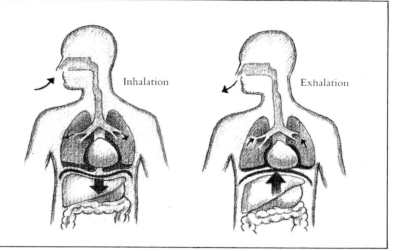

Yogic breathing
This principle of correct breathing combines the three basic levels: clavical (shallow), intercostal (middle), and abdominal (deep). To achieve correct breathing, you must breathe through your nose inhaling and exhaling deeply to bring all of your lungs fully into use. When you inhale, your abdomen expands and the diaphragm moves down, massaging the abdominal organs. When you exhale, your abdomen contracts and the diaphragm moves up, massaging the heart. Of the three stages to each breath you take – inhalation, retention, and exhalation – it is exhalation that is most important. The more stale air you exhale the more fresh air you can then inhale, and the more energy you absorb.

Inhalation

Exhalation

died. "Clean-air" legislation in many industrialized countries has reduced smoke pollution visibly and dramatically, but city air is now becoming increasingly contaminated by more invisible gases, such as sulphur dioxide from power plants and carbon monoxide and nitrogen oxides from vehicle exhausts, and by particles such as lead. Nitrogen oxides are acid gases that react in sunlight with hydrocarbons to make ozone – the main ingredient of the modern photochemical smogs that hang over the world's cities from Los Angeles to Sydney. When sulphur dioxide and nitrogen oxides dissolve in rain they form dilute sulphuric and nitric acids – known as "acid rain".

Indoor air pollution

You are not necessarily any safer indoors, and most indoor air pollution does not come from outside – it is generated from within. Research in the US has shown that indoor air can be up to ten times more polluted than outdoor air samples. But even if levels are low, you are exposed to them for long periods. The problem has arisen recently (over about the last two decades) because of the widespread introduction of synthetic building materials and finishes, furnishings, fabrics, and household chemicals. All of these have joined established pollutants, such as

dust, bacteria, and fungi, to create a far more dangerous environment for us all.

Sealed buildings

Since the energy crisis of the 1970s, and the overall increase in energy costs since then, buildings have become more energy conserving. Sealing all gaps in the structure and around windows and doors has been extremely effective in reducing energy leaks. This has been enhanced further in new buildings by the introduction of vapour barriers and draught-proofing of all windows and doors.

In doing this, however, the amount of ventilation in buildings has been dramatically reduced. Whereas in older homes indoor air would be exchanged with fresh outdoor air on average of once every hour, in modern, energy-conserving homes this rate may drop to about once every five or six hours. The build-up of pollutants and stale air can therefore reach much higher levels than in the past. Artificial ventilation and air-conditioning systems can provide an energy-intensive answer, provided that they do not recirculate too much already polluted air rather than exchanging it for fresh, outdoor air. But by using Baubiologie principles (see p. 26) the building structure itself can regulate the quality of indoor air.

The indoor life

Surprisingly, we spend up to 90 per cent of our time indoors (depending on climate) – at home, work, in stores, restaurants, or travelling. Children, the sick and elderly, and those without work or working at home may be indoors even more than this. So, added to the generally higher levels of pollution you find indoors is your increased exposure to it. Although little confirmed data is available for all building types, you would be safest to assume that most have poor or even harmful indoor air.

Offices, stores, and public buildings are now full of synthetic materials, chemicals, and electrical equipment, all of which are known contributory factors to the "sick building syndrome" (see pp. 52–3). Tightly sealed car interiors are worse than buildings in this respect, since they are composed entirely of chemically synthetic materials known to be associated with the release of more than a hundred organic compounds, especially when new or in hot and humid climates – hence the "new-car" interior smell. This, combined with exhaust pollution sucked into the interior by windows and unfiltered vents and heaters, must make city driving one of the worst modern indoor air experiences.

So, at a time when pollutants have increased everywhere, we are in the process of exacerbating the problem by sealing them in around us and by experiencing these unhealthy indoor conditions for longer and longer periods.

Ionization Inside the home, negative ions are depleted by electrical fields from TVs and VDUs, metal ducts, static from synthetic fabrics, and particularly by smoking and polluted, dusty, or dry air. Ions are positive and negative electrically charged molecules. Outdoors in unpolluted places, the air contains from 1000 to 2000 ions per cubic centimetre, in a ratio of five positive to four negative. This natural balance gives a feeling of general wellbeing. But in certain conditions – before thunderstorms or when the "evil winds" such as the Mistral of France, the Foehn of Europe, and the Sharav of the Middle East are blowing – the negative ions lose charge and a surfeit of positive ions is generated. This imbalance, no matter how it is caused, brings unpleasant feelings of tension, irritability, and depression and even physical disorders. Accidents rise and hospital operations are often postponed.

A simple vision of open doors and windows filling the house with clean, fresh air (left) is, for many of us, becoming difficult to achieve. City, town, and some country air is increasingly polluted and, as a result, our homes are insulated and shut off from the outside world.

So conditioned have we become that even when the surroundings are beautiful, the weather fine, and the air pure, we are often still inclined to sit inside behind sealed windows (right).

Do you have a problem?

Assessing the situation

It can be difficult to be certain if you have an indoor air-pollution problem. The Consumer Federation of America has advised that you should be alert to the following symptoms: headaches, itchy or watering eyes, nose or throat infection or dryness, dizziness, nausea, colds, asthma, bronchitis, and allergies. Also, be alert to:

○ The onset of symptoms following a move to a different home.
○ Symptoms occurring following home remodelling, the purchase of new furniture, drapes, or carpeting, or pesticide treatment.
○ Symptoms that disappear when you leave your home or office, but recur when you return to that environment.

○ Symptoms that develop after energy-conservation work is carried out.
○ Symptoms that trouble those members of your household who spend most time indoors.

These symptoms may be acute during warm, humid weather and when your home is tightly sealed in cold weather.

Testing the air

If you persistently experience any of the problems described above, you should have the air in your home tested. Unfortunately, measuring many airborne pollutants, especially at low concentrations, requires delicate, complex, and expensive equipment. If needs arise, you should be careful to select a competent company to conduct these measurements or to supply and install permanent monitors. Consult your local health authority or relevant professional institutes for guidance.

Evaluating the results of these tests is not straightforward, since there is no real consensus on the maximum safe levels of all but the most common air pollutants in homes. You should also bear in mind that there will be a wide range of individual sensitivities and reactions to set standards (if they exist), and that those levels accepted today may be considered unacceptably high in the near future.

Therefore, as a guide only, an international range of standards set recently are compared in chart form on page 272.

Controlling air quality

If you have an air-quality problem in your home, there are a number of ways you can deal with it depending on the types, concentrations, and sources of the pollutants and the needs of energy conservation in your home.

Your primary control approach is to find the main sources of pollutants, remove or restrict them, and then increase natural ventilation. Once you have done everything possible along these lines, you must then decide if the pollution problem warrants the introduction of further measures, such as mechanical ventilation and filtration systems (bearing in mind that overfiltered air inhibits the build-up of negative ions). In most homes, however, such simple measures as opening the windows more often will lessen or even eradicate the problem.

There may well be situations where you cannot remove the sources of pollution – foul city air, for example, or building materials that are an integral part of the structure – and you will have no choice but to introduce more complex and expensive mechanical ventilation and filters. Chemically sensitive people or those suffering from allergies may also need clean and purified air. If you do install filters, humidifiers, or dehumidifiers then you must pay attention to proper maintenance procedures. Unless you keep them clean they can themselves become the breeding ground for bacteria that could then be spread throughout your home.

The following list summarizes the steps you should take, depending on the severity of the pollution problem.

○ Remove or reduce the pollutants at source.
○ Remove or seal sources of radon if possible or increase ventilation to reduce concentrations.
○ Increase natural ventilation – the simplest and most traditional methods are windows, air vents, ducts, and diffusion through the walls.
○ Use mechanical ventilation, from extractor fans close to sources of pollution to whole-house systems (see pp. 102-3) using air ducts (when linked to air-conditioning systems).

○ Use electronic, fibre, or charcoal filters for incoming or recirculated air and ionizers to increase the proportion of negative ions in the air.
○ Use heat-exchange or heat-recovery systems (see pp. 102-3). These will retain some of the heat of the outgoing air and transfer it to the fresh, incoming air. This will go some way to help meet energy-conservation needs.

Removal at source

Repair or replace such things as a defective gas cooker or wood-burning stove, ban tobacco smoke and aerosols, replace or seal materials containing formaldehyde (common sources include chipboard and synthetic carpets, curtains, furnishings, and fabrics), and prevent the entry of radon. Additionally, avoid polyurethane foam and soft-plastic goods as well as carpets with foam underlays. Oil tanks and garages should be away from the house.

Radon

Radon is an example of a natural substance that is definitely a major health risk. It is only recently that it has been realized that radon 222 – a tasteless, odourless, invisible gas – can account for up to 50% of all the radiation we receive from natural sources. It is now thought to be the second biggest cause of lung cancer after smoking. These concentrations vary enormously between different regions of the world, but indoors at radon hot spots (particularly in sealed buildings with low ventilation) they can be far higher than outdoors. Extreme concentrations of radon have been found in Sweden and Finland (5000 times that of outdoor air) and in the UK and US (500 times).

Such building materials as certain bricks, cement, and aggregate made from uranium or phosphate mine trailings or stone (particularly granite or rocks used as heat stores in solar-heating systems) can all be sources of radon. But emissions from these are thought to be small when compared with that from the ground beneath structures in radon regions. In general, concentrations are greater in ground-floor rooms but the type of flooring material and even wall construction have a great effect.

Water and natural gas can also be sources of radon. In the bathroom, for example, radon in the water can be released into the air from showers creating levels up to 40 times greater than those found in living rooms.

Remedies for this problem are still at the developmental stage, but from radon-mitigation work in a number of countries it appears that you can take some broad, preventative measures. First, however, contact your local health department to establish whether you live in a radon area, the levels of radon in your home, and the appropriate local remedial actions. If you have been exposed to high concentrations, have a medical check-up immediately.

For suspended floors (ground floors with an air space underneath):
○ Seal all cracks around edges, pipes, ducts, and walls. Cover the floor with radon-impermeable material such as sealed heavy polythene sheeting. Lay protective boarding on top.
○ Increase natural ventilation under the floor. Either install more airbricks or, preferably, install a fan and block up most of the airbricks (to allow the fan to expel the radon).

For solid floors (laid on hardcore with no air space, but usually with a vapour barrier):
○ Seal cracks in floor and edges, pipes, and walls (especially in basements).
○ Reduce air pressure underneath the house. Build a "radon sump" and expel the radon to the outside (see below).
○ In both cases, ensure that the outlet from the fan is well away from windows and doors.
○ Ventilate basements, cellars, crawl spaces, and the home generally.
○ Use extractor fans to expel moisture (continuous use may reduce air pressure and increase radon entry).
○ For energy conservation, install a mechanical ventilation and heat recovery system.
○ Install radon detectors and monitor levels regularly.

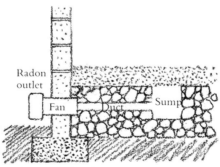

Prevent radon from entering the home by sealing ground floors and increasing ventilation underneath. With a solid concrete floor, radon collects in a sump beneath the floor and is drawn outside by a fan.

Natural ventilation

Air moves naturally through the home due to pressure and temperature differences. Air entering through windows can be increased by cross-ventilation – opening windows and doors in other walls. Winds cause a difference in pressure from one side of the house to the other, and this draws air through the home. So, too, does the convection currents of heated air and the "stack effect" causing air to rise upward.

Filters and ionizers

If you decide on filtration to remove pollutants then portable filter units might be appropriate. But they are not always very effective, particularly for radon. These are designed to filter areas ranging in volume from single rooms to whole houses. The air is drawn through a number of filters: a prefilter of fibreglass or polyester to remove dust; main filters of coconut shell carbon or Purafil (a nontoxic odouroxidant consisting of activated alumina impregnated with potassium permanganate) to absorb vapours and small gas molecules; and a particulate filter.

Another, but less-effective, option is an electrostatic air cleaner, which charges airborne particles either negatively or positively. The charged particles are then attracted to special collector plates or any items in the room with an opposite charge.

A negative ion generator that you use to ionize the air is similar, but it removes only smoke, dust, and some allergens. Although there is no consensus among researchers that ion concentrations in the air significantly affect comfort and wellbeing, many users of ionizers are convinced that they are fundamental to air quality. Perhaps your best approach is to buy or borrow a small room ionizer and see if you experience any benefits before investing in larger, whole-house units. Use the ionizer in rooms with a TV or VDU where negative ions are low in concentration; ionizers are also thought to be beneficial in bedrooms.

Air control systems

How you balance air quality and energy use will largely depend on climatic conditions. If you live where it is hot and humid, for example, or where it is cold for long periods and energy saving is paramount, you may have to choose mechanical systems that, ideally, incorporate heat-recovery features. In newly built Scandinavian and North American low-energy houses it is now the norm to have integral whole-house mechanical ventilation.

In more temperate climates, where houses are less tightly sealed, you should aim to continue to rely on passive ventilation. Such a system uses the "stack effect" principle, where, due to differences in inside and outside temperatures and pressures, and the height of the stack itself, fresh air is drawn through the house. Polluted and moist air then rises to an outlet in the roof. You can supplement this with extractor fans in kitchens and bathrooms or in specific pollution-generating areas, such as basements containing central-heating boilers, home offices with VDUs, or home workshops containing paints and adhesives.

Whole-house systems

Integral whole-house systems, either active or passive, extract air containing pollutants, odours, and excess moisture through ducts or designed airflows. Depending on the design of the particular system, dry air from, for example, living rooms can be directed through kitchens and bathrooms to ensure that excess moisture is removed and the likelihood of unsightly and damaging condensation lessened. Whole-house systems can also be designed to be "intelligent", in as much as they respond, via sensors, to changes in conditions in each room.

Ideally, you should have indoor air monitored by permanent sensors that detect pollution and automatically regulate ventilation. Although sensors capable of carrying out this function do exist, the truly effective ones are expensive and measure only certain pollutants, such as carbon dioxide, radon, or formaldehyde. Less-expensive detectors for radon or formaldehyde are available in some countries, but you should check their accuracy with your local product standards office.

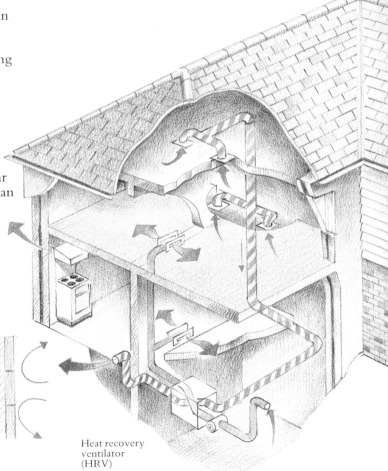

Active whole-house ventilation systems use air ducting along with the heating system (see right). This delivers fresh, filtered, and warmed air at floor level to each room and extracts it at high level. It also removes moisture, odours, and pollutants. Kitchens are usually vented separately to prevent high concentrations of smoke and oil accumulating in the system. Heat exchangers (see p. 82) are necessary to provide adequate ventilation while still maintaining energy efficiency.

Sealed wall

Heat recovery ventilator (HRV)

Design, siting, and orientation

These three factors have a significant effect on the balance in your home between the needs of energy conservation and those of ventilation. If home design was generally improved to take advantage of the natural benefits of sun and shelter (or micro-climates), they would be much better conservers of energy and would not, therefore, need to be made so airtight. The earth-covered home highlights this point admirably – by remaining at a fairly constant year-round temperature it requires very little extra energy for either space heating or cooling. Since energy conservation is not so necessary, it is possible to use simple, natural ventilation to keep the air inside the house fresh and comfortable.

The breathing house

One form of ventilation that is frequently over-looked is the natural diffusion of air through porous building materials, such as brick, stone, timber, and plaster (see pp. 132-55). The "breathing" effect of the whole outer (above-ground) shell of the struc-ture – the "third skin" – can add significantly to the air exchange with the outside. Ventilation by diffusion also has an advantage because porous materials can absorb and release excess moisture, thereby helping to regulate indoor humidity and expel pollutants. But with the current trend toward airtight homes with nonporous materials, and surfaces sealed with paints, varnishes, and plastics, ventilation by diffusion is becoming impossible.

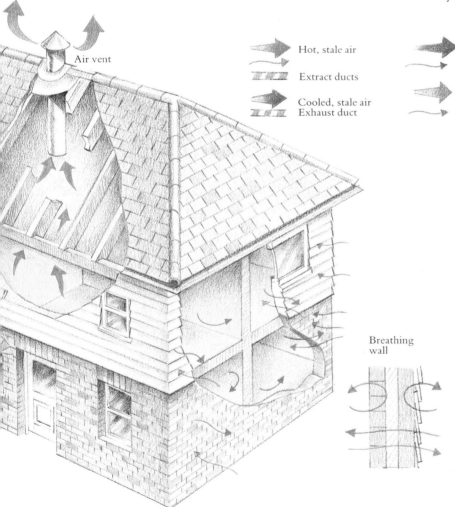

Air vent

→ Hot, stale air	→ Cold fresh air
⇢ Extract ducts	
→ Cooled, stale air	→ Warmed fresh air
⇢ Exhaust duct	

Breathing wall

Passive ventilation relies on the porosity of traditional materials, such as clay bricks and tiles, lime mortar and plaster, and timber and weatherboarding. They allow air and moisture to pass very slowly through their minute pores by diffusion – the natural difference in air pressure and temperature between the inside and the outside gradually drawing fresh air through the building structure and into the home (see left). This process filters and rids the air of dust and reduces pollutants and excess moisture. There are no draughts or loss of heat – the process is so slow that heat is retained in the materials. Once inside, the fresh air rises by convec-tion, permeating throughout the home and either filters out via the roof and walls or, to increase flow when necessary, through a closable roof vent. This Baubiologie prin-ciple regulates indoor air quality, humidity, and electrical balance, dilutes and expels pollutants, and works without any powered systems.

Scent

Due to the environment many of us live in, the sense of smell is becoming increasingly less important. The full capacities of this once vital sense are being subconsciously subordinated to the other senses of hearing and seeing. In other species the sense of smell is much more highly developed as, indeed, it is in those human societies today that remain in close contact with nature and depend on this sense, in conjunction with all the others, for day-to-day survival.

Denying your senses

Your nose is an extremely sensitive sensory organ and your sense of smell is many thousands of times more acute than your sense of taste. Because of this, you, like everybody else, have probably experienced a sudden and vivid association evoked by a particular smell, perhaps reminding you of a person, place, or event often from long ago and until that moment quite forgotten.

But air pollution, both indoors and outdoors, dulls and damages the sense of smell. By reacting badly to an unpleasant smell your body is warning you that you should not be breathing that air. But if you have no choice, as many of us don't, then the warning goes unheeded. But you do pay a price. By denial, you can add to your already overtaxed stress level, which can lead on to stress-related symptoms and eventually to illness. And the more you deny your senses the less the warning bells ring. Few people, for example, seem to notice the strong chemical smells associated with detergents, cleaners, and cosmetics on supermarket shelves, or the sharp and irritating smell of synthetic fabrics in clothes or carpet stores.

Often you will find the most overpowering accumulations of smells in newly decorated and furnished offices or hotel rooms where almost everything used is now chemically based. However, many people do suffer from stress and allergic reactions to just these sources and never realize what the cause might be.

You often find that a thoroughly unpleasant smell of some new purchase, perhaps made of plastic, seems to diminish after a few days and you assume that because the odour has lessened so have the chemical vapours. But what probably has happened is that olfactory fatigue has set in. This is a condition where your sense of smell adapts but the danger remains the same. You may even come to like a smell that is harmful to you – another facet of the adaption syndrome. For example, a weekend woodworker might come to enjoy, or even become addicted to, the smell of adhesives in the workshop, and never suspect that exposure to those same fumes is the cause of fuzzy thinking on Monday mornings. As Dr Alfred Zamm, an American physician and clinical ecologist, says: ". . . if you can't eat it, don't breathe it."

Your sense of smell

Some of the most common pollutants that erode your ability to smell include: vehicle exhausts; factory emissions; smog; vapours from chemicals inside buildings; decorating products; plastics; artificial fragrances from household cleaners; cosmetics; and air fresheners.

Unfortunately, many of the odours you will come across in your everyday environment are not only unpleasant, they are also toxic and damaging. Examples include: tobacco and fuel smoke; nail polish remover; air fresheners and aerosols in general; many plastics and adhesives; and paints, vinyl wallpaper, and paper removers.

Some naturally occurring scents, such as those from the *terpene* family, resins from coniferous woods, and rubber, can also cause allergies in some people, as can dust, damp, mould, and bacteria.

Any of the pollutants listed above can cause a range of symptoms, including respiratory problems, congestion, blocked nose, asthma and allergies, headaches, nausea, increased intolerance to chemical odours, and a range of nervous disorders.

Aroma as part of design

It is an interesting fact that when interior design or architectural magazines describe a home, colour, form, space, and texture are all frequently mentioned – but smell hardly ever. It is as if this was of no consequence, or that all interiors are expected to be odourless and sterile. But unfortunately many modern interiors have a decidedly unpleasant smell, which gives warning of an accumulation of pollutants, stale air, condensation, and cooking odours. The design of a home, in order to be complete, must embrace aroma, too.

Detoxifying the home

To avoid harmful and unpleasant smells in the home and to create an environment that is naturally scented, first you will need to detoxify and clean your home. As a starting point, you should try the following suggestions:
○ Remove or reduce all sources of pollution and unpleasant smells. Gradually replace all offending items with safe and natural materials, furnishings, fabrics, and floorcoverings, and decorate your home with natural paints (see pp. 264–5). These natural materials all have their own subtle and pleasant aromas and it is extremely therapeutic to be surrounded by them.
○ Keep all rooms and cupboards clean. Use safe and nontoxic cleaning materials, such as herbal soaps, furniture creams, floor polishes, and fabric shampoos. These should be either odourless or have a natural fragrance. Use bicarbonate of soda to remove unpleasant smells from fabrics, refrigerators, and rooms generally (see pp. 266–7).
○ Ventilate all rooms adequately (see p. 102), particularly bathrooms, toilets, and kitchens, in order to remove both cooking smells and moist air.

The odourless home

Many chemically sensitive people can lose their entire sense of smell but it usually returns following a course of treatment by a clinical ecologist. For allergy sufferers, it may be necessary to make part of the home, or at least one room, a "sanctuary" that is completely free from odours (see p. 241).

Sufferers may find it difficult to pinpoint the sources of the problem smells and some allergy and environmental medicine hospitals have resorted to the help of former patients as "super-sniffers", who because of their peculiarly sensitive noses can detect the type and source of many chemical smells. Natural gas can be a powerful sensitizer and, if this substance is diagnosed by a clinical ecologist as a cause of the problem, the gas supply will have to be cut off before it enters the home. The repercussions of this can be extreme – heating, cooking, etc – and it should be considered only as a last resort. Any other sensitizers should also be removed and it may be necessary to install a filter system.

Aromatherapy

This is an ancient branch of herbal medicine and is thought to have originated in either India or China. Essential oils are extracted from flowers, leaves, roots, seeds, barks, and resins and these are usually massaged into the skin, inhaled, or used in a bath. These oils have been found to be particularly beneficial in treating a range of common ailments and they are also generally revitalizing and energizing for the body and mind as a whole.

There have been many theories to explain the effects of aromatherapy and, although not scientifically proven, it is widely accepted that the oils stimulate the olfactory responses and nerves in the skin surface. These effects are passed on to the brain area controlling the emotions and, via the nervous system, to the pituitary gland, which controls the other major glands in the body.

Aromatherapy is used as an aid to relaxation and as a way of bringing you back in touch with all your senses, including that of smell.

Essential oils

You can use aromatherapy essential oils generally around the home. Add a few drops to a hot bath, for example, and relax in the water for at least ten minutes, or add fragrance to any room by placing just a drop or two in a vaporizer ring on a lightbulb or stove. You can also use the oils in home-made soaps, polishes, candles, pot-pourris, and herb or flower sachets and pillows. From the wide range of oils available, you can select some, such as those following, for their relaxing and soothing qualities.

Lavender Well known for its ability to heal wounds, it is also a powerful relaxant. Dilute a drop and add it to a baby's bath to help it to sleep.
Rose The oil from the damascena, centifolia, and gallica varieties of the rose is much valued for its ability to relieve stress and depression. The very astringent oil of "attar" from the petals is more antiseptic than carbolic acid.
Sandalwood A heavy, luxurious oil good for relieving tension and anxiety. Use a few drops in a vaporizer in the evening.

Chamomile Frequently used in aromatherapy to calm the nerves. Use five or six drops in a bath or add two drops to five teaspoons of soya oil for massage.
Melissa The oil from the lemon balm plant; it is soothing and helps lift depression. It has been used since medieval times to scent beeswax furniture polish, as has myrtle and sweet marjoram.
Neroli Used for nervous tension and anxiety, this oil comes from the bitter orange tree. For massaging, add five drops to two teaspoons of soya oil.

The naturally fragrant home

The use of scented plants and herbs in the home is very ancient and the first recorded use was by the Egyptians, who also used them in their tombs.

Spices brought from the East were used widely by the Greeks and Romans, and every culture since has recognized the pleasures and benefits of these natural fragrances. In the medieval world, herb gardens became fashionable and cultivated herbs were used in cooking and medicine, as well as in the home – rushes and herbs were often strewn on floors and pomanders and pot-pourris placed in rooms to make them smell sweet and fresh. It is only comparatively recently that artificial scents have displaced these old and natural products.

You can almost smell the sweet fragrance of the honeysuckle and the savoury sage that fills the air of the living room in this French farmhouse (right). Natural paints and beeswax polishes add their own pleasant aromas and combine to make this house a place where you can fill your lungs deeply and slowly regain your full sense of smell once more.

Adding fragrances

○ Place sweet-smelling flowers around the home and grow pots of savoury, aromatic herbs, or hang bunches of herbs in the kitchen.
○ Grow aromatic plants and flowers in window boxes or in the garden close to windows and doors. Many varieties of flowers, such as night-scented stocks, roses, pinks, tobacco plant, violets, wall-flowers, carnations, lilies, jasmine, and so on, have captivating scents, and many herbs are pungent and savoury.
○ Use bowls of flower water (out of reach of children), pot-pourris, pomanders, scented candles, room sprays (not aerosols), and a vaporizer with a variety of essential oils. Woodruff gives any room a particularly pleasant freshness.
○ Use aromatic woods such as cedar, sandalwood, juniper, and hickory for storage chests and boxes as well as natural herbal-scented polishes and oils (see pp. 266-7).
○ You can subtly emphasize the quality and atmosphere of each room by using different combinations of herbs and flowers. This can be even more satis-fying if you live in a city apartment without access to a garden.

Using herbs

As well as flavouring and preserving food, many herbs make excellent domestic cleaners, air fresheners, fumi-gators, and insecticides. They are mar-vellous for scenting linen, freshening cupboards and drawers, or used in pot-pourris and herbal pillows. You can also make your own dyes and herb-scented candles.
○ To make sweet herb sachets, fill small cotton bags with pot-pourri mixtures of any blend of dried herbs. Add a few drops of oil of rosemary or oregano. To intensify or renew the aroma of laven-der, use a little oil of lavender. Place the sachets in closets and drawers or tie them to clothes hangers.
○ To make a dry pot-pourri, dry leaves and flowers separately and place alter-nate 2.5cm (1in) layers of them in jars. Over each layer sprinkle 1/2 a teaspoon of coarse salt and the same of orris root powder. Close the jars tightly and store them in the dark for three weeks. After this period, mix the contents in a bowl with spices and one or two essential oils. For "herb garden" pot-pourri, mix tablespoons (the number in brackets) as above: peppermint or spearmint (6); rosemary (4); lemon balm (4); marjoram (2); sage (1); crumbled bay leaves (1); thyme (1/2); salt (2); orris root powder (2); plus 1 teaspoon of oil of rosemary and 1/2 teaspoon of oil of oregano.

○ To make a pomander, prick an orange, lemon, or lime all over with a knitting needle, leaving a central "cross" free to tie a ribbon. Press a clove into each prick until the surface of the fruit is entirely covered (except for the cross). For extra scent, roll the pomander in powdered cinnamon, nutmeg, ginger, and orris. Leave the fruit somewhere dark until it is dry and hard, tie on a ribbon along the clear central cross, and hang it up.
○ To make a herbal pillow, fill one or two sachets and tuck them between the pillow and its case. Renew the sachet each year. Mix dry ingredients in parts (numbers in brackets): for a "country pillow" – meadowsweet (3); agrimony (3); and honeysuckle (2). For a "hop pillow" (for peaceful sleep): hops (4); woodruff (2); and chamomile (2).

Sound

Sound is, like light, a basic energy source and it has a powerful sensory effect on the whole being – mind, body, and spirit. "Pleasant" sounds (which are very much culturally defined) can help induce feelings of wellbeing and tranquillity and they are supportive and healing. Additionally, there are the universally recognized sounds of nature – the wind in the trees and grass, the babble of running water, or the calls of birds and other animals – which all help to reinforce your connectedness with the natural world.

Conversely, "unpleasant" sounds can be harmful and stressful. At intense levels, these sounds represent a serious health hazard. And just like the fatigue your other senses suffer when subjected to continual bombardment, constant noise (defined as unwanted sound) will cause auditory fatigue as the mind tries to minimize the intrusion. But unlike sight and smell, which have specific receptors, it is thought that the cells of the body have some sort of sound perception and that you react to sound even if it is below the level of conscious awareness. When you are asleep, for example, you might still be reacting to the constant drone of traffic along busy city streets outside your bedroom window.

Noise pollution

Noise is one of the least recognized and regulated of all pollution sources. Although noise is slowly becoming seen as a real health hazard and there are now noise-abatement laws in many countries, enforcement is generally far too relaxed and standards far too low.

Most of us are exposed to high levels of noise stress at work, while shopping, and even when travelling. And often you are not much better off in the home, with intrusive traffic noise, nearby construction or roadworks, low-flying airplanes, mechanical garden equipment, barking dogs, and screaming children. Added to this is the noise generated indoors by washing machines, vacuum cleaners, food mixers, refrigerators, boilers, air conditioners, flushing toilets, noisy plumbing, extractor fans, and fluorescent lights, as well as by radios, TVs, and stereos. And for many, especially those living in badly constructed apartments and terraced houses, the noise from neighbours can represent an intolerable extra burden. You can reach a point of near desperation where it seems almost impossible to find a peaceful space.

Noise in the home There are three main ways in which noise can travel into and around the home: *airborne sound*, *impact sound*, and *flanking transmission*.

The efficiency of walls and floors in preventing sound transmission depends on their mass. The heavier and thicker the construction the less it vibrates. Thus brick, earth, and concrete are usually better sound insulators than wood. Impact noise through floors, however, is not controlled by mass but by an absorbing surface, such as carpet, or by separating the floor into a "floating floor" resting on a resilient quilt above the structural floor.

Typical noise-pollution sources

Perceived decibels	Typical sounds
140–130	Jet engine at 30m (100ft); pneumatic rivetter; hydraulic press at 1m (39in)
120	**Threshold of pain**; 1 billion times greater than the least audible sound; loud thunder
110	Discotheque speakers at 1.2m (4ft); pneumatic drill
100	Food blender at 61cm (24in); nearby chain saw or motor cycle
90	Heavy truck; automatic lathe
80	**Danger level**; inside small car; noisy office; alarm clock; window air conditioner
70	Busy shopping street; large department store; building noise; vacuum cleaner, food mixer washing machine
60	Normal conversation at 1m (39in)
50	Quiet street; inside average home
40	Quiet office; quiet conversation; residential area at night; refrigerator
30	Ticking watch; rustle of paper; whispered conversation; bedroom
20	Quiet country lane
10	Leaves rustling in wind
0	**Threshold of hearing**

What is sound?

What the ear perceives as sound is a disturbance of the air usually caused when a surface is vibrated. This produces alternating waves of compression and rarefaction. The number of vibrations per second determines the *frequency*, or pitch, of the sound, and these cycles of alternating waves produced are measured in hertz (Hz). The human ear can respond to vibrations between about 20 and 20,000Hz, although the higher pitches become increasingly difficult to hear as you grow older. People are most disturbed by higher frequencies, between about 500 and 6000Hz, and low-frequency sounds are generally more relaxing.

The *intensity*, or loudness, of sound is the amount of acoustic energy transmitted through the air, and this is measured in decibels (dB).

Whether or not you perceive the frequency and intensity of sound around you in the home as pleasant or unpleasant depends to a considerable extent on the *ambient*, or background, noise. You tend not to notice external noise of, for example, traffic to the same extent if there is conversation or music inside. Tightly sealed and sound-insulated homes exclude the majority of outside sounds and, as a result, can seem almost oppressively quiet. Too little sound entering the home from outside can lead to feelings of isolation and unease. Internal sounds will then become more apparent and take on increasing importance.

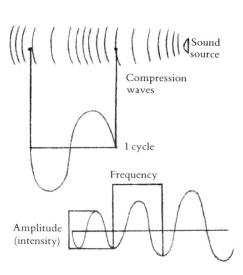

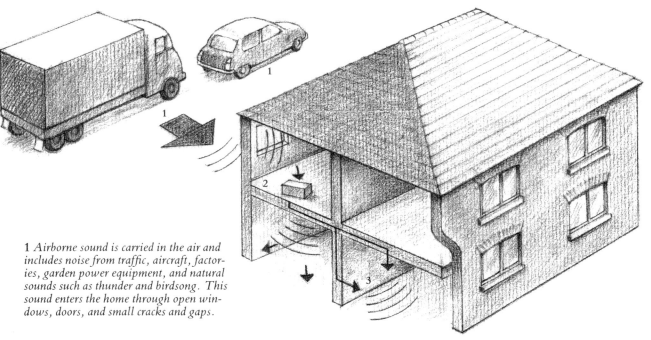

1 Airborne sound is carried in the air and includes noise from traffic, aircraft, factories, garden power equipment, and natural sounds such as thunder and birdsong. This sound enters the home through open windows, doors, and small cracks and gaps.

2 Impact sound occurs when you drop an object on the floor or a refrigerator vibrates the floor. This travels through floors and walls and will be heard quite loudly on the other side. Heavy objects and hard surfaces transmit most sound; softer surfaces absorb impact sound.

3 Flanking sound is heard because impact sound travels along walls and floors, so even distant impacts can be heard. In a structure such as a concrete building, impact sounds from plumbing, lift motors, and so on will travel a long way.

The sound-healthy home

Reducing noise

In the first instance, just listen to the noise you and your family make. You could even carry out an audit and note down all the sources of noise in and around your home and decide how to deal with them. Think also about the types of pleasant sound you would like to introduce – running water from a fountain in the garden or wind chimes are just two suggestions.

In all cases of unwanted sound, prevention is better than cure, and a few simple behavioural changes could make life more pleasant.

In the home

○ Place refrigerators, washing machines, and other household appliances away from partition walls.
○ Stop noisy do-it-yourself jobs once night falls.
○ Keep the volume of radios, TVs, and stereos as low as possible, especially late at night.
○ Inform neighbours beforehand if you intend to do any drilling or hammering.
○ If your dog barks constantly when left alone indoors, try to leave it with a friend or neighbour.
○ If you are having a party, let the neighbours know beforehand and keep noise to a reasonable level.
○ Wear slippers or go barefoot indoors.

About the home

○ Don't allow your dog to bark outside for long periods, especially at night.
○ Don't carry out noisy car maintenance or rev the engine unnecessarily at night.
○ Don't slam doors.
○ Use the car horn only in emergencies.
○ Maintain car and motorcycle exhaust systems.
○ Use lawnmowers and other power garden tools only at reasonable times.

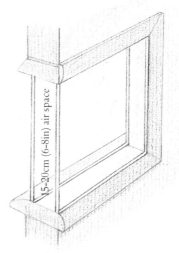

15–20cm (6–8in) air space

Together with entrance doors, windows are the weak points that let in most outside noise. To reduce sound entering, add secondary glazing (with a wider gap between panes than for energy conservation) and seal any cracks around the edges of both windows.

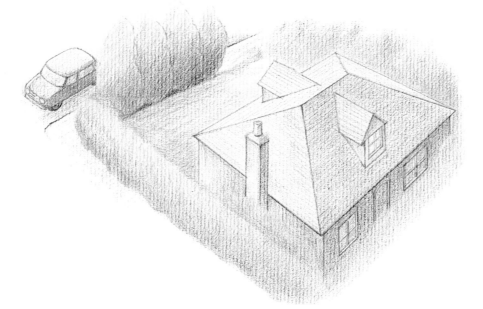

Many homes are sited next to noisy traffic routes (above) and suffer from constant disturbance inside. A dense barrier of trees, high walls, hedges, and earth mounds, plus planting and thick creepers over the house walls will help to absorb and dissipate the noise. Rear living and bedrooms will be quieter, too.

One of the worst problems with apartments, especially those created when large houses are converted into smaller units, is noise from neighbours above. To make a "floating floor", lay a dense mineral fibre quilt and fix floorboards to battens on top. For a ceiling, line it with quilt, battens, and plasterboard.

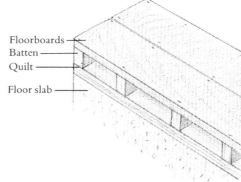

Floorboards
Batten
Quilt
Floor slab

Excluding outside noise

There is the unfortunate minority of homes that are located in areas subjected to intolerable levels of noise and vibration. Homes close to airports, busy roads, noisy factories, and so on really should not be there at all. But for most of us, intrusive outside noise is normally only at nuisance level and you can do much to minimize its impact.

As well as adding to the aesthetic appeal of your environment, trees, shrubs, and soft ground-cover plants deaden the effects of a great deal of outside noise. Plant-covered fencing and hedges, high walls, and grassy mounds also act as efficient sound barriers. If you have a garden, think about installing a small fountain or waterfall to provide a relaxing background of natural sound. If you are designing or building a new home, place kitchens, bathrooms, and halls on the noisy side of the structure to act as buffers.

Your next line of defence is the external fabric of your home. Since windows and doors let in most noise, it is here you need to pay most attention. In fact the techniques needed to reduce sound transmission do not differ from those used to conserve energy (see pp. 82-3). First, seal all edge gaps and, secondly, install secondary glazing (to reduce sound, though, the minimum air space between glazing has to be 15-20cm/6-8in). Consider adding window shutters or heavy curtains.

External and common walls between apartments or terraced houses should be of rigid mass construction (brick, block, or concrete). Lightweight, timber-frame walls will not be effective as sound insulators unless you modify them by adding a second, independent, inner-frame wall covered with a double layer of plasterboard.

You will need to take expert advice on these types of modification, especially since sealing your home and lining the walls will have an effect on ventilation (see pp. 102-3).

With intrusive external noise reduced, noise generated inside the home will become more obvious. Simple measures you can take to reduce this include placing noisy appliances (washing machines, refrigerators, etc) on thick rubber mats or concrete floors; replacing older appliances with low-noise models; moving boilers away from living areas; renewing faulty water valves; and installing silent-flush toilets.

If you are planning a radical reorganization of your living space, you might be able to change the function of rooms so that noisy areas are away from living rooms and bedrooms, or soundproof one room to make a "quiet area".

For some respite in unavoidably noisy environments you could consider the simple solution of wearing earplugs for short periods. A more satisfactory solution, though, is a flotation tank, which you can install anywhere in your home. This full-length tank contains sufficient thermostatically controlled warm salt water for you to float in comfortably. The tank also has a door that you can close to exclude extraneous light and noise. It provides a secure and extremely relaxing experience.

An acoustic atmosphere

Once you have solved, or at least minimized as far as possible, the problems of internal and external noise, you will find it much easier to create within your home the sounds you positively enjoy and an acoustic environment designed for relaxation and pleasure.

The quality of sound inside a space is dependent on the mix of *direct* sounds travelling from the source to your ear and *reverberent* sounds reflecting off surfaces within that space. Reflected sound is influenced by the type and amount of surfaces present – a room with predominantly hard surfaces and a bare floor, for example, will tend to echo and feel spacious as a result.

If you want a room to have a cosier, more intimate and relaxed acoustic effect, you need to introduce absorbent surfaces. Add thick drapes to the windows and carpet the floor (or use deep-piled rugs). Fabric wall hangings will also help, especially over thick wallpaper or hessian-lined surfaces. Soft furnishings, screens, and plants will all add to the sound-softening quality.

On a more active level, you can experiment with introducing sounds into different rooms in order to create a range of varied atmospheres. The types of sound you would like to hear in the background will depend on personal preference, but they generally should be at a level where you are not necessarily even consciously aware of their presence. In the appropriate indoor setting you could, for example, build a small water sculpture to create this level of background sound. It would be an obvious choice in a plant-filled conservatory, but it could also become a fascinating focal point in a living room, bedroom, or dining room. Wind bells and chimes made of glass, metal, or bamboo can add delicate and subtle shades to ambient sound levels, and they would not be out of place in any room or balcony in your home.

In addition to ordinary music there is an ever-widening selection of "natural sound" recordings to bring the wilder places of the world into city-bound living rooms.

You can also do much in the garden by planting broad-leafed trees and shrubs, all of which move and rustle with every breeze. And to attract song birds, plant berry-producing species and provide nesting sites, bird tables, and a pond or fountain. Bamboos, reeds, and tall grasses not only look superb, especially when associated with water, but they, too, respond with their own individual voices to even slight movements of air through the garden.

Light and colour

The evolution of the human race and all other living things on the planet has occurred only because of the continuous radiation of the sun. Over the millennia, we have become attuned and adapted to its daily and seasonal cycles; our bodies' circadian rhythms and inner biological clocks are timed to follow these cycles of light and dark. We wake with the morning light, are most active while the sun is high in the sky and the light brightest, and rest and sleep as day slips into dusk and then night.

Other patterns linked to levels of sunlight can also be discerned: we tend to be sluggish and depressed during short, grey winter days and more energetic and generally happier in the long, bright days of summer. After all, winter sunlight in temperate latitudes is only about one-tenth its summer intensity. Significant changes occur in our hormone patterns due to these seasonal cycles that affect our endocrine glands. The hormone melatonin, secreted by the pineal gland in the brain during darkness or dim light, causes sleepiness, but its overproduction is an indicator of a medical condition known as seasonal depression.

But today, most of us do not live in harmony with the natural cycles of the sun. Our lives are spent mostly indoors where our activities are extended by artificial light sources. Modern offices, stores, and public buildings usually have intense levels of artificial lighting of a harsh, regimented, and shadowless type, which has rightly been termed workhouse or malign lighting.

SAD syndrome

Research in the US and the UK has shown that there is a marked seasonal variation in depression. Suicide rates, for example, tend to peak in late winter and manic depressives also feel worse during these months. This syndrome, known as "seasonal affective disorder" (SAD), is characterized by annually occurring winter depressions associated with increased somnolence, fatigue, weight gain, and carbohydrate craving. During spring and summer there is a reversal of these symptoms.

Treatment for sufferers with bright, full-spectrum lights (five times brighter than normal room lighting) inhibits the production of melatonin.

Patients sit a few feet from a lightbox of this intensity for a minimum of two hours a day. This seems an effective cure for many, but not all, sufferers, but UV radiation can be a problem (see p. 120). If you think you may be suffering from SAD, seek professional medical advice.

Colour

Another vitally important aspect of light is its effects on colour. Exposure to particular colours has been shown in clinical studies to have significant effects on the mood and personality of subjects. Colour consultants are often employed to plan the colour schemes of offices and factories in an attempt to provide an atmosphere that is both pleasant and productive. In the home, too, there is now widespread appreciation of the importance of colour schemes to live with, but here you have the complication of selecting the most appropriate artificial light source as well.

Light and shade are modifiers of colours. Even in a white or pastel-coloured room, natural light and reflections will cause the walls and ceiling to vary subtly in hue and tone – the wall with the window set into it being the darkest. The natural spectrum of sunlight changes with the cycle of the sun – moving from the rosy light of dawn to a more neutral effect at noon and then to the bluer light of dusk. You may want to take this into account when planning the colour of rooms receiving sunlight at different times of the day.

Artificial lighting has even more drastic effects on colour. An incandescent or tungsten-filament lamp is deficient in blue wavelengths but rich in red and yellow. Under this type of illumination cool colours will lose their brilliance and purity but warm colours will gain in intensity and richness. Fluorescent lighting, however, is deficient in the warmer end of the spectrum and casts a cooler, more blue/green light – although you can offset this by using warm-white tubes. Special daylight fluorescent tubes have been used for many years in commercial environments where accurate colour matching is important. Recently, however, full-spectrum fluorescent tubes and incandescent lamps have become more widely available.

Designing with light

Natural outdoor light is variable and subtle. It changes in intensity during the year as well as during the day – diffused by morning mist, obscured by clouds, or dappled by trees. Moonlight varies, too, according to both the lunar cycle and the weather. These natural variations and cycles help to keep us stimulated, alert, and well.

We need to be more aware of these subtle varieties and qualities and try to introduce them into our own homes. Unfortunately, though, many houses have windows only at the front and back, and some apartments may only look in one direction. This type of limitation is difficult to overcome, but you could try to add windows with different orientations if, for example, you are building an extension. You could also add skylights or clerestory windows to existing rooms.

Cross-lighting is always more pleasant than light coming from only one direction. If you decide to add new windows, make sure they do specific jobs – such as catching the morning sun in bedrooms, kitchens, or breakfast rooms, for example.

The quality of light

Light can be direct, reflected, or diffused and it also has a colour quality depending on the season, the time of day, and the weather. Direct sunlight shining straight through a window is the strongest, casting shadows and causing glare. Reflected light is light bouncing off surfaces outside and/or inside the room. Depending on the brightness and texture of the surface, the light will probably be muted and tinted the colour of the reflecting surface. Light is diffused when it passes through a filter, such as net curtains, frosted glass, blinds, or screens. It is then soft and almost shadowless.

You should vary the amount and quality of the light according to the needs of each space. Use direct lighting for kitchens, offices, workrooms, stairs, and sunspaces where bright light is essential for safety or plant growth. Highlight focal points and add dramatic contrasts, too, with small windows or shafts of light. But for a more relaxed and comfortable atmosphere in living rooms, use reflected and diffused lighting.

Types of light
There are three basic types of artificial lighting – general, task, and atmospheric. Most rooms are provided only with a central overhead fitting for general lighting, and this produces an unattractive and inflexible form of illumination. In most rooms, try to use several light sources, such as downlighters, tungsten-halogen uplighters, or spotlights. For task lighting, use spotlights, mini-spotlights, and desk lights close to the work area, or fluorescent lights well shaded to avoid glare. You can create mood and atmosphere by using low-level lighting, such as table, floor, and wall lamps or concealed shelf lighting using decorative, soft-toned incandescent bulbs. Dimmer controls give you extra flexibility and variety.

Electromagnetic spectrum

Visible light spectrum

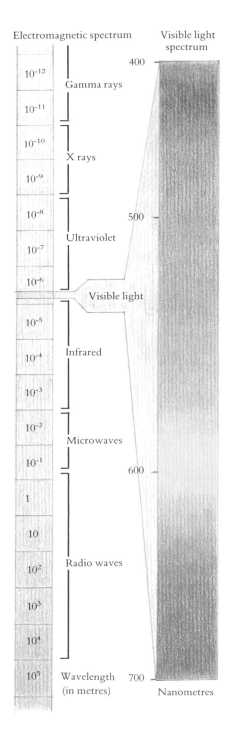

10^{-12}	Gamma rays
10^{-11}	
10^{-10}	X rays
10^{-9}	
10^{-8}	Ultraviolet
10^{-7}	
10^{-6}	
	Visible light
10^{-5}	
10^{-4}	Infrared
10^{-3}	
10^{-2}	
10^{-1}	Microwaves
1	
10	
10^2	Radio waves
10^3	
10^4	
10^5	

Wavelength (in metres)

400

500

600

700

Nanometres

The spectrum

The wavelengths of the different colours of visible light are a minute part of the range of energy we know as electromagnetic radiation. You can demonstrate that visible light is made up of many different colours by passing light through a prism. A similar effect is achieved naturally when sunlight shines through water droplets in the air and is broken up into the spectral colours of the rainbow.

Being part of the electromagnetic spectrum, light and its constituent colours are, in fact, minute packets of energy known as photons. The wavelengths of these photons are so small that they are measured in nanometres (nm), each unit being one-millionth of a millimetre.

The wavelengths of visible light extend from violet, the shortest at about 400nm, to red, the longest at about 700nm. Beyond these are the invisible wavelengths – the shorter ones of ultraviolet, X rays, and gamma rays and the longer ones of infrared, microwaves, and radio waves.

It is, however, the property of the surface of the object receiving the light that determines your perception of its colour. A red object, such as a tomato, absorbs all the wavelengths of the visible spectrum with the exception of red, which it reflects.

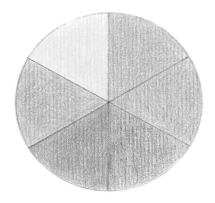

Daylight floods this airy Swedish living room (above). The light, reflective surfaces and bright splashes of colour enliven the atmosphere and lift the spirits. Bright sunlight and daylight produce an atmosphere of optimism, which is especially important in climates where there are too many grey cloudy days and depressingly long, dark winters.

The wooden shutters (left) shade the strong Southern sunlight and give the impression of coolness and greenness in this porch of the house where John James Audubon, the famous American artist and naturalist, was born.

Increasing and decreasing daylight

Daylight is a crucial feature of any natural home, and yours can be adapted to be far more "daylight healthy" and, thus, far less reliant on artificial light. The potential for admitting daylight into your home varies greatly depending on location and climate. Homes in temperate regions of the world, for example, can be daylight deficient, while those in more tropical, hotter areas can suffer from the opposite problem. Well-designed new homes being built in temperate regions should (but very often don't) make allowances for the lack of daylight for large parts of the year, but if you are trying to make improvements to an existing building, concentrate your attention on rooms that do not receive direct sunlight, those that are overshadowed, and basement or sub-basement areas.

Maximizing sunlight

The following points are more applicable to people living in the daylight-deficient areas of the world, but many homes, because of their orientation, overshadowing, or local aspects of environment, in the sunnier areas can also suffer from daylight deprivation.

○ Wherever possible, increase penetration and reflection of daylight from outside by using, for example, light-coloured paving underneath windows, applying light-coloured paint to garden walls or outside walls adjacent to windows, installing a pond, and by pruning overshadowing trees, shrubs, and climbing plants.

○ Increase the reflection of daylight from interior surfaces by using light-coloured decorations, furnishings, and carpets. Mirrors can greatly increase the background level of light in a room.

○ Increase daylight penetration into rooms by keeping the glass clean and clearing away physical obstructions at windows – especially, make sure you draw curtains fully and use a curtain track that allows curtains to clear completely the window area. If possible, add splayed window reveals (above left) or use reflective surfaces, such as mirrors or ornaments, at window reveals.

○ If you are contemplating building work or major redecoration, then think

To gain the most from natural light, site bedrooms facing toward sunrise, breakfast rooms to the early morning sun, and kitchens, living rooms and sunspaces anywhere in the sun zone. Store rooms can take advantage of the no-sun zone. The diagrams and cross-sections (top) give you an indication of the increased light penetration when you add a splayed reveal to a new or existing window.

Evening — Morning

Studio, office
Storage
NO-SUN ZONE
Constant light
Sunset   Sunrise
SUN ZONE
Noon
Kitchen, dining
Living, entrances
Bedrooms
Playroom
Sunspace
Sun's path during the day

about adapting your existing windows. Raising the height of windows is more effective than widening them because you gain more sky area.

○ Install new windows in positions that admit most daylight. Toplighting is most efficient via rooflights and sky-lights. Clerestory windows high up in walls allow light to reach to the back of rooms and also admit sunlight to pre-viously sunless rooms. Orientation will affect the amount of sunlight gained this way and you might have to pay atten-tion to controlling ultraviolet (UV), glare, and solar gain.

○ To capture the maximum amount of winter sunlight yet still have necessary shade from the heat of the summer sun, grow only deciduous trees, climbers, and bushes near windows on the sunny side of the structure.

○ Additionally, add a sunspace, an atrium, or light shafts with mirrors that track the sun and reflect its rays into sunless or windowless rooms.

It is necessary to strike a balance between any increased window area you might create with heat gain or loss and energy conservation needs. (Also, you will probably have to take into account local building and planning regulations.) Before making any changes, think about how the room is to be used, where you will place the furniture, and the amount and quality of light you will want for different activities.

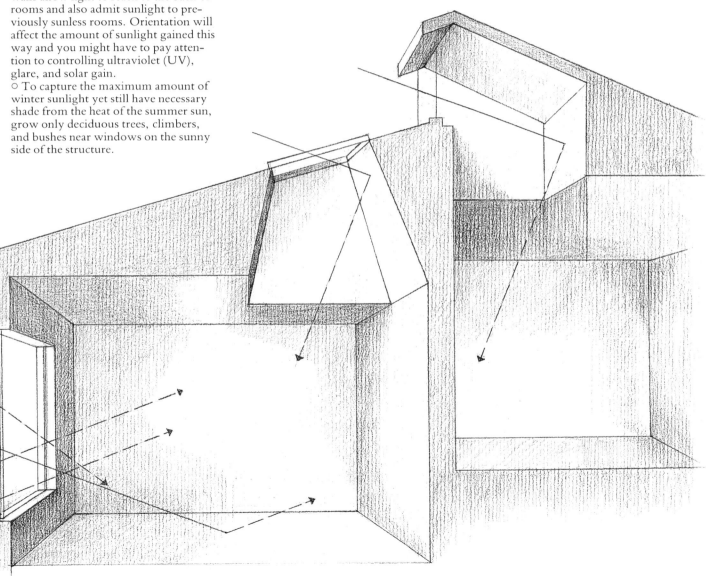

Minimizing sunlight

The following points are largely addressed to those living in areas benefiting from high levels of intense sunlight. Although these areas tend to be more equatorial, the types of problems associated with a surfeit of daylight can also apply to many other locations for part of the year or at specific times of the day.
○ Use shading and antiglare devices around the outside of your home. These include: extending the roof at the eaves; building verandahs on the sunny side of the structure; installing awnings, canopies, window shutters, blinds, screens, louvres, and skylight sunshields; planting trees, shrubs, and climbers to provide shade; and using tinted and solar-control glass.
○ Reduce the number and size of window openings on the sunny side (depending on prevailing breezes) and rely more on reflected light than direct light. This will help to keep the interior much cooler and it is the principle of subdued lighting employed in traditional Japanese homes.

Glare

In order to avoid glare from windows you need to reduce the contrast between light entering the room from the sky and the interior lighting of the room. If you light the room from two or more directions you will almost certainly reduce glare, as will making the walls near windows as bright as possible and increasing the amount of reflected light by using light-toned decoration, carpet, and furnishing. Another approach to the problem of internal glare from windows is to reduce the amount of light entering in the first place. To do this you can use shading devices (such as those listed on the left) on the outside or, on the inside, splayed window reveals or net curtains.

Minimizing
sunlight

Minimizing glare

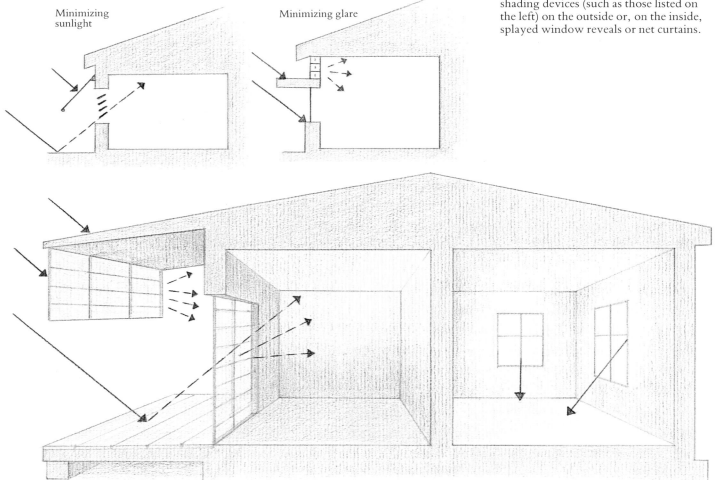

Artificial light

Although the principal aim in a natural home should be to rely as much as possible on daylight, and thus reduce the use of artificial light, you will inevitably be forced to use supplementary light at night and probably also during some daylight hours in winter. But despite the importance of the correct type and level of artificial illumination for your home, in terms both of health and safety and mood and atmosphere, it is surprising just how little attention most people pay to this subject.

The type of artificial light source you choose and where you position light fittings have a very considerable impact on the wellbeing of all the members of your household. The object of good artificial lighting is not simply to avoid any health problems, such as headaches and eyestrain, it should also contribute in a major way toward a supportive mood and atmosphere within the home. Here, you need to consider the colour rendering of the spectrum produced by different types of light source (see right), as well as the colours cast by lampshades. And leading on from this, lighting colour will then affect the colour of walls, ceiling, and furnishings and you need to take this into account when planning decorative colour schemes.

The lighting design itself should be as natural looking as possible (in other words, simulate the effects of daylight), and in this respect it is best to arrange lights in such a way that not too many of the actual fittings are visible. Naked bulbs or bright light sources need shading or they immediately draw the eye and can become unwanted and stressful focal points in a room.

It is not easy to lay down hard-and-fast rules concerning the placement of light fittings – so much depends on the individual characteristics of each room, the amount and placement of furniture, and the style of decoration. But you should be able to use the information here as at least a starting point to help you relate the principles of good, healthy lighting to your particular environment. You will probably find that the ideal arrangement is arrived at only by a process of trial and error – place lights where you think they might work best, live with them for a while, and then make any necessary modifications before fixing them permanently.

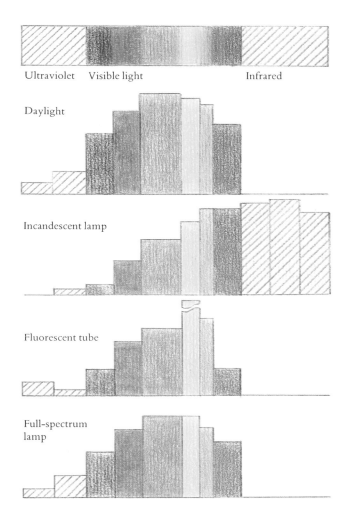

Ultraviolet   Visible light   Infrared

Daylight

Incandescent lamp

Fluorescent tube

Full-spectrum lamp

Using the spectral distribution of the colours of daylight as the norm, you can see how different artificial lights compare. Incandescent lamps – ordinary lightbulbs – are heavily weighted toward the red end of the spectrum and have little blue or green light. This is why these lamps give a yellow cast. In fact, most of the electricity used produces infrared heat rather than light. Fluorescent light is the reverse – it has more ultraviolet, blues, and greens and less yellows and reds, although "warm-white" tubes correct the "coldness" of the light. Electricity used produces mostly light and tubes are much cooler. Full-spectrum lamps more closely resemble the spectral balance of daylight, and its ultraviolet.

Lighting and health

Ultraviolet radiation

Of all radiation from the sun, the ultraviolet (UV) end of the electromagnetic spectrum has the most significant effects on your health. At low levels of exposure it can be beneficial, but exposure to high levels for long periods can result in premature aging of the skin, melanoma, and eye damage. But there is no real agreement among medical experts on where to draw the line between healthy and hazardous exposure to UV radiation, mainly because so much depends on the type of skin you have (light or dark), climate, altitude, the amount of time you spend in the sun, and your age (children being more susceptible).

One thing researchers are agreed on, however, is that the depletion of the ozone layer, which shields the planet from the worst effects of UV, will allow more of the highest-energy radiation (UV-C) to penetrate. Thus, both moderation and proper protection are thought to be even more essential than ever before.

At present, the construction of our homes and the use of ordinary glass shield us from current levels of lower-energy UV-A and UV-B. But windows and skylights made of certain plastics, such as polycarbonate and acrylic, do not. When these are used, as is often the case in mobile homes or as sheeting to cover home extensions (sunlounges or greenhouses), UV radiation will penetrate. In sun-deprived areas this can be beneficial for occasional sunbathing, but you need to take care, particularly in summer, if you sit for long periods by these plastic windows and skylights. UV radiation can also cause the deterioration of and offgassing from furnishings and curtains, especially if they are made of synthetic fibres. Full-spectrum lamps (see right) also emit small amounts of UV.

Full-spectrum lamps

These light sources are produced in the form of incandescent bulbs and fluorescent tubes for general interior lighting. They are designed to replicate more closely the spectral balance of daylight and they emit slightly higher levels of UV than ordinary bulbs and tubes. Manufacturers of full-spectrum lamps claim that their products are beneficial if you are sunlight deficient, improving your mood and performance. But with the increased concern about UV and as yet no satisfactory medical definition of safe levels, caution is advisable. In the US, these lamps cannot be advertised as health products.

In some offices, full-spectrum lamps have been overused and have had to be changed because the increased level of UV reacted with hydrocarbon pollutants in the air to produce a photochemical smog.

PCBs and other pollutants

Many older fluorescent fittings (pre-1978) have starting devices, known as rapid-start ballasts, containing highly toxic polychlorinated biphenyls (PCBs). These starting devices can leak and produce high concentrations of PCBs in rooms where this older type of fluorescent lighting is installed (usually kitchens and bathrooms). As a precaution, check the age of any fluorescent fittings you have in your home. Even if you cannot be certain of their age, it is safest to replace them, preferably with incandescent lights.

Bear in mind, however, that the most common incandescent lamps become hot when in use and they can cause plastics and paints in or around the fittings and shades to vaporize and pollute the air. The heat produced also disturbs dust and this, together with other indoor airborne pollutants, can act as irritants and cause allergic reactions.

Fluorescent lighting and stress

Although fluorescents are energy efficient, many people report symptoms of irritability, eyestrain, headaches, allergies, and hyperactivity when working by fluorescent lighting. Flicker, hum, glare, and UV all cause problems. The flicker you sometimes notice with fluorescent lighting occurs at a rate of either 50 or 60 cycles per second (depending on your electricity supply). This means that the tube is effectively switched on and off 100 or 120 times every second. Although it is supposed to be imperceptible when the light is functioning properly, with old or malfunctioning lights the flicker becomes distressing (as does the associated hum).

New fluorescent tubes have been designed to accelerate this cycle up to a thousand times. Manufacturers claim that the flicker should be invisible and the hum so high pitched as to be inaudible. But until health tests are carried out, these claims should be treated with caution.

Fluorescent lights also emit higher electromagnetic fields (EMFs) than other light sources, and these may affect some people (see pp. 80-1).

Energy-efficient lighting

More than 20 per cent of the electricity generated in the US is used for lighting, and approximately half this amount of energy is wasted lighting empty rooms or as heat produced by inefficient lamps. As an example, 95 per cent of the energy consumed by the most commonly used incandescent (tungsten-filament) lamp is given off as heat.

Efficiency is a measure of how much visible light is produced (lumens) per unit of electricity (watts). The more efficient a source the more light per watt it generates. By way of comparison, a 100w incandescent bulb produces 1200 lumens and, therefore, 12 lumens of light per watt, whereas a 20w warm-white fluorescent tube delivers 60 lumens per watt. It is thus five times more efficient and uses only 20 per cent of the electricity

So, from the point of view of energy conservation, it is far more efficient to use fluorescents. In financial terms, fluorescents can make savings of about 80 per cent of the amount spent on lighting.

Compact fluorescent lamps These are now available as replacements in incandescent fittings. Although the initial purchase price of the lamps is high, their long life and efficiency make them by far the cheaper long-term option. Because they do not produce excessive amounts of heat in operation, they also avoid the problem of dust and pollution associated with incandescent lamps. Ordinary fabric or paper shades do much to improve the quality of the light output of fluorescents.

Tungsten-halogen lamps These are a new generation of incandescents. The miniature quartz glass bulbs give a bright, white light close to daylight in quality. There are two types: first, powerful high-voltage lamps best used for general illumination, such as uplighters; and second, more energy-efficient, low-voltage halogen lights ideal for accent lighting. Both are expensive but lamps can last as long as 4000 hours and can represent savings as high as 60 per cent on lighting energy costs.

Metal-halide lamps This type of light produces the same powerful white illumination as tungsten-halogen lamps but is as efficient as fluorescents. Again, they are expensive to buy but you should expect up to 6000 hours of use from them.

Creating energy-efficient lighting

The following points are generally applicable and by following them you will not only create a healthier environment in the home, you will also make noticeable savings in the energy consumed by light fittings.
○ Reduce as far as is possible your reliance on artificial light (see pp. 116–17) and eliminate unnecessary sources of artificial light.
○ Use lighting only when and where it is needed (but excessive switching on and off of lamps will adversely affect their working life).
○ Create a lighting scheme that is well designed and specific to the activities in each room – adequate, but not too much, light in the right position and casting illumination in the right direction.

○ Increase the effectiveness of illumination by using light-coloured sources (but be careful of creating glare).
○ Bear in mind that a low-wattage lamp close to where it is needed is more energy-efficient than a stronger lamp positioned farther away.
○ Use energy-efficient instead of regular incandescent lamps.
○ Eliminate the unnecessary use of electricity by using control devices such as timers, dimmers, and cupboard door contact switches.
○ Carry out a regular maintenance routine with all your lamp fittings. Dust all bulbs and tubes regularly to increase light output and reduce potential pollutants. Replace lamps before they become too old and inefficient.

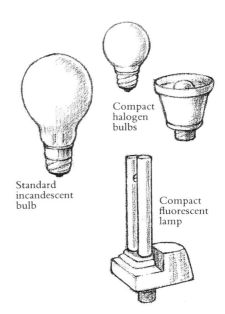

Compact halogen bulbs

Standard incandescent bulb

Compact fluorescent lamp

Using colour

Colour is extremely influential in everyday life. It expresses the type of person you are, your changing moods, and how you wish to appear to other people. Emotionally, colours are associated with feelings – seeing *red*, feeling *blue*, being *green* with envy, or simply feeling *off-colour*. The young are attracted to bright primary colours, while the old usually prefer subdued or more neutral hues.

Although the increasing use and availability of colour has brought the benefits of a brighter and more cheerful world, you are now bombarded by colour everywhere in your life – in what you eat, touch, and wear, from advertising in magazines, newspapers, and on TV, and on every shelf of every store you go into. But because colour is so all-pervading, and forever changing with current fashions, the tendency is to see it less and less and to regard it merely as superficial and cosmetic.

But colour has deeper spiritual and psychological effects, and many of us have lost touch with these more intuitive and personal associations. Colour and light can also have healing and rejuve-nating effects and many cultures have used colour medicinally for thousands of years. The Egyptians, for example, attributed certain colours to their gods and perfected a way of building rooms in their temples where the rays of the sun were used for healing. Illnesses were diagnosed as being partly due to a colour imbalance and were treated by bathing the patient in the deficient colour. The drinking of "solarized" water (water exposed to absorb a colour from the sun's spectrum) and the use of coloured gemstones were also prescribed. Colour occupied a similarly important place in the healing practices of China and India from earliest times (see p. 125).

Manipulating colour

Through its ties with advertising and "moving products", colour has become bound up with ex-ploitation and overconsumption. Market research has shown that, although it is not possible to be exact, certain families of colours convey a certain image, atmosphere, or feeling to most people.

The vibrant colours of this hallway and stairway act as strong youthful signals. Bright and jazzy, the jukebox image throbs with colour and impact and is a compulsive focal point.

The Itten colour system illustrated here (left) is only one of many that exist to describe the relationship of different colours. Devised by Johannes Itten, a member of the German Bauhaus until it was closed in 1933, it is made up of 12 pure hues, or colours. According to Itten, each of these pure colours can be tinted toward white or shaded toward black.

The subtle differences between the colours of each glazed tile (below) give the impression of a large mosaic. They harmonize to form the perfect background to the gentle colouring of this unusual French washbasin.

Warm colours, such as red, orange, and yellow, are usually seen as active, dynamic, and youthful; cool colours, such as green, blue, brown, and earth colours, are seen as passive, static, and conservative. In order to enhance these links, high-intensity colours are often associated with potency, strength, and masculinity; low-intensity or pastel colours are linked to soft, gentle, and feminine products.

The problem with these types of association is that they often act against traditional local tastes and submerge individual and personal needs. But in Japan, where the cycles of fashion and novelty are perhaps the fastest moving in the world, there appears to be the beginnings of a change. Traditionally in Japanese culture there has never been much emphasis on the interplay of different colours. Of greater significance has been the balance created by the relationship between the colour and the material to which it is applied. There is now a movement to try to recapture these colour associations, which are more in line with the Japanese cultural inclinations.

Environmental costs

Far worse than the colour pollution of our senses is the damage done to the environment by the various processes involved in the manufacture of colour pigments. Although the connection between colour and the environment, from the ecological point of view, is not immediately apparent, the increasing use of colour has a considerable impact on the consumption of natural resources.

With the majority of colour pigments and dyes having nonrenewable petrochemical or mineral origins, the more colour that is used in paints, fabrics, plastics, cosmetics, and so on, the faster these irreplaceable resources are consumed. In addition, commercial manufacturing processes may result in serious pollution of both the atmosphere and water supply.

Colour in the natural home

In the natural home, colour will tend to come more from the materials used to build and furnish the interior. Natural materials, such as wood, plaster, stone, brick, and clay, and natural fibres and fabrics all have their own beautiful and subtle colours and textures. In the vast majority of instances you simply do not need to decorate them at all: just allow the natural finish to become your basic colour theme. You may have to treat the surfaces of some materials in order to enhance the colour and grain, but if you use traditional finishes, the underlying materials will age gracefully over the years and become more attractive in the process.

For additional colour in your home, consider the possibilities inherent in woodstains and transparent colour washes. As opposed to conventional paints, which cover up the surface, these products give a special vibrancy when applied to white and pastel walls and plaster, allowing textures and grains to show through. Rugs, cushions, wall hangings, flowers, and plants all add bright accents and focal points that you can easily change according to your mood or the season.

Natural paints and plaster As an alternative to petrochemical-based paints and finishes, you can use natural paints made from plants, minerals, and resin oils (see pp. 264-5). These natural products have slightly different and more subtle hues than those derived from chemical sources. You could also try making your own paints and mixing your own colours or inventing your own patterns and textures. The process is not difficult (see pp. 264-5).

If you are applying new areas of plaster, instead of simply painting it, consider a decorative scheme using several different types, textures, and colours of plaster. You could even add pigments that enhance the natural texture of the material or try your hand at attractive decorative finishes such as marbling (see pp. 164-7).

Natural dyes Until the 19th century, colours for dyes were obtained mainly from plant sources. The muted and soft colours of natural dyes give a quiet beauty that is often missing from the hard colours of synthetic chemical dyes. Plants provide a good range of colours, the most common being shades of yellow, orange, brown, and grey. Some plants also yield purples and blues. You make plant dyes permanent by using mordants, mineral compounds such as alum, tin, iron, and chrome. You need to exercise care, though, since some (such as chrome) are poisonous. You can achieve an extensive colour variation depending on the mordant you use and the timing of the processes.

Creative colour

Colours have always been associated with certain fundamental feelings and symbols. Although there are cultural and personal variations and preferences, there appear to be underlying themes far more permanent than the transient and ever-changing dictates of style and fashion. In China, for example, colours represent Yin and Yang qualities. Warm and vitalizing red, orange, and yellow are Yang colours, while cool and withdrawing blue, indigo, and violet are Yin colours. Green is considered the balance point in the spectrum and is thought of as being neutral. And the roles of black and white have been reversed, with white being associated with death and worn at funerals.

Colours in the broad groups of warm, cool, and neutral usually, but not always, evoke certain responses. Warm colours, such as red, are the most exciting, auspicious, and stimulating; orange and yellow are joyful, lively, and happy; pink suggests health and wellbeing. Cool colours, such as green, are fresh, pleasant, and restful; blues and greys are peaceful and distant; purple and mauve suggest richness, dignity, and spirituality. Black and white are not colours, but they have powerful associations – white, for example, with purity and life (but death in China), while black is considered ominous, deathly, serious, and sombre.

Warm colours seem to *advance* and tend to dominate the cool colours, which appear to *recede*. You can use these attributes to modify the apparent shape and proportions of rooms by, for example, making the ceiling seem lower, or a long, narrow passage or room seem shorter.

Light colours and tones tend to make a room look larger, while bold, dark tones have the opposite effect. Although dark tones can make a small room feel oppressive, they can make a large room feel more intimate. You can also use colours to modify the apparent aspect of a room – warm colours will make a sunless room more cheerful, while you can use cool colours to make a room exposed to lots of sun seem more comfortable.

But bear in mind that the room's natural daylight and orientation are important starting points, as are your own preferences and feelings about colour. Colour is deeply expressive and when used creatively can be a powerful therapy.

Colour therapy

The use of colour as a therapeutic medium is ancient to many cultures, such as the Egyptian, Indian, and Chinese, and colour therapy, as it is known today, has developed as a natural healing remedy for many illnesses as well as a general restorative technique.

Colour therapists believe that colours (and the other invisible wavelengths of the electromagnetic spectrum) react with the body and mind because we are able to absorb them physically through the eyes and skin and in our breath, food, and drink, and mentally by meditation and visualization techniques. The vibrations from the various wavelengths of the complete spectrum radiate energy and are thought to be visible to some people as an aura of glowing colours surrounding all living things. If a person is healthy and happy, the aura will appear bluish with a balanced spectrum of colours around the body emanating from the *chakras*, or energy centres, and chief glands in the following order:

Spirit, individuality	Magenta
Pineal/crown	Violet
Pituitary/third eye	Blue
Thyroid/throat	Turquoise
Cardiac plexus/heart	Green
Solar plexus/stomach	Yellow
Adrenals/kidneys	Orange
Sacral/base	Red

If a person is unhealthy or emotionally and spiritually under stress, the aura is said to change colour and show irregularities, such as flaring oranges and reds if angry or flecks and flashes if unwell. Colour therapy seeks to redress these imbalances by treating the area of the body or the mind with the appropriate balancing colour. Counselling offers the client advice on the colours of clothes, cosmetics, and diet and the colours that are best for the home and place of work.

There are numerous examples of the therapeutic use of colours in hospitals, schools, and homes for the care of children. Unexpectedly, it has been found that hyperactive children tend to become calmer in rooms with bright colours and that slow-learning children are stimulated by cool colours. If you would like to apply the principles of colour therapy in your own home you will find further sources and advice on pages 273-7.

Chapter Four
MATERIALS

Building materials are the "building blocks of life". We depend on them for shelter as we do on food, water, and air for sustenance. The world consists of a vast number and variety of natural chemicals and materials, all interdependent and all interlinked in a planetary organism. Our personal health and well-being are affected by what we eat, drink, and breathe and also, to a surprising degree, by our houses and, in particular, by the materials we use to build them.

The third skin

A house is effectively a "building organism" that interacts with us, the inhabitants, and with the environment. It can be supportive to our health and to the environment or, as is too often the case, it can be harmful to both. Just as clothes provide our "second skin", so a house acts as our "third skin", offering extra protection, comfort, and shelter. It is vitally important that we surround ourselves with buildings that are healthy and life-giving.

Until the development of extended transport systems, house–building materials were usually of local origin. Transport was difficult and expensive, often costing more than the materials themselves. Some materials tended to be locally dominant, such as stone in rocky areas and adobe, brick, and tile in clay areas of Europe and North America. Others, such as timber and grasses, were more widespread than stone and brick and lent themselves more to log and timber-framed construction, with reed and straw for thatching. Over many centuries individual regions developed homes and crafts that were harmonious and appropriate to particular localities. Skills and crafts handed down over generations, often through families, led to an intimate under-standing of local materials from the points of view of their selection and use in the home.

Naturally, some areas were less well endowed than others, and the lack of sound and varied building materials was a definite disadvantage. However, with improved transport systems – by canals, railways, and better roads – local materials could be dispersed to distant places, there to be used in inappropriate and discordant ways. The process of our gradual and inevitable alienation from local materials and craft traditions had begun.

The log cabin is the house of American myth. Chopped from the forest, erected with-out nails or sawn timber, this homestead, like the Arkansas cabin (right), symbolizes the courage, frugality, and inde-pendence of the early pioneers. Although the American Indians used logs for their "hogans", it was the old Norse, German, Scot-tish, and Irish building tradi-tions that provided the basic shelters for the pioneers as they pushed westward.

Natural materials have always played a vital role in the traditional Japanese home (right). The floors are laid with light green and fragrant rush tatami mats, the walls are a series of sliding shoji mulberry paper screens or infilled with scented cedar wood or natural-coloured clay plaster, and the ceiling is wood or bamboo. Surfaces are seldom painted but are left plain. The naturalness is often enhanced by some mate-rials "in the raw" – a timber post with the bark retained, for example.

The Industrial Revolution speeded the process. It also introduced new factory-produced materials – iron and steel – which required *engineering* rather than craft skills. The reaction of a concerned few in England to the replacement of traditions by mass-produced and standardized goods was expressed in the efforts of such people as John Ruskin and William Morris. In the second half of the last century they established the Arts and Crafts Movement, which sought to maintain local design and crafts. But the stage was set for change and the transformation of society into an industrial age.

The challenges and opportunities of the new age were taken up by architects and designers of the Modern Movement. Through the influence of architects, such as Walter Gropius (the founder of the Bauhaus in Germany), Le Corbusier, and Mies van der Rohe, an international style was established. Since the 1930s mainstream architecture and building design have developed further and further along these lines, a trend reflected until recently in the anonymity and alienation of so many of our modern buildings and homes.

Today, the Chemical Revolution has placed us in a situation similar to that following last century's industrialization; except that now we are faced with increasing production as well as the use of synthetic products, mainly from petrochemical sources. Although nonsynthetic materials are still very much in use and popular, they often lose out against the lower cost, concerted advertising, and ready availability of the newer alternatives. But strong reaction is growing to the Chemical Revolution. This time it comes from a much broader base of environmental campaign and consumer protection groups, health and occupational safety organizations, the "Green Party", and, most important of all, from a growing body of public opinion. The greater the ground-swell of consumer concern, the better the chance of influencing the course of future events.

It is difficult to ascertain the composition of synthetic materials and substances, especially since many products are a mixture of several synthetics. It is much simpler to choose, where possible, tried-and-trusted natural materials and fibres. You will not always be able to do this, but every time you do, you lessen the chemical load on yourself and on the environment. Choosing natural and acceptable products, however, is not that simple; the term "natural" has no tight definition, and even some truly natural products are treated with potentially harmful chemicals during processing. The following sections on natural materials will help you here and allow you to make more informed choices.

Sustainable materials

The materials we use affect the environment. Their production and transportation deplete resources and consume energy. More and more building materials are becoming scarce – not only the raw materials but also the energy needed to produce them – and if present trends continue, some of the most common raw materials and energy sources, such as oil and natural gas, will be exhausted within about the next thirty years. And it is on these that we have become increasingly dependent since World War II as natural materials have been supplemented with synthetic chemicals and plastic products.

Traditional materials – clay, lime, chalk, stone – still abound, and timber (especially softwoods) can be replenished by properly managed forestation. In addition, these materials are easily reused or recycled, they produce little or no pollution, and they are reabsorbed into the natural cycles of the environment once their use as building materials is over. We have long experience of them and know how to work with them and cope with potential problems. Don't, however, fall into the trap of thinking that sustainable materials are necessarily

Production energy costs

The energy consumed in felling, sawing, and transporting timber has been estimated at 580kWh/tonne. Taking this as a guide, the energy costs for other common materials are (see right):

Aluminium	timber x 126 times	Plastic	timber x 6 times
Steel	timber x 24 times	Cement	timber x 5 times
Glass	timber x 14 times	Bricks	timber x 4 times

traditional ones – cellulose and rayon, relatively modern products, are derived from plant fibres, and are examples of the potential for new materials from other than petrochemical sources.

Energy costs

Energy is becoming scarce and the amount used in the production and transportation of materials is high. The best materials are, therefore, those that need little processing and/or are local. Locally grown and used timber entails only a low energy expenditure, a simple log cabin perhaps least of all. Clay, dug from the site of the house and used as adobe or unbaked brick, is another example of a material that uses almost no energy, except that required for the building work. In contrast to natural materials, synthetic and processed products, such as plastics, aluminium, steel, glass, and oven-fired bricks and clay tiles, require a high energy expenditure on both production and transportation.

The information gap

Weighing the relative merits and disadvantages of the properties of different building materials has become a complex science. Most materials are classified and listed according to national and international standards. These specify such features as strength, density, weight, porosity, durability, performance under stress, and thermal and flammable characteristics. All materials have to be tested and comply with the approved standards of an official body such as the British Standards Institution, the European Agrément Board, or the Standards Associations of Australia and the US.

Many countries, however, do not include standards specifying adequate consideration of the health hazards faced by building workers and occupants. The lack of environmental-impact and ecological information, particularly for synthetic materials, is also disturbing. Manufacturers and suppliers generally fail to give such information and may not know it themselves.

As consumers, we do not know how much energy is used in the production and processing of various materials, nor whether a hardwood timber comes from a plantation or an endangered rain-forest. It is difficult to discover if the raw materials in metal products are new or recycled, or what impact their manufacture and use has on the environment. Manufacturers and suppliers of these products consume massive quantities of the Earth's resources; they have an undeniable responsibility for the environmental consequences.

The power of the consumer

Consumer pressure on the food industry has been successful in curbing the use of additives and preservatives and in promoting healthy foods. Similar pressure must now be applied to the building industry to provide healthier and more sustainable materials. If producers think there is a demand they will respond; and that demand is growing as consumers become more conscious of their power. Consumers make known their opinions of products by exercising choice. They are increasingly interested not only in the product itself but also in the various raw materials and processes by which it is made. And the introduction of some cleaner products indicates that the commercial world is beginning to respond. "Green" products are now available that promote an environment-friendly lifestyle. But building and decorating materials are still largely dominated by petrochemical products. Traditional brick, timber, and stone, however, have had a recent renaissance, and materials such as linoleum, vegetable oil and resin paints, and natural fabrics are also reappearing.

The "Blue Angel"

In 1977 the West German government launched a scheme under which safe materials could display the "Blue Angel" symbol. But a manufacturer could use the symbol on a product simply by reducing a harmful ingredient, such as formaldehyde, by 20%. To prevent this, private laboratories now conduct independent tests. But an acceptable product can be used in unacceptable ways.

The new criteria

A reclassification of all building materials and products is long overdue. It must take account of the growing concerns for health and ecology and provide proper information and labelling to help consumers make informed choices. What exactly are healthy and ecological materials? Assuming that a product complies with the technical requirements laid down by the various government standards authorities, it should also meet certain other criteria relating firstly to personal health and, secondly, to the health of the environment.

Healthy materials

Look at the materials and products in your home in the light of the following criteria and try to apply them when you buy new products. You can derive much satisfaction from being in control of the materials that will help to create a healthy and safe home. All new products you buy should be:

○ Clean and contain no pollutants or toxins, emit no biologically harmful vapours, dust, particles, or odours, either in manufacture or use. They should also be resistant to bacteria, viruses, moulds, and other harmful micro-organisms.
○ Quiet, producing little or no noise themselves, or have good sound-reduction properties.
○ Radioactive safe and not emit any harmful levels of radiation.
○ Electromagnetic safe and not allow the conduction or build-up of static electricity or emit harmful electric fields of any type.

Ecological materials

For materials to be environmentally sound they should meet as many as possible of the following criteria. Products should be:

○ Renewable and abundant, coming from diverse natural sources and whose production has low impact on the environment (whether this is local or in developing countries).

○ Nonpolluting, emitting no harmful vapours, particles, or toxins into the environment, either in manufacture or in use.
○ Energy efficient, using low energy in production, transport, and use, and generally coming from local regions. Additionally, they should be good energy conservers with high insulation values that retain heat in winter and keep the home cool in summer.
○ Durable, long lived, and easy to maintain and repair, tested and tried over several generations – as is the case with natural materials.
○ Equitable and produced via socially fair means, which include, as a minimum, good working conditions, fair wages, and equal opportunities. Direct sales from co-operatives in the developing world to consumers in affluent countries should be supported.
○ Low waste and capable of being reused and recycled, thereby saving the vast amounts of energy spent on processing raw materials. Recycled steel, for example, saves more than 70% of the energy used in manufacturing new steel from primary ore. Using salvaged doors, beams, stone, bricks, tiles, slates, shingles, and even furniture is an environmental option even cheaper than recycling materials.

Many traditional stone masons believed that if a stone wall was built properly it should need no mortar. As with this new dry stone wall home in France (above), the skill lies in carefully selecting the stones and bonding them tightly together. With experience, this becomes intuitive – the eye quickly sizes up the space and the hand automatically picks up the appropriate stone.

The Elizabethan housing boom and the use of wood for fuel and ship building had exhausted the great forests of England by the 17th century. Before this, as with the 15th century half-timbered thatched cottage at Bignor, Sussex (above), oak was the dominant building material. The upper floor is jettied and the oak frame is infilled with flint, brick, and plaster.

On the volcanic Greek island of Santorini (Thera) the local natural materials are black lava stone, pumice, and china clay. The lightweight and heat-insulating pumice is ideal for the semi-circular barrel vault roofs and domes so characteristic of the island (left). Building into the hillside and whitewashing the outsides help to maintain an even indoor temperature.

Stone

Natural rock caves are the earliest dwelling places and ritual sites we know of. Rock paintings, tools, and animal remains are evidence that these sites were used by Stone-Age peoples thousands of years ago. Even today, though, in places such as Shaanxi province and the "dragon" caves of Henan province (both in northeast China), in rock-cut villages in Central Anatolia (Turkey), in the Matmata Mountains in southern Tunisia, in remote mountain regions of Spain, and elsewhere, some 40 million people live in what are basically cave dwellings.

Since prehistoric times stone has been used as the strongest and most enduring of building materials. Megalith builders employed stone for their huge burial mounds, pagan temples, and solar observatories. Worked stone has survived thousands of years – the pyramids of Egypt, the temple of Karnak near Luxor, in the Kaaba, the holy shrine of Islam, at Mecca, the Great Wall of China, and in the Roman roads and aqueducts throughout Europe.

Until the 15th century AD, worked stone was used mainly for palaces and castles, temples, and fortifications. It remained the prerogative of the rich and powerful. The élite Mayas built stone cities for themselves while the populace lived in mud huts; the Incas retreated to their granite city of Machu Picchu high in the Andes. In Europe, increasing prosperity among the middle classes elevated stone to the favourite material for ordinary houses.

Traditional stone buildings

Lack of transport made local stone the obvious and most aesthetically pleasing choice; from this sprang distinctive building styles that typify particular regions. In Britain, limestone houses and cottages belong to the Cotswolds, flint to East Anglia, and granite to Cornwall and the Hebrides. Sandstone was the local material for New York's brownstone townhouses and Sydney's early terraces, and blue basalt for Melbourne. Away from quarrying areas, stone was used for facing brick and timber houses, for lintels and window frames, steps and paths. Today, the expense of quarried stone again limits its use to facing, although a renewed interest in stone building has resulted in "Lithotecture", a form of underground, cave-like housing.

Dramatically sited on the saddle between two mountains, a stone building of the Inca city of Machu Picchu seems to be a natural outcropping, growing out of the rock beneath.

This classic New York brownstone (below) was designed in the Tuscan mode and, like an Italian palazzo, has its main rooms on a piano nobile *raised above the street. The stonework is ashlar, with a heavier rusticated semi-basement.*

Types of building stone

All stones come from one of three main groups: igneous, sedimentary, and metamorphic. Granite is the main igneous building stone, a crystalline, granular rock made up of feldspar, quartz, and mica. A hard, strong, and durable stone, weather resistant and impervious to water, granite varies in colour from silver-grey to white and red. Flint, another igneous rock, is almost pure silica; the round, hard but brittle stones range in colour from black to grey, brown, and white. Basalt, solidified lava flow, usually in columnar strata, is blue, green, brown, or black.

Sedimentary rocks are formed by the erosion of igneous rock. Particles deposited in ancient river beds formed sandstones, ranging from brown and buff to gold, grey, pink, and lavender-purple. These stones are harder than limestone, another sedimentary and the most common rock type, originally laid down under the sea bed and containing deposits of fossil shellfish. The most popular building stone in England, limestone, is grey-blue, tawny-brown, or creamy-white, as in Portland stone, one of the few limestones that will weather away from its locality – many colonial houses in Virginia, for example, are faced with Portland stone.

Metamorphic rocks are igneous or sedimentary rocks changed by enormous pressure or great heat; they include slate, marble, and alabaster. Dark grey to green in colour, slate can be split along its natural planes into thin roofing and wall tiles or into thicker slabs for floors and window sills. Marble, in origin compressed limestone, is found in a great variety of colours, pure white or richly stained or marked with mineral deposits; it is easy to carve and polish but loses its lustre when exposed to the weather. Alabaster is also too soft for external use in cold climates. But because of its translucent, creamy-white colour, sometimes veined with pink, it was the favoured material for sculpture in ancient civilizations.

Processing and using stone

Small stones and boulders are collected from the surface while large blocks are excavated from quarries, sawn into regular pieces and slabs, or broken into irregular chunks. Some are polished to highlight the grain and texture, others are left coarse with finishes such as hammer-dressing, scabbling, and vermiculation. Most old stone houses are rubble-built from irregular stones laid either at random or coursed dry-walled or set in mortar. Squared and dressed stone is known as ashlar and is used to face rubble or bricks. Ashlar is laid in level courses and bonded with fine mortar joints.

As the expense of quarry stone from deeper and deeper beds grew, stucco became a popular substitute. Made from a blend of sand, lime, and cement, stucco was rendered over brick and painted to simulate local real stone or incised with lines to suggest mortar joints. Because stucco needs frequent repainting, it has declined in favour of artificial, or reconstituted, stone made from stone dust and cement, sometimes with powdered colour agents, and often with a concrete core.

Health and ecological criteria

Traditional stone houses give a feeling of strength and security. Stone is healthy and nonpolluting if it is set in plain cement mortar and on a damp-proof foundation. Radon can be a problem, however, in some granite and slate areas, and quarry workers and stone masons may contract silicosis from inhaled stone dust. From an ecological viewpoint, quarries disfigure the landscape, and high energy costs are involved in the quarrying, handling, and transporting of stone.

Problems The chief drawback with using stone is its expense, in terms of the raw material and labour costs. In spite of its structural strength stone does not always weather well when removed from its locality; water and frost may split the stone unless it is protected by overhanging roofs, copings, and drip stones. Limestone is liable to be damaged by acid rain.

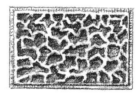

Much stone walling is built from rough and irregular rubble stone of varying sizes and laid (with plenty of mortar) in random courses (left). Hammer-dressed and vermiculated stone is squared and cut to present a heavily textured surface (above left). The ashlar arch (above) is built of wedge-shaped stones, each individually shaped to "course-in" with the wall.

Choosing stone

Few people will be fortunate enough to build a new house in stone, but many live in old ones. Most experience today concerns renovation and repair, where the emphasis should be on using salvaged stone and matching the original style. For interior alterations, use local stone; it is cheaper to transport and will look more "at home". Stone is enduring, although in the northern hemisphere marble and alabaster are suitable only for interiors.

Strong in compression, less so in tension, stone is ideal for walling rather than horizontal planes over wide spans and openings where it may crack. Ancient stonebuilders solved this problem with arches and domes to spread the load.

Old stone walls are often covered with crumbling plaster; rather than repair or replace it (provided that the stones are well laid and in good condition), remove it to reveal the textures and colours of the stones beneath. The stones will breathe again and help to regulate room humidity. Because stone is easy to cut and shape it has many ornamental and practical uses, such as mouldings and cornices, balustrades and mullioned windows; it is used for window and door surrounds, for lintels and steps, for paving and cobbles, roof and wall tiling. And stone finds its ultimate expression in carvings and sculptures – "the conscious stone to beauty grew". (Ralph Waldo Emerson)

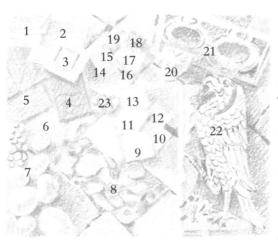

Key

1–4 *marble tiles;* **5** *black roofing slates;* **6** *York paving stone;* **7** *pebbles and cobbles;* **8** *knapped flint;* **9** *Portland Whitbed stone;* **10** *Portland Fancy Beach stone;* **11** *Bath Westwood stone;* **12** *Bath Monk's Park stone;* **13** *Portland roach stone;* **14** *Portland yellow square stone;* **15** *Brecon Beacon stone;* **16** *Derbyshire buff gritstone;* **17** *lilac sandstone;* **18** *red sandstone;* **19** *Derbyshire gritstone;* **20** *Romanesque carving;* **21** *pierced stone screening;* **22** *stone griffin;* **23** *fossilized coral.*

Glass and plaster

The Romans perfected the art of glassmaking, but as long ago as 3000BC the early Egyptians had created delicate drinking cups by carving rock crystal, a translucent, colourless quartz. Other craftsmen used obsidian, a naturally occurring black volcanic glass with shiny fracture surfaces. Stone and wooden tools and weapons, unearthed in Turkey, Greece, and the Near East, were tipped with carved obsidian; smaller pieces were used as inlays in jewellery and furniture, and large pieces were polished for mirrors. By 2500BC, the Sumerians had fashioned crude glass beads and Egyptian glassmakers had made the first glass vessels.

Early glass was opaque or greenish coloured from the iron oxide in the sand, but the Romans produced plain glass to which they added brilliantly coloured mineral oxides and gold particles. The revolutionary breakthrough, however, was the Roman invention, in about 50BC, of glassblowing. Skilled craftsmen combined the art of stone carving with that of glassblowing to produce cameo vases in which a glass blob of one colour was inserted into one of pure white and the two blown simultaneously. After cooling, the outer white glass was carved in a relief design.

From Imperial Rome, glassmaking spread to other parts of Europe and the Near East, with much of the industry concentrating on the production of window panes – plain or coloured. France in particular was famous for stained-glass architecture. For centuries, glass windows were for use only in churches and palaces; in houses, window openings were closed against the elements with wooden shutters or coverings of parchment, oiled cloth, skins, horn, or mica. During the 16th century, glass became more generally available, and "leaded lights" (small diamonds or rectangles of blown glass fixed in grooved lead bars, known as cames) were fitted between masonry mullions to side-hung casement frames that opened outward.

The evolution of glass

Blown glass soon failed to meet demand, however, and clearer crown glass became the next technological step. The addition of lead oxide made the brilliant lead crystal glass with its improved softer and refractive qualities, allowing engravers to carve intricate designs. This had an uneven surface and needed grinding and polishing by hand until the introduction, in 1773, of machine-cast plate glass. Householders in Britain were penalized, however, if they had more than six windows. The Window Tax applied to all private homes and it was not repealed until 1851. Bricked-up window openings are still a common sight today on many older houses.

Joseph Paxton's magnificent Crystal Palace, which opened in London in 1851, was the beginning of a new era that has given us rolled, float, laminated, toughened, and double- and triple-glazed glass. Solar glass (see pp. 72-3) has added yet other dimensions to an ancient material.

Plaster and cement

The first village settlements consisted of huts made of wood, reeds, stone, or mud bricks finished with a thick layer of mud or lime plaster bound with chopped straw, animal hairs and feathers, or cow dung. An early example is the Neolithic mud-built town of Catal Hüyük, Turkey, of the 6th millennium BC. Plastering protected the walls from the effects of the weather – ancient Greek and Roman architects waterproofed aqueducts and water-storage cisterns with plaster – and it also gave the walls a smoother, more pleasing appearance. Often the plaster was decorated: in Mexico, the Mayas of the first centuries AD adorned houses with coloured plaster frescoes and reliefs, and to this day many African houses are embellished with ornamental designs in mud plaster. The traditional timber-framed houses and wattle-and-daub cottages of Europe were also rendered with lime plaster. As extra weather protection, the exterior was coated with washes of lime or lime and tallow, linseed oil, or colour washes in white, cream, or pastel shades.

By the 16th and 17th centuries, plain plaster walls were decorated with ornamental designs, known as pargetting, which were incised in the wet plaster or modelled as raised, coloured reliefs. The later pebbledash concrete rendering was much less impressive – the greyish mixture of stone chippings or gravel, coarse sand, lime, and cement merely giving a rough, protective surface.

Glass and plaster products

Ordinary glass is inexpensive but fragile and breaks easily. Tempered, or safety, glass is up to five times stronger and, if broken, disintegrates into harmless fragments. Laminated safety glass consists of two or more panes layered with plastic; it may crack but the glass sticks to the tough plastic. Wire mesh incorporated into window panes prevents the glass splintering and it also acts as an effective safety barrier in areas such as skylights. Solar-control glass is tinted to reduce glare and heat gain, and it also protects fabrics from fading by strong sunlight. As a conservation measure, low-emissivity glass reflects heat back into the home.

Lime plaster is the oldest and the finest plaster. Plaster of paris is made from gypsum and is used for interior ornamentation and moulded objects. Various other versions include translucent Parian plaster and Sirapite, which can take on a glossy sheen. Portland cement, a modern rendering material, is stronger than other plasters and does not need the protection of paints or washes if used outside.

Raw materials and manufacture

Glass consists of silica (sand), sodium oxide (soda), and calcium oxide (limestone), with mineral oxides, colorants, and cullet (broken glass). These are melted at temperatures of more than 1500°C (2730°F), shaped, and then cooled to prevent crystallization and cracking. In the early days of crown glass, a globe of molten glass was gathered on the end of a blowing iron and blown until it was the desired shape, size, and thickness. Window glass was blown and spun rapidly into circular discs, each bearing the central "bull's eye", or "bullion", of the blowing iron.

Improved glassmaking techniques introduced thin sheet glass and thicker plate glass, but most flat glass is now produced by the float process, in which a continuous ribbon of molten glass is floated along the surface of liquid tin.

Lime plaster is a compound of slaked lime and sharp, coarse sand mixed with water; fibrous materials, such as animal hair, provide extra binding. Plaster of paris is produced by heating and grinding gypsum (calcium sulphate) and mixing it with water; while Portland cement is made from lime and clay, which, when mixed with aggregate, such as sand or gravel, makes mortar and concrete.

Shutters frame the small leaded lights of a Dutch farmhouse window (far left), while the 13th-century stained-glass window in Bourges Cathedral, France, depicts Christ and symbols of the seven churches of Asia (left). An innovative approach is the detail of Buckminster Fuller's geodesic dome at Expo 67, Canada (below left).

Criteria and problems

Glass and plaster are both made from abundant, natural resources. They are healthy and nonpolluting, and while glass is an inert material, natural plasters have good breathing qualities. Glass is a poor thermal and noise insulator unless it is double or triple glazed or has a low-emissivity coating. Water and frost action causes exterior plasters to crack and badly polluted air discolours them. You must renew protective washes on a regular basis.

Extraction and manufacturing processes can disfigure the environment and glass production consumes vast amounts of energy, as well as creating combustion pollution. On the positive side, glass is easily reused and recycled, but all too often glass bottles and jars are simply discarded. Bottle banks are still few and far between, and local authorites fail to arrange collection of sorted glass waste. Scandinavia, though, has begun to tackle this problem by enforcing deposits on all bottles and also by charging local authorities with the responsibility of collection and removal of glass to recycling plants. Old bottles have even been used like hollow bricks to build glass and cement walls.

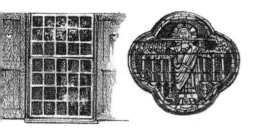

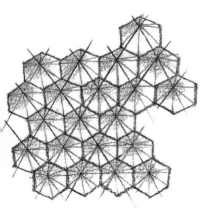

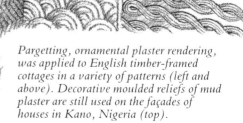

Pargetting, ornamental plaster rendering, was applied to English timber-framed cottages in a variety of patterns (left and above). Decorative moulded reliefs of mud plaster are still used on the façades of houses in Kano, Nigeria (top).

Choosing glass and plaster

Glass is extremely versatile with a huge range of applications in the home. It is a basic ingredient of solar design, incorporating such features as energy-conserving windows, solar panels, and sunspaces (see pp. 70-3). Today's larger areas of glass can admit more daylight, when needed, into our homes, thus reducing dependence on artificial light (see pp. 114-21). For safety, glass is tempered or laminated in high-risk areas, such as patio doors, low-level glazing, and bathrooms. But it is the area of decorative glass that offers the most exciting potential for creating spaces filled with a varied display of light and colour. You can choose from the huge range offered by manufacturers or, even better, have some glass etched, sand blasted, or silk screened to your own patterns and designs.

Natural plasters can have such pleasing colours and finishes – white, cream, pink, or grey in mat or high gloss – it is a pity always to cover interior surfaces with paint or wallpaper. As a background for natural materials and fabrics, unpainted plaster can enhance the "natural" ambience of a room. You could also try some of the older techniques where pigments were used for such effects as imitation marble. If you decide to decorate plaster surfaces, use porous, water-based paints (see pp. 264-5) or paper wallpapers (not vinyl) that still allow the plaster to breathe.

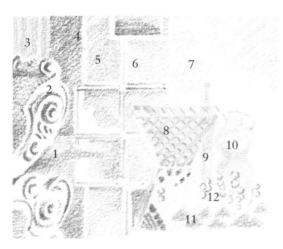

Key
1 *pink, white, and grey plaster;* 2 *moulded plaster bracket;* 3 *marble-effect travertine fluted column;* 4 *white plaster column;* 5 *reeded and textured glass;* 6 *glass bricks;* 7 *ground glass;* 8 *glass vase by Yanush (The Glasshouse, Longacre, London);* 9 *Victorian moulded medicine bottle;* 10 *Victorian crackleware glass jug;* 11 *glass ingredients – silica, sand, limestone, soda ash;* 12 *iridescent glass marbles.*

Metals

The types of materials used and the invention of metals have been so fundamentally important to our cultural development that some of the major phases of humanity's early history – the Stone Age, Bronze Age, and Iron Age – are delineated solely in terms of their widespread introduction and use. But it was the Industrial Revolution that brought metal engineering to building construction, using first cast iron, then wrought iron, and finally steel and steel-reinforced concrete.

Cast iron was used as early as 1780 for single columns, but engineering techniques advanced rapidly and iron soon replaced wooden supporting beams. As a result, iron was formed into the frameworks of factories, warehouses, huge conservatories, railway stations, and bridges. Paxton's Crystal Palace and Brunel's Clifton Suspension Bridge, both of which are in Britain, and Eiffel's magnificent tower in the heart of Paris are poetic essays in iron and steel. But more than that, these structures transformed the technology of building, as did the introduction of the rolled steel joist (RSJ) and the early skyscrapers in Chicago and New York. The new and exhilarating ethic of glass and steel was to become a central influence on architects of the Modern Movement; an influence that is still evident in the work of architects worldwide.

Types and uses

The range of metals used in the home today is enormous. The most common are: mild steel for RSJs; zinc, copper, galvanized steel, and aluminium for roof coverings, gutters, and flashings; zinc-coated steel for ducts and expanded metal laths for plastering; aluminium-foil-backed plasterboard and vapour barriers; steel reinforcing rods in concrete; coated steel windows; enamelled cast-iron and steel baths; copper pipes; and brass for electric wiring, plumbing, and hardware.

Apart from construction, metals are used for kitchen and laundry appliances, light fittings, furniture, and even cooking foil. Cans are made from aluminium, tin, or steel, or of mixed metals, which makes recycling impossible. Most, though, are now of one metal to aid recycling.

Criteria and problems

All metals are precious. The mineral ores from which they come are a non-renewable resource. Although about 75% of the 80 minerals on which we depend are abundant enough to meet our anticipated needs, there are about 20 (including lead, tin, tungsten, and zinc) that even with greater recovery, stockpiling, and recycling are becoming increasingly scarce.

Although almost half the iron for steelmaking now comes from scrap and nearly a third of the aluminium produced is recycled, the percentages need to be much higher. Recycling saves energy to such an extent that secondary aluminium, for example, consumes only 5% of the energy used to extract and process primary ore.

Health factors From the point of view of health, many metals can be harmful if ingested in sufficiently high concentrations. Arsenic and lead are the best known of these but others, such as mercury, nickel, zinc, aluminium, silver, cobalt, cadmium, titanium, selenium, and chromium (VI), can also be harmful if leached into drinking water or ingested in the form of, for example, paint. Mostly, however, the concentrations of these metals in the home is negligible and should not be of concern.

But there are other factors that should make us look again at the use of metal in the home. Steel beams and water-filled radiators and pipes can, for example, disturb natural electromagnetic fields, while steel frames and metal laths and decking as well as metal furniture and magnetized bedsprings (see pp. 80-1) may cause adverse effects. Metal ducts used for space heating and ventilation can also affect the ion balance of the air. Despite this, metal furniture is inert and free from chemicals and resins and is often essential for chemically sensitive and allergic people.

Living sensibly with metals

○ Recycle cans and scrap metal. Trade-in old appliances and don't dump.
○ Choose durable and repairable metal appliances and equipment.
○ Campaign for local recycling schemes and for manufacturers to stamp products showing metal type for recycling.
○ Avoid aluminium or zinc-coated cookware.
○ Have your drinking water tested for metals and filter if necessary (see pp. 84-91).
○ Replace lead pipes and lead-solder joints in copper pipes.
○ Don't collect rainwater from lead roofs or gutters.
○ Carefully remove and dispose of old flaking paint – it may contain lead.
○ If you are sensitive to electromagnetic fields, sleep away from radiators and pipes and use natural-fibre-filled mattresses.
○ If you are chemically sensitive, consider metal furniture.

Earth

Earth is the most ancient of all worked materials. In the origin myths of many cultures, the human race itself is fashioned from clay, the inert material breathed into life. Earth is a simple, durable, and an adaptable material, abundant locally, plastic yet strong, rot and termite proof, cool in summer, and warm in winter. Mud walls, dried in the sun and protected from excessive wet, can last for centuries and, once fired, earth can survive for thousands of years to provide buildings and artefacts of extraordinary beauty and diversity.

In Mesopotamia, where civilization is said to have been born 5000 years ago, the Sumerians built large cities on the plains between the rivers Tigris and Euphrates (as we know from the excavations at the temple at Ur). Houses, temples, and ziggurats (temple towers) were all built with sun-dried mud and burned bricks. In the Nile Valley, the Egyptians lived in mud and reed shelters that later gave way to plastered and whitewashed mud-brick villas. The Babylonians knew how to fire and glaze clay bricks; the Ishtar Gate (see right) at the palace of Nebuchadnezzar was decorated with blue-glazed bricks.

The ancient Greeks and Romans lived in mud and timber dwellings, a building construction that spread throughout Europe. In England, many "cob" and wattle-and-daub buildings (see p. 144) still exist, hidden behind new facings of plaster, brick, or cement. Earth buildings were constructed by the American Indians and Spanish conquistadors, and by the Pilgrim Fathers who brought the

The Ishtar Gate at the palace of Nebuchadnezzar (605-562BC)

brick building style to the Americas, and English settlers who introduced it to Australia. Rammed earth and adobe buildings are found in Europe, Asia, the Americas, and Africa – the world's oldest-surviving mud building is the 14th-century mosque at Djenne, an ancient trading centre in Mali, northwest Africa.

Ironically, when many people in the developing world are losing their knowledge of their ancient building traditions, earth building is undergoing a revival among self-builders and environmentalists in Australia, the US, and Germany. This is hardly surprising, since, in today's synthetic world, earth houses, whose sturdy walls are formed of the land itself, comfort and reassure us of our links with the past.

The advantages of earth
Earth is an abundant material easily dug at little or no cost. In many arid regions, earth may be the only material available. Shaped into bricks or tiles and dried in the sun or kiln fired, earth has excellent thermal-storage qualities. A properly built earth house is durable as well as fire, rot, and termite proof. It has an indoor climate that regulates air moisture and sound and helps to absorb and expel polluted air. In construction, it uses only about 3% of the energy expended on a similar concrete building.

Earth as a raw material
Although many types of soil can be used for earth buildings, the best soil for bricks contains 75% sand and a minimum of 10% clay. For rammed earth, less sand and more clay and silt is preferred. Well-compacted soil usually requires no stabilizers, but poor soils will – cement and bitumen for sandy soils and lime for clay soils. The laterite soils of the tropics are ideal for mud bricks (the Latin word *later* means brick). Mixed with lime as a binder, laterite soils produce adobe blocks and they are also the best for rammed earth.

Problems with earth
Earth in its natural state is vulnerable to water and has a low resistance to impact. An earth house is less suitable in wet, temperate regions of the world unless it is built up on a well-drained damp-proof foundation and with a wide roof overhang. Unless they are reinforced and well sited, earth buildings can be destroyed by floods and hurricanes.

Choosing bricks, tiles, and pottery

Baked clay has been known for thousands of years.
It is a warm, breathing material, in perfect harmony
with the earth from which it comes, and in temperate and wet climates, fired bricks are more durable
than sun-dried clay varieties.

Hand-made bricks have a marvellous individuality and character, ranging in colour through
shades of red, brown, yellow, grey, and blue, and in
surface texture from granular to smooth or sanded.
For the finest work, nothing can better mellow terra
cotta used for ornamental brickwork. These bricks
are still available today, either newly made or
salvaged from older buildings.

Clay tiles share the characteristics of brick and
are traditional as roofing for all but stone houses.
Red, brown, brindle, grey, and near-black roof tiles
vary in shape from plain (peg) to the tapered
Spanish tile and the Roman tile with rolled edges.
The larger and more distinctive pantile has upturned
and downturned edges so that each tile hooks on to
the next. For vertical wall cladding you can choose
between plain or shaped tiles.

Early potters coiled ropes of clay into vessels
and cooking utensils and moulded sculptures and
tiles that were intricately decorated and glazed.
Delicate, translucent porcelain was made under the
Han dynasty of China (206BC–AD220), fashioned
from the pure white kaolin we still call china clay.

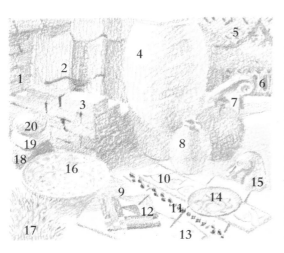

Key

1 *plain clay (peg) tiles;* 2 *terra-cotta pantiles;* 3 *hand-made facing bricks;* 4 *coiled pot;* 5 *terra-cotta frieze;* 6 *edging tiles;* 7 *ridge tile;* 8 *salt-glazed pots;* 9 & 10 *floor tiles;* 11 *strip tiles;* 12 *glazed mosaic tiles;* 13 *blue and white Delft tiles;* 14 *Roman-ian slipware plate;* 15 *Han dynasty sculpture;* 16 *Ming bowl;* 17 *turf;* 18 *terra-cotta clay;* 19 *china clay;* 20 *Limoges porcelain clay.*

Working with earth

Earths can be fired to make long-lasting bricks and tiles or they can be used "raw" from the site and worked by the dry or wet method. Traditional raw-earth houses are experiencing a revival among ecologically orientated architects and self-builders in the US, Australia, and Europe, and the technique is proving to be a low-cost option in developing countries. The Chinese have built rammed-earth constructions for more than 3000 years, and Hannibal is said to have introduced the method to Europe, where it is known as "pisé". Two of the oldest buildings in the US, in Santa Fe and St Augustine, Florida, are rammed-earth houses.

Raw earth

Using the traditional wet method, earth is bound with chopped straw and then mixed with water and trodden until it has the correct plasticity. Today, to stabilize the mixture, lime, cement, and bitumen are also often added. A mud or cob wall is usually built up in layers, or "lifts", up to 1m (39in) high; each lift is left to dry before the next is added. The traditional mud or cob cottages of northern Europe were built on stone foundations to prevent rising damp and given overhanging thatch roofs.

An alternative method of using wet earth is to mould the mixture, by hand or machine, into bricks or blocks and leave them to dry in the sun. Earth brick or adobe houses are traditional throughout Latin America and are also found in East Anglia, England, where they are known as "clay lump" houses. The bricks are laid in courses bonded with wet mud mortar; when completely dry the walls can be rendered or lime washed to protect them against rain. The wattle-and-daub method is a variant used as in-fill in timber buildings. In Kenya, Masai women cover their timber-poled and woven *kraals* with a mud and straw daub and render them with cattle dung.

Using the dry pisé method, loose, dry earth is rammed down hard between temporary shutters, or forms. The forms are then moved along or up the walls as each section is completed. Extremely strong and durable walls result, and if the composition of the soil is appropriate no extra binders or surface finishes are necessary.

In the Middle Ages, peasants were given the right to cut turf sods for cottage building. Similar sod houses were known in many parts of central Europe and in the US, where early pioneers built their low-slung homesteads from tough prairie sods laid grass-side down.

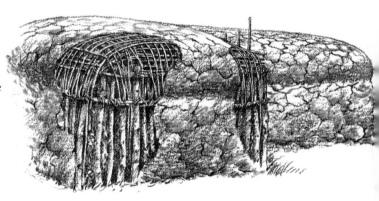

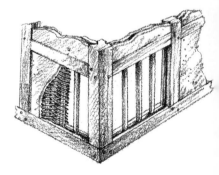

Wattle-and-daub cottages were common in medieval Europe. A mixture of wet earth and straw was spread over interwoven wattle panels (above right) and coated, when dry, with lime wash. Native mud huts in tropical regions are built on much the same principle (above).

Fired earth

When a clay pot first fell into the fire and was found later in the ashes hardened and subtly coloured, the craft of fired earth was born. The early potters had no wheel but coiled and moulded the clay into pots, tiles, and bricks. They also knew how to select the types of clay that could be fired.

Bricks and tiles are made from "brick earths", a mixture of clay and shale found as surface deposits of ancient lakes and rivers; fine pottery from the white clay formed in granite bedrocks. Local clays contain different proportions of minerals (such as iron and magnesia), salts, and limestone that give the fired bricks their distinctive colours. Before firing, each brick is rolled and kneaded, "dashed" into a sanded mould, turned out, and left on drying racks to go through a natural shrinkage stage. These "green" bricks are fired at great heat, to a maximum of 1100°C (2012°F) dropping to 300°C (572°F).

Colour variations occur during the firing, with bricks placed in the centre of the kiln burning the deepest shade. Hand-made bricks can be ordered to specific shapes, but most fired bricks are now machine made to uniform shapes, sizes, and colours. Depending on the qualities of the clay, machine-made bricks are extruded and wire cut or mechanically compressed in moulds prior to firing.

Although fired clay has much greater compressive strength and better weather resistance than raw earth, you should be aware of the impact on the environment in terms of energy and pollution from combustion and fuel consumption in the firing.

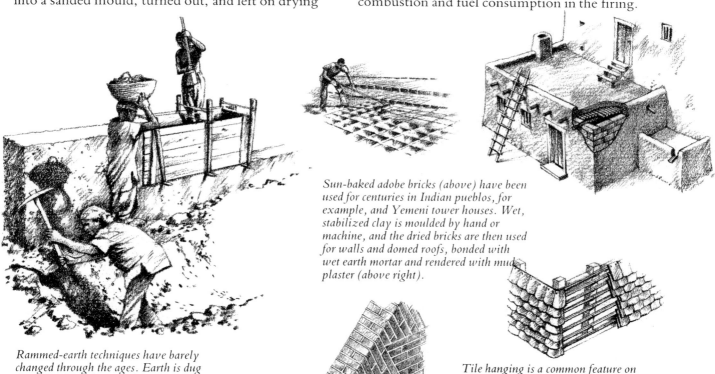

Rammed-earth techniques have barely changed through the ages. Earth is dug from the site and rammed into wooden forms. When full and compacted, the forms are moved to a new position. Pisé walls are very resistant to rain and if they have a wide roof require no extra surface finish.

Sun-baked adobe bricks (above) have been used for centuries in Indian pueblos, for example, and Yemeni tower houses. Wet, stabilized clay is moulded by hand or machine, and the dried bricks are then used for walls and domed roofs, bonded with wet earth mortar and rendered with mud plaster (above right).

Tile hanging is a common feature on English timber-framed houses (above). Fired clay tiles are hung on wooden battens and, like clapboards, protect the walls against rain. Brick patterns, such as Dutch "tumbling in", where bricks are laid diagonally to form a series of triangles (left), are both very strong and ornamental.

Earth buildings

Earth buildings are excellent moderators of local climate and have evolved in certain cultures using brilliant colours and forms. The earth walls and floors of open courtyards and roofs, as in this example in Oualata, Mauritania, West Africa (top left), absorb the heat of the sun in the day and radiate it back out again during the cool of the night, making them comfortable sleeping areas.

Urban courtyard houses of Djenne, Mali (far left) are built of clay and straw bricks. The traditional flat roof of this type of house is made of split poles covered with branches, leaves, and a layer of clay. The symbolic façade is dominated by tall earth pilasters, or kadye – columns attached to the face of a wall.

The modern use of adobe by the American architect Charles Johnson in the Boulder House, Arizona (above) is a brilliant exposition of the new Santa Fe style. Gently undulating earth walls and Mexican-style fireplaces blend perfectly with the natural rock of the desert location.

Timber

Huge forests once covered much of the primeval world, making wood, branches, and leaves readily available to the hunter-gatherers as shelter for their temporary campsites. Frameworks of branches were covered with hides or cloth, palm fronds, or woven grass mats. Such shelters have not completely disappeared today and they are still used by the bushmen of the Kalahari and the Mbuti pygmies of central African forests. American Indians moved their tepees and the nomadic Kazakhs of Asia their felt-covered yurta to summer pastures.

With the development of village settlements, timber and organic materials were still the preferred building materials, from the circular kraal of central and southern Africa to the pole-and-thatch huts of Yucatan Mayas and the Maoris of New Zealand. In northern climates, dwellings were constructed with solid log walls, which were sometimes further insulated with earth to form the earth-covered lodges and hogans of the North American Indians.

In Europe, and especially in Britain, the mighty oak was the universal timber used in the building of churches, monasteries, and palaces. This early timber technology developed into the medieval timber-framed houses, which ranged from crude post-and-beam structures to cruck or A-framed and box-framed buildings with jettied or cantilevered upper storeys. For reasons of economy, European timber-framed houses had a framework of halved timbers with an infilling of wattle-and-daub, which consisted of interwoven hazel sticks covered with clay mixed with straw, cow hair, and dung.

In North America, with timber in more plentiful supply, most timber-framed houses were also covered with wood, usually clapboard, painted in bright colours against white window surrounds – a typical feature of New England. Cedar shingles were also a common feature, used as both a roof and wall covering, on buildings ranging from the Connecticut saltbox to the Californian bungalow.

Although wood is a perishable commodity and can be destroyed by fire, the sturdy, thicker structures of the past have endured for centuries. Japan can boast of the oldest wooden buildings in the world – the pagoda and the cloisters of the Horyuji Buddhist temple near Nara date from the 7th century AD.

Health and ecological criteria

Timber is one of the healthiest building materials. Wood is a natural regulator of the indoor climate; it "breathes" and assists ventilation; it stabilizes humidity and filters and purifies the air; it is warm to the touch and absorbs sound. It also does not disturb the natural, subtle electrical and magnetic fields (see pp. 80-1) as do most other materials. However, some people have an allergic response to the aromatic terpenes in pinewood resins.

Worldwide, continuous tree felling without adequate reforestation has diminished forests alarmingly (see pp. 260-1). In the developed world acid rain and pollution are damaging and killing large areas of woodland. In the developing world overcutting for fuelwood or timber is causing a serious shortage. The worst affected and most vulnerable are the tropical rainforests in Africa, Asia, Malaysia, and South America. In addition, the widespread burning of Brazilian forests, producing vast amounts of carbon dioxide, has made a serious and permanent contribution to the "greenhouse effect". It is the concern of each individual to avoid buying endangered hardwoods and to use instead more sustainable softwoods and the more carefully managed temperate hardwoods tree species (see p. 279).

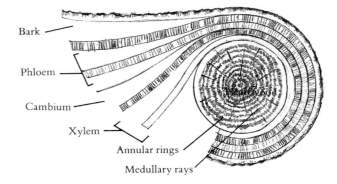

Tree heartwood is surrounded by sapwood layers: cambium (cell-generating) plus xylem and phloem (sap-circulating). Annular rings show yearly growth and medullary rays radiate from the centre.

Types of timber

Timber is divided into softwoods and hardwoods, a botanical distinction that does not always reflect the relative hardness of the wood. Softwoods come from coniferous tree species, chiefly evergreen, and hardwoods from broad-leaved trees that are usually deciduous in temperate regions, evergreen in the tropics. They are slower growing than softwoods, denser, and more resistant to fungal and insect attacks, to moisture movement and distortion – and also more expensive.

Trees intended for timber are felled at maturity, which varies from species to species: ash at 50 years, oak at 100, and pine anywhere between 60 and 120 years. After felling, timber must be seasoned to remove excess sap and reduce, not eliminate, the moisture content. Seasoned wood should not shrink, warp, or split and it is stronger, lighter, and easier to work than green wood.

In relation to its weight, timber is stronger than any other building material except bamboo. The strength/weight ratio of structural timber is greater than either mild steel or reinforced concrete, yet a timber building might weigh only one-eighth as much as a similar structure in concrete and brick.

Using timber

The most traditional use of timber is as unsawn poles (or roundwood). Cheap and readily available in many parts of the world, roundwoods are mostly used green (unseasoned) in the construction of roofs for timber-and-earth homes. This is the most conserving way to use timber: the cost and wastage associated with sawing is eliminated and poles can be cut annually from thinnings.

The old method of joining poles (using rope or bark strips) is not as strong as the modern wooden dowel or metal connector. But, with either method, even the unskilled can build a strong supporting framework. These same methods can be adapted to build domes and wide-span roofs out of triangular sections – ideal for the self-built ecohome of today.

In industrialized countries, log buildings are enjoying something of a revival and complete log houses can now be supplied for the owner-builder or for erection by specialist companies.

Most modern timber construction, however, is with sawn wood. The virtual worldwide use of timber stud frame indicates its popularity and practicality. One of the major advantages timber has over brick- and stone-built houses is that the structure can be pre-assembled and the house shell erected very quickly, allowing work on the inside to commence almost immediately. Another advantage it has is that, being a dry-construction method, you do not have to wait for a lengthy drying-out period before you move in and decorate.

Apart from its structural uses, timber can be split into shingles, carved, fretted, bent, and inlaid into many decorative styles to suit different climates and different cultures.

Shingles and clapboards

Until the Middle Ages, roofs were made from shingles, thin slices of wood. Clay tiles superseded them, but today shingles are popular again for roofing and wall facing. Local wood should be used as it withstands local conditions best and weathers in keeping with the surroundings. Oak, fir, and larch are the usual shingle timbers in Europe; cedar and cypress in North America. Like shingles, weather or clapboards give extra weather protection; they are usually fixed horizontally and overlapping at the joints.

Swedish two-room cabin, Darby Creek, Pennsylvania c1654 (above); 14th-century cruck cottage, Didbrook, Gloucestershire (above right); Timber frame of Wealden house, Sussex c1600 (right); Frank Lloyd Wright's own Shingle Style house, Illinois 1889 (above far right).

Choosing timber

Wood is a living, breathing material with myriad colours, scents, grains, and textures. It endures for centuries, maintaining our links with tradition and with nature, and grows more beautiful with age.

There is a vast range of hardwoods and softwoods to choose from, many of which are imported. When deciding on timber, first consider reusing older material. This is often of better quality and of thicker section than that produced today. Keep solid-wood doors, for example, rather than replacing them with inferior, hollow-core doors, and buy older solid-wood furniture and renovate it – it is likely to be better built than modern products.

If you are buying new sawn timber and furniture, try to find out exactly the type of wood it is. Avoid all endangered tropical hardwood species (see below) and, for preference, buy indigenous hardwoods and softwoods rather than imports.

If you are an allergy sufferer you may have to avoid fresh pinewood, although sealing its surface with varnish or paint may solve the problem. For exterior use, choose more durable woods from managed forests. Many softwoods can be used outside if you first protect them with a natural "breathing" paint, varnish, or stain. But the more common use of softwoods is inside the home, where they are fine for all uses except surfaces where there is a lot of wear and tear and moisture.

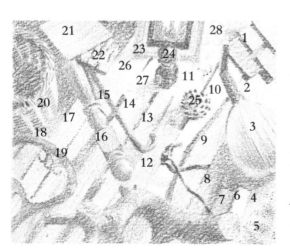

Key *(endangered species marked ★)*
1 *cedar shingles;* **2** *teak★;* **3** *lute;* **4** *Canadian maple;* **5** *sawdust;* **6** *pear;* **7** *western red cedar;* **8** *Russian redwood;* **9** *English ash;* **10** *English sycamore;* **11** *plywood;* **12** *American white oak;* **13** *American ash;* **14** *English lime;* **15** *bentwood walking stick;* **16** *lauan★ newel post;* **17** *American ash;* **18** *European pink ash;* **19** *mahogany chair;* **20** *willow log basket;* **21** *cork tile;* **22** *cork bark;* **23** *walnut picture frame;* **24** *African carving;* **25** *pine cone;* **26** *particle board;* **27** *medium-density fibreboard;* **28** *wood shavings.*

Timber products

Although timber is a renewable, natural material we are using the resources at such an alarming rate that they may cease to be sustainable. The tropical rainforests are fast disappearing and, in the West, acid rain and the indiscriminate use of chemical fertilizers are damaging vast tracts of woodland. The practice, for commercial gain, of replacing slow-growing deciduous forests with the faster conifer plantations places increasing demands on the import of hardwood, and causes the degradation of the landscapes from which they come. And the demand is not only for construction and joinery timbers; we fell millions of trees annually for the production of woodpulp for paper and packaging materials.

We can help to conserve the dwindling supplies of timber by making better use of existing resources. We can reuse old construction timbers, purchase second-hand furniture, and recycle others; for interior use we can also use certain composite boards if they meet health and ecological criteria (see right). Cork and linoleum are again popular and far healthier than their synthetic counterparts.

Cork

Made from the outer bark of the cork oak (*Quercus suber*) of southern Europe, compressed cork strips and granules are made into sheets, wall and floor tiles, and cork wallcoverings. It is a natural, healthy material with good thermal- and noise-insulating properties. Cork is resistant to rot and moulds, hardwearing and elastic in texture, and its natural colour and grainy surface require little or no treatment except when used on floors. Always check with the supplier that tiles have not been treated with synthetics or vinyl backed. Corkboard insulation is available for roofs, floors, and walls. Smaller granules are used in the production of linoleum. Cork is a sound ecological product, too. Not only does the cork oak regenerate itself after stripping, but all the bark is used without waste.

Linoleum

Linoleum is made from powdered cork, linseed oil, wood resin, and wood flour mixed with chalk and pressed on to a backing of hessian (burlap) or jute canvas. Linoleum has all the advantages and none of the disadvantages of PVC floor covering. It is strong and flexible and comes in sheets or tiles but it needs a firm, damp-proof surface, since moisture can rot the fabric backing. Avoid toxic petrochemical adhesives and use a wood lignin paste instead. You can use lignin paste for all cork products, too (see left).

Rubber

The white, milky latex extracted from the rubber tree (*Hevea brasiliensis*), is known as "caoutchouc" in South America, its natural habitat. The British imported the tree to Malaysia and established huge rubber plantations prior to World War I. The latex is vulcanized with sulphur under heat and pressure to impart resilience and elasticity and to remove its odour and stickiness. Synthetics lack the strength of natural rubber, for which demand outstrips supplies. Latex is obtained from other sources, notably the guayule shrub (*Parthenium argentatum*) native to the southwestern states of the US. Rubber is tough and waterproof, and was a popular flooring material for bathrooms until it was replaced by plastics. It is still available in sheets and tiles, though some people have an allergic reaction.

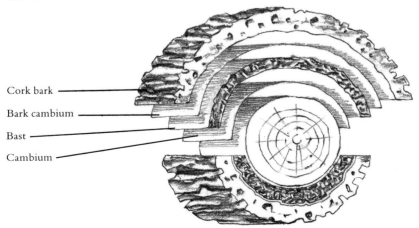

Cork bark

Bark cambium

Bast

Cambium

The cork oak is a small, broadleaved evergreen tree that grows to a height of 12 to 18m (40 to 60ft) and lives for 150 years or more. Although the formation of a corky outer bark is common to many trees, the cork oak is unique because its bark can be removed without harming the tree. The tree must grow for about 15 years before it is first stripped and then it will yield better-quality cork every eight to ten years.

Paper

The ancient Egyptians used the pithy stems of the papyrus reed to produce writing material, but it is the Chinese who are credited with the invention of paper, in the first century AD. Made principally from woodpulp, paper uses enormous amounts of precious timber resources in the form of newsprint, cardboard, and packaging materials. Northern Europe has traditionally produced most woodpulp, but now virgin rainforests are also being used. In the UK alone it is estimated that more than a million trees are used annually in paper and board production. And most of that is thrown out as waste that could be recycled, cutting the demand for fresh woodpulp by up to 30% and, just as important, energy costs by 40%. Some countries are beginning to accept their ecological responsibilities. In Scandinavia, local authorites are now legally obliged to collect household paper waste for recycling. And there is no need to rely solely on woodpulp; paper production from other materials, such as bagasse (a sugar-cane residue), bamboo, mulberry bush, and esparto grass, all of which yield fibres suitable for papermaking, could be stepped up so as to reduce the demand worldwide for woodpulp.

Types of composite boards (left to right): Particle board (such as chipboard); medium-density fibreboard (MDF); blockboard; plywood (5-ply).

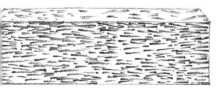

Composite boards

Waste timber and vegetable matter are used to make many composite boards. But in order to meet demand, much comes from fresh timber grown in already hard-pressed forests. The health risks due to formaldehyde, phenols, and adhesives added in manufacture also prejudices their use. Some manufacturers produce formaldehyde-free, or "low-emission", products, and if you use these with nontoxic adhesives they should not present a health problem.

Fibreboards These are made from compressed and dried wood and vegetable fibres without the use of adhesives. They are available as hard or soft boards and as medium-density fibreboard (MDF). MDF, however, is usually treated with urea formaldehyde.

Plywood Both exterior- and interior-grade plywood is composed of several thin layers or veneers of wood bonded with glues that often contain phenol and urea formaldehyde (see pp. 46-51).

Blockboard This product is similar to plywood in composition, but it is made up of a core of blocks of wood.

Particle board This is a nonspecific term covering such products as chipboard, flaxboard, and bagasse board. Chipboard consists of wood chips blended with synthetic resins and pressed into sheets. Flaxboard is made from particles from the residues of the linen industry and bagasse board is obtained as a byproduct of the sugar industry. Particle boards are known to give off formaldehyde and can be a serious health risk.

Timber treatment

Properly seasoned timber can last for hundreds of years. But it is prone to moulds and to fungal decay, encouraged by damp conditions, and to attacks by wood-boring beetles and termites, which, in Australia and the US, can demolish whole timber constructions. Hardwoods, such as oak and teak, are generally resistant to water and to insect attacks. Softwoods, except for redwood (*Sequoia* species), are more susceptible. Building authorities often insist that timber is impregnated with a preservative containing highly toxic insecticides and fungicides. The most common treatments may include lindane, pentachlorophenol (PCP), and dieldrin, although these will vary from country to country.

When you buy an older house, or build a new one, it is usually a condition of the finance company that structural timbers and floorboards are treated with an "approved", and highly toxic, preservative. The alternative and safe approach is first to ensure that all timber is kept dry or, if it becomes wet, that it dries out as soon as possible by eliminating the source of the problem. Sensible constructional techniques and detailing will go a long way to avoiding trouble – wide roof overhangs, waterproof membranes, good ventilation, and drip edges, for example.

Central heating will keep internal wood dry and deny wood beetle larvae the conditions they need to live. Termite infestations can be avoided by elevating the structure on steel supports (if building from new) and using foundation shields and grooves. These measures will greatly increase the durability of timber and reduce the need for additional protection from toxic preservatives.

If necessary, you can use safer, yet effective, treatments – borax, soda (sodium carbonate), potash, linseed oil, and beeswax. Painting timbers with natural resin-oil stains, varnishes, and paints will also help. If you must use toxic products, move out until all vapours have dispersed.

Timber, reeds, and bamboo

Beside Lake Titicaca, the world's highest lake, the Aymara Indians of Bolivia build their houses of woven reed mats made from the local tutora marsh reed (above). They also use bundles of reeds to build their distinctive, banana-shaped fishing boats.

This modern garden room (above right) follows the traditional style of Balinese house, where each room and the family temple has a separate structure or open pavilion grouped within a walled compound. The thatched covering is supported by a magnificent roof structure of native teakwood and bamboo.

The massive stone houses of the Swiss Engadin valley are adorned with incised decoration (sgraffito), paintings, oriels, and iron window grills. The interiors, with carved timber beams, panelled walls, and wide boarded floors, are fine examples of the beauty of wood and the subtle patina of age (right).

Canes and grasses

Where timber and stone were scarce, grasses, reeds, sedges, and bamboo, as well as plant fibres and leaves, have been used as traditional building materials. Along the river delta of the Tigris and Euphrates, the Sumerians (of about 5000BC) constructed reed houses whose style barely differs from that of today's marsh Arabs of Iraq. The ancient Egyptians of the Nile Valley covered their reed houses with mud and wove tough sedges into comfortable beds. In tropical Africa, the nomadic pygmies still erect temporary shelters from branches interwoven with grass and topped with a roof of palm or banana leaves. Their village settlements consist of houses with low mud walls and pointed or domed roofs thatched with reeds or the bright yellow elephant grass (a type of gigantic reedmace).

Bamboo-framed houses, with bamboo mat walls and a thatch of grass, leaves, or rice straw are known as far afield as China and Japan, India and Bangladesh, Borneo, Brazil, and Peru. Bamboo canes are used for house building and scaffolding, bridges and rafts, utensils, and furniture. But it is the rattan from southeast Asia that provides most of the cane furniture found in so many homes in Europe, Japan, Australia, and the US.

In Germany and Austria, architects of the biological building school are introducing grass roofs on many contemporary buildings (see also p. 75). This is no modern invention, but a revival of old traditions common in places such as Scandinavia and Alaska where the severe winter climate demands extra protection. In much of northern and central Europe, straw and reed thatch were common, along with broom and sedge where cereal crops could not be grown. Because of the fire risk, thatch was largely replaced by stone, tile, and slate roofs; today it is again a favoured roofing material and is even obligatory in certain conservation areas. But thatching is an expensive and rare craft, and suitable reeds and straw are becoming scarce as many traditional reed beds are reclaimed for agricultural land. The straw that remains after mechanical harvesting is either too broken up and burned or turned into compressed panels for wall insulation. In Denmark, this same "waste" straw is burned in industrial plants and straw-burning furnaces provide district heating for large towns.

The mudhifs, or guest houses, of the Ma'dan (marsh Arabs) of Iraq are built from reeds to a technique that evolved long ago (above). The seal from the late Uruk period (right) shows how similar the houses of the Sumerians were as long ago as the 4th millennium BC.

Disappearing species

Reeds and long-stalked straw may be in decline but they are still sustainable compared with rattan and some species of bamboo (see pp. 262-3). Managed bamboo canes are cut selectively to leave young shoots to reach maturity; cutting by mechanical means and land clearing set regeneration back decades. Such destruction poses other environmental dangers. In China, for example, the giant panda is under threat, due in part to disappearing natural habitats but also because of the bamboo's unpredictable flowering pattern. Bamboos flower only once and then die. The Chinese have now prohibited the cutting of bamboo near known panda habitats. Even more serious is the rate at which rattan is being overharvested and the destruction of the rainforests that form its natural habitat. Unless plantations can be combined with reforestation, many rattan species will disappear.

The raw materials

Grasses will grow in inhospitable conditions where trees and other vegetation refuse to flourish and, being annual crops, they are in continuous supply. Cut turfs are used in sod houses (see p. 144), or grasses can be tied in sheaves and bundles or twisted and woven for structural use or for roof thatching and wall panels.

Straw, which belongs to the grass family, is a byproduct of cultivated cereal crops, such as wheat, rye, oats, and barley, and a traditional material for thatching. Rye straw is the longest, strongest, and most weather resistant but little cultivated – wheat straw is the most readily available. Outside of the cereal-cultivating areas, palm and banana leaves are common roofing materials; for weaving purposes, raffia, the tough leaf fibres of the African palm tree (*Raphia ruffia*), is locally popular.

Reeds and sedges, the tall perennial grasses of fresh and saltwater marshes and lake and river edges, are strong and durable. The Norfolk reed of England grows to a height of about 2.7m (9ft) and the giant qasab reed of Iraq to more than 6m (20ft).

Bamboo, another perennial grass with more than 1000 species, is the tallest, and the largest can reach 35m (115ft). It is the world's fastest growing plant, capable of increasing in height by up to 1m (39in) in a day. Culms can be cut after three years, but for construction purposes mature culms of five or six years are essential.

Rattan is not a grass but a palm that climbs high into the tropical forest canopy. The most common rattans are species of *Calamus* found in the Malay peninsula, Borneo, Indonesia, and, to a smaller extent, in the Philippines and India. Mature stems, often more than 76m (250ft) tall, are hauled down and cut at the age of ten years. The twining stems often damage their tree hosts in the process.

Manufacturing processes

Grasses are harvested at the end of the growing season, tied into bundles of equal length, and used for thatching or woven into mats. Reeds and straw are also tied in bundles or "yealms" ready for the thatcher, who fixes them in overlapping courses to the roof timbers with wooden sticks and iron hooks. Sometimes, for structural building, reeds are tied together to form thick bundles and curved columns, with the spaces between filled by woven wall panels and sunscreens.

Bamboo is a unique plant, lending itself to a multitude of applications and craft techniques that can support whole village communities. A single hectare can yield between 20 and 40 tonnes annually. The culms are harvested in the dry season, left for a few days to allow the sap to drain, and then immersed in water for many weeks to reduce the sugar and starch contents. Bamboo can also be pulped for paper, used either by itself or combined with wood pulp to ease timber shortages. A technique originating in China, where timber shortages are acute, is the production of ply bamboo. The decorative surface of the bamboo is removed, flattened, and applied as veneer strips to the ply, creating an attractive zigzag effect not dissimilar to herringbone. Bamboo's remarkable lightness and strength under tension makes it ideal for building and scaffolding purposes.

The barbed rattan canes are dragged to the ground, stripped of leaves, and left to dry in the sun before they are cut into lengths and graded according to size. After being washed and scoured with sand, the canes may be left whole or split in half. Strips of bark are used for the weaving process.

Health and ecological criteria

In their natural, untreated state, all these vegetative materials are healthy. And, until recently, the impact of harvesting and processing on the environment has been negligible. The resources are generally renewable, and harvesting and processing involve neither energy costs nor heavy machinery. In addition, they provide local employment and help to maintain traditional local crafts. Now, however, following close on the destruction of tropical rainforests is the erosion of the natural habitats of reeds, bamboo, and rattan, and with that the disappearance of wildlife. You should make sure that you buy products only from managed plantations.

Problems Once harvested, these materials are often treated with chemical preservatives and finishes. Bamboo, rattan, and reeds, for example, may be treated with toxic DDT and lindane. It is possible to order untreated products direct from village craft centres in developing countries via Alternative Trading Organizations. Then you can prolong the life of these materials by treating them with borax, linseed oil, or beeswax, or by coating them with natural varnishes.

The earliest evidence of prehistoric houses includes the Yayoi pit dwellings at Toro, Japan. They had low, rammed-earth walls encircling four wooden posts and beams that supported roof rafters to the ground. The thick thatch was probably the perennial miscanthus grass.

Choosing canes and grasses

These natural materials have inherent "easy-living" qualities, evoking feelings of warmth and shelter in winter and the touch of sun and airy breezes in summer. Thatched houses are part of our inheritance. They represent an unbroken line from the past in the form of a continuation of local craft traditions.

Under good conditions, straw thatch can last 30 years, reed for 50. They are lightweight materials and have fine insulating and acoustic qualities. But there is always the risk of fire, and birds and mice can cause extensive damage. Bamboo is extremely versatile – the tensile strength and rigidity of mature culms make them suitable for structural building as well as furnituremaking, while thinner and split canes are flexible enough to be bent and woven into wall and roof panels, blinds, and screens. Bamboo can also be carved and shaped into a wide range of everyday utensils, toys, and musical instruments. Look for bamboo in its natural warm honey colour (dark-flecked goods have almost certainly been treated), and finish it yourself with natural waxes, oils, and varnishes. The fibres of bamboo – and raffia – can be woven into basketware, mats, and sunhats. Rattan is almost as ubiquitous. The largest demand is for furniture made from whole or split canes plaited or woven in various designs; the bark, too, is split into strips and woven into chair seats, decorative screens, and baskets.

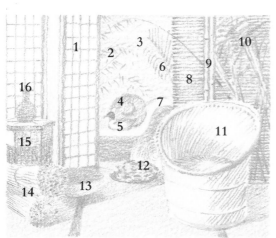

Key
1 *mulberry paper shoji screen;* 2 *bamboo plant;* 3 *reed blind;* 4 *Chinese bamboo hat;* 5 *bamboo duck;* 6 *rattan* (Calamus) *plant;* 7 *rattan chaise-longue;* 8 *split bamboo blind;* 9 *unprocessed rattan canes;* 10 *bamboos;* 11 *split bamboo and rush chair;* 12 *raffia Somali winnowing basket;* 13 *rattan basket;* 14 *thatch reeds;* 15 *banana leaf linen basket;* 16 *bamboo vase.*

Natural fibres

Natural plant fibres, animal skins, and bird feathers have always been the staples of our clothing, furnishing, and bedding. Remains found in eastern Europe indicate that 20,000 years ago people lived in tents of hide stretched over frames of wood or mammoth tusks. But it was another 13,000 years before we see any evidence of weaving.

In China, silkworm farms flourished in the Yellow River Valley 5000 years ago, and wall hangings, carpets, and scrolls in intricate and beautifully worked patterns were woven on bamboo looms. Carpetmaking probably originated with nomads as a means of keeping their tents warm. Later it became an art form, finding its finest expression in the carpets of Persia. Wool and silk were dyed with chamomile flowers, madder root, and acorns and carpets and rugs were made in geometric designs or symbolic patterns of flowers and birds. In the 19th century, the subtle, slowly fading colours were replaced by the brighter hues of synthetic dyes.

Historically, wool has been the favourite fabric in Europe. The ancient Romans wove woollen blankets, wall hangings, and togas and, much later, the Medicis of Florence made their fortune in the wool trade. By the middle of the 13th century, Britain had a near monopoly on wool, forbade the import of cotton, and decreed compulsory burial shrouds of wool. This supremacy lasted until Australia began to breed the Iberian merino sheep in the 18th century. Australian merino wool today constitutes more than one-third of world production.

Synthetic fibres

Just before World War II the first commercial synthetic fibre, nylon, was invented by Wallace Carothers. Since then natural fibres have been largely supplanted by "artificial" fibres of two main types. *Cellulosics* are derived from the cellulose in trees and plants – the major fibres being rayon and acetate. *Noncellulosics* can come from hydrocarbons, glass, and graphite – the major fibres being polyester, nylon, acrylic, and polypropylene. Noncellulosics account for 90 per cent of all synthetics. This is unfortunate, since cellulosics can come from renewable plant resources and offer possibilities of environmentally sustainable synthetics.

Fibres and the ecosystem

Natural fibres come from abundant and renewable resources and are produced as annual crops or animal byproducts. But "natural" does not necessarily mean "healthy", mainly due to the prolific use of chemicals and pesticides during cultivation or afterward as additives. Cotton plantations are sprayed with pesticides and fungicides in spring and with defoliants in the autumn. Most chemical residues are removed when cotton is processed and when it is first washed. Formaldehyde, used to produce finishes that appear on labels as "easy-care", "non-iron", or "crease-resistant", can be permanent. Legally enforced flame retardants can be health hazards, too. In the US, the carcinogenic TRIS is banned in children's sleepwear but is legal in adult clothing. Wool or wool/cotton mixtures are alternatives, but they may have been mothproofed with sodium fluorosilicate, dieldrin, or DDT. Such pesticides are difficult to identify, and it is safest to use wool that has not been mothproofed. Some people are allergic to wool and to feathers.

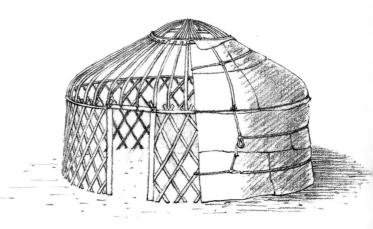

For centuries, nomads of central Asia have used felted wool as a building material. It is lightweight, water and wind resistant, and still used today for the portable yurta, or tents, from Turkey to Mongolia.

Linen
Made from the annual flax (*Linum usitatissimum*), long linen fibres from the crushed stems are combed and spun into yarn. Woven or knitted linen produces a fabric with a natural sheen and slightly uneven texture, but it is moisture absorbent and cool as well as strong and durable. Linen is finished by calendering or pressing through rollers to prevent shrinking and a tendency to fray. It is sold unbleached or dyed and printed.

Cotton
Natural cellulose fibres are produced from the hairs around the seed pods of the annual cotton plant (*Gossypium*). Cotton gins separate the pods into seeds that yield cooking oil and cattle fodder, soft fibres (lint) spun into yarns for woven fabrics, and coarse linters used in cotton padding, rayon, and papermaking. Cotton is soft and nonirritating, absorbs body moisture, allowing the skin to breathe, and is cool in summer, warm in winter. But some finishes involve harmful chemicals (see left); mercerized and sanforized cotton, treated to resist shrinkage and to accept dyes, can be regarded as harmless.

Wool
Most sheep fleece is washed or scoured and, when carded and combed, the fibres are ready for spinning, weaving, or knitting. Finishes – to increase the bulk, reduce shrinkage, and absorb grease – include fulling of the cloth and, sometimes, mothproofing at the dyeing stage. Wool is warm in winter, cool in summer, water resistant on the outside, absorbent on the inside, and naturally flame resistant. It may be mixed with other fibres, so you should look for the official woolmark guaranteeing 100% wool content. Other wool sources include silky Kashmir goats and Angora rabbits, yaks, and llamas, vicunas, and alpacas. The coarser wool of Angora goats (mohair) is usually mixed with fine lamb's wool; fibres from the Bactrian camel have a texture midway between the two. Felt is made by matting together woollen fibres.

Silk
Luxurious, soft, and lightweight, silk is made from the tough filaments spun by silkworms around their cocoons as they feed on mulberry leaves. The long, elastic fibres are woven to make warm fabrics of various weights and textures, while the short fibres are spun or used as silk waste.

Kapok
Seed pods of the tropical silk-cotton tree (*Ceiba pentandra*) yield silky fibres with a downy texture. Although unsuitable for spinning, the fibres have excellent thermal and waterproof qualities and they are used to fill bedding, cold-weather clothing, and life-jackets. After prolonged wear, especially in mattresses and quilts, the fibres break down and can release allergenic dust.

Jute
The long stems of the jute plant (*Corchorus capsularis* or *C. olitorius*) must be softened in water before the fibres can be beaten out. Too coarse for clothing, the fibres are processed with hemp to make hessian (burlap) and similar fabrics, for use in sacking, wall coverings, and as a backing for linoleum. Several crops are produced annually from managed plantations in the Ganges delta. Even so, demand exceeds production and other stem fibres are used as a substitute for jute. Some of these include ramie, kenaf, and roselle.

Hemp
Stems of the annual *Cannabis sativa* yield strong, coarse fibres used for cord, rope, matting, and cloth. Their use for these purposes has declined, and cultivation is strictly controlled or banned in many countries due to the plant's other use as the source of cannabis.

Sisal
This Mexican agave species (*Agave sisalana*) is renowned for the strength of its long leaf fibres. They are extracted from the leaves once they reach 1m (39in) in length, cleansed of pulp, and made into cord and matting.

Coir
The tough, coarse fibres from the husk of the fruit of the coconut palm are known as coir. Strong and hardwearing, the dark-brown fibres are used for matting and ropes. Most coir comes from the tropics.

Rayon
Rayon is a synthetic fibre made from cellulose derived from wood and plant pulp, and has a cotton-like texture. It tends to crease unless treated and it is often blended with natural fibres. Rayon illustrates the possibilities of using plant-based chemistry rather than petrochemicals to produce healthy and sustainable fibres and fabrics.

Feathers and down
Gathered, ideally, during the moulting season, feathers and down are the traditional fillings for bedding and cushions. They are washed and air cleaned without the use of chemicals that would destroy their heat-insulating properties. Down is softer, lighter, and warmer than feathers and eider down is the most expensive, followed by goose down. Mixed feather and down fillings vary in quality: the higher the proportion of feather, the bulkier the filling. Some people are allergic to feathers and down.

Skins and hairs
Natural, undyed leather is usually acceptable although some tanning processes contain formaldehyde. Horsehair comes chiefly from the mane or the tail and was the traditional material for stuffing furniture. It is hardwearing but increasingly scarce, and a good filling for mattresses or chairs. But it is expensive and some people are allergic to it. You should avoid all wild animal products or those involving cruelty – some would say that all animal products are cruel and should not be used.

Choosing fabrics and fibres

The choice of fabrics and fibres for the home can be confusing. But the hidden environmental costs of petrochemical-based synthetics (see pp. 42–3) make it clear that they should be avoided. Not all natural fibres are problem free, however, but on the whole they do come from abundant, diverse, and renewable sources, it is possible to produce them without pollution (although certain chemical treatments and pesticides are real problems), and processing them usually requires far less energy than is used for producing synthetics.

In the home, different fibres and fabrics are suited to different purposes, depending on such factors as durability, rot and flame resistance, strength, and cost. For durability, choose coarser, hardwearing fibres such as coir, sisal, and stain-resistant wool mixes for floor mats and carpets. Use felts for underlays and hessian (burlap) or canvas for wall finishes, linings, and screens. Linen, although expensive, is very long lasting; cottons and wools are the most versatile and diverse, with good thermal and "breathing" qualities. Silk – the finest of the fabrics – can be as soft as chiffon, as stiff as taffeta, or as brilliant as shantung.

Look for the international logos on labels to ensure that they are 100 per cent natural fibre. For colour, choose the soft tones of untreated fabrics or the subtle beauty of natural, nonchemical dyes.

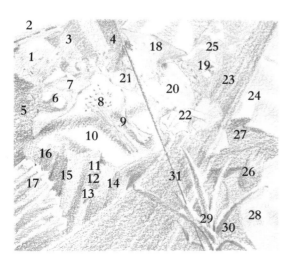

Key
1 *raw wool;* 2 *unbleached wool fabric;* 3 *wool poncho;* 4 *felted wool;* 5 *tanned leather;* 6 *cellulose;* 7 *rayon;* 8 *flax seed;* 9 *flax fibres;* 10 *linen;* 11 *silkworm cocoon;* 12 *silkworm cocoon case;* 13 *silk fibres;* 14, 15, 16 & 17 *silk fabrics;* 18 *feathers;* 19 *cotton seed;* 20 *raw cotton;* 21 *cotton rug;* 22 *cotton lace;* 23 *cotton hammock;* 24 *unbleached cotton fabric;* 25 *recycled cotton;* 26 *coconut;* 27 *coir mat;* 28 *hessian;* 29 *agave leaves;* 30 *sisal matting;* 31 *hemp rope.*

Paints and varnishes

More than 15,000 years ago Stone-Age artists decorated their cave walls with exuberant paintings of animals, birds, and fish. Outstanding examples of artistic skills have been found at more than a hundred sites in the Dordogne area of France and in northern Spain. The most impressive paintings, however, are those at Lascaux near Montignac, France, which were discovered in 1940. Our early ancestors made paints from ochre, a clay-like natural earth containing ferric oxide, silica, and alumina, which produces yellow, brown, and red pigments, or from hematite, obtained by grinding iron-rich rocks to yield a bright red to near black powder (black pigments came from charcoal). There is evidence that prehistoric people sprinkled their dead with powdered red ochre, and the early Australian Aborigines are thought to have used hematite in their burial ceremonies. For painting, the pigments were mixed with animal fat to bind them and make them waterproof.

Stone-Age artists also knew the art of stencilling: they would place a hand against the wall and spray around it with paint blown through a hollow bone. The pattern was repeated until it formed a row of handprints.

The ancient Egyptians decorated mud-plaster walls with water paints using gum arabic or size as the binding agent. To achieve a range of colours, they ground minerals into powder: cinnabar to produce red; azurite for blue; malachite for green; and orpiment for yellow. But it was the Minoans who perfected the art of fresco – applying pigments to wet lime-plaster – and they produced magnificent images of birds, animals, and flowers on the walls of their Cretan homes and palaces. The Roman contributions to this growing repertoire of colours were the famous Tyrian purple, made from whelk shells, and a blue-green pigment from the verdigris on copper. But it was from the Arabs that the two "great" colours came – the bright red of vermilion, made from mercuric sulphide, and the vivid deep blue of ultramarine, made by powdering the semi-precious stone lapis lazuli.

By the 14th century egg tempera paint was in wide use. With this technique, pigments were mixed with egg yolk to produce colours with a particular brilliance and luminosity. Gradually, tempera was superseded by the introduction of oil paints, which used the drying and hardening properties of linseed, poppy, walnut, and hempseed oil mediums mixed with the thinner turpentine and pigments on a gesso glue ground.

Few new colours were discovered, with the exception of Prussian blue and Naples yellow in the 18th century, until the advent of chemical synthetics in the 19th century, when many new colours were introduced, including mauve, cadmium and chrome yellow, and synthetic ultramarine.

Varnishes and oil paints

By the 15th century, linseed oil had become the favoured medium in varnishes. It fulfilled the basic requirement of hardening on contact with the air and it was also the most readily available. Along with lead, linseed oil also became the established base for decorators' oil paints. Turpentine, distilled from pine resin, was used as a thinner, and pigment pastes were added as colorants. New oil paints and varnishes with superior weather resistance replaced the traditional external finishes of lime wash and plaster rendering and were also used to give a gloss finish to interior wood.

By the beginning of the 20th century various additives had been incorporated in oil paints to improve their durability and drying properties and to impart a higher gloss finish. Since World War II petrochemical synthetics have largely taken over from natural vegetable oil and resin bases.

The attendant health hazards of using synthetic oil-based paints and varnishes may be small for the householder, but this is not necessarily the case for those involved in its manufacture or for professional decorators exposed to potentially harmful fumes throughout their working day. Labels on paints and varnishes inform us that the product should be applied with windows and doors wide open – a clear indication of the toxicity of the pollutants released into the atmosphere. A few companies, predominantly in Germany and the US, now offer natural, pollutant-free paints, stainers, and varnishes. Consumer – and government – pressure is now needed to force manufacturers to initiate more environmentally acceptable products.

Unacceptable synthetics and additives

The criteria for a healthy product are that it should be harmless to the user, the manufacturer, and the environment. Synthetic paints, varnishes, stainers, sealants, and adhesives meet none of these criteria. Paint, varnish, and thinner solvents contain volatile organic compounds, such as xylene, epoxy, toluene, and ketones, as well as toxic heavy metals. These offgas during application and while drying, and even after they are dry. Urethane varnish and latex paint fall into this category and, like many paints, they also contain synthetic rubber, acrylics, and other additives (such as insecticides and fungicides) that offgas indefinitely.

Lead, formerly a common additive in paint, has been gradually phased out and its inclusion in paints is legally controlled or even, as in the UK, US, and Australia, banned. But cases still occur of lead poisoning in children who have been in direct contact with old, flaking paintwork or with some imported toys. Always check that lead-free paint has been used with any product you buy.

But the problem does not stop with lead. Epoxy paints and varnishes contain synthetic resins and phenols. These are possibly carcinogenic and have been banned in many countries. Bear in mind, too, that all synthetic paints are serious fire risks; once alight they emit toxic gases and dense smoke that can prove fatal.

Raw materials

Paint is a compound material consisting basically of a solid pigment, ground and suspended in a liquid medium such as water or oil. Pigments give opacity, colour, and consistency to paints. They are mainly of mineral origin, such as those quarried from the earth – the red, brownish, and yellow ochres, the brown umbers, and the red oxides. Brighter colours come from metal ores. Paris green was prepared from acetate of copper and arsenic trioxide; it is highly poisonous and has long since been dis-

continued. White pigments come from zinc oxide, titanium oxide (the most opaque), and from antimony oxide, now that white lead has been banned.

Pure plant pigments, similar to those used in natural dyeing, were also used and are now being reintroduced. They are ideal for translucent colour washes or glazes on a white wall base. Some natural pigments tend to fade gradually in sunlight, endowing surfaces with a delicate coloured patina.

Oil-based paints

Today, most oil paints are made with synthetic alkyd and epoxy resins and white spirit (a petroleum product that has taken the place of turpentine). Synthetic varnishes are included in some paints to produce a gloss finish. More recent nondrip paints contain polyurethane. New microporous synthetic paints and varnishes are now available and these permit the underlying wood, stone, or plaster surface to breathe and help overcome the problem of trapped moisture and rot.

Water-based paints

These paints basically consist of pigments thinned with water, and types include lime distempers and whitewashes. This type of paint is easy to apply and is thus suitable when you need to cover large areas of walls and ceilings. It dries quickly and has a healthy, pleasant smell during application. However, it flakes easily and is neither durable nor washable.

Improved water paints thinned with milk casein or natural glue/oil water emulsions give a smooth, mat finish that is washable and durable enough to be used on exterior walls. Lime wash is a natural antiseptic and deters insects, making it ideal for use anywhere food is stored – provided that the walls are dry.

You can make your own water-based paints by mixing lime-based whitewash or casein emulsion with artists' pigments. Unlike oil-based paints, water-based paints are hygroscopic and allow the surfaces to breathe; you can apply them to plaster before it has fully dried.

Thinners and removers

Turpentine is distilled from a volatile essential oil, oleoresin, tapped from the bark of certain pine trees. A basic thinning and solvent ingredient in oil paints, turpentine has been replaced by synthetic, inflammable liquids derived from petroleum, known as turpentine substitute or white spirit. Paint strippers contain highly dangerous solvents, including methylene chloride, that give off toxic fumes and burn on contact with the skin. If possible, avoid using products containing these ingredients, but if you have no choice try to work outdoors with proper protection, or indoors only in a well-ventilated area.

Natural paints and varnishes

Subtle colours, pleasant scents, and a healthy environment are some of the advantages of paints, varnishes, and waxes derived from natural plant and mineral ingredients. Many different parts of a plant can be distilled to make pigments: roots (madder), bark (oak), leaves (birch), stems (reseda), flowers (coreopsis, chamomile, and saffron crocus), and fruit (walnut).

All pigments require a medium and thinner, and here, too, plants oblige by yielding resins, oils, starches, and waxes (all with their distinctive scents). Linseed oil is truly versatile – on its own it is suitable for external or interior use, and it deeply impregnates wood making it water resistant. Raw linseed oil dries slowly, however, so it is often boiled and mixed with a varnish and various drying agents.

Natural varnishes combine resins, such as larch or copal, with scented turpentine oil and pigments. They are less durable than synthetic varnishes, but have an added depth of colour and scent and they also allow underlying wooden surfaces to breathe. Pure beeswax lends lustre and golden tones to all types of interior wood surfaces. It is also antistatic and its scent improves the room climate (see pp. 264–5).

Choosing paints and varnishes

There is often a contradiction in the way we decorate our homes. We restore old brickwork and stone, lay wooden floors, and install wooden cabinets – and then destroy these healthy materials with synthetic finishes. The lack of biological compatibility between natural and synthetic materials can adversely affect the room climate and create barriers that prevent surfaces from breathing.

The only treatment needed for new and restored wood is a finish of linseed oil or beeswax; exterior wood, which should be chosen for its durability, can be protected with stains, oils, and varnishes with a natural resin or linseed oil base. Finishes for exterior stone and plaster walls include lime wash and natural resin, casein, and silicate paints. In the home, consider leaving new plaster untreated. If you do decorate, use paper wallpaper and a nontoxic paste; or, instead of emulsion, use water-based paints tinted with natural pigments.

Use synthetic oil-based paints sparingly and with caution; decorate during the warm, dry season, when you can leave doors and windows wide open. Avoid spray paints and toxic chemical paint strippers. Be sceptical about paints that are labelled low-odour or biologically friendly. Choose instead healthy products from specialist manufacturers who have recreated paints from resins, oils, and pigments using Earth's "gentle chemistry".

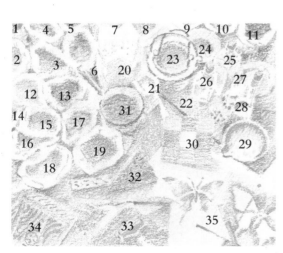

Key
1 *Chinese red;* 2 *mid chrome yellow;* 3 *vermilion;* 4 *magenta lake;* 5 *burnt sienna;* 6 *ultramarine;* 7 *yellow ochre;* 8 *raw sienna;* 9 *raw umber;* 10 *silver;* 11 *black lake;* 12 *new yellow;* 13 *violet;* 14 *mid Brunswick green;* 15 *rose-pink;* 16 *chromate green;* 17 *cerulean blue;* 18 *neptune green;* 19 *red ochre;* 20 *whiting;* 21 *casein;* 22 & 23 *rabbit skin glue and size;* 24 *fish glue;* 25 *linseed oil;* 26 *turpentine;* 27 *beeswax;* 28 *white spirit;* 29 *damar resin crystals;* 30 *varnished wood;* 31 *pigment with casein & water;* 32 *printing blocks;* 33 *pigment & PVA;* 34 *wood block printed papers;* 35 *butterfly stencil & brush.*

Plastics

Although we think of plastic as a modern material, the term can apply to any material that is softened by heat and then set or moulded into another shape. Concrete and steel go through plastic stages and amber, horn, bone, tortoiseshell, and shellac are all centuries-old, natural "plastics". Charles Goodyear in the 19th century produced the first semi-synthetic plastic by combining natural rubber with sulphur to make vulcanized rubber – Vulcanite. But Leo Baekeland invented the first wholly synthetic plastic, known as Bakelite.

Types of plastics

There are more than 50 types falling into two main classes: thermosets and thermoplastics. Thermosets once hard cannot be softened, whereas thermoplastics can be softened by heat any number of times. Surprisingly, though, they are all organic. About 90 per cent of plastics are produced from petroleum and natural gas and some, the cellulosics, come from wood and plants. With a few exceptions, they burn quickly, producing intense heat and often emitting dense smoke and toxic gases.

Thermoplastics This type accounts for more than 80 per cent of all plastics produced today. Among the most common around the home are polyvinyl chloride (PVC), polypropylene (PP), polyethylene, acrylics, nylon, polystyrene, polycarbonate, polyvinyl butytal, and cellulose.

Thermosets In this category are phenolics, urea formaldehyde, melamine formaldehyde, polyesters, polyurethane, and silicones. Around the home, you can find them in the form of particulate, composite, and laminate boards used for floors and walls, and as paints, furniture, carpets, fabrics, pipes, vapour barriers, insulation, electrical fittings, plastic glazing, and as adhesives and sealants.

Ecological criteria

Plastics are obviously useful and convenient but from the points of view of health and the environment, they do not rate well. As well as using nonrenewable resources of oil and natural gas, they also consume vast amounts of energy during their production, which is often dirty and polluting. In addition, most are not biodegradable and cannot be recycled, and increasing volumes of plastic waste litter both the land and sea. Many, particularly the soft thermoplastics, may be a health risk due to off-gassing or leaching when warm or in contact with food and drink. Synthetic fabrics and carpets also allow electric static to build up and synthetic clothes are poor absorbers of perspiration.

To overcome the problem of plastic waste that cannot be recycled, many countries are turning to large-scale incineration. The "Energy from Waste" idea turns refuse, including plastics, into energy and heat (see pp. 78–9), but air pollution results and there are worries of dioxin being emitted from burning PVC. Although improved techniques could eliminate toxic fumes (but not CO_2) many governments feel it better to ban plastics for certain uses – Denmark has banned plastic bottles and Italy plastic shopping bags.

Problems and solutions

The polyethylene terephthalate bottle for drinks is the latest plastics success story but another problem for the environment. Sold at first as nonreturnable, now experimental bottle-bank schemes are being tried with deposit refunds.

The plasticizer in PVC clingfilm can migrate into foods, particularly fatty ones. Microwave cooking with cling-film-covered dishes also causes a high level of migration. Use greaseproof paper, solid containers, or non-PVC films instead.

Polyurethane foam – used extensively in furniture and cushions – is highly flammable and gives off dense smoke and toxic cyanate fumes. It has now been banned in the UK, and only safer "combustion-modified" foam will be allowed in new furniture.

Recycling

The problem with plastics is the number of different chemical compositions involved. At present, classification and separation are only possible via specialist plastic recycling companies, and it would obviously be better if consumers could sort different plastics for recycling. To achieve this the plastics industry needs to devise a labelling system.

Living with plastics

Plastics are undeniably useful and there is no point in trying to eliminate them completely from the home. But we need to be far more discriminating about what we use them for.

○ Avoid plastic packaging, bags, and nonreturnable bottles. Use your own shopping bags and baskets.
○ Opt for alternative materials and nonplastic products when possible.
○ Don't use plastics, particularly soft ones, to store food or drink, or plastic water pipes for drinking supplies.
○ Campaign for proper recycling and disposal schemes in your area.

PART THREE
SPACES

Introduction 170

SPACES

We have become so accustomed to thinking of our homes as a collection of separate rooms – living room, dining room, bedroom, bathroom, kitchen, and so on – with a garden outside, that it is difficult to conceive of them in any other way. But by using these terms, we are already limiting the scope and potentialities of these areas. Think in fresh ways about the things you do at home – how you do them and why. Think "activities" and "processes" rather than "rooms". Instead of "bathroom", consider "bathing and cleansing" – both for hygiene and relaxation. Instead of "kitchen", think "food chain" – its source, processing, freshness, and what you do with all the waste. Rather than "bedroom", imagine "peaceful sleep" – deep uninterrupted rest to rejuvenate mind and body. And rather than "garden" or "yard", think of "living ecosystems" integrated with the home, both inside and out.

Then, instead of "rooms", think "spaces" – like the following six chapters – living spaces, sleeping spaces, kitchen spaces, bathing spaces, health spaces, and greenspaces. Rethink every space in your home, how it is furnished, and how you could make it better suit your lifestyle.

Everything you do in your home affects your health and wellbeing, as well as the general environment. And even simple changes to the way you use your home's spaces and the type of materials and furnishings you use can help support a healthier and more conserving lifestyle. A simple thing such as separate bins for sorting waste, for example, is an important first step toward recycling. In terms of your wellbeing, better posture is much easier if you adapt or buy chairs and beds to give correct support. For exercise, you can make health spaces, and for contemplation, quiet spaces. And to enjoy the benefits of nature, you can create greenspaces, both indoors and out.

Particular activities are not exclusive to certain spaces in the home, though – they often overlap or can be combined in fresh and innovative ways – living space extending into sunspace, for example, or health space and bathing space linking indoors and out. And the transitions between spaces are also extremely important – doorways and windows provide the yin-yang contrast of dark to light, enclosure to emptiness, outer world to the inner world of home and self.

The change between home and street should not be abrupt. We need an in-between space to allow our minds to make a more gradual transition from inside to outside, and vice versa. Steps, paths, plants, views, fences, and gates all help us to adjust. This shingle-roofed gateway at Sotaseter, Norway (right), offers a partial glimpse of what is within, but does not reveal it all at once.

There are many types of transitional space. Porches, verandahs, and balconies are half-way spaces between in and out. Glazed sunspaces, such as the wintergarden of this Norwegian home by the Gaia group (right), insulate against noise, collect solar heat, and provide a sunny place to relax and grow plants. Here, interesting views into and across the sunspace break down the normal hard divisions between rooms (see also pp. 6-7 and 31).

The Spaces chapters

The six following chapters deal with each of the main spaces and functions of the home and garden. Their basic activities and processes are redefined in the context of personal health, wellbeing, and the environment, drawing together all the information of previous chapters concerning ecological design, the hazards of modern homes, and the choice of life systems and materials. After practical advice on location, orientation, and layout for health and energy saving, each space is illustrated with a design that highlights the chief points you will need to consider. Each space is set in a different locale and suggests just one interpretation of the principles behind the design in that particular context, using typical materials, colours, scents, and sounds.

Photographs of many interiors, simple and stylish, ethnic and modern, illustrate the beauty and individuality of a range of environments. And the potential hazards and health and ecological concerns peculiar to specific areas are highlighted along with practical advice on safe alternatives and solutions. But above all, these chapters aim to change the way you regard the spaces in your home.

Knowing your own space

Sit quietly in your favourite spot at home and think of the places where you have been happy and at ease. Perhaps some of these are early memories of childhood homes or places where you stayed. Perhaps they are not in the home at all, but outside in the garden, the countryside, or abroad. What was it that you liked and why? Then, in your mind, come to your own front gate or door and make an imaginary tour round your home or apartment. Move from space to space, gaining an impression of what you like and what you don't, and why. Imagine the light, colours, sounds, smells, and textures, and the changes by day and night and at different seasons. Your thoughts, feelings, and intuitions are powerful indicators of whether your home is a good place for you, and you need to take notice of your reactions.

Where were you sitting while on this imaginary tour? Why did you choose this spot? We all have our own special place where we feel most at peace with ourselves and the world. Wherever it is – at the kitchen table, by a window, in the loft, or a garden hideaway – this is your "place of power", your healing centre, and the emotional centre of your home. Recognizing it will give you more insight into how you respond to the other spaces in your home, and to the world beyond.

Creating intermediate space

In our crowded and polluted cities, the space around the home becomes a vital barrier, protecting it from noise, pollution, and the feeling of the city pressing in on all sides. We are all social beings, tending naturally to live within communities; but we are territorial and private, too. Different cultures have different ways of expressing the interface between private and public space. In the West, the division is usually abrupt: house and street, and house and garden, being very distinct. The traditional Japanese house, on the other hand, purposely blurs the hard distinction using a variety of features, including soft, natural landscaping, perimeter verandahs, paper *shoji* and bamboo screens, and a formal entranceway. These features form ambiguous or intermediate spaces that extend living areas beyond the walls into the garden. Nature is drawn into the house and gardens can be likened to rooms. Removing the shoes symbolizes the transition from exterior to interior; and a sense of distance, rather than walls, provides privacy – the most secluded space being referred to as the "deep, inner recess".

Although the Japanese house is a special case, it serves to demonstrate the principle of adding extra buffer zones to our homes. In hotter parts of the world, the verandah or porch has been popular for hundreds of years, not only for shade or as a place to grow plants, but also as a place to sit and watch the world go by. In the new urban development of Seaside, Florida, a verandah looking on to the street is one of the conditions of all new housebuilding. In Europe, the balcony has traditionally fulfilled a similar social function.

Creating intermediate space can be as simple as growing a few plants on a balcony, in a window box, or in tubs outside the front door. A glazed porch with some plants and flowers buffers the home, makes a pleasant, welcoming entrance, and saves energy too. Almost any tiny patch of ground can be transformed into a pocket garden and even the most barren façade, hard on the street, can be softened and distanced with creepers. A plant-filled bay window or a greenhouse window (see p. 245) is an excellent insulator against noise, heat loss, and visual intrusion. Even better, add a full sunspace addition linking the house and garden.

Creating spaces in the home

Before making any changes, you and all the members of your household need to understand how you react to the present arrangement of spaces in your home and how you want them modified, and why. You have to know what you are aiming for even if the achievement of it seems difficult or a long way in the future.

The simplest change – introducing natural colours and scents, more plants, a water filter, recycling paper – made in response to these feelings is an important first step. It gives you confidence to go on and gradually make more ambitious changes. Use your own ideas and, as you become more health and environment aware, one thing will lead to another. Doing things yourself, within reason, is much more creative and satisfying (and also far less expensive) than always buying something ready made or employing professionals. It depends on the level of the change and your skill – be sensible and don't try to do too much at once. Always bear safety in mind and avoid hazardous jobs, such as electrical work, that need a qualified person.

For most people faced with an existing building, the choice comes down to which area to use for which activity, and the effects of colour and light and natural materials are the main tools you have for creativity within spaces. You may be able to make spaces more dynamic by expanding them upward into roof areas, outward into gardens, or downward into basements. Adding new windows can have an even greater effect – skylights dramatically change a room. You can also add levels within a room – from sitting platforms or sunken "dens" to mezzanines – or create mini spaces with screens and hangings and shelving for books or ornaments.

But there is no point in doing all this only for effect. In the natural house, these methods of utilizing space serve a deeper function – to create healthy and conserving living areas. In Baubiologie terms, you need spaces where heat, humidity, air flow, colour, scent, sound, materials, and green plants combine to create a "living climate".

An integral part of the spaces you create is the way you furnish them. Solid furniture built of natural materials can last for centuries, and thus conserves resources. Wooden furniture must, however, be built of sustainable timber grown in managed plantations (see pp. 260-1). Younger designers are now using innovative techniques with local timbers rather than imports, as well as using the normally wasted roundwood thinnings.

Timber furniture with natural finishes, fillings, and upholstery is not only a pleasure to own and use, but healthier than synthetic products, and safer than furniture filled with polyurethane foam. Like the rest of a healthy interior, natural furniture "breathes" and contributes to a pleasant indoor climate. Being porous and absorbent, natural materials in furniture, curtains, and carpets help to stabilize room humidity and temperature and prevent the build-up of electric static, so common with synthetics, and unpleasant chemical smells. To be truly healthy, though, all furniture must also promote good posture and relaxation – firm support, correct height, and the right body position. The new "bio furniture" of West Germany expresses the best features of natural design: solid wood, traditional joints, organic glues, fillings of natural latex, wool, kapok, linen, cotton, and horse hair, finished with beeswax polish, and designed for posture. Many other items of natural furniture are increasingly available, from Japanese futons to "back chairs".

The first time you enter a natural house you can instinctively sense the difference. As one such visitor remarked: "The house immediately struck us as being unusual. The furnishings were all natural and the atmosphere relaxing. As we entered, we felt a sensation of being welcome."

Chapter Five
LIVING SPACES

The living room is regarded by many as being the most important room in the home. It is where you can relax by yourself or with the family or where you can entertain your friends. But in Western homes, the comfort we have learned to associate with the living room means wall-to-wall synthetic carpets (foam backed or laid on top of a foam underlay), the foam-filled, synthetic-covered three-piece suite, and with the TV and stereo forming the most important focal point. More often than not, the room will be decorated with synthetic paints or vinyl wallpapers and any "wooden" furniture is likely to be made of composite board finished with plastic laminates and varnish. Air fresheners and spray polishes will be used to keep surfaces clean and the air fresh. It is all so normal, how could anything possibly be wrong?

Well, first of all there are the materials. On both health and environmental grounds, synthetics rate poorly and fall far short of the criteria for healthy and sustainable products (see pp. 126–31). And the polyurethane foam still found in much living room furniture is a serious fire hazard, which, fortunately, is now being controlled in many countries by law. Many spray polishes and air fresheners, apart from containing a range of toxic chemicals, also use ozone-damaging CFCs in the propellant gas.

Then there is the question of comfort. Do, in fact, oversoft armchairs and sofas really give your back the support it needs? And furniture designers often make their products too soft and low for the elderly to rise from without effort. Everybody likes the idea of sitting in front of a blazing open fire on cold winter evenings. But not only should your fireplace operate efficiently to avoid indoor pollution, it must also limit outdoor emissions. As well as the control of smoke, the fireplace of the future (if it is to have a future at all) must be designed to limit the emission of greenhouse gases, too.

But beyond these undeniably important aspects, the stereotype of the modern living room, with its mass-produced furniture and prepackaged "style", often lacks that important individual touch that you could describe as emotional warmth. But by listening to your own intuition and by using natural materials and products, you will be able to create a truly "living" room.

A simple and graceful dining room (left), made all the more so by the gently opposing curves of the unusual centre window. The plain white walls, the timber ceiling, and the brick floor form a clear and understated space – a perfect setting for the elegant dining table and chairs. Architect: Frank Lloyd Wright

The clean simplicity, so much a tradition of Scandinavia, is also elegant and comfortable (right). Instead of overstuffed sofas and chairs, fitted carpets, and clutter, the gentle light, soft greenery, delicate wicker furniture, and plain wooden floor, all create a peaceful and informal space.

Orientation and location

Good daylight and sunlight are essential for living spaces. In cold and temperate climates, these rooms should be located on the sun-facing side of the building (see p. 103); spaces oriented within a 30° segment east and west of due south (north in the southern hemisphere) all have the advantage of midday sun, particularly valuable when this is low in winter. Spaces facing east catch the morning sun and are ideal for bedrooms and breakfast rooms, while those facing west avoid the hot noon sun and overheating and enjoy sunset views. A northerly aspect (southerly in the southern hemisphere) gives a constant and shadowless, cool light considered ideal for an artist's studio (or a food larder). In hot, dry climates, living and sleeping spaces are conven-

tionally shielded from the sun and either look on to cool, shaded courtyards or they are protected with wide verandahs and porches. Trees, climbing vines, large water surfaces, and softly playing fountains also help to disperse excessive heat. At the same time, winters can be extremely cold, and it is then vital that living spaces receive the uninterrupted warmth of midday winter sun. It would be helpful if you could move your living and sleeping spaces around as the seasons change, avoiding the sun in summer and taking advantage of it in winter – an unfortunate impossibility. In hot, humid areas, you should give priority to the prevailing winds so that living spaces can be located in the path of through-ventilation or cross–ventilation.

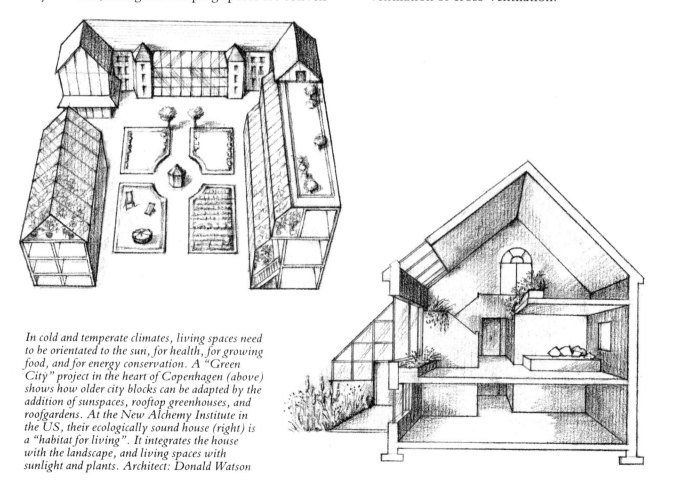

In cold and temperate climates, living spaces need to be orientated to the sun, for health, for growing food, and for energy conservation. A "Green City" project in the heart of Copenhagen (above) shows how older city blocks can be adapted by the addition of sunspaces, rooftop greenhouses, and roofgardens. At the New Alchemy Institute in the US, their ecologically sound house (right) is a "habitat for living". It integrates the house with the landscape, and living spaces with sunlight and plants. Architect: Donald Watson

Front and back rooms

You must balance climatic considerations against other factors, such as the advantages and disadvantages of good views and your position in relation to external and internal sources of noise. Internally, the choice of suitable living spaces will usually also depend on the types of activity the rooms will have to accommodate. Conventionally, the main living space has been the "front room", usually located on the ground floor. But for optimum balance between sun and daylight, peace and quiet and pleasant views, a relocation of living space to the back of the house may be a better option. You might even consider an upstairs back room, away from traffic noise and pollution and where there is clearer light and finer views over the garden. Such a choice, however, may then conflict with the best place for sleeping spaces (see pp. 194-205).

Much will depend on your lifestyle; many elderly and disabled people spend most of their time at home and would prefer a quiet living space at the back of the house overlooking the garden. The front room, facing the street, can be fitted with secondary double glazing to make it a quieter, warmer, and more secure sleeping space. Teenagers will appreciate a separate living room where they can make noise and entertain friends without too much interference from the rest of the family. In built-up areas, converted roof spaces can become green and welcome refuges from the pressures of urban life. Likewise, balconies and rooftop gardens can extend the feeling of being "on top of the world".

The late 1980s have seen a revival of living areas combined with indoor gardens. Many new houses are designed with the living space adjacent to or extending into a greenspace (see p. 242). These types of structure can also be added to older houses; in Britain, the Victorian conservatory is enjoying renewed popularity and, in West Germany, the former *Wintergarten* is again incorporated into many homes. Like the sunspaces or solar greenhouses of North America, it is designed with optimum orientation to the sun and has built-in storage for solar heating. In Denmark, "green façades" of glassed-in balconies are added to city apartment blocks so that each unit has access to sun, growing space, and solar heating. Window greenhouses, that open from the inside, can be fitted to the outside of sunny windows and allow you to grow flowers, herbs, and even some food crops.

In the feng shui discipline (see p. 196), circles, squares, and rectangles make the best room shapes. The living or receiving room should be large and light, with the host's chair in a "safe" position, facing the entrance (although not directly opposite it). Seating should be arranged for ease of conversation, and guests should have a commanding view of the room and the door; in less than ideal situations, mirrors can be used to reflect the entrance. Mirrors can also enhance the living space by drawing in views and light and making the room seem more spacious. They are also useful for hiding oddly shaped corners and discordant features. Fireplaces are warm and auspicious, but should not be obscured by furniture; round tables are fortuitous. Windows and doors that open outward improve the occupants' ch'i and their fortunes by allowing ch'i to spread beyond the house. A window/door relationship is like that of parent and child: the door, symbolic of the parent's mouth, should be the more impressive or the child will be rebellious; if the window is the larger, it should be divided into smaller panes and a wind chime should be hung in the doorway so that the parent's voice can be heard.

Creating living spaces

The beautiful treetop view and its dappled sunlight were the inspirations for this spacious window sitting area (above).

A West African interior in Oualata, Mauritania (left) with its thick and softly moulded earth walls and ceiling of tangled branches is a textural delight. The raised palmwood sitting and sleeping platforms provide for a different tradition of sitting and resting (see also p. 146).

"Regarding posture there are two camps: the sitters-up (the so-called western world) and the squatters (everyone else)." Witold Rybezynski Home. *The dining room at Charleston (above – see also p. 191).*

Seating and posture

In the West we are so used to sitting on chairs that it is difficult to perceive being seated in any other way. Sitting on the floor or the ground does not feel right and is uncomfortable for our stiff muscles and joints. In many other cultures, though, sitting on the ground has always been, and still is, the most natural and comfortable position.

At different points, many people will experience back problems caused by poor posture. The spinal column, which keeps the body upright, is often held rigid, with muscles clenched or, more often, sagging and slouched – a posture encouraged by poorly designed furniture. You can avoid much back pain by keeping the spine straight and, when in a sitting position, supporting it in a good chair. A poor sitting posture leads to back, neck, and shoulder aches, numb buttocks, and encourages circulatory and respiratory problems.

When you sit crosslegged on the floor, on the other hand, the spine tends to stay straighter and breathing and circulation are more relaxed. It is also easier to change from one position to another, bringing different sets of muscles into play and keeping them more flexible.

Low seating

Although many cultures have adopted the Western habit of sitting on chairs, they still retain their older traditions. The Japanese, for example, still relax best by removing their shoes before entering the house and sitting on *tatami* floor mats. In many modern urban Japanese homes there is a revival of the old custom of changing into loose-fitting clothes before sitting down on low cushions or legless stools around the *kotatsu*, a low table with a built-in covered heater to keep the feet warm, or close to the old-fashioned *irori*, a central hearth and brazier.

Low-level seating is gaining in popularity in the West, and new designs are being introduced to cater for such sitting options. Low tables and reading and writing desks with sloping worktops are teamed with firm cushions or low stools, sometimes known as meditation stools. These have tilted seats designed to promote good posture as well as be relaxing. Some futon beds have frames that fold into comfortable daytime sofas or low

reclining chairs. Much of the best design in low-level furniture comes from West Germany and conforms to Baubiologie principles. Chairs are constructed from solid timber with natural finishes of beeswax or resin wood stains and varnishes, and with covers and fillings of natural fibres. Other variations on this theme include low sitting platforms without arms or backs (similar to the Turkish ottomans) and covered with rugs and cushions.

Correct sitting postures

Sitting in a conventional chair is the most widely adopted position, but posture and chair design are of the utmost importance. Poor posture when lying down, sitting, standing, and walking, and badly designed chairs and beds trigger avoidable back and neck pain. Fitness-conscious designers now produce a range of posture furniture and accessories that encourage correct sitting postures and prevent back problems; other designs relieve chronic backache.

What then are the components of a good chair and correct sitting? Basically they are identical whether you are working at a desk, driving a car, eating, or relaxing. These activities all require different positions and different seats, but in all instances the body should be free of tension, with good support for the lumbar part of the spine. The seat should be firm and wide enough to support the back of the thighs, without digging into the knees, and high enough to allow the feet to rest lightly on the floor. Arms take the weight and stress off the neck and help in getting up and sitting down.

For relaxing, a wide angle of more than 90° between the hips and the lumbar region of the spine is usually the most comfortable. The back of the chair should support the whole length of the spine as well as the head, and the seat should be firm enough to prevent slumping when the spine sags into a "banana" shape. The height of the seat is equally important: too high and the feet are left dangling uncomfortably, too low and you are forced to cross the legs and increase tension in the whole body. Old-fashioned rocking chairs and porch swing sofas are ideal relaxers – and sleep inducers – the steady movement gently easing the muscles. Don't confuse relaxing with a slumped posture; those whose ideal of blissful relaxation is to "curl up in a chair with a good book" more often than not end up with a stiff neck and aching back. Sitting is the worst possible position for anyone with acute back pain; reclining on a *chaise-longue* is much more comfortable. If you suffer from leg problems or varicose veins, put your feet up, ideally higher than the hips. For the elderly and the physically handicapped, there are chairs with seats that can be tilted to facilitate getting up, or reclined to a more comfortable angle.

Driving seats should conform to the principles of firm back and thigh support; the best are fully adjustable Recaro seats as fitted in some Swedish and German makes. When you sit down to work or eat, the back should be straight, with the lower part of the spine well supported, and a 90° plus angle between the hips and lower spine. The height

relation between table and chair should be such that it necessitates neither slouching nor leaning forward (see also p. 188).

Sitting areas

Our comfort depends on more subtle factors than just good chairs and proper posture. Seating arrangements are important and most of us prefer an informal circle where we can easily see and talk to each other. A circular seating arrangement also breaks down social barriers and gives equal importance to everybody. Subconsciously, we prefer to sit with our backs to the wall or the windows and with a clear view of anybody entering the room. Avoid seating that is in the path of through traffic but try to arrange seats around a central feature, such as the traditional hearth or a circular table.

Too many of us sit badly and cause ourselves unnecessary fatigue and backache. Instead of slouching in the "banana" position (below), sit on a firm chair that supports the lower back (below centre), or use a posture back chair (right). With a meditation table and stool (below right) you rest your legs and feet on a soft mat.

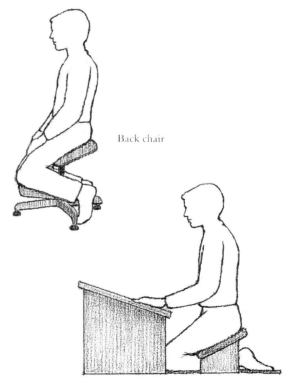

Back chair

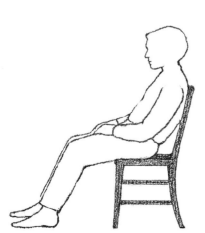

Incorrect sitting position

Correct sitting position

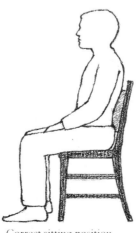

Meditation stool and table

Natural living spaces

The family living space needs to be versatile enough to be put to a variety of uses: it should be a sociable gathering place; a peaceful retreat for relaxation; and also a happy setting for special events, such as anniversaries and parties. The changing seasons bring different rhythms and moods, and our living spaces should harmonize closely with them. In 19th-century Russia, large country houses contained separate summer and winter apartments, and in Scandinavia and Germany it is still common practice for affluent city people to migrate to their summer apartments or houses in the countryside, just like people in hot climates would move from the stifling summer heat of the valleys to the cooler mountain locations. This practice is reflected throughout the Western world in the growing popularity of second, or weekend, homes and retreats. Even if such options are not open to all of us today, we can still adapt our living areas to be more flexible and responsive to climate.

This traditional living room in Santa Fe, New Mexico (see right) illustrates how the best of a vernacular style can be combined with new design ideas to create an adaptable living area. The focal point is the corner hearth, where a circular seating platform becomes the natural gathering area and, on winter nights, a warm and intimate room enclosed by heavy curtains or folding doors. Beyond, on the sun-facing side, is a new, semi-circular sunspace, which is light and airy and acts as a transition between the private inner room and the outside garden – a feature enhanced with plenty of indoor plants. The roof canopy shields the inner room from the high angle of the summer sun, while the solid insulated floor of the sunspace acts as a solar collector that releases heat into the room on cold winter nights. Double-glazed solar windows, with top and bottom vents to regulate the temperature, are insulated with outside shutters or interior padded blinds that prevent the heat from escaping in winter; in summer, through-ventilation from front to back keeps the interior cool.

Thick, solid adobe walls are moulded into flowing curves, platforms, and alcoves that, with old timber beams, avoid rigid, straight angles. The earthy hues of the adobe form a natural background for bright rugs and cushions and local pottery.

The hearth is at the heart of this natural living space, but here the fireplace has been fitted with a high-performance combustion stove. This feature increases output via conducted heat vents, and complete combustion and filters minimize emission of pollutants. The adobe walls, left untreated or finished with nontoxic, water-based paints, allow the room to "breathe" and assist natural diffusive ventilation and heat transfer. The timber ceiling, like the walls, absorbs and releases moisture naturally and further helps to regulate room climate. Clay quarry floor tiles have been laid on a thick concrete and rock base that acts as a solar heat store, insulated to retain the heat and release it as required. The adaptability of the tile surface makes it cool underfoot in summer, warm in winter. Underfloor hot-water pipes, heated by the stove, can boost space heating if this should become necessary.

Traditional focal points

Doors and windows are obvious focal points in the home. They are vulnerable because while they are welcoming to friends they are also meant, traditionally, to deter the entry of unwanted guests, evil spirits, and harmful energies. The threshold is the dividing line between the external, frightening world and the inner sanctuary of the home. In earlier times, the doorstep was protected against evil with cast iron, knives, or crossed scissors buried beneath the threshold. Well into the 20th century it was common to see iron horseshoes nailed to the lintel and front doors as good luck symbols. Step charms and "tangled thread" patterns were common in Scotland and are still used in India where doors, doorposts, knockers, and hinges bear protective patterns; in China, the front door is painted red as a sign of happiness. Orientation of front doors to face the rising sun is of ancient origin, as are solar symbols. Windows were protected with various protective designs, and shutters often had heart-shaped cut-outs as representations of Mother Earth. Glass balls and mirrors hung in the windows were thought to ward off witches and evil spirits.

The inglenook *was a common feature in early houses. The hearth was often protected from evil by a witch post and runic X-symbol of the fire god, Ing.*

Since the earliest human settlements, the hearth has been the traditional and most important focal point. It represented the heart of the home and the centre for family gatherings and social activities. Protection was essential, and witch posts by large ingle-nook fireplaces with built-in seating were carved with protective symbols. Today, an open fireplace remains a centre of attraction for most people, and a brightly burning fire immediately becomes the natural focus. Sadly, though, an open fire is very wasteful of fuel, inefficient as a heating source, and responsible for much pollution. From an ecological viewpoint we should never light a fire again, but the delight gained from this simple act echoes through thousands of years and is difficult to extinguish. Provided that the fire is contained within an efficient, pollution-controlled stove and is used as an occasional, supplementary heating source, the hearth should remain the happy and traditional focal point in the home.

Spiritual and social centres

Neolithic peoples built shrines within their settlements and homes; the ancient Greeks and Romans built house altars for the gods that protected home and hearth; and almost every religious faith has manifested itself in the home with focal points for meditation and prayer. Such spiritual symbols have largely disappeared from modern Christian homes in the West, although a house icon or small shrine in a candle-lit alcove can often be found in orthodox religious homes.

The sharing of a meal is a bonding experience – an extended welcome to friends or a breaking down of the social barriers between strangers or associates. Family members gravitate to the kitchen to congregate round the table for confidential talks or simple idle domestic chatter in a relaxed and informal atmosphere.

In warm climates, the focal points of the home are often extended to the outdoors, where shaded terraces, porches and verandahs, cool courtyards, and even pools and hot tubs become the gathering place for family and friends. Informality and a sense of being at peace with the world always appear easier to accomplish when close to nature.

Personal living space

The home, like the clothes we wear and the food we eat, is an intensely personal expression of our lives, experiences, and values. Although the home may be expressive of your own personal lifestyle, it is more often the combined result of several family members who all need to define their personality.

Sometimes the most satisfying personal spaces are not in the house at all, but are outside in the garden, a shed, workshop, or the garage. Indoors, it may be the attic, basement, or an unused room to which we withdraw for a spell of solitude and quiet contemplation. Childhood memories of hideyholes and hideaways under the stairs where we played "sardines" and "houses", of the junk or attic room for illicit reading on rainy afternoons, of hours spent up treehouses or in precariously built dens where grown-ups were strictly forbidden, all have powerful associations; they have helped to influence our later lives and define the places where we feel happiest and most secure as adults. Visits to the homes of grandparents, aunts, and uncles also hold a special fascination, with their memories of old-fashioned furniture, distinctive smells of must and furniture polish, moth balls in unused bedrooms, and hot sultry days in secluded gardens.

All members of the household need a space of their own where they can be entirely themselves, free from disturbances. The bedroom, home office, or the study are the usual places of retreat. Self-expression can also take the form of a particular interest or hobby, such as collections of objects or memorabilia. They don't have to be antiques or valuable paintings; buttons and old bottles, weird stones, fossils, driftwood, and shells can be just as fascinating. Items bought on visits abroad are reminders of foreign travels and adventures, and can be the basis for collections displayed to best advantage on shelves or in small, well-lit alcoves.

Personal spaces are also those favourite spots where, for some reason, we feel totally happy and at ease. Most of us have a favourite chair or seat, the usurpation of which we find unsettling or annoying. The old inglenook within a large fireplace and the rocking chair by the kitchen range must have been such happy spots, warm and secure. A half-hidden window seat, secluded corners, nooks and crannies, the seat on a verandah are other personal spaces, or, in the words of A. A. Milne's Christopher Robin: "Halfway down the stairs is a stair where I sit. There isn't any other stair quite like it."

The places that we feel closest to and most at ease in are often those that we find or make ourselves. Christopher Alexander is an architect who believes that people, themselves, are the best designers. Over the generations we have come to feel most comfortable in certain spaces and traditional designs. Like the window seat and alcove (left) and the balcony (right), these are the archetypal "words" in a timeless "language" of building that we must all relearn.

Focal points

The hearth, with its brightly burning fire, is one of the most powerful focal points in the home, traditional or modern. Everybody feels drawn toward a fire, and gathering around it on a cold, bleak day soon excludes any gloomy thoughts. The flames and warmth have a soothing and comforting effect that are almost hypnotic, often creating an almost tranquil reverie. The open fire, unfortunately, is inefficient, pollutes the air, and uses scarce fuel resources. Although open fires can be made more efficient, you will need to install a high-efficiency stove to reduce the pollutants that contribute to acid rain. But until the technology is developed, the only way to avoid adding to greenhouse gases is not to light a fire at all.

Unusual and eye-catching features, such as the recessed window with its amber-coloured panes and lattice doors (top left), are an immediate focus of attention, as is this unique design for a stained-glass window (above left), which is further reflected in the glass table top. Tables, especially the kitchen table, tend to *become family gathering points, especially when the setting is as attractive as this (top right). A bay window filled with plants and light, and with good views outside, also has a special attraction as a sitting place, either in a comfortable chair, on low window seats, or at the table (above right).*

Workspace

A modern office was considered, just a few decades ago, an enviable and healthy working environment. We now know that today's workplaces can actually make you ill. Surrounded by fluorescent lighting, VDUs, photocopiers, and synthetic furnishings and carpets behind sealed tinted windows, in stuffy, dry air full of hazardous substances, you are likely to suffer from continuous stress and health problems. This environmental illness is officially recognized as the "sick building syndrome" (see p. 52). On top of this you have the additional strain of commuting to work in often appalling traffic conditions. It is hardly surprising that working at home is becoming an attractive alternative.

Combining work and home life can be satisfying for many people and often less divisive for partner and family relationships. In our high-technology, post-industrial world, forecasts predict that large parts of the office workforce will operate from a home base by the end of the century. The Henley Centre for Forecasting, in England, estimates that one-sixth of the workforce, comprising about 4 million people, will be "teleworking" in Britain by 1995, communicating with head offices via personal computers and the telephone network. The survey also revealed that two-thirds of the high-flying generation, the 25 to 35 year olds, would prefer to work from home.

But there are disadvantages. It takes time, patience, and much self-discipline to adjust to an isolating working environment where there is a lack of companionship, support, and inspiration from colleagues. You may miss seeing new faces and a change of scene, and the close proximity of your partner for 24 hours each day can put a strain on even the best relationship.

Creating a workspace

A home workspace needs careful organization to ensure that you are able to operate efficiently, in a healthy and relaxed environment. Home working covers a range of mental and physical activities and requires office, studio, or workshop space. The best work is produced by people who truly enjoy what they are doing. If you feel good in yourself, your work is more likely to be satisfying; and the choice of workspace can be a decisive factor. It should be quiet and undisturbed, separate from the rest of the home so that you can concentrate, and shut the door on work when you have finished for the day. If you cannot set a whole room aside for a home office, consider adapting an attic, outbuilding, or a basement, or putting up a small extension.

The desk is the centre of the home office and should be in a prominent position, ideally next to a large window, with good daylight, ventilation, and outside views. Choose the desk and chair as a unit; recommended average desk height is about 71-74cm (28-29in) and chair height about 43cm (17in), but both should be adjustable to suit individual needs. Height depends on the type of work and equipment you use: lower for typing than for writing, and electric typewriters slightly lower than manuals. Sloping surfaces and raised reading lecterns for books and papers avoid eye strain and ensure good posture. Choose nonreflecting surfaces, in good daylight and low-voltage halogen or full-spectrum lights rather than fluorescent.

A chair designed for office use should support the small of the back. Avoid soft and bucket-shaped chairs and make sure the backrest is adjustable, that the seat swivels, and that the base, preferably a five-leg base, is sturdy. Avoid castors, since they reduce support and stability. A foot rest can help to lift thighs to a more comfortable position. Chairs, such as the Balans posture chair (illustrated right), have a forward-sloping seat with a waterfall edge that does not cut into the thighs and the backs of the knees, and a knee rest to keep the spine straight without a back support. Balans chairs help prevent backache and fatigue, and once you have become used to a tilting seat, when different muscles come into play, it is surprisingly comfortable. Choose firm chair upholstery, never inflammable polyurethane foam, and covers of natural, nonslip cotton fabrics.

A personal computer or terminal is now common in many homes. Ideally, the screen and keyboard should be separate so that they can be arranged to suit individual needs. Sit as far away as possible from the screen so as to reduce the positive electrical charge. The screen should be at eye level; looking down or up puts tension on the neck and shoulders. You can avoid glare from the screen by placing it at right-angles to the window; when keyboarding, the forearms should be horizontal, and hand rests can help to reduce muscle strain. Views differ on the best working method at a terminal; the majority favours an upright position with the keyboard at elbow level, but many users adopt a semi-reclining position with the keyboard slightly above elbow height. Fit a conductive safety filter in front of the screen to prevent reflection, enhance contrast, and reduce static and radiation.

The working environment

Keep the workspace tidy, or at least free from irrelevant clutter, storing and filing all materials in low cabinets that fit under the worktop. Set up recycling routines for used and unwanted paper and cardboard and use stationery made from recycled paper. Avoid plastic products and accessories, synthetic furnishings and carpets, and toxic cleaning aids, glues, and fixatives; never use aerosols and keep photocopiers out of the home office (site them in a separate, well-ventilated place). Office electrical equipment causes much indoor pollution; it is essential, therefore, to ventilate the room properly and to maintain adequate air humidity. An ionizer will boost the negative ions depleted by electrical equipment. Use natural materials for interior decoration and furnishings; they disperse electrostatic charges from yourself and help to regulate the room climate.

Today, more and more people use personal computers and, apart from the electrical and radiation hazards, users can suffer from poor posture, eyestrain, and headaches. If you work at home, invest in a well-designed desk and posture chair and an adjustable document holder. Use an anti-radiation and anti-glare screen and keep the room well ventilated. Spider plants (Chlorophytum clatum) *in the room help to clean the air (see p.245). Regular breaks also help to relieve strain.*

Living and work

The home is an intensely personal place;
somewhere where we can develop our individual interests. Rather than spending too
much time in passive leisure pursuits, such as
watching TV or listening to the stereo or
radio, developing your own talents and
interests would be helpful (see above).

Artists can rarely resist the temptation of a
plain plastered wall. Every room of Duncan
Grant's and Vanessa Bell's home (right),
including the studio at Charleston, Firle,
Sussex, was decorated by them and other
members of the Bloomsbury group of the
1920s. The house has been preserved as it
was when they lived there and retains the
paintings, murals, pottery, furnishings and
memorabilia, all evoking the intensely individual character of their lives and their home.

Health and conservation

The living room is a place for relaxation and entertaining. But it also poses potential health dangers and is a serious polluter of both the indoor and outdoor environment. The traditional focal point of the home, the hearth, has made a welcome reappearance after decades of unpopularity, but its very presence poses a dilemma. Air pollution is increasing and global climate is threatened by the greenhouse effect caused, to a large degree, by carbon dioxide in the atmosphere. We must ask ourselves whether it is responsible to burn fires in our homes or should we settle for clean energy sources. The furniture in our living rooms is often badly designed and filled with plastic foams that are very real – and fatal – fire hazards. Synthetic paints, wallpapers, fabrics, and carpets as well as chemical cleaners contain toxic substances that damage our health and pollute the indoor atmosphere. And, finally, the TV, computer, stereo, and video all contribute their own, unseen, electrical hazards.

Hazards	Don'ts	Dos
Sitting Deep, soft sofas and armchairs do not give sufficient support, especially to the lower back, resulting in poor posture, undue pressure on the spine, and, eventually, backache. The physically handicapped and the elderly find them difficult to get into and out of, more so if they are low.	Avoid slouching in an easy chair so that the spine sags into the "banana" position. This interferes with digestion and restricts the lungs and the diaphragm. Don't sit too long in one position, and if you suffer from acute or chronic back pain, lie down.	Use a firm chair that supports the back and base of the spine; if necessary, insert a cushion in the small of the back. Extra, firm cushions add height to low chairs, and arm rests or tilting seats make it easier to get up. Rest your legs on a footstool and get up and stretch every now and again.
Furnishings Polyurethane foam-filled furniture is a serious fire hazard. The foam burns quickly and fills the room with dense, acrid smoke and toxic gases that often prove fatal. Plastics and synthetic carpets and fabrics, especially when new, contain chemicals that offgas and pollute the air; they also cause static build-up.	Never smoke when sitting in polyurethane furniture. Don't leave an unguarded open fireplace, and make sure the fire is out before you go to bed. Avoid synthetic fabrics and carpets and all toxic cleaning aids. Don't let the air become too hot and dry because this increases static.	Replace all polyurethane with natural fibres and fillings or with "combustion modified foam". Place a fine-mesh metal guard in front of an open fire. Use furnishings made from natural fibres, and felt carpet underlays and rugs rather than fitted carpets. Regulate air moisture to reduce static.
TV Videos, TVs, stereos, and personal computers generate radiation, EMF, static, and high levels of positive ions. They also emit unpleasant odours and dust and offgas pollutants from inner components and from the plastic casing when they are switched on.	Don't sit too close to a TV and never let children squat in front of one. Avoid long periods working or playing computer games at a VDT screen. Don't watch TV in unventilated or darkened rooms, and don't watch TV for long, uninterrupted periods.	Radiation diminishes by the square of the distance, so always sit well away from a TV. Some countries, notably Sweden, make low-radiation sets. Fit an anti-radiation screen to the VDT, earthed to eliminate static. Install a negative-ion generator, improve ventilation, and balance humidity with plants and bowls of water.
Cleaners and air fresheners These and carpet shampoos and aerosols contain chemical substances that pollute the indoor air and mask it with odours.	Avoid chemical cleaners and polishes, and especially air fresheners and aerosols; if you must use them, make sure of plenty of through-ventilation.	Use natural waxes, polishes, and herbal shampoos. Scent the room with flowers, bowls of pot-pourri, pomanders, and drops of fragrant essential oils.

The hearth

The sight of a cheerfully burning fire and the delicious scents, especially from wood, stimulate all our senses and increase our feeling of wellbeing. Despite efficient central-heating systems, the traditional open fireplace has undergone a revival and is again being installed as a focal point in many modern homes. As much as we appreciate an open fire, it does bring problems of pollution and health hazards, for the individual and for the environment. But the worst offenders in respect of atmospheric pollution are industry, power stations, and the motor car, and it is the emissions from these that must be curbed. Although domestic fuel combustion adds to the atmospheric load, it is on a smaller scale, especially since the introduction of Clean Air laws. You can help of course, by ensuring that all heat sources and the chimney are kept as clean as possible. Bear in mind, too, any local regulations that may apply to your actions – some places, such as Oregon, in the US, for example, have stringent control measures on all emissions.

Most people enjoy an open fire on occasions despite this apparent conflict of interests between ecology and comfort. While reliance on oil and solid fuels as our chief heating sources must be avoided in the future, the occasional enjoyment of an open fire or stove as a back-up to an efficient and nonpolluting heating system is reasonable.

Hazards

Although there are positive associations with open fires (see above), wood- and coal-burning fires and stoves do release potentially dangerous combustion gases, including benzopyrene, into indoor air. The problem does not stop there, since they also add carbon dioxide to the outdoor pollution load, the chief contributor to global warming. Smoke and gases are mainly created because of poor and incomplete combustion of the fuels being used.

If fireplaces and chimneys are badly constructed, with insufficient draught, or where they are blocked by soot or loose bricks, any down-draught will allow the smoke and gases to enter the room. In homes that are well sealed or where the air flow has been altered by mechanical ventilation systems, the situation is made worse. In reality, an open fireplace is an attractive but inefficient heating device, since most of the heat is wasted up the chimney, with only about 10% actually heating the room. And if the fireplace is located against an outside wall, the heat loss will be even greater.

Actions

There are various precautions you can take to make open fires cleaner and more efficient as heating sources.

○ Reduce indoor pollution dramatically with a well-designed fireplace, a flue with smoke shelf and air damper, and an underfloor duct that brings plenty of outside air directly to the fire.
○ Increase the heating output to about 30% by incorporating a heat-circulation system that draws convected heat from the fireplace surround and the chimney into the room.
○ If you are contemplating a new fireplace, ignore the outside wall and build in the centre of the house as a heat store or even in the middle of the living room. Use solid masonry for the fireplace and the chimney, since it is a better heat store.
○ To reduce pollution, use only clean-burn solid fuels. This will exclude wood, which is in any case prohibited in urban areas under many of the Clean Air laws around the world.

○ Install a high-performance, airtight stove if you have to rely on coal, oil, or wood for space and water heating. Such stoves are designed to meet stringent standards for low-emission outdoor pollution and they increase heating efficiency to 70%. They can be fitted into existing chimneys and reinforced glass doors allow you to enjoy the sight and glow of a fire in the living room. A combination of higher temperatures, secondary burning of smoke and gases, and filters help to reduce, if not completely eliminate, air pollution.
○ Alternatively, install a traditional closed tile stove, such as the German *Kachelofen*. Tile stoves are still popular in northern Europe, and although they are not usually designed as low-emission stoves, they are considered a particularly pleasant and efficient form of heating by Baubiologists (see pp. 26 and 79).

Chapter Six
SLEEPING SPACES

Where and how we sleep can have an enormous effect on us. If, for example, we sleep in a healthy and undisturbed environment, we will be in a better position to remain fit and well and to cope with the stresses and strains of our daily lives. If, though, we use badly designed beds in a disturbed type of environment leading to consistently poor sleep, our whole lives may suffer. The stresses of the day will become more intrusive, our mood irritable, and our bodies more open to fatigue and illness. One of the notable things about sleep is that it takes up such a large percentage of our lives and happens almost always in the same bed. This is no problem if the bedroom and the bed both form part of a healthy environment. If they don't, you may be storing up long-term problems.

Children, the elderly, and the infirm all spend extra time in bed and will, therefore, be all the more susceptible to damage. Sleeping for years in a bed that is too soft, for example, can lead eventually to poor posture and will almost certainly inhibit the proper rest and regeneration you should expect from sound sleep on a firm bed. Sleeping in a bedroom full of synthetic carpets and furnishings, in beds made of unhealthy materials, and between synthetic sheets and covers, means we are in close contact with numerous, potentially harmful chemicals every night – again for years on end. And there is now a growing body of international concern about the health effects of sleeping near electromagnetic fields (EMFs), especially those associated with high-voltage power lines. And the spotlight of concern is now being turned toward the EMFs of domestic supplies as well. A similar worry is the long-term exposure to harmful concentrations of EMFs emanating from the ground beneath the house. This "geopathic stress" (see p. 201) caused in certain locations is thought to contribute to disease that may even lead to cancer.

Our sleep does not have to suffer from these problems. Most problems can be dealt with using a little common sense, once our eyes are opened to see the potential hazards. Start by assessing your sleep patterns (and the factors in your lifestyle that may affect your sleep), and look around all your bedrooms to see if you can find the problem areas. Many people now consider the bed to be the most important piece of furniture in the house. Either adapt the ones you have or, if you can, invest in really good beds and bedding.

Sleeping in this bedroom (left) on the Greek island of Patmos would be difficult in the sultry afternoons and humid evenings without the cooling breezes through the open window. The net curtains at the windows and around the four-poster bed, together with the wooden shutters, soften and subdue the penetratingly bright sunlight, helping to create a relaxing retreat. Design: John Stefanidis

The round window and gently curving ceiling of this Californian bedroom (right), are the perfect contours for a restful and tranquil atmosphere. The starkness of the window and the plain white interior into which it is set, are a perfect frame to focus attention on the trees and valley beyond.

How we sleep

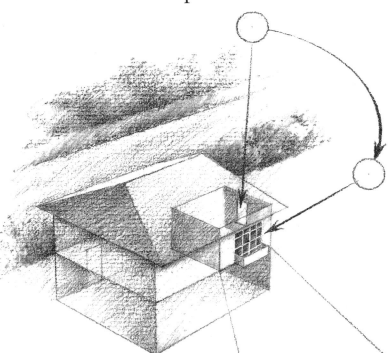

Sleep and dreams are healing, bringing physical, mental, and spiritual relief. But the amount of sleep we need varies greatly: infants sleep nearly all the time, toddlers nearly 12 hours, adolescents 10, active adults around 8 hours, and elderly people much less – at night. In old age, as in hot climates, we tend to sleep in the afternoons. Personal sleep patterns vary, too, depending on whether you are a "lark" or an "owl".

Much more important than the amount of sleep you get each day is its quality, and this is influenced by the location, layout, and furnishing of your sleeping space. Choose bedrooms at the back of the house, away from loud street noises, and if possible shielded by trees. Avoid areas that are noisy, such as those above or next to utility rooms, kitchens, and bathrooms (although elderly people will need one nearby). Try to create a restful atmosphere, excluding television, telephones (again, the elderly or infirm should have access to one), and intrusive clutter. And consider applying the Chinese art of placement, *feng shui*, to layout (see below).

Correct orientation to the path of the sun in different climates is important for our natural waking/sleeping rhythms. In feng shui, the correct siting of sleeping areas can bring health and good fortune. The ideal place for a bedroom is as far as possible from the main entrance and nearest road, behind the meridian/midline of the building and overlooking a peaceful natural landscape. (If the bedroom is at the front, hang a mirror, facing the bedroom door, behind the midline of the house, to "draw" the room back.)

Feng shui places importance on the position of the bed which should ideally be diagonally opposite the door, and with the head away from it. This allows the best view of anybody entering, and gives control of one's destiny. If the bed is wrongly placed, especially opposite the door – the position of a coffin in China – nervousness and ill health may follow. The remedy is to hang wind chimes between the bed and door and place a mirror facing the entrance.

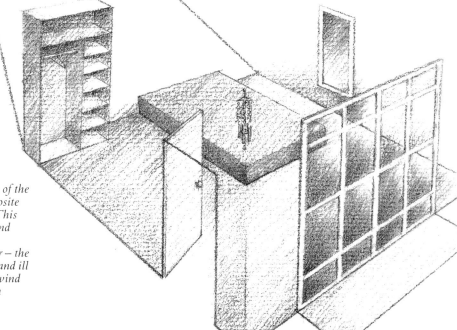

Our natural rhythms of sleeping and waking hours are influenced by the daily and seasonal cycles of the sun. In temperate climates, sleeping spaces with windows that catch the early morning sun will assist awakening, and a balcony facing the setting sun is restful. In hot climates, where direct sun is intrusive, sleeping and siesta spaces should be on the shady side of the house, or screened and shuttered, or protected by verandahs, plants, and creepers. Headlamps and streetlighting should not penetrate bedrooms at night. But a skylight showing the moon, stars, and clouds can help to reaffirm our links with nature.

Dream time

In an average night, sleep passes through four or five cycles, the first four known as "orthodox sleep" and the fifth as "dream sleep". During the orthodox period, our brain waves and body functions slow down and healing takes place. In the fifth stage when dreaming occurs, there are rapid eye movements (REMs). Some dreams may last only a few seconds but they allow us to consolidate experience and deal with unresolved tensions; problems are often eased by "sleeping on them".

REM sleep in a quiet, undisturbed, and comfortable space is necessary for health. Stress and tension can spoil our sleep and cause insomnia. It is important to relax before going to bed: a warm bath with soothing essential oils or a few minutes spent tensing and then relaxing each part of the body are excellent ways to unwind. Some people place a natural rock crystal by the bed or use an ionizer (see p. 101); others prefer hop pillows, herbal aids, or dietary supplements that encourage production in the brain of serotonin, a natural sleep-inducing compound. Don't worry if you sleep badly for a night or two – you will be able to cope as long as you have adequate nourishment and rest and do not become too anxious.

Most of all, good sleep depends on a good bed and sleeping posture. Choose a mattress and base that provide the right support – neither too soft nor too hard. Generally, the heavier you are, the firmer the support should be, and couples may prefer separate mattresses on the same base. A strong, slatted timber base with a quality pocket-sprung mattress made from natural fibres, or a futon, will provide firm support and allow air to circulate.

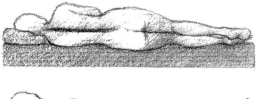

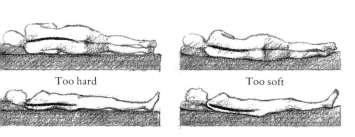
Too hard   Too soft

The wrong bed *If it is difficult to roll from side to side, the mattress is too soft and not giving enough support; old beds are more likely to be weak. The spine will then curve downward in a hammock effect (above), whether you sleep flat or on the side. A board under the mattress may help. If you can slide a hand easily under the small of your back when lying flat, the mattress is too hard. The spine will then be too straight and will curve upward when you lie on your side. This type of bed causes discomfort in the hip and shoulder joints and strains the natural curvature of the spine, leading to later back problems.*

The right bed *This supports the spine while allowing the hips and shoulders to lie comfortably in their natural curvature. The spine should form a shallow S-shape when you lie flat, and a straight horizontal line when you lie on your side (above). The position of the neck and shoulders is also extremely important: the cervical spine should be straight when you lie on your side, curved gently upward when on your back. Use a pillow, neither thin nor bulky, that supports the nape of the neck and correctly aligns the head. If you have neck strain, try an anatomical pillow, a neckroll, or butterfly pillow.*

The natural bedroom

On average we spend a third of our lives in bed, and the bedroom is one of the most important rooms in the home. That is why we should spend time and effort on creating a peaceful, harmonious, and more soothing atmosphere within it. Here we can relax and unwind, rest, study, meditate, or exercise. The bedroom is a private and personal place where we can take refuge during periods of ill health and bad humour or when we need to retreat from the world and be by ourselves. And the bedroom is the most popular place for making love.

Above all, the room should express tranquillity. The economy, simplicity, and understatement of the traditional Japanese bedroom evokes this atmosphere perfectly. The natural materials have soft textures and subdued colours: wood and bamboo, plain plaster, shoji paper, and pale green tatami mats all create that soothing atmosphere that is conducive to peace of mind and physical relaxation. An awareness of our spiritual needs, our bonds with nature, and the passing seasons are expressed and symbolized in the traditional alcove, or *toko-noma*, with its rustic pillar and changing display of wall scroll, objects of beauty, and ikebana flower arrangement. Reflected and indirect natural light creates a soft and subtle illumination; you could further diffuse the light with net curtains, blinds, or, as here, with translucent shoji screens. The shoji floor lamp adds gentle artificial illumination.

Peace and quiet are essential. Double glazing the windows and double doors or a small enclosed entrance lobby may be necessary to shut out the sounds of the city; noisy apartments can often be improved by soundproofing the walls and ceilings. But for complete relaxation, the sound of softly falling rain and the wind in the trees is ideal.

Western bedrooms are often too dry, warm, and stuffy. The ideal temperature is 13–15°C (55–60°F), slightly higher for children and the elderly, with adequate humidity and fresh, clean air for good ventilation and easy breathing. But avoid creating any through draughts; very low temperatures can easily induce hypothermia in the vulnerable. Natural and untreated, nontoxic materials and fabrics breathe and will help to regulate the room climate.

The apparent simplicity of a Japanese-style bedroom is the result of detailed attention given to the individual features that all together create a perfect space for relaxation and meditation.

The alcove, a miniature replica of nature with its rustic post, small boulder, and plant, serves as the focal point for meditation. During the day, the bed can be moved or folded and the cotton futon rolled up and stored behind the sliding doors. That will then leave sufficient clear floor space for practising meditation, yoga exercises, or massage on the symmetrically arranged tatami mats of springy rice straw.

Lighting is subdued: shoji screens of mulberry paper on sliding glass doors diffuse the natural light, which diminishes toward the back of the room. The screens can be raised to permit low-level views of the garden, and outside shutters can be closed to shut out the glare and heat of the noonday sun. Artificial light from the floor lamp is also softened by a shoji paper shade; the light in the alcove is concealed. Large, loose-filled floor cushions provide seating or reclining supports around a low wooden reading table with ornamental inlay.

Sleeping space options

In our modern Western culture, sleeping is a private activity, the bedroom a retreat. But in those cultures that have stronger ties with their past, people often sleep in groups. The comfort, warmth, security, and companionship that this offers seem to them more natural and beneficial than sleeping alone. The architect Christopher Alexander acknowledges that while adults in Western societies do need bedrooms of their own, the isolation of a small child in a private room can be incompatible with healthy development. Children, he suggests, might prefer a bed cluster arrangement similar to the raised bed alcoves of many ethnic cultures.

But as children grow into their teens, they will usually want their own space as an expression of their growing sense of independence and maturity. The teenage years are often a period of rejection of family lifestyle and habits; the need to express such rebellion can cause violent conflicts unless provision can be made for some kind of private refuge. The bedroom usually fulfils this role and it is essential that individual design ideas and creativity are given the opportunity to flourish there. Even better than a bedroom, and more exciting, would be a quite separate part of the house – an attic, perhaps, or a basement or garage. Such spaces effectively grow into multipurpose rooms: living/sleeping/study/ entertaining all rolled into one.

It requires some ingenuity to squeeze so many functions into a small space, but the bed could be raised on a platform, for example, leaving floor space for a worktop, storage area, or den. It could also be folded away in a cupboard, or be exchanged for a sofa-bed or a roll-up futon. The noise from stereos and TVs can be reduced with sound-proofing, beginning with the windows. You can also soundproof the door, or it may be possible to fit another door on the inside of the frame or even to build a lobby with space for coats, shoes, and sports gear. Absorbent wall finishes, curtains, and fur-nishings in natural materials also lower noise levels.

Young people experiment, quickly exchanging one fashion for another, so the layout of their rooms should be flexible and adaptable. Furniture that can be moved or folded out of the way is best, while decoration is less important than walls lined with cork or pinboards for posters and other parapher-nalia. Recycled old furniture can be adapted for a variety of purposes and then painted or stained. It is often a better option than buying new items. But you should spend money on a firm bed that ensures good posture (see p. 197), and on bedding of natural materials. Flooring should be hardwearing – ideally plain timber boards, untreated cork, or linoleum, covered with scatter rugs and cushions to create a warm, informal atmosphere.

"Place the children's beds in alcoves or small alcove-like rooms, around a common playspace. Make each alcove large enough to contain a table, or chair, or shelves – at least some floor area where each child has his own things. Give the alcoves curtains looking onto the common space, but not walls or doors which will tend once more to isolate the beds too greatly." (Christopher Alexander, et al, A Pattern Language)

Reducing the health hazards

Geopathic stress

The site where your home is built may be affected by positive or negative ground energies (see p. 50). Places "disturbed" by negative energies can be disruptive to sleep and where these are particularly strong they may contribute to serious illnesses. Typical symptoms are: unwillingness to go to bed, cold and cramps during the night, and general exhaustion and depression. Children are especially sensitive and try to avoid such forces by sleeping at the end of, or across the corner of, the bed. The worst locations are where Curry or Hartmann Grids cross at an underground fault or a watercourse, known as a "black stream".

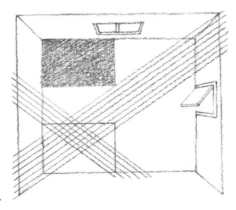

Action

Many people begin to suspect they have a problem only when they suffer from continuous poor sleep or when they fall ill for no apparent reason yet improve rapidly away from home. Moving the bed to a different part of the room or to another room altogether often alleviates the problem. In Germany, professional dowsers are employed to check if beds are located over geopathic zones and particularly if they are "cancer beds". Use an insulating blanket beneath the bed or special electronic devices to neutralize the zone. The traditional remedy was a copper or iron rod driven into the offending zone.

Electromagnetic radiation

The link between close proximity to overhead power-transmission lines and the incidence of leukemia and cancer is gaining official recognition. The risk is increased if you sleep close to such danger areas, and children are the most susceptible. In the home, the bedroom itself can be a source of radiation from electric wiring, alarm clocks, radios, bedside lights, and power sockets. Iron and steel in bedframes, sprung mattresses, beams, radiators, and plumbing equipment can become magnetic and distort the natural magnetic field of the Earth (see pp. 80-1). Electrostress is not fully understood but it may disturb sleep and the rejuvenating processes.

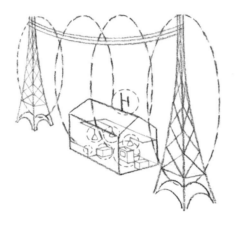

Action

Make sure that the bedroom is well away from high-voltage external cables. You can check magnetism by running a good compass slowly over the mattress – if it deflects from north, the springs or mattress are most likely magnetic. Check all metal objects. Move the bed away from magnetic sources and replace the mattress, frame, and bedding with a wooden base and a natural-fibre-filled mattress. Align yourself with the Earth's magnetic field by sleeping in a north-south direction. At night, switch off the electric current in the bedroom via a "demand switch" and choose shielded cables for new wiring. Use battery-operated radios and alarm clocks and avoid electric blankets.

Allergies and toxins

The last place you would expect to be bombarded with toxins and chemicals is in your own bed. But synthetics have come to dominate the bedroom as they do most other rooms. Polyurethane foam pillows and mattresses, polyester-filled quilts and duvets, "non-iron" sheets containing formaldehyde (which never washes out completely), synthetic wall-to-wall carpets, and particle-board furniture and built-in units all emit chemical vapours that pollute the bedroom. Petrochemical-based paints and vinyl wallpapers add to the chemical load, as well as sealing surfaces and preventing vapours escaping. When breathed in every night, they pose serious health hazards and often produce such allergy reactions as breathing difficulties, itchy eyes and skin, headaches, irritability, and tiredness. Dust, mites, and certain natural fibres, especially wool and feathers, also act as allergy triggers in some people. As well, polyurethane foam is a serious fire risk.

Action

Replace all synthetic materials with non-allergenic natural fibres and fabrics. Use 100% pure, untreated cotton or linen sheets and pillow cases; cotton flannel needs no ironing and is usually untreated. Sleep on natural-fibre-filled or nonmagnetic spring mattresses covered with natural fabrics. Latex foam is also non-allergenic as well as hygienic; but for sheer luxury, use a tufted lambs' wool underblanket. Cellular wool blankets and down duvets are light, warm, and comfortable.

Creating sleeping spaces

Tatami mats, a futon, and a few carefully selected items of furniture and ornaments, show how the main ingredients of a traditional Japanese interior can be introduced to bring a sense of peace into a modern bedroom (right).

The all-timber Swedish home (far right) is bright and sunny and filled with plants. Furniture and fabrics, including the bed in the sleeping loft, are all made of natural "breathing" materials – everything, for a healthy, living room climate.

Low platforms are used for sitting and sleeping in this bedroom in southern France (below). Thick stone walls and heavy wooden shutters absorb sound and protect the interior from strong sun, and create a comfortable sleeping space.

The nursery

A new baby brings excitement to the family. Long before the expected arrival, elaborate preparations of the nursery begin. At the very least it is cleaned thoroughly, but often it is redecorated and refurnished as well. New carpet, curtains, cot, bedding, clothes, and toys may be bought to welcome the baby. But, ironically, far from turning the nursery into a healthy place, these preparations may be harmful. Synthetic fibres and plastics with unknown deodorizing chemicals and dyes are not compatible with a new-born's skin. Fresh paint fumes blend with vapours from synthetic bedding, carpets, and cleaners to create chemical smog.

Babies and small children are more vulnerable than adults to the effects of a toxic environment. Because of their size and their faster respiratory and metabolic rates, babies ingest more pollutants from air, food, and water, and the build-up in the body is more concentrated. And since many pollutants are heavier than air, they tend to collect at lower levels, just where babies and youngsters breathe. Paints should be lead free, preferably water-based or quick-drying acrylics. Check that furniture, toys, and clothes meet national safety standards and avoid any made from plastic and metal. Fit safety covers over all electrical sockets or have them repositioned high on the walls. Avoid any possible dangers from electrical radiation and other hazards (see p. 201). The cot should be sturdy, with no sharp edges, and preferably made of unpainted wood. Spacing of the side bars should not exceed 37-50mm (1.5-2in), and the drop side should be fitted with a locking device. Choose 100 per cent natural fibres and fabrics for the mattress and bedding – cotton flannelette and terry sheets and cotton cellular blankets are light and warm, but wash them before their first use. Don't use plastic undersheets; rubber with a cotton terry facing or a washable cotton mattress is better.

Colours, patterns, and textures are important for a child's visual and tactile development, but boldly patterned wallpapers and fabrics soon pall, while a neutral background can be livened up with mobiles and pinboards of simple drawings and pictures. Fit thermostats to radiators to ensure an even temperature. Washable floors of wood or untreated linoleum or cork, with cheerful rugs, are preferable to carpets.

In this loft nursery, walls and ceiling are finished in water-based paint, beams and timbers are painted with natural resin stain, and washable rugs and dhurries cover the cork or lino floor. Natural daylight is increased by a rooflight above the casement windows. Safety measures include detachable bars fitted to the double-glazed windows, a radiator guard, and a gate at the top of the stairs. A "demand switch" cuts off electricity at night. The wooden cot, finished with beeswax, has an adjustable mattress base and a drop side with safety lock. The wooden chest has a padded top and a rollguard for nappy changing, with herbal oils, creams, and powders. A low-legged chair or rocker is ideal for nursing. The bedding consists of 100% untreated cotton flannelette sheets and cellular cotton blankets. No pillow is included because of the risk of smothering.

Chapter Seven
KITCHEN SPACES

The kitchen is the heart of the house, the centre of consumption, the hub of daily life. It is the place where family and friends gather to eat, drink, and chat, share their joys, or solve their problems. It is the base of all domestic operations and the one place where we can "act locally", and play an active part in protecting the health of ourselves and that of the wider environment.

The kitchen of childhood dreams is a place full of appetizing and tantalizing smells, a farmhouse kitchen, perhaps, hung with polished copper pots and pans and warmed by a glowing fire. However, behind that dream lay the reality for the housewife of long hours of tiring work stoking fires, heating water, hand-washing and ironing, scrubbing and polishing, and cooking.

The modern kitchen evolved largely from a desire to eliminate the worst of the laborious and time-consuming chores and to create an easier, safe, and hygienic environment. It soon took us far beyond the basic improvements and became a status symbol. Streamlined and super-efficient, every wall crammed with designer fitted units and a profusion of handy gadgets for every imaginable task, the kitchen had become no more than a fast processor of overpackaged supermarket goods and overpriced convenience foods, and a depository for electrical appliances. As fashion changed, the former country style returned and the strident, white laminated surfaces have now been replaced with softer, more rustic façades. But behind these carefully contrived nostalgic exteriors, the modern kitchen is still unhealthy and overconsuming; it is sometimes dangerous and it is always polluting.

The modern kitchen is wasteful of energy and water and fails to recycle valuable waste materials. The continuing problems of condensation, fumes, and gases from stoves and cookers still make the air unhealthy. Worse still are the new dangers from the chemical kitchen – formaldehyde in particle board units, toxic vapours from adhesives and paints, and offgassing from plastics and synthetic materials. Food stored, prepared, and consumed in a chemical atmosphere may absorb the harmful substances and itself become polluted. Hazardous detergents and strong, non-biodegradable chemicals pollute the waste water from washing machines and dish-washers and this in turn pollutes the environment. But most wasteful and most damaging are the mountains of throwaway cans, bottles, plastic packaging, paper, card, and food garbage.

More and more people are changing to a healthier lifestyle and becoming increasingly aware of their responsibilities for the environment. What we need now is a new type of kitchen, a new focus for our daily life that is not intended for surface show but stands for the sounder principles of personal health and universal ecology. A kitchen where we can enjoy the pleasures of healthy food without it costing, literally, the earth.

". . . at once they found themselves in all the glow of a large fire-lit kitchen. The floor was well-worn red brick, and on the wide hearth burnt a fire of logs . . . Rows of spotless plates winked from the shelves of the dresser at the far end of the room, and from the rafters overhead hung hams, bundles of dried herbs, nets of onions, and baskets of eggs." Badger's kitchen, in The Wind in the Willows *by Kenneth Grahame.*

A kitchen doesn't have to be clinical – lined with plastic laminate surfaces and mass-produced units all made of composite board. It can be, like the kitchen in this Swedish timber house (right), a comfortable and mellow living room. Built of solid wood, the worktops and cupboards blend in well; the cornflower blue complimenting the warm-toned wood.

The food chain

At its most basic, the kitchen is the engine room that drives the long food processing chain. This stretches from the farmlands and oceans that produce our food to the landfills, rivers, and seas that take the eventual wastes and rubbish. But the chain does not start with the food growers and processors – it starts with *you*. For it is what each individual consumer decides to buy that ultimately determines the produce – and the price – from the growers and the food industry. The purse is very influential and we, as consumers, have both power and responsibility for making choices. Hard on the heels of the outcry over additives and artificial colouring in processed foods, we now have mounting concern over the dangers inherent in our most basic foodstuffs: salmonella in eggs and poultry, listeria in milk and soft cheeses, hormones in meat, heavy metals in fish, pesticide residues in fruit and vegetables, and pollutants in our drinking water. We daily become more and more conscious that something is going very wrong and that something must be done, and we are willing to try alternatives as long as we are given proper information and can find the safe, clean foods.

Food has one advantage over many other consumer goods: we can produce, process, and dispose of much of it ourselves. As home producers of at least some of our food we begin to be more self-reliant and can break a link in the chain that binds us to the whole producer/consumer complex. If you don't have a garden, you can still grow some vegetables and fruit, perhaps on a balcony or even a wide window sill. Growing, harvesting, and eating your own food can be a powerful stimulus for a change in attitudes and lifestyle. Once you start growing, or buying, food produced by healthy and conserving methods, you may want to apply the same principles when you store, prepare, cook, and eat the food, and when you clear up and dispose of the waste. The process can then become wholistic, with each stage relying on the others, and change from being one geared to wastefulness to one concerned with health and sustainability.

While you may not be willing or able to change all the kitchen functions at once, a few simple and gradual alterations should be rewarding enough for you to want to experiment further. Start, for example, by growing some fruit and vegetables. Then you might want to try your hand at making preserves, jams, and pickles, or bottling fruit and making home-made wines and beers. Herbs are easy to grow and make a wonderful difference when used fresh in your cooking. And for the health of the environment, you can compost organic waste, fit low-flow taps, avoid plastic packaging, and sort bottles, aluminium cans, and paper for recycling. Although the activities mentioned here are small in themselves, each contributes to a healthier and more sustainable lifestyle by helping to safeguard the environment. You can start anywhere, as long as you make a start – today.

Kitchen layout

Changes to your cooking and eating habits affect the design, function, and layout of the kitchen. A natural kitchen differs from the conventional type in needing more space for fresh, home-grown produce, for storage, as well as for preparation. Large, deep cupboards or, preferably, a walk-in larder or pantry provide ample space for preserved and bottled produce and for bulk supplies of dry goods. Herbs and salad crops grown on window sills need plenty of sun and good daylight. In the natural kitchen, worktop space is more generous and is designed as work centres of different heights and surfaces, with tools to suit various purposes ready to hand. Kitchenware and tools are practical rather than gimmicky, and there is less dependence on mechanical preparation.

Separate recycling bins in or adjacent to the kitchen assist presorting and assignment of waste to the compost heap. All equipment, furnishings, and materials are healthy and nontoxic, and water and energy systems are designed to be conserving. The natural kitchen is, in reality, a new expression of the older, family-style kitchen. It can be fun to adapt to a natural kitchen, even if it requires a little thought and effort at the start. Planning it involves the whole family, and the ideas may be taken up by friends and neighbours. The kitchen is a source of strength and inspiration, often the first place where people begin the changes that will transform their homes and their lifestyles.

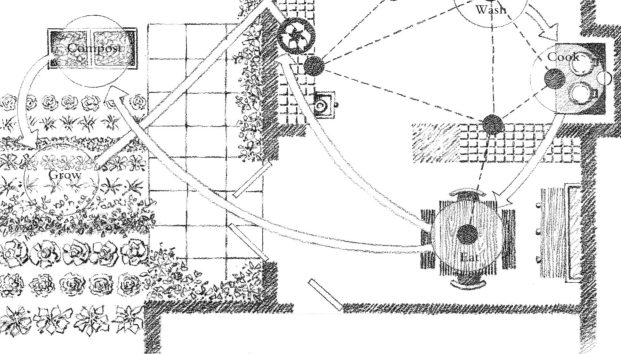

The new kitchen

The new natural kitchen is a healthy and conserving processor at every stage. Unlike the ordinary kitchen with its "open" system of high consumption and throw-away waste, the natural kitchen is designed as a "closed" system, conserving water and energy, recycling all packaging, and linking organic waste to compost and new growth in the garden. It has storage and work centres designed for home-grown and organic produce, and more basic tools and equipment for cleaning, preparation, and cooking.

Work centres

The main activities of storing, preparing, cleaning, and cooking need separate work centres. These should be close to each other, though, to reduce unnecessary walking. Heights, surfaces, and tools are designed for specific purposes, such as a large double sink for washing vegetables, a marble slab for pastry making, a chopping block, and a generous-sized table for social and family gatherings.

Out

Buy

Store

Compost

Grow

Wash

Cook

Eat

○ Main processes

● Work centres

⊛ Recycling bins for
    paper, glass, metal, plastic

Food

To ensure that food is as healthy and wholesome as possible, both home-grown produce and that bought in stores should be organically grown. A combination of raw and least-cook dishes ensures a diet rich in nutrients and fibre, and vegetarian and low-meat dishes reduce the intake of saturated fat. Freshly grown herbs add flavour and help to reduce the need for salt as a seasoning.

Recycling

All waste is presorted for recycling, first into separate kitchen bins and secondly into larger, outside bins for collection or delivery to recycling centres. Organic waste is consigned to the garden compost bins where it breaks down into humus that is used as manure and organic fertilizer for the garden and for indoor growing spaces.

The vernacular kitchen

An original wood-burning stove and "Kamin" range is the centerpiece of this spacious family kitchen (above). The stove is still used for back-up heating and occasional cooking, but the modern oven and hob is more efficient for everyday use.

Even a compact galley on a houseboat (left) can have all the basic ingredients of a working kitchen. And attention to detail also makes this a pleasant place in which to work.

An archetypal French provençale farm-house kitchen (right), has been built in a former stable. Its sturdy open-beamed ceiling was conserved and simply sanded smooth. The handmade tiles are the work of François Vernin.

Storage and preparation

When you change from processed to fresh and whole foods you will need less room for packaged, canned, and frozen produce, but at the same time more space for fresh leaf and root vegetables, fruit, dry staples, such as pulses, rice, pasta, dried fruit, and home preserves. Modern kitchens are rarely designed for storing bulky items and hardly ever have access to the old, efficient larder or pantry, or to a cellar or basement. A healthier diet, with raw or lightly cooked vegetables and less meat, will cut down on cooking but requires more varied preparation space. You will also need extra bins for sorting waste for recycling and composting.

A simpler lifestyle requires fewer gadgets and less equipment, necessitating fewer built-in cupboards. Ideally, you will have a larder, but if this is not possible, you will need a food cupboard sited against a cool external wall with several vents to the outside. Built-in cabinets are not essential and many functional and attractive kitchens have freestanding furniture – corner cabinets, worktops and benches, dressers, floor cabinets, and tables and chairs. They are made from solid, durable, and natural wood and are far healthier than the ubiquitous formaldehyde-impregnated particle board units covered with plastic laminate. The recent trend toward the "unfitted" kitchen is an indication of people's desire for rooms that are also warm, practical, and comfortable living areas rather than streamlined, uncomfortable, food-processing centres.

Since you will be spending less money on food, you can afford better quality, as well as kitchenware that is well designed, functional, and looks attractive when displayed by the work centres and preparation areas, rather than hidden away in cabinets and drawers until needed.

You must store perishable foods correctly, probably in a combined refrigerator/freezer. And you must keep dairy produce, meat, fish, and poultry at a constant low temperature, or buy it fresh and cook it on the day of purchase. In cold climates, a food safe built against an outside wall is likely to be at a safe low temperature; in temperate regions, you can store milk and butter in containers of water covered with porous clay pots or wet muslin and allow the process of evaporation to keep the produce cool.

The old-fashioned larder has largely been replaced by the refrigerator and freezer. But this large, walk-in pantry is ideal for storing bulky items, dry goods, fresh vegetables and fruit, preserves, wines, beer, and soft drinks. Best sited on the cool side of the house, it should be dry and well ventilated, ideally through a window with a fixed vent as well as air vents in the other walls, all covered with fine, fly-proof wire mesh. Healthy, natural materials, such as marble or solid wood shelves, quarry tile floor, and water-based paints, ensure that the larder is both practicable and hygienic.

Preparation

The campaign for labour-saving and efficient kitchens has not necessarily freed women from the drudgery and isolation of housework – that needs a change in attitudes. And, although modern equipment has eased certain chores, shopping, cooking, and cleaning for a household, even a small one, still take time and effort. In reality, many of the gadgets and equipment on the market have much more to do with advertising and the manufacturers' desire for continuing profitability than with actual needs and demands of the consumers. In addition, these labour-saving products are not always in the best interest of ourselves or the planet. In terms of the environment, labour saving usually means that energy-intensive processes are involved; packaged convenience foods that are quick to cook and serve have consumed a vast amount of energy during their preparation – the end-product of a series of steps, including processing, packaging, storage, and transportation. Also, convenience foods are less nutritious than fresh types and their preparation removes us from the world of real food. Handling fresh ingredients is a pleasure and can be as much part of the stimulating process as eating the finished meal. Rather than a chore, food preparation can be regarded as a relaxing and sensual activity that brings out and highlights your creativity and appreciation of colour, texture, smell, and taste. For a dedicated cook, these are the permanent inspirations and values of even the simplest meal.

Work surfaces

A good cook will insist on an efficient kitchen that saves unnecessary work. Careful planning must go into the kitchen layout. The most satisfactory plan often links, in a triangular path, the three basic elements – cooker, sink, and food storage – to the preparation centres. They should be located in a compact sequence and not too far apart in order to save unnecessary movements. But personal preferences and styles and methods of working are also important, and you may want to have cookware and utensils within easy reach, as well as such ingredients as oils and condiments. If you spend much time cooking and baking, you may decide to have mini work centres conveniently located around the kitchen for such activities as chopping vegetables, mixing ingredients, baking, and other space-demanding tasks, such as bottling and making preserves, beer, and wines.

Work surfaces in an L- or U-shape arrangement are good options, although unfitted kitchens can have tables and workbenches instead. Preparation often involves much standing and, in order to avoid poor posture and backache, the work surfaces should be designed to suit the activity and the person who is going to do most of the work. You may have to allow for the heights of several different people. Waist-high surfaces are generally the best; standard units with a height of 85-90cm (34-36in) can be adjusted by mounting them on plinths of various heights. Make sure there is ample foot room at the plinths so that you can adopt a comfortable stance with one foot in front of the other. Wooden platforms can be used at surfaces that are too high, and thick chopping boards on top of surfaces that are too low. Heavy tasks, such as kneading dough, rolling pastry, and chopping root vegetables, are easier on surfaces that are below waist height so that you can put your weight behind the activity. You can make prolonged standing easier by wearing soft-soled shoes with arch supports, or by installing cushioned floors or mats. Sit down to as many tasks as possible and include in the kitchen plan several sitting spaces at the counter or work surfaces as well as at the table.

All work surfaces should be generous in width – 65-70cm (26-28in) – to allow plenty of space for food preparation and room, too, for plumbing and cables behind the worktops. There are practical and sounder alternatives to plastic laminates for the surface covering, and you can choose different types to suit different tasks: ceramic and quarry tiles, solid wood (such as maple), and, for real durability, stainless steel, slate, granite, or terrazzo. Or you can have insets of marble or wooden slabs.

A double sink is a must so that dish washing can be kept separate from food preparation. Invest in good-quality knives, pots, and pans, and avoid nonstick and aluminium cookware. Electrical time savers, such as liquidizers, food processors, and mixers are a matter of personal choice.

The natural kitchen

The kitchen should, ideally, be a warm and friendly place, somewhere full of activity, busy, and comfortable so that family or friends will naturally gravitate there to chat or eat or even to read or work. For some, the traditional farmhouse kitchen with its central table is the ideal; while others prefer a clear and uncluttered space in which to prepare and cook food and a separate area for eating and relaxing. With young children, you will need a corner out of harm's way but where you can keep an eye on them; you will also want a clear view of any outdoor play area.

Since food is handled in the kitchen, it, more than any other space, must be toxin and pollution free. Hygiene is obviously important, but there is no point using products that leave surfaces with a "sparkling clean" shine disguising a residual slick of harmful chemicals. Many safe, natural alternatives are available (see pp. 266–7). Ventilate the kitchen and food storage areas, fit an extractor hood over the cooker, and consider a heat–exchange system (see pp. 82–3). Filter tap water at the supply or in a filter jug, and avoid plastic containers for food storage. Use natural materials for flooring, cabinets, and surfaces and decorate with natural paints. Make sure work surfaces are brightly lit and make maximum use of daylight.

Every culture has a different appreciation of food and different rules for preparing, cooking, and serving it, but all cultures require a rapport with the kitchen and with the ingredients. The sight of fresh food, herbs, and the culinary tools in daily use creates an emotional reassurance that is as important as the physical elements of the kitchen. Healthy diets that contain plenty of fresh fruit, vegetables, and salads, as well as pulses and grains bring more colour into the kitchen and determine the layout and arrangement of work spaces. The traditional larder extends the possibilities for preparing and storing home-grown food and preserves (see p. 212), and you can feast your eyes on pots of fresh herbs and sprouting seeds on the window sill and even grow salads and vegetables in a greenhouse window. Don't hide gleaming pots and pans and handsome tools away in cupboards: hang them around the kitchen along with strings of onions and garlic and bunches of dried herbs.

The natural kitchen is a family room with a separate but not isolated cooking area. As well as storage, preparation, cooking, and cleaning centres, there are deep drawers with large bins for recycling paper, plastic, metal, glass, and organic matter for composting. A large, walk-in larder for bulky items is supplemented with a small refrigerator/freezer for perishables. The wooden units, furniture, and dresser are polished with beeswax, and the worktops are clay tile set in mortar, with an inset wooden chopping block and a marble slab for pastry making. The large central rooflight increases illumination, while bright artificial light is directed on to work surfaces and low-level light on to the kitchen table. Full-spectrum and low-voltage halogen lights are used throughout. An extractor hood is fitted over the cooker. A filter water jug removes some pollutants (even better, use a full filtration system – see p. 91).

Health and conservation

How should you cook in a healthy and conserving way and yet still be able to enjoy the results of your efforts? Consider in the first place whether the food, in fact, needs to be cooked for lengthy periods of time. A healthy diet depends to a large degree on foods that are as near to their natural state as possible, thus retaining their vitamin content and nutritional value.

Vegetables should be absolutely fresh, preferably young, and they should be prepared with the minimum of wastage. Fresh raw vegetables and fruit are highly nutritious and retain most of the minerals, vitamins, trace elements, and fibre often destroyed by cooking. They are also good for the teeth and digestion. You can eat the overwhelming majority of vegetables raw, after thorough preparation, which includes washing them thoroughly to remove any trace of possible pesticide residues. You should peel some vegetables, including commercially grown carrots, for the same reason. Raw root vegetables, potatoes apart, are excellent grated and have better, more distinct flavours than when cooked. Leaf and stem vegetables should always be perfectly fresh whether you intend to eat them raw or cook them, since the vitamin and mineral contents decline rapidly once they are harvested.

With such an endless variety of ingredients available there really is no reason for us not to eat a fresh salad every day. Apart from the poor, overworked lettuce, you can use young dandelion leaves, spinach, coriander leaves, wild sorrel, and nasturtium. You can also include raw beans and peas, cauliflower florets, beansprouts, grains, raisins, nuts, and fruit. These are the true "convenience foods" for they are easy to prepare, healthy, and full of flavour.

However, many foods must be cooked to be safe for consumption and for preservation, especially in hot climates where food can spoil very quickly and in regions where food poisoning is a problem. In colder climates, too, food hygiene is vitally important and many foods are improved in the cooking. A skilled cook should be familiar with all the basic cooking techniques, from boiling, poaching, and steaming to grilling, frying, braising, roasting, and baking. But to be a conserving cook, you must also have knowledge of the most efficient cooking methods and how you can save energy.

Energy-saving measures

○ Always use a saucepan wider than the hob ring and cover the pan with a lid.
○ Don't boil more water than needed at a time or overfill kettles and pans.
○ On electric rings, use saucepans with flat and thick bases. Use double or stacking saucepans on one hob ring, or steam a quick-cooking leaf vegetable above a pan of boiling potatoes.
○ Replace old stoves. Modern cookers are more energy efficient and will save about 10% of fuel; fan-assisted ovens save another 10%.
○ Get maximum efficiency from the oven by using all shelf space. Cook a whole meal or several dishes simultaneously. Choose ovens with glass doors and timers so that you observe progress without opening the door.
○ Cook vegetables in minimum water, just enough to prevent them from sticking to the base.

○ Include least-cook dishes in the diet. Many cuisines, including the Chinese, are traditionally based on least-cooked and stir-fried dishes. Alternatively, try recipes for lightly poached, steamed, or grilled food.
○ Use a pressure cooker, one of the most economical cooking utensils ever invented. It is safe and easy to use, and retains most of the nutrients. Whole meals can be cooked at the same time and cooking time is reduced to a fraction of conventional cooking. The quality and flavour of pressure-cooked food are superior to that produced in a microwave oven. Large model pressure cookers are being installed in domestic kitchens in some countries.
○ Choose energy-efficient cookers and stoves, such as the legendary Aga. Created in the 1930s by Dr Gustaf Dalen, a renowned Swedish physicist and Nobel Prize winner, the Aga uses heat storage combined with a small heat source to bring cooking rings to simmering or boiling point and to heat 2-4 large ovens. Heat is retained by insulation around the ovens and on the hot plates; it is precisely controlled and always instantly available, using the minimum of fuel. Agas can be fuelled by gas, oil, solid fuels, or electricity, and can also provide hot water and central heating. Although more expensive than conventional cookers, Agas are high-quality products, lasting a lifetime with care and will repay the investment over the years with economy and high performance.
○ Try a hay box. Foods, such as stews and casseroles, pasta and vegetable dishes, rice and puddings, are brought to boiling point, then packed in their cooking pots into a thickly insulated hay box (or thermal cooker) where it continues to cook for hours or overnight.

Waste and disposal

The kitchen is the prime generator of waste in the home. Throw-away packaging is the worst offender, yet we have become so accustomed to this aspect of life that we hardly notice it, let alone feel guilty about it. Interestingly, though, consumer surveys show that there is now steady and growing public concern, and in the UK a surprising 90 per cent of householders interviewed said they would be prepared to sort their rubbish and co-operate with local councils in recycling schemes. In some countries, this type of responsible attitude already carries the weight of law and recycling schemes are established facts of normal life.

Next time you do the week's shopping, count the number of cans, bottles, plastic containers, plastic food trays with clingfilm, and cardboard cereal packets. Then, at home, see how much you throw away. The first to go will probably be the plastic packaging around the fruit and vegetables (which makes them sweat and decay). During the week, the kitchen bin will keep rapidly filling up with all the rest – cans, bottles, paper, plastics, and toxic chemicals all mixed together with food scraps and vegetable waste. Finally, you will probably make matters even worse by confining all this in plastic bin liners.

But this final action for you is only the beginning of the global waste disposal and pollution problem. The damage has already been done by mixing everything up, rendering the individual materials worthless. The only thing left to do is to dump them on the land or out at sea, or perhaps burn them in order to recoup some useful energy in the form of heat or electricity.

But you don't have to continue to support this senseless waste. You can decide right now to reduce the problem, and help yourself and the environment at the same time. The biggest obstacle you are likely to encounter is the slowness of the public refuse agencies, manufacturers, and stores to respond to changing consumer attitudes. In West Germany and Denmark, city authorities have introduced radical waste collection systems that supply houses with separate bins for sorted wastes. Heavy bonuses for sorted rubbish encourage everyone to co-operate with the scheme. But even without this degree of official encouragement, you can still do a lot for yourself (see below).

Reducing waste

○ The cardinal rule is to stop buying overpackaged goods and bringing waste into the home in the first place. "Don't choose what you can't reuse".
○ Grow more of your own vegetables and fruit or buy them fresh rather than frozen or prepacked in cans and bottles. Buy them loose and avoid plastic wrapping and bags.
○ Buy fresh fish, meat, and poultry, and also dried goods such as pulses, rice, and pasta. Avoid processed or convenience foods – they have more packaging.
○ Buy fresh cuts of cheese and cold meats at delicatessen counters or stores rather than pre-wrapped in plastic film.

○ Buy glass rather than plastic bottles. Buy returnable bottles if possible. Have milk delivered (in the UK and Australia) in returnable bottles rather than cartons.
○ Stop buying toxic oven and drain cleaners, bleach, ammonia-based products, disinfectants, detergents, washing-up liquids, and aerosols. Buy environment-friendly products (see pp. 266-7).
○ If you cannot avoid packaged goods, look for those packed in cardboard, cellophane, or paper, which are all biodegradable or can be recycled.
○ Buy cans made of a single metal only to permit recycling.

○ Sort your rubbish into separate bins: one for paper and card; one for plastics; one for glass; one for metals; and one for organic waste for composting. Reuse or recycle everything you possibly can (see pp. 268-9).
○ Don't dump old equipment, large or small. Trade it in on a new product or take it to a scrap dealer.
○ Compost all kitchen vegetable and organic wastes. These can also be a useful part of the compost in a waterless toilet (see p. 228). Don't use sink garbage disposal units.
○ Don't empty medicines, chemicals, paints, or other toxins down sinks or toilets. Always dispose of them safely.

Creating kitchen spaces

A tile oven and pine wood dresser are attractive as well as very traditional and practical features of a German kitchen (above left).

Well-designed, professional cookware and utensils are both functional and appealing to the eye (left), and it is a pity to hide them away in cupboards and drawers. Instead of this, why not display them openly and have them ready to hand whenever they are needed?

A large, built-in pressure cooker oven (right), makes a practical fast-cooking alternative to the ubiquitous microwave. And there are none of the health worries associated with radiation leakage.

The simple kitchen in a new American home (left), is not an isolated room – it is part of the living space. The wood burning stove provides extra heat and a comforting glow to keep the space warm on cold and snowy winter days. Architect: Turner Brooks

Fresh courgettes, tomatoes, and herbs grow in this passive solar greenhouse attached to the kitchen of the Cooley House, Connecticut (below). Double-skin roof panels admit light yet insulate and prevent overheating. Design: Solsearch

Kitchen hazards

Health hazards

Formaldehyde Particle board and ply-wood used in wall and floor units give off vapour, especially when new and in hot and humid conditions.
Action Build all cabinets of solid wood or low-emission boards. Seal new particle board surfaces with nontoxic paint or varnish (see pp. 264-5). Ventilate the kitchen area.

Combustion byproducts Gas, coal, and wood-burning cookers produce carbon monoxide, nitrogen dioxide, cooking odours, and other pollutants.
Action Fit an extractor fan and hood over the cooker. Open the window when cooking. Use an electric cooker or a gas cooker without a pilot light. Regularly maintain equipment.

Food storage Clingfilm may contain the plasticizer DEHA, which, when warm can be absorbed by foods. Soft plastic containers may also offgas. Insecticides and fungicides in paint, wallpaper, and flypapers can be absorbed. Paper products may have been bleached and contain dioxin. Mould and bacteria found in porous surfaces and cracks can contaminate food. Food not stored at a low enough temperature can lead to bacterial growth. Uncovered food may be contaminated by insect pests. Raw food coming into contact with cooked food is a health hazard, as is thawed and refrozen food. Pesticide residues, hormones, and preservatives pollute many of our foods.
Action Use glass, ceramic, and stainless-steel containers. Use nontoxic paints and paper (avoid tea bags and paper coffee filters). Use herbal insect deterrents and metal gauze screens and covers to exclude them. Seal surface cracks. Keep surfaces clean and dry. Store food in a cool, dry larder or cellar; perishable items in a fridge or freezer. Keep cooked and raw food separate; do not refreeze food. Eat organically grown food.

Plastic laminates and toxic adhesives Vapours can arise from adhesive solvents and some laminates will offgas.
Action Use alternative surfaces such as ceramic tile, solid wood, stainless steel, slate, and marble slabs.

Particle board units Plywood, chipboard, blockboard, and other composites usually contain formaldehyde, which can contaminate food.
Action Use solid wood units with traditional joints and timber glues. Metal cabinets are good, too.

PVC tile floors Tiles and toxic adhesives give off vapours.
Action Use sealed timber strip floor, clay quarry tiles, stone, sealed cork, or linoleum.

Cookware Aluminium pots and pans increase the risk of Alzheimer's disease and other neurological disorders. Copper pans, if not cleaned, accumulate toxic verdigris. Nonstick coatings can contaminate food.
Action Use stainless-steel, toughened-glass, cast-iron, lined-copper, enamel, or ovenproof earthenware pots and pans. Don't use abrasives on metal cookware. This may free small metal particles that then enter the food.

Microwave ovens These can leak radiation from a faulty door. Microwaves interfere with the formation of living cells. Safe levels of exposure are still controversial – US regulations limit them to $1mW/cm^2$ in new ovens, $5mW/cm^2$ in existing ones.
Action Have ovens checked and maintained regularly. Use other fast cooking methods, such as pressure cookers.

Cleaners Washing-up and dishwasher liquids, bleach and chlorinated scouring powders, detergents, fabric softeners and whiteners, oven and drain cleaners, and all-purpose cleaners all contain complex toxic chemicals. Many aerosols produce CFCs.

Action Use biodegradable and nontoxic materials and products. Don't use aerosols containing CFCs.

Air and water pollution For health effects and actions, pages 88 and 100.

Home-grown foods In cities, garden soils may be polluted with lead and other chemicals. Lead, in particular, can be absorbed by vegetables as they grow – lettuces, cabbages, and blackberries being the worst affected.
Action Have soil tested for contaminants. If there is a problem you may have to dig out the old soil and replace it with organic topsoil. Grow vegetables under glass or in greenspaces if airborne pollution is a continuing problem.

Accidents The kitchen is where most home accidents occur. Fire and scalds are a risk from frying pans, pots, kettles, and irons. Poisonings are also not uncommon, as is electrocution from faulty equipment and proximity to water. Cuts from sharp knives or cans and falls are the commonest dangers.
Action Keep a first-aid box in the kitchen, and a fire blanket near the cooker. Use a thermostatically controlled deep-fat fryer and the safer types of kettle and iron with cut-out switches. Site the cooker away from doors and busy routes. Keep cleaners locked away from children and knives and glass jars out of reach. Use sliding cupboard doors, particularly at high level, to avoid banging your head. Use steps to reach high shelves, not chairs, but avoid having high shelves if at all possible. Always turn pan handles inward on hobs. Earth all metal objects, such as the sink and cooker, and keep electrical sockets away from water. Never hurry when carrying full pans, knives, or electrical equipment.

Ecological hazards

Water pollution Toxic and non-biodegradable cleaners pollute sink wastewater and increase treatment costs. They also make household greywater recycling impossible. Both old lead and new plastic pipes contaminate water, and sink waste-disposal units add solids to wastewater.
Action Only use nontoxic products. Remove lead pipes and replace with copper and lead-free jointing. Avoid sink waste-disposal units.

Air pollution Aerosols, especially those with CFCs, air fresheners, fly strips, and combustion byproducts from cookers and heaters are all exported from the kitchen and pollute the outdoor air. The refrigerant liquid in refrigerators and freezers contains CFCs.
Action Avoid chemical products and use herbal alternatives instead. Make sure all equipment is regularly serviced and nonpolluting.

Kitchen wastes Common examples include packaging, plastics, cans, bottles, paper, card, and organic wastes, plus toxic chemicals.
Action Avoid packaged goods, use your own containers, bottles and bags, buy goods in refillable or returnable containers, buy durable goods and avoid throwaways, presort wastes, and reuse or recycle. Campaign for local recycling services. Compost organic matter.

Water consumption Dishwashers and automatic clothes washers use a lot of water. You may use about 20% of your domestic water supplies in the kitchen, especially if you do the laundry there too. Hot water uses large amounts of energy (see also pp. 92-3).
Action Fit low-flow taps and handwash dishes in bowls, not under running water. Avoid dishwashers or choose a small, energy-efficient model.
Use full loads in washing machines and choose an efficient, low-water, hot-fill model (for example, one that doesn't heat cold water in the machine), and use economy cycles.

In dry areas you may want to recycle kitchen greywater for the garden, as well as that from the bath, shower, and washbasin (see pp. 94-5). Usually there is too much grease, food particles, and detergent in kitchen wastewater for you to incorporate it.

Energy consumption Cookers, refrigerators, freezers, dishwashers, washing machines, tumble dryers, and other equipment use considerable amounts of energy. So too does the host of gadget-intensive food-preparation activities – mixing, grinding, blending, peeling, juicing – that were once mainly manual tasks. Here also, you can economize without losing the practical advantages of these labour-saving devices.
Action Choose energy-efficient appliances and have them serviced regularly. Use economy settings whenever they are available. Fit heat-recovery devices to extractor fans and wastewater pipes. Consider if you really need all those labour-saving gadgets: some hand work is satisfying, as well as being good for your health.
Dry clothes outdoors or hang them indoors in a well-ventilated space. Put the refrigerator and freezer in a cool place, not next to the cooker. Use least-cook methods.

Planning utility space The modern kitchen can be likened to the engine room of a ship – the power house that keeps the whole vessel moving. But all typical kitchen machinery creates electrical fields, in addition to the other safety hazards and ecological costs. In fact, much kitchen machinery is better located elsewhere.

Refrigerators and freezers These need to be in a cool space for greatest energy conservation – but not in the larder, since the refrigerator produces heat (and possibly CFCs if it is old). In the kitchen they are noisy and again may be polluting the air and food products. The best place would be adjacent to the kitchen in a separate, ventilated, cool space with a heat-recovery unit attached.

Dryers and washing machines Most models have to be located on an outside wall – the dryer for venting and the washing machine for wastewater outflow. It is not hygienic to have a washing machine outflow feeding into a kitchen sink where dishes, and food, may be washed. These machines also give out heat, which could be used to partially heat a drying area or room. Again, these machines are better out of the kitchen (and bathroom) and in a separate, airy space with a heat-recovery and ventilation system.

Dishwashers These create electrical pollution and noise and generate heat. Although they are usually in the kitchen, there is no reason why in the healthy home you should not locate them elsewhere – probably in the same convenient utility area as washing machines.

Cleaning space If possible, locate this area away from the kitchen, too. A utility sink, where nonfood washing and cleaning up, and generally dirty jobs can be done, is necessary. Store brooms, mops, vacuum cleaners, and all cleaning materials in their own utility closet which can be safely secured if there are children about.

Chapter Eight
BATHING SPACES

For affluent Victorians, cleanliness was next to godliness. But ideas of hygiene change, and it is Queen Victoria herself who is credited with the pronouncement that she bathed once a month – whether or not she needed it. This sentiment, accurate or not, does, however, highlight the puritanical 19th-century attitude that bathing was strictly a private and necessary function, a cleansing operation largely devoid of pleasure. In fact, to take pleasure from your bath was regarded as sinful.

In contrast, the ancient Greeks and Romans were great believers in the benefits of the shared bath and mineral spa, for relaxation, socializing, and for the exchange of political ideas and gossip. But the undoubted benefits of the bath were not just for mere mortals: in the bas-relief below, Hera, queen of the Olympian gods, wife and sister of Zeus, steps with due modesty from her bath as her two hand maidens arrange her robe.

The word spa comes to us from the Belgium resort town of that name, which was discovered to have healing mineral waters in the 14th century. Many European countries boasted at least one important spa town, and as late as the 17th century, mixed bathing was common at Bath, a city in England famous for its healing mineral waters and first established as a spa by the Romans in AD44.

Despite the widespread introduction of piped water to the home at the beginning of the 20th century, the Western bathroom remained a closeted and private place. In the East, however, bathing had retained its strong tradition as a social activity where water not only cleansed the body but also refreshed the soul. In Japan, the therapeutic qualities of the numerous natural volcanic springs, combining relaxation with spiritual rejuvenation, have always been regarded as one of life's pleasures – a source of benefit and enjoyment. While public baths and spas may have waned in popularity, the traditions of communal bathing have been maintained in the modern Japanese home.

Influences from California, Scandinavia, and Japan have begun to change the Western attitude to the bath and have reintroduced concepts of pleasure, health, and relaxation. Though health centres are often better equipped to cater in this regard, bathing provisions in the home can still be made far more imaginative and flexible. Many individuals now want the options of home hot tubs, whirlpools, saunas, and spas, but it is essential that such bathroom extras are designed and sited with conservation in mind so that they do not become additional strains on already stretched water provision and energy resources.

Bathing spaces need to be organized so that they cater for relaxation and pleasure, as well as for hygiene. This combination has been achieved in the imaginative and elegant American bathroom, designed by Nelson Denny (right), which is flooded with light from a large semi-circular window. The sunken bath is, though, the focal point in the middle of the bathroom, and is ideal for long, relaxing soaks. And the shower curtain can be drawn around the bath to retain the heat.

Bathing and showering

Bathing space in the home should focus on aspects other than mere hygiene. It should be a soothing and comforting place, offering health, relaxation, and intimacy, as well as cleanliness. The Western tradition of mixing both cleansing and relaxation in the same room and, worse still, in the same tub, is considered by other cultures to be unhygienic and disagreeable, and a change of water for each person is regarded as wasteful.

A variety of modern water therapies can be economically integrated with the simplicity of Japanese bathing styles. Thorough cleansing of the body is the important first step, and this you should do as a separate activity if you are going to soak in a bath or tub. A shower is the best and most water-conserving place for washing. Use a loofah, friction glove, or bathing brush to scrub away dead skin, and rinse thoroughly before entering the bathtub for a hot, relaxing soak.

Water is a symbol of purity; in many cultures and religious faiths it represents the immortality of the soul. It is also therapeutic and soothes the sympathetic nervous system; in hydrotherapy, water is used for treating muscular complaints. Underwater exercises and massage in a whirlpool tank, a swimming pool, or sitz bath help restore weak muscles, relieve arthritic and related pains, and promote healing. Depending on the temperature, water relaxes or stimulates the body, increasing physical health and pleasure. For stimulation, try alternate hot and cold baths; they are beneficial to the nervous system and the brain, and at the same time soothe stiff, tired, and aching muscles. Hot water opens the pores of the skin, increases circulation, and draws out body wastes and toxins. Cold water closes the pores, stimulates the skin, and produces a glorious afterglow. You can increase the stimulating effects of a hot/cold treatment with a sea salt rub or massage or with vigorous scrubbing before immersing yourself in a hot, deep bath for up to 20 minutes followed by a cold plunge. Hot and cold showers use less water and time and have similar effects.

Soaking in warm or hot water is a wonderful way to relax, promoting a deep sense of pleasure that you can share, on occasions, with family and friends. Ideally, the bathtub should be larger than normal and sufficiently deep for the water to cover your shoulders completely, producing a feeling of buoyancy and weightlessness. A hot tub can be the perfect solution and a boon for the elderly or anybody suffering from muscular complaints, but not for those who have high blood pressure or a heart condition (see p. 229). A relaxing bath can become a truly sensuous experience if you add herbal or mineral bathsalts or essential oils. You can elevate the experience to sheer luxury with soft candlelight and pleasant music from a (battery-powered) radio or tape recorder. A warm, soothing bath followed by a brief, cool rinse and vigorous towelling, is ideal before bedtime and produces sound and restful sleep.

The bath
The Western bath has evolved from oval tubs and chair and hip baths. The standard size is about 70 x 170cm (28 x 67in) and 36cm (14in) deep and is designed for lying full length. Due to its large surface area, the water cools fairly quickly. The Eastern soaking baths are shorter, often wider, and much deeper. They come in a range of sizes: 99–137cm (39–54in) long, 74–92cm (29–36in) wide, and 61–81cm (24–32in) deep. They usually have one or two inside seats that act as steps for getting in and out of the water, and often an outside step as well. Since the water is deeper with a smaller surface area, it stays warmer for longer.

The shower
Showers use less water and energy than baths and can be set by thermostat to deliver water at a constant temperature. They can be just as invigorating as baths provided you have good water pressure and the shower head has an adjustable nozzle for soft, needle, and pulsating sprays. Power showers which use a booster pump are more expensive than conventional ones while impulse showers, designed to alternate high-pressure jets of hot and cold water, use about 50% more water. Shower heads should be adjustable for a range of heights as well as detachable for easy cleaning or hand holding.

Whirlpools
The Jacuzzi brothers pioneered the modern whirlpool bath and introduced the pleasures of the home spa. Through the combined action of water pressure, air agitation, and heat the body receives an invigorating "micromassage". Total immersion at a temperature of 35–40°C (95–104°F) gives a sense of buoyancy, stimulates the muscles and the flow of blood to joints and skin tissues, and helps to expel toxins and reduce stress. Whirlpools can replace standard baths or you can use them as spas for family and friends. Although an excellent health aid, they are expensive and use more energy than both baths and showers.

Bath accessories

Use natural materials for all your bath-room accessories: cotton mats and towels for drying, cotton flannels for rinsing, sea sponges for soaping, and hemp or sisal friction gloves and mitts, loofahs, backstraps, or bristle brushes for scrubbing. The best soaps are made from natural plant extracts, and there are types to suit all skins. Natural body and hair shampoos and conditioners are also available, which you should rinse off thoroughly after use. You could remove the alkaline scum left by commercial shampoos with a solution of water and lemon juice or vinegar, and you can improve the quality of branded conditioners and shampoos with infusions of chamomile, rosemary, or natural henna. After a bath or shower, don't forget to apply a moisturizer to your still damp skin to replace body oils.

Bathsalts and oils

You can add salts, crystals, gels, and oils to warm bathwater to moisturize and perfume the skin. Once dissolved in the water they will be absorbed directly through the skin into the bloodstream. Many have curative effects: epsom salts ease swollen ankles and feet and relieve early symptoms of colds; sodium bicarbonate crystals soothe skin irritation and sunburn; and mineral salts from natural spas and volcanic springs, available in powder form, can alleviate muscular and rheumatic aches and pains. Many herbs have relaxing or sleep-inducing properties; you can add a few drops of essential oils or make infusions from such herbs as lavender, mint, rosemary, and marigold and add them to your evening bath; sage, lovage, and orange are stimulants, ideal for a refreshing early morning bath.

Water treatment

Since earliest times water has been known to have therapeutic and healing powers. Homer, the Greek poet of the 8th century BC, extolled its virtues as a cleanser of body and soul; the father of medicine, Hippocrates, treated even serious diseases with cold-water cures; and throughout the world people journey to health spas and springs seeking relief from physical and spiritual problems. Water therapy, or hydrotherapy, was developed for the treatment of muscular and joint ailments; it uses baths, pressure jet showers, and pools for the treatment of the whole body, and sitz baths, douches, and compresses for specific limbs. During pregnancy, and also if you are diabetic or suffer from circulatory or heart disease consult your doctor before undertaking self hydrotherapy in whirlpools or home spas.

In Japan, the body is thoroughly scrubbed and cleansed as a separate operation before the bath itself is entered. It is customary to scrub each other's backs before bathing, and children usually bathe with their mother or father. The Japanese bath, or furo, is designed for the use of more than one person; it is shorter than a Western bath and deep enough to allow the water to cover the shoulders of a seated person. Soaking in an unhurried manner in deep, hot water creates a feeling of weightlessness and warmth in which the whole body relaxes. Since the water is used for soaking only, it can be shared by several people one after another without changing it after every use. This type of bath is extremely economical: it uses less water than a Western bath and it stays warm for longer because of the smaller surface area. Water heat is further conserved, and humidity reduced, with a cover over the bath between each use; the water is fed through a small boiler and reheated before it is returned to the bath.

The natural bathroom

Bathing spaces in the home must necessarily serve several purposes, combining a place for cleanliness with room for stimulation and relaxation as well as a healing atmosphere. And it sometimes becomes a more social environment. Ideally, you should choose a large room that can function as another type of living space, a pleasant space where you will want to spend time. For practical reasons, the toilet is better sited in a separate, adjoining room and fitted with a wash basin.

Ideally, the natural bathroom will have a closer and more intimate relationship with green space than an ordinary one. The bathing space featured here was designed for its view over the secluded garden. The bath itself can be the conventional Western type, but a deep tub with a built-in seat is better for soaking; water is recycled through a small heater to keep it at a constant temperature. A raised floor area can accommodate the depth of the tub or access can be via a step. The adjoining wet area is larger than usual and handy for quick showers or a thorough cleansing and scrubbing prior to soaking. The nonslip, tiled shower tray can be stoppered to provide a shallow bathing and water play area; small children should *never* be left unattended. Babies are best bathed in a bowl with only a few inches of water, at a temperature of 30°C (86°F); you can avoid backache by placing the bowl on a low stool – also useful for elderly people while showering.

The bathroom provides ample space for simple exercises and massage or for resting after bathing. The materials are natural – ceramic, nonslip clay tiles for the wet areas, and ceiling and wall plaster painted with a water-based microporous paint that allows the walls to breathe. You could also finish them with untreated cork or timber; the heat and moisture from hot baths bring out the delightful aroma of timbers, such as Japanese cypress and cedar. Good and permanent ventilation and windows that open are essential to expel excess moist air and, in radon "hot spots" (see p. 101), you will also need an extractor fan. Warm floors are pleasant in the bathroom, and underfloor heating and hot towel rails are optional extras. Wicker or cane furniture, moisture-loving plants (such as ferns and aroids), soothing colours, natural fragrances, and soft lighting all help to create a restful space.

Bathing is a time for relaxation and contemplation. Sun and daylight, entering through double-glazed safety windows giving a view into the quiet garden, increase the feeling of wellbeing. It is a safe and secure place, with nonslip rubber mats inside and outside the bath and shower tray, and safety grips designed for the elderly. A "low-flow" shower head is more conserving than the standard nozzle. Condensation and humidity are controlled through open windows and doors, permanent ventilation, moisture-loving plants, and absorbent wall finishes. All lights are enclosed for safety and operated by ceiling pull-cords or switches outside the room; the only power socket is for an electric shaver. Metal pipes, baths, and fixtures have all been earthed. The recessed cabinet with sliding mirror doors, holds essential oils, shampoos, soaps, and bath salts. Fit it with a lock to protect small children.

Conservation and hazards

In the bathroom the philosophies of health and ecology often come into conflict. Healthy and relaxed bathing usually requires generous amounts of water while, as conservationists, we should use as little as possible. Campaigners' usual advice is to take showers – and to be economical even with these – in preference to taking baths. Obviously, it would be better if we could return to the custom of earlier days of visiting local public baths. These usually had better facilities and were better conservers of water and energy than individual home spas. But most people have a strong desire to bathe in the privacy of their own homes, and, fortunately, some bathroom designers and manufacturers have already responded to the growing demand for home health with better, more energy-efficient, and also more water-conserving designs.

It is not impossible to combine the best of both worlds. Conservation devices can be incorporated in most bathroom designs, and the present dependence on drinking water supplies for bathing purposes can be drastically reduced by using alternatives. Stored rainwater, processed if necessary to make it safe for bathing, is an option, as is treated greywater for flushing the toilet; in Scandinavia and Germany, the waterless toilet is steadily gaining in favour. Solar water heating and heat exchangers can greatly reduce the need for conventional heating sources (see also pp. 82–3 and 92–5).

"There is no guano comparable in fertility to the detritus of a capital", said Victor Hugo, the French novelist. But except for China where so-called "night soil" is made into fertilizer, this human resource goes unused. Moreover, we waste huge amounts of water and energy in its disposal. The Swedish alternative, the Clivus Multrum waterless, or compost, toilet, encourages the aerobic decomposition of human and organic food wastes. In the waterless toilet (right), beneficial bacteria and other microorganisms break down waste to compost and fertilizer. Given a steady air flow, the bacteria generate heat up to 70°C (160°F) that kills harmful pathogens and eliminates odours.

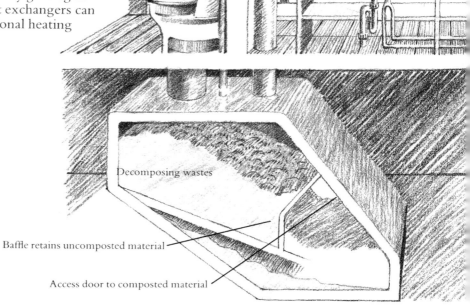

Insulated exhaust vent allows escape of waste gases above rooftop level

40w fan promotes air flow

Kitchen organic waste

Toilet

Decomposing wastes

Baffle retains uncomposted material

Access door to composted material

Hazards

Radon

If you live in a radon hot spot or if your water supply comes from a radon-rich source, you may be exposed to excessive radioactivity, particularly in the bathroom. When water is heated and produces steam or a fine spray, as in the shower, radioactive particles are released into the air and can easily be breathed into the lungs. A recent Finnish survey found that radon concentration in bathrooms were three times higher than in kitchens and up to 40 times higher than in living rooms. A Canadian study revealed that radon in bathroom air increased rapidly during a seven-minute warm shower and that it took more than 90 minutes to disperse it.

Action Ventilate the bathroom well, while it is in use and afterward. Open a window during showering and bathing and install one or more vents in walls or windows for permanent ventilation. An extract fan or a mechanical system, linked to a heat-recovery device, can be installed, but make sure that the system is perfectly balanced so that fresh air is supplied to the room at the same rate as air is extracted. If the pressure is too high, more radon can be drawn from the soil into other parts of the house (see also p. 101).

Water temperatures

Acceptable bathing temperatures vary greatly from culture to culture and from one person to another. Some people swear by the benefits of regular cold showers or outdoor plunges in icy water while others prefer to luxuriate in very hot water. Mineral hot springs from the ground often flow at temperatures well above boiling point and must obviously be cooled. While most people in the West find natural spring temperatures of 42°C (108°F) perfectly comfortable, the Japanese prefer water temperatures of 43-49°C (110-120°F).

Action In the West, the recommended temperatures for indoor bathing, based on medical advice, are: hot water, 37-42°C (99-108°F); warm water, 33-36°C (92-97°F); cold water, 15-20°C (59-68°F). Some doctors recommend maximum bathing temperatures of 37.8°C (100°F) for adults, 35°C (95°F) for children and the elderly, and 30°C (86°F) for babies. Common sense and moderation are the keys, and if you are feeling too hot, cool off for a while outside the bath or shower. If you stay in a hot bath for more than 20 minutes, you may become dizzy and light headed when you step out due to a fall in the blood pressure. You can stay in a warm bath for up to an hour. Cold showers and baths should be quick; towel briskly afterward. Or you can follow the hydrotherapy routine of hot-cold- hot-cold shower bursts; this, like the Taoist philosophy of Yin and Yang, brings to the body and mind the balance of both extremes. When you visit mineral hot springs and baths, always check the temperature; have the water cooled if necessary or bathe for a very short time only. People suffering from high blood pressure or heart problems should avoid hot springs (and very hot baths) completely.

Electricity

The chief danger in the bathroom is electrocution. Water is an excellent conductor of electricity.

Action Safety regulations vary from country to country, and you should familiarize yourself with them. For safety reasons, all metal pipes, taps and fittings, including the bath and shower, should be earthed or grounded. In the UK, the only permitted socket outlet is for an electric shaver unit incorporating an isolating transformer. All light switches should be of the pull-cord type or be located outside the room. Lights, heaters, and heated towel rails must be wired to a fused connector unit out of reach of the bath and shower. No surface wiring is permitted; washing machines and driers cannot be installed except by a qualified electrician and they must be sited at least 1.8m (6ft) away from the bath or shower.

Damp, mould, and bacteria

Bathrooms, unless properly ventilated, are liable to be damp. Condensation encourages moulds and fungal growth as well as unpleasant smells and general deterioration. Warm, humid conditions are also ideal breeding grounds for bacteria, and shower heads, waste pipes, and wash basins that become clogged from use add to the problem. In recent years there has been an upsurge in Legionnaire's disease, spread through poorly maintained ventilation systems, humidifiers, and whirlpools.

Action Use waterproof materials around the bath, shower, wash basin, and on the floor; seal all cracks between fittings and walls. Fit doors or washable curtains around the shower; finish wall surfaces and ceilings with materials that breathe and permit moisture to disperse and surfaces to dry. Synthetic finishes, such as vinyl wallpapers, emulsion paints, and plastics are impermeable and trap moisture. Heating and good ventilation counteract condensation, and strong sunlight destroys bacteria. Regular and thorough cleaning of the bathroom is important. Use mildly antiseptic solutions of borax and lemon or vinegar or other nonpolluting aids (see pp. 266-7). Wash shower curtains and bath mats frequently, and keep shower heads, spray taps, and waste pipes and traps clear of clogging scum or scale.

Hygiene products

The bathroom is often a depository for dangerous medicines, toxic products, and harmful aerosols. Chlorine bleach, strong disinfectants, drain and toilet cleansers, air fresheners, deodorant and hair sprays, perfumes, and shaving creams affect the bathroom climate. Even talcum and face powder can be inhaled, irritating the lung passages.

Action Avoid all aerosols and toxic cleaning products and replace them with healthy alternatives. Use herbal and vegetable extract soaps, creams, shampoos, and personal cosmetics. Dispose of old medicines and keep others locked away from children.

Creating bathing spaces

A greenhouse window (left), brings sunlight and nature right into the bathroom. The humidity in this type of location can be perfect for growing healthy plants, and the plants provide an extremely attractive form of screening. By absorbing carbon dioxide and releasing oxygen, they keep the air fresh and lively, too. The timber-clad walls and cork tiles, if treated with beeswax or another type of porous finish, will, along with the plants, help to regulate the room's humidity and temperature. The unusual shape of the bath is big enough for two and incorporates a whirlpool feature.

This bathing space in Australia (above) is on the roof, next to the sun deck, and has uninterrupted views of the surrounding natural countryside. Designed for social occasions, as well as for family bathing, the generous bath cum spa has a built-in whirlpool. As a natural adjunct to the outdoor lifestyle, this space is ideal for promoting friendly and informal evening and weekend gatherings.

For seclusion, while still allowing the cool winds to penetrate, this area (left), screened by sliding wooden louvre doors, can be an optional indoor or outdoor bathing space. The large circular bath set in a raised tile surround, doubles for personal bathing or as a social place for family and friends.

Outdoor bathing

In warm climates, you can enjoy the pleasures and benefits of outdoor bathing. Tubs and spas cost far less than a swimming pool and you can integrate one into any underused area of a small garden or patio. They also use less heat and water than a pool. Common tub sizes are 1.5–1.8m (5–6ft) in diameter, with a depth of 75cm–1.5m (30in–5ft), although 1.2m (4ft) is typical. A standard 1.5 by 1.2m (5 by 4ft) tub holds about 1893 litres (415 gallons) of water, and a 1.8 by 1.2m (6 by 4ft) tub about 2650 litres (583 gallons). When the bathers are included, a tub is heavy, weighing between 3175 and 3630kg (7000–8000lb). Apart from space for the tub, you should also calculate for decking and the support system of water heater, pump, filter, and perhaps an optional blower for whirlpool jets.

You must give careful thought to the choice of outdoor bathing space, including consideration of privacy, access, sun and shade, shelter from winds, safety, views, and local planning and building requirements. Usually, the need for privacy and effective screening from adjoining properties will mean siting the tub close to the house. Surrounded by decking, the space becomes the perfect place for sunbathing and entertaining. Evergreen trees and shrubs create a shelter belt that ensures quiet and seclusion; on the windward side you can erect wooden, glass, bamboo, or canvas screens.

Saunas

Many cultures have found ways of enjoying outdoor bathing, from the ancient Greek and Roman *thermae* to the Turkish baths and the sweat lodges of the North American Indians. But it is to the Finns that we owe the joys of the sauna. To them, saunas are so important that they would commonly build the sauna before the house! The sauna combines physical revival with mental relaxation and quiet contemplation, on a communal basis. A sauna can be sited in the house or outdoors and can be as small as 1 by 1m by 2m high (39in by 39in by 7ft). An innovative Austrian domestic heating system also incorporates, in the middle of the house, a brick sauna that acts as a heat store for the whole house. This can be used as a family health area without incurring additional energy costs.

A natural setting enhances the pleasures of outdoor bathing. The tub here, sited where it catches the full sun, is surrounded by mature trees and shrubs, and sweet-smelling herbs and flowering plants scent the air. The water is heated by independent solar collector panels, but these could also be connected to the home's solar water-heating system. Depending on climate, the panels can provide all the necessary heat or be supplemented by a back-up heater. With sun for more than six hours a day, a solar heating system can provide 70-100% of the heat needed for a tub or spa. With fre-quent use of the tub, you can recover the cost of installing solar heating in two or three years. Keep the tub covered with a lid or insulating blanket when not in use. Have regular checks carried out on the tub, pump, filters, and water quality, including the correct pH balance. For wooden tubs choose hardwood timber from plantations, and local solid-wood furniture in preference to plastic furniture and foam-filled cushions. In cooler climates, site the tub in a gazebo or in a sunspace/conservatory attached to the house. You could also use an outdoor tub for a cold plunge after a soak or sauna.

Chapter Nine
HEALTH SPACES

In a world where pollution is increasing and most of us live in artificial, indoor, city environments, keeping healthy is of paramount importance. Our physical and mental systems are under constant attack and our natural defences to infections – our immune responses – have become weakened as a result, making us vulnerable to many new allergies and new viruses.

Many of us lead unhealthy lives, ignoring routine maintenance and turning a blind eye to warning signals. If something goes wrong, we assume that medical help will arrive and put right years of abuse. Western medicine has tended to see the body as a working machine made up of various components; when illness occurs, diagnosis will try to isolate and repair the part that has gone wrong. But the body is not a machine, it is a living entity and must be viewed as a whole organism in which any stress or malfunction affects all of its parts, leading to "dis-ease" of body, mind, and spirit.

The older, Eastern health traditions have always embraced this wholistic view and are concerned with harmony and balance of the whole system, and with the flow of vital energy. Alterna-tive therapies, such as homeopathy, acupuncture, osteopathy, and herbalism, are becoming increasingly popular, partly as a reaction against the immoderate and often unsuccessful use of drugs and partly from a new awareness that we must take personal responsibility for preventive health care. The natural home is designed, in its entirety, as a wholistic and healthy environment, with fresh air, clean water, organic foods, and nontoxic materials and furnishings – a place where the chemical load is reduced to a minimum and where our bodies can gradually detoxify and restore themselves. But it should also cater for more specific fitness activities, ranging from purely physical workouts to mental and spiritual requirements. It is often difficult to find the time and opportunity to organize regular exercise, and many public facilities are oversubscribed and crowded. But we can accomplish a lot during leisure hours in our homes without the help of sports facilities and expensive equipment. Aerobic exercises, for example, can be balanced with daily relaxation through meditation, yoga, or t'ai chi, and home massage. With a little thought, you can adapt your home to suit these activities.

The human body is designed and made to move. Dance exercises (see right) are, in many ways, better than aerobics or jogging – they not only build fitness gradually, they also make you more aware of your own body. Once proficient, you will walk with more grace, stand with more poise, and become generally more comfortable within yourself. To practise dance at home, you need only a clear, nonslip floorspace, a wall bar, and a mirror.

Amid the stresses of modern living we all need reassurance and the comfort of human contact at times. Massage and shiatsu are soothing and healing therapies that require only a small, warm space and a relaxing atmosphere. Massage is the easier technique to learn. Shiatsu (see right), originating in Japan, involves applying pressure to the acupuncture points, or tsubos, along the body's energy channels – the meridians through which the vital energy, or ch'i, flows.

Health and exercise

Preventive health care is a concept we all need to embrace. But most of us worry about our health only when we fall ill, and then we blame such factors as germs, the weather, or the stresses of work, home, and travel. Illness, though, is often linked to lifestyle – a factor within your control. You can make a positive contribution to healthier living through eating a proper diet and having a reasonable division between work and rest, and by creating a healthy home environment.

For health of the whole person, you have to care for all facets equally – physical and spiritual – for each of them affects the other. Once you start a programme of regular exercises, the need for such stimulants as coffee or tobacco usually reduces, as does stress, while vitality increases and sleep improves. Similarly, quiet meditation and relaxation can release physical as well as mental energies. Any adjustments to your lifestyle or your home should be gentle and gradual; indeed, sudden, dramatic changes can be disruptive.

Exercise

Regular exercise increases the metabolic rate, improves circulation, digestion, and skin tone, and strengthens the heart muscles. Exercise also lowers blood sugar, cholesterol, and fat levels and increases strength, stamina, and suppleness. The benefits to posture brought about by exercise can also influence your general health. Exercise is not all strenuous, however; brisk walking, cycling, and gardening are excellent fitness activities.

For maximum benefit, all exercise programmes should include relaxation and stretching movements. Take into account body type, age, weight, level of health, and temperament. And seek advice from a physician or a fitness consultant before starting a new and strenuous exercise programme.

Different exercises are geared to developing, to different degrees, stamina, strength, flexibility, or co-ordination. Aerobic exercises, which speed up breathing and increase the consumption of oxygen, stimulate blood circulation and improve physical strength and stamina. The gentle stretching poses of yoga or the movement-awareness exercises of the Feldenkrais method are more suited to flexibility, posture, and co-ordination. Meditation, yoga, relaxation, and massage techniques relieve physical and mental stress and bring calm and harmony to the body and spirit. A good programme for maintenance of health will include all three basic elements – aerobics, stretching movements, and relaxation. Set aside time for them every day and, ideally, practise them in an attractive space with good daylight and plenty of fresh air.

Aerobics and workouts

These can be strenuous and you should attend classes for expert tuition before practising at home. Have a check-up by a physician before starting any demanding exercise programme. Aerobics combine dance steps with keep-fit exercises, running, jumping, and jogging on the spot, all set to music. Starting with a 10-20-minute warm-up of stretching and flexing, the exercises gradually increase in aerobic content, designed to increase the efficiency of the heart and lungs.

Workouts include fast walking, jogging, running, swimming, and cycling to improve stamina and endurance. All you need at home is rhythmic music, a nonslip floor, and perhaps a full-length, wall-mounted mirror.

Calisthenics

Calisthenics, a Greek word meaning beauty and strength, were originally devised as a routine of simple exercises for developing muscular tone and improving fitness. You do not need specialized equipment for this mixture of static and dynamic exercise and you can fit them in any time. Calisthenic sessions for toning muscles and improving posture should preferably last about 30 minutes a day. This may be too strenuous for all but the young; beginners should attend classes with trained instructors. Popular fitness routines include the Royal Canadian Air Force 5B-X and XBX programmes where 10 to 12 exercises are designed to be performed in a specific order and in a maximum time of 12 minutes.

Isometrics and weight training

Both these types of exercise are designed to build up and tone the muscles and to improve strength. Isometric exercises involve the contraction of different sets of muscles for short periods of time.

Weight lifting can be dangerous unless you are extremely fit and have been through a training programme under expert tuition at a health club or gymnasium; even so, you should not commit yourself to more than one or two sessions per week. Weight training machines, designed to improve almost every muscle group, are expensive, but in the home you can try exercises with lighter weights or dumb bells as part of your keep-fit programme.

Eastern exercises

Indian, Chinese, and Japanese philosophies have all developed disciplines
for health based on releasing and balancing the flow of vital energy to unite
body, mind, and spirit. All these disciplines involve exercises with controlled
movements, breathing, concentration,
and a meditative approach. Yoga, from
India, is the most commonly practised
in the West. The martial arts – Japanese
Aikido and a range of Chinese forms –
are also popular. Within the family of
Chinese arts there is a group of "soft" or
"internal" forms that have evolved into
methods of personal development and
health. Once taught, you can easily
practise them at home, especially T'ai
Chi Chuan and Chi Kung, which are
usually taught together. Though "soft",
these arts still contain a self-defence
element. The arts are founded in the
ancient philosophy of Taoism, in which
nature is the key to self-knowledge and
internal harmony.

T'ai Chi Chuan

This is perhaps the ultimate "soft"
martial art and it is widely recognized
for its great powers of creating and sustaining health. Studies in China of the
effects of T'ai Chi found that it benefited
circulation and respiration and reduced
insomnia, anxiety, and emotional illnesses. As a subtle and effective self-
defence, its practice goes far beyond the
martial aspect. The slow and expressive
exercises are like moving meditation.
They take absolute concentration and
gradually bring you a sense of rhythm
and harmony with life and a calm
detachment from temporal concerns.
Like millions of Chinese who do the
exercises daily, you can practise them in
the park, in your garden, or indoors in
an uncluttered space.

*Ba Duan Jin Touching the
Sky exercise.*

Chi Kung and Ba Duan Jin

The simplest "soft" art to learn is Chi
Kung, which means "energy work". Its
aim is to cultivate *ch'i* and build the
strength to practise other arts. Decep-
tively simple, Chi Kung involves deep,
natural breathing and focusing the mind
using slow, meditative postures. For the
master, Chi Kung brings extraordinary
powers of endurance. For the beginner,
it maintains health, improves vitality,
and helps recovery from illness at any
stage of life.

Ba Duan Jin is a set of simple exercises
that are often practised with Chi Kung.
The *Touching the Sky* exercise, illustrated here, is the first position you
learn. The sequence is performed eight
times, holding each posture for 1 second
while breathing deeply.

Meditation and exercise

Today's homes should promote a healthy lifestyle, encouraging the healing of mind and spirit. Few homes are designed for indoor exercise but you can create personal health spaces that combine exercises with quiet contemplation. You will need two spaces: an active and aerobics area for strenuous exercises, such as workouts, weight training, dance, or gymnastics; and one that is passive, quiet, and relaxing for such things as massage, meditation, yoga, or one of the Eastern therapies that are well suited to solo practice.

The active space should have a firm, nonslip floor and allow unrestricted movement. A space of about 3 x 3m (10 x 10ft) is probably adequate if it is equipped with exercise mats, benches, chinning bars fixed between door posts, and perhaps dance practice bars on a wall. A high-ceilinged room will allow climbing ropes and suspended bars and rings. Expensive fitness equipment, from mini trampolines, exercise bicycles, and rowing machines to fully equipped mini gyms, needs more space, even if it is often consigned to gather dust after the initial enthusiasm wears off.

The passive space – safe, warm, and tranquil – can be small and intimate, with just enough room for yoga mats, a portable massage table, and a focus point for meditation. A small bedroom, a converted attic, or an outbuilding can be the perfect location, especially if it is close to nature with a fine view and plenty of fresh air and sunlight. In warm climates, a sheltered, private outdoor place can be even more satisfying. Keep it simple, with soft rugs, comfortable pillows or cushions, and one or two personal objects of beauty.

An ideal health space has been created in this airy New York loft. A mezzanine divides it into a lower-floor living area with little furniture and an uncarpeted floor suitable for exercises. The upper floor is for sleeping and bathing, with a quiet corner for yoga and meditation. The circular, inscribed Chinese "moon gate" symbolizes the entry into the inner spiritual world evoked by the 6th-century Chinese poet-recluse Pei Di:
"I come to the bamboo studio,
Having grown more fond of you each day;
Only mountain birds enter and leave here,
No worldly man is found at this secluded place."

Relaxation techniques

Modern life constantly throws up stressful situations. Although not all stress is bad, it could eventually wear out your ability to respond, unless you learn to relax and to release tension. Stress management is really learning how to lead a more relaxed life. For a start, you can try to remove the obvious stress factors; then alter your diet and work and rest patterns. More exercise, correct breathing (see p. 97), and a healthy and relaxing home environment are therapies within everyone's reach. For the release of tension you must learn the art of relaxation, where the mind is alert and aware while the body is resting. A daily relaxation session, with massage, meditation, yoga, or other therapies, is a pleasant and effective way of unwinding at home and relieving day-to-day pressures.

Yoga

There are many kinds of yoga, an ancient philosophy that originated in India, but all are directed toward achieving a personal union of physical, mental, and spiritual health, and a joining of the self with the Absolute. The wholistic system of yoga maintains the health and wellbeing of body and spirit and establishes harmony between the individual and the outside world. Yoga postures, or *asanas*, work on all parts of the body, stretching and toning the muscles and ligaments and keeping the spine and joints supple; breathing exercises increase oxygen in the bloodstream and tissues and regulate the flow of the life force, the *prana*, or ch'i. Anyone can practise yoga, but it is advisable to join a class with an experienced teacher where you can learn correct breathing and the structure and sequence of the postures. All you need are loose-fitting clothes and a yoga mat or folded blanket.

A session involves practising an ordered sequence of *asanas*, which works all sides of the body, starting and finishing with relaxation in the Corpse Pose, or *Savasana*. Lie on your back, feet apart, and hands (palm upward) at the sides; let legs and feet roll outward. Now tense and relax each part of the body in turn, from feet and legs through hands and arms to neck and face. Close your eyes and concentrate your mind on the rise and fall of the abdomen as you breathe in and out. Relax in this position for at least 5 minutes before slowly rolling to your side and rising.

Massage

Touch therapy is a marvellous experience, bringing pleasure to receiver and giver alike. Many of the physical and mental stress-related illnesses of life can be eased with massage, and the warm and tender touch of human hands lifts us out of isolation and despair. Simple massage techniques are easy to learn, but more complex ones, such as Japanese shiatsu, and reflexology foot massage, need expert tuition. For a home massage, you need a warm, quiet, and draught-free room, cushions, blankets, warm towels, and massaging and essential oils and essences. A clear space of 2.4 x 1.8m (8 x 6ft) is enough. You can give a massage on a table or on the floor; if it has soft rugs, cover them with a folded blanket beneath a cotton sheet or towel. Cover a hard floor with extra folded blankets or a futon with sheets or towels. Avoid using sprung mattresses since they will not give adequate support.

If massage is a regular part of your lifestyle, you might consider buying a folding massage table. Tables are generally about 1.8m (6ft) long and 75cm (30in) wide, firmly supported on six legs, and should be hip height. Some people like soothing music while receiving a massage, others prefer silence, but constant warmth is essential, with a temperature of about 21°C (70°F). Create a soothing, relaxed atmosphere with subdued lighting and colours; daylight is fine, but candles or the soft glow of a fire are better. Scent the room with flowers, incense, or aromatic essential oils, which also improve breathing.

Meditation

Practised regularly once or twice a day, meditation harmonizes mind and body and can help to overcome many problems, from addictions and insomnia to migraine and depression. You can sit or kneel and rest on your heels, depending on which position feels most comfortable. First, relax the body by breathing slowly and deeply from the diaphragm, and then try to empty your mind of all thoughts; if it wanders, concentrate on breathing and focus on an inspiring, peaceful object – a flower, for example, or a lighted candle or a mandala (a Hindu sacred symbol). You can also try the simple meditation technique of closing your eyes and repeating a mantra (a single word or sentence) silently within yourself; or you can visualize an idyllic setting, such as a forest or an ocean, its gentle waves lapping a sandy beach.

With practice, you can meditate anywhere, even in crowded places and traffic queues, but for the deep and healing benefits of meditation you should choose a quiet, comfortable, and safe place. You don't need a lot of space, merely enough to sit or lie down. But quality rather than quantity of space is important: meditation space is essentially a separate world, far removed from everyday life, a tiny cosmos to which you can retreat and find harmony and look inward toward the centre of your being. Like the tiny Japanese *chashitsu*, the ceremonial tea room, meditation space is a natural place of the utmost simplicity – a spiritual shelter or mountain hut in the middle of the city.

The sanctuary

For an environmentally sensitive person, it may be necessary to create a special refuge and healing place in the home. This sanctuary must be scrupulously clean and free from vapours, moulds, dust, bacteria, or any offending allergy sensitizers. Clear the room of all furnishings and have doors, windows, and all cracks, including those around electric switches and sockets, thoroughly sealed. Some specialists on environmental sensitivity advise lining walls, floors,

and inner ceiling with plastic or aluminium foil to prevent the entry of structural pollutants. But in Baubiological terms, provided that internal air pressure is maintained slightly higher than outside pressure, any pollutants will be expelled by the process of natural diffusion through the walls. A mechanical ventilation system is needed to create this differential in air pressure, possibly with a separate filtered air supply.

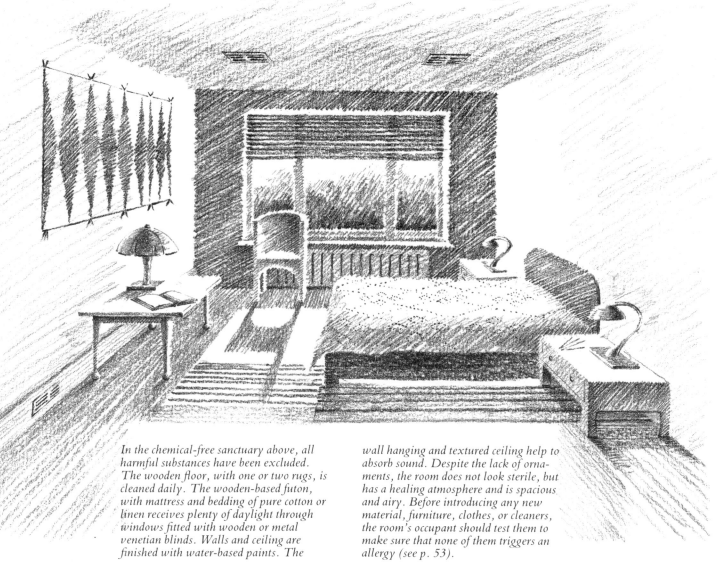

In the chemical-free sanctuary above, all harmful substances have been excluded. The wooden floor, with one or two rugs, is cleaned daily. The wooden-based futon, with mattress and bedding of pure cotton or linen receives plenty of daylight through windows fitted with wooden or metal venetian blinds. Walls and ceiling are finished with water-based paints. The wall hanging and textured ceiling help to absorb sound. Despite the lack of orna- ments, the room does not look sterile, but has a healing atmosphere and is spacious and airy. Before introducing any new material, furniture, clothes, or cleaners, the room's occupant should test them to make sure that none of them triggers an allergy (see p. 53).

Chapter Ten
GREENSPACES

No home is really complete without its greenspaces. Without soil to grow plants or trees, without water to nourish them, and without the wildlife attracted by the sustenance thus provided, a house or apartment has not the fully rounded completeness of a true home. And when we are denied this rich and natural world of subtly changing light, colours, and scents, as well as the special sounds of wind through leaves and the visual indicators of the changing seasons, we are diminished. Children growing up in an environment without close and caring contact with nature, run the risk of being ignorant of the need to protect and enjoy the natural world, not only for their own sake and that of their families, but also for their children's children.

Ecology parks and city farms fulfil a vital role, for they allow city children (and their parents) to experience nature and wildlife where they live and to see that the wilderness is not something to be observed secondhand via the television. Greenspaces inside and outside the home also need to be understood more in terms of ecology – as an interface between us and the natural world. They are in fact mini ecosystems – the sun, water, and soil supporting plants, animals, and microbes that all depend on each other for survival, as in planetary systems. Our gardens do not only belong to us,

they are homes to many other living things, too. How we treat these greenspaces, and the lifeforms they support, affects us and the environment. Pollute them with chemicals and we, and everything else, will suffer; enrich and protect them and we all benefit.

On another, but equally important, level, greenspaces are places for us to slow down and feel more at ease with the world; where we also begin to "put down our own roots". Front and back gardens, balconies, verandahs, and porches make it easier for people living in the same street and community to get to know one another.

A greenspace, no matter what its form or size, can quickly personalize an otherwise anonymous home. And in the stressed inner city, gardens added to ground-floor apartments can even help to calm violence. Gardens, sunspaces, and conservatories – the smallest glass entrance lobby – are effective buffers, providing intermediate spaces to soften the often abrupt change between home and the outside. These spaces make us feel more secure and they can protect us against climate extremes, noise, and pollution. And like the small city gardens of the Japanese, our greenspaces can be spiritual landscapes linking us with wilderness and solitude far away and bringing rejuvenation and peace of mind.

Spaces can be ambiguous, not necessarily having rigidly defined functions. This unusual seating area (right) by the innovative French furniture designer Pierre Paulin, has been installed within a wintergarden, thus extending the living area into the greenspace.

Rather than formal flower beds fringing a carefully tended lawn, consider instead an informal arrangement of native plants and herbs (right). An attractive, circular pattern of laid bricks forms an entirely practical, low-maintenance surface, ideal for just sitting in the sun – or shelling peas.

Indoor greenspaces

Indoor plants are often perceived merely as visual ornaments – decorative items to add a touch more colour and interest to a room or to enhance interior design. Exotic specimens are bought on the spur of the moment, but once home they soon begin to fail through lack of care or proper conditions. As with outdoor gardening, you need to see plants, not as isolated things, but as part of a living ecosystem. Indoors this is more difficult, since your home is an alien environment for plants, and so their existence depends totally on the way you treat them.

In effect, what you have to do is create mini ecosystems to provide sufficient light, water, food, and warmth. Whereas house plants generally like humidity of around 60 per cent, most homes are only about 20 per cent humid in living rooms and 50 per cent in kitchens and bathrooms. The right level of light and exposure to the sun is also important, but most vital of all is the correct amount of water. The most common mistake is overwatering.

Many plants will gradually adapt, within limits, to less than ideal conditions provided that you meet their main needs. In view of this, the first decision you must make concerns the plants' positions – whether a sunny living room window, a gloomy hallway, a moist bathroom and kitchen, or a cool bedroom – and then choose appropriate specimens. Bear in mind, too, the size they will ultimately attain and the amount of care they will need to remain healthy.

Growing your own indoor plants or taking cuttings could mean the plant will be hardier and more readily adapted to your home than a mature one bought from a nursery. You can also bring garden specimens indoors in the winter, and tubs or pots of savoury-smelling herbs or lemon-scented pelargoniums in a sunny window will give your home an aromatic magic and be a reminder of warm, summer days.

Plants and health

Indoor plants filter and purify the air by sedimentation and absorption. Leaf surfaces, especially hairy ones, trap dust and soot. Using a process known as *photosynthesis*, plants convert sunlight into chemical energy, absorb carbon dioxide in the air, and replace it with oxygen. This not only gives you fresher air, it also dilutes any airborne pollutants. By *transpiration* through leaves and drinking via roots, they also help regulate humidity, modify temperatures, and balance ions in the air.

To the surprise of US space scientists researching ways to recycle wastes in space stations, they found that plants are also excellent absorbers of

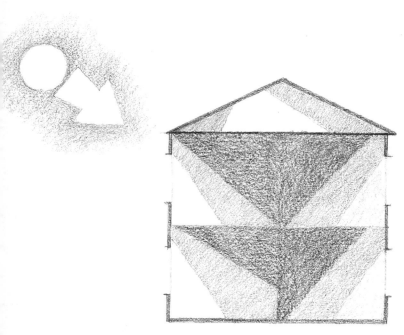

The diagram (left) of a typical house type shows the three main light zones indoor plants have to contend with – bright, direct sunlight; indirect daylight; and shade. All plants need the correct combination of light and humidity in order to grow happily, so always try to find the right plant for a particular room, and position within that room.

certain pollutants. The common spider plant (*Chlorophytum elatum* var *vittatum*), in particular, is an efficient absorber of formaldehyde, one of the most prevalent indoor pollutants. And, although 70 large plants were needed to purify constantly the air in a sealed capsule, in the home with other forms of ventilation, four or five plants in polluted rooms should be sufficient. Soil, too, cleans the air – its microorganisms act as sponges and absorb gases and vapours, especially carbon monoxide, a main constituent of cigarette smoke.

In fact, plants and soil make the perfect ecological air-conditioning system. And they could do more for our homes and buildings. A single tree, for example, can evaporate 455 litres (100 gallons) of water a day and generate 230,000 calories of heat – equivalent to 20 hours cooling of five room-sized air conditioners. Moreover, a beech tree absorbes carbon dioxide equivalent to the amount produced by 800 homes. Imagine what fully grown specimens included in office atriums or smaller varieties in our home can do for our indoor environment.

Apart from these health benefits, the scents and subtle fragrances of plants and flowers enhance the quality of the air and (avoiding those that may trigger allergies) can encourage us to breath more deeply. Plant a scented garden near the house or next to doors and windows or use tubs of fragrant plants that you can move around to suit the mood. Enjoy morning scent with summer jasmine, evening scents with night-scented stocks or honeysuckle trained over a sun-facing wall, and grow the resilient thyme on garden paths where it can release its scent every time it is stepped on.

Not only is growing your own herbs much more satisfying than buying them dried, they also taste better and are milder and fresher. You can easily grow a selection of your favourite herbs on a kitchen window sill or balcony if you don't have a garden. Parsley, chives, sweet basil, pot marigold, and nasturtium all do well in pots.

Indeed, plants are so good for us that rather than thinking of them as something we introduce into our homes, we should really choose to live more in their habitats. This is not a new concept – the glasshouse and conservatory have long been used as a refreshing place in which to sit and relax. The growing popularity of sunspaces, wintergardens and conservatories indicates that we have begun to understand this vital relationship once more. Some people even move their offices into greenhouse environments, while others have made the decision to build their homes inside greenhouse structures (see p.62).

If you like growing your own flowers, fresh salad vegetables, and herbs but don't have a garden, you can build a simple window greenhouse. Made of timber and glass and fixed to the outside of a sun-facing window, it has slatted shelves to take pots and trays of seedlings or cuttings. It extends the growing season and also has the added bonus that it insulates the window and acts as a solar collector to heat the room. Remember, however, to include shading and ventilation.

Solar greenhouses

A solar greenhouse is not the same as a sunspace or conservatory. Whereas a sunspace does provide a good environment for many plants, it is more of a recreational area that also provides solar heating for the home. A solar greenhouse follows sound solar principles (see pp. 70–1), but it is designed more specifically for year-round food production using the sun as the main energy source. It is also different from a conventional greenhouse in that it is not free standing but attached to the sun–facing side of the house. Oriented carefully to the sun-sector, its glazed roof and walls are sloped to the exact angles of the winter and summer sun.

To maximize solar gain from the low winter sun, the glass should slope between 40 and 50°, depending on latitude. The roof and walls are double glazed for insulation and the sun's heat is stored in heavy masonry house walls and an insulated solid floor, as well as other heat stores such as water-filled drums, for release in cold weather. Insulating shutters, vents, and roller blinds control air flow, overheating, and cooling. Like a sunspace, it provides solar heat and, having more plants, is an even more effective air filter to improve air quality inside the home.

With close planting and overlapping plants of different sizes and species, as well as careful harvesting (only picking outside or larger leaves to allow the plant to continue to grow), it is possible to produce in an urban greenhouse of only 20 sq m (215 sq ft), about 70 per cent of the salads and vegetables and 30 per cent of the fruit for a family of three or four. Organic wastes from the kitchen, house, and greenhouse are converted into rich compost using worms in a wormbox, so that you can regenerate the soil organically. Maintaining the greenhouse and year-round food production needs a commitment of about an hour a day on average, with some additional weekend time spent during the planting periods.

For this investment of time you can grow a wide variety of vegetables, salads, herbs, and fruit, as well as ornamental plants and flowers and what would otherwise be expensive, exotic species of plants. And what a wonderful place to spend time in – a calming, reflective atmosphere, with healthy, fragrant air, surrounded by living greenery.

This triangular, two-storey greenhouse (modelled on a real one in New Mexico) built between two wings of a house, is like a modern version of the old Spanish central courtyard. It combines space for growing plants and fruit trees with a sunspace for relaxation that also provides solar heat for the home. Even in a cold area (the original has over two hundred days a year below freezing point), this greenspace will always be filled with sun and light and an abundance of plants and flowers. The thick adobe walls, solid masonry floor, soil, and drums filled with water, store the heat of the day and release it at night. Double-glazed roof and walls plus the roller insulation blind conserve the heat. But the main problem, especially in places with hot summers and sunny winter days, is overheating. Use a good flow of air (cool air from low vents, warming and rising through high roof vents). You will also need to shade the outside in summer by growing deciduous trees, tall sunflowers, or climbing plants such as grape vines and runner beans. Alternatively, use bamboo or canvas screens. Free from chemical pesticides and fertilizers, the organic soil and biological pest control keep the plants robust and healthy.

Natural landscapes

The key to creating a natural greenspace outside your home is understanding and working with the processes of nature. First, you will need to find out what the landscape was like before it was developed, and what were the native species of trees, plants, and wildlife (the local history society might be able to help). Next, you will need to find out about the local soils and the seasonal patterns of rainfall, winds, and temperatures. The ecology of an area is very variable and your garden or yard may be different from that of your neighbours.

The real advantages of introducing native plants are that they are better adapted and, therefore, less trouble than imported ones. If you look at the wild vegetation growing locally in conditions similar to your own garden, you will soon discover the types to plant. Observe, too, how and where they grow in relation to each other: are they on the fringe or in the centre; what species grow next to, or underneath, each other; and how big are they at maturity? Return and observe them throughout the changing seasons.

A wild landscape is diverse and has the full span of life within it, from seedlings to the fully grown. It also relies on the self-sustaining cycles of death and decay to regenerate itself every year. Although it is impossible to recreate this sort of "climax" ecosystem in the span of your lifetime, even if you had sufficient space, it is possible to design and plant your garden to include a cross section of the major local species. In temperate climates, this may include elements of meadow, hedgerow, woodland, and pond; in hot, arid climates, cacti, succulents, desert trees, palms, sand, boulders, and rock (with a more easily maintained green courtyard oasis). Even in a city apartment, window boxes and balcony tubs can pioneer natural planting of native species typical of wilder habitats nearby.

Organic gardening

As well as naturalizing their gardens, many people are turning away from chemical fertilizers and pesticides and returning to the old methods of cultivation. Organic gardening is now spreading fast as people rediscover the delicious taste of natural produce and know that it is healthy and chemical free.

The three main concerns of growing organically are soil, composting, and insect control. The organic gardener knows the soil is a living, breathing organism of great complexity and, being alive, it needs to be fertilized and cultivated using nature's own way. Natural mineral and organic fertilizers actually create soil, whereas chemicals and pesticides overstimulate and eventually drain it of life. As well, they pollute our food, rivers, and groundwater. The organic gardener is a contributor to the cycle of life, not only taking from the soil but also giving and restoring it.

Most gardens bear no resemblance to their natural state. They have been carefully planted with exotic trees and plants and will probably feature lawns and clipped hedges. But it would be senseless to cut down healthy, mature trees and plants simply because they are not indigenous.

Composting is the basis of healthy soil. Instead of using chemical fertilizers, you can make your own compost using the original Indore method invented in the early 1900s by the father of organic gardening, Sir Albert Howard. With his 14-day method, leaves, grass cuttings, and garden debris are interlayered with organic kitchen wastes, sawdust, and livestock manure in a compost heap. Bacteria, air, water, earthworms, and the heat they generate rapidly decay the organic matter into a loamy humus similar to that found in woods. In cities and small yards, the anaerobic, or airless, composting method – covering the compost with black impermeable sheeting – is more practicable.

The other main concern of organic gardening – controlling insects – does not have to involve toxic sprays and pesticides either. In fact, plants grown in good organic soil tend to suffer less from insects and disease than do those grown in chemical soils. An established organic and naturalized garden will anyway contain a more self-regulatory ecosystem, with fewer pests and diseases, and its own microclimate will also benefit the home.

The most fully developed natural system is that of "permaculture". It is based on the natural farming approach developed in Japan by Masanobu Fukuoka since about 1940. The four principles of "do-nothing" farming let the rhythms and processes of nature do the work. They are: *no cultivation* (no ploughing or turning the soil – roots, worms, small animals, and microorganisms do this); *no fertilizer* (no chemicals or prepared compost – use ground cover, straw, and manure); *no weeding* (use ground cover and mulch); and *no pesticides*.

The term permaculture, coined by an Australian, Bill Mollison, in 1978, means permanent agriculture. It uses ecological principles to plan self-renewing and sustaining systems for food, water, and energy. Every available space is used with close, multilayer planting: ground plants under trees; vine trellising on walls; and trees and plants with multiple uses (shelter, food, fuel, and animal fodder). Edible landscaping is combined with planting in order to create a wholistic balance of shelter, food, and environment.

In gardens, the emphasis is on growing a wide variety of perennials for food, using crop rotation, increasing the number of earthworms, saving energy and water (especially in dry areas with rainwater and recycled greywater), using garden compost and manure, and keeping small animals and poultry. In the city, permaculture can be used in greenhouses, small yards, and lofts converted into greenhouses. Homes with glass roofs and walls covered with climbing plants provide shelter, insulation, air cleansing, a home for wildlife, and soften the visual impact. Perhaps the ultimate is the proposal of German architect Rudolf Doernach that we live in "biotecture plant houses" – houses not only covered with plants but made in and of them.

In this garden the house rear is sun facing, with a solar greenhouse and, from left to right: shelter trees on street side; rainwater tank; pond; trellis with vines; organic vegetables and herbs; fruit bushes; composting area; nut and fruit trees; raised meadow area; and wild, naturalized woodland.

Creating greenspaces

Lush tropical vegetation envelopes this Australian sunroom (above). Allowed to grow close to the house, the dense trees and ferns not only give shade but also regulate room humidity.

Exotic and tender plants thrive in the indoor green-space of this modern American home (left), designed by architect Denis Davey. It is more than simply an attractive space, though; it also heats the home with passive solar power and keeps the indoor air fresh. At night, insulating blinds retain the heat.

Outdoor greenspaces

Your garden or yard does not have to be large to
have all the elements of a natural, conserving, and
healthy outdoor environment. By scaling down the
main types of habitat, you can have many ecosystems represented in microcosm. Collect rainwater
and use it for a pond and marsh garden; leave an area
to go wild to make a meadow; plant native trees at
the end or sides to form a small woodland; grow a
mixed hedgerow or thick wall cover; and use
plantings to create both sunny and shady places.
Vegetables are ornamental as well as edible, and
espaliered fruit trees or scarlet-flowering runner
beans can make an attractive trellis or pergola.
Culinary and medicinal herbs, too, are a fragrant
alternative to exclusively ornamental plants, and
herbal lawns planted with chamomile or thyme are
a substitute for grass.

The manicured lawn is a heavy consumer of
water, fertilizers, pesticides, and energy. Motor
mowers are also noisy. Fortunately, there are
options. First, mow less often, use less water and
fertilizer, and leave clippings on the lawn. Second,
reduce the lawn size and use more varieties of
groundcover, garden beds, and food-producing
plants. Third, let native meadow grasses grow.

*Creating a natural outdoor
greenspace does not mean let-
ting everything go wild –
there is a design to it. First,
assess your garden's assets
and problems – sunlight and
shade, shelter and exposure,
vegetation and wildlife, soil
and water. Next, see how
you can naturalize it and
even turn problems to advantage. In this small city garden
(right) rainwater is collected
in butts and is used to feed the
pond or water the garden.
Greywater from the house is
filtered and also irrigates the
garden by a drip-feed process.
Instead of a lawn, brick and
stone paving make a warm
sitting area against the garden
wall, shaded by a large fig
tree and bordered with herbs.
A stone wall niche provides a*

*focal point, and espaliered
fruit trees and runner beans
trained over a pergola screen
the vegetable garden behind.
At the end is a wild area of
meadow grass and a small
grove of native trees.*

*To attract wildlife you
have to provide protection
from the weather and predators and grow plants rich in
seeds, berries, or nectar. This
is better than feeding wildlife
directly, since it avoids creating a dependency on you.
And in the pesticide-free garden there will be small prey
and insects for wildlife to feed
on. If you are lucky enough
to have a colony of bats in
and around your garden, bear
in mind that they may be
protected by law and should
not be disturbed.*

Light and shade

Climate plays a vital role in the development and refinement of any successful style of architecture. The Spanish courtyard of El Casaba, Andalucia, Spain (left), is a good example, with its Moorish archways, colonnades, and closely planted trees all employed to give protection from the often fierce heat of the day. In summer, the pools at either end are filled with water and the fountains used to cool and moisten the air.

Sheltered above and surrounded by dense foliage, giving both privacy and shelter from winds, this setting (right) is perfect for an outdoor spa. When not in use for bathing and relaxing in, it becomes a beautiful pool reflecting the light, and the surrounding ferns and creepers.

Spiritual gardens

Many of our grand Western gardens have evolved largely from Classical and Renaissance traditions and are greatly admired for the formal beauty of their large sweeps of lawn, the careful symmetry of paths, clipped hedges, and buildings, and the impressive vistas through park-like settings. This style of garden, more suited to courtly palaces or fine country houses, is one of status and also of overconsumption. By contrast, the cottage garden with its herbs, vegetables, and informal plantings echoes more the monastic tradition of healing and sustenance and implies an intimate relationship between gardener and garden. In modern cities, we need gardens more than ever to provide a quiet space for contemplation. Wild natural places, rather than tamed landscapes, more deeply release our innate yearnings to be close, still, to nature.

Eastern cultures have always seen their gardens more as spiritual landscapes. Motivated by a desire to be reminded of their country's remote, natural wilderness, the Chinese built palace and city gardens that recreated, on a smaller scale, the effects of vast rugged mountains, flowing rivers, or still lakes. Miniature hills and valleys, craggy rocks, waterfalls, streams, ponds, picturesque trees, and undulating paths all represent the wild and the distant. Blending unobtrusively into this are the buildings, kiosks, pavilions, and walls, all contrived to allow long vistas or intimate glimpses as you wander through this imaginary landscape. Features of the real landscape outside are "borrowed scenery" and even the sky, sun, and moon are included in the form of reflections in water. Everything becomes a metaphor of a timeless world beyond and expresses the ancient Chinese ideal of the hermit-philosopher, meditating deep within the far away mountains or forests.

The Japanese garden stems from the Chinese tradition but was strongly influenced by the Shinto faith. This viewed the human race as a part of nature, rather than being the dominant force, and accepted the need to submerge one's being into the endless cycle of nature. In the spirit of Zen, gardens became simpler and more austere: water often being represented by dry, raked gravel and stone. The tea garden was devised to create the right mood of serenity and purity for those about to partake of the tea ceremony. The *roji* (garden path) was intended to break the connection with the outside world and become the first stage in meditation. Today, the Japanese still use the same ancient ways to build themselves peaceful gardens, even in the middle of the most crowded city. Here, they can sit quietly and contemplate not only a garden, but also the landscape evoked beyond.

The naturalized garden, too, can express through its design a spiritual perception of the world and our place within it. By its layout, it can lead from the tame to the wild, light to shade, water to "mountains" and "valleys", and conduct us to a quiet meditative centre – a pool, a shady seat, or a sunny, secluded space.

The distancing effect of the roji *is seen in the modern garden below, with the stepping stone path weaving between mossy boulders and a stone lantern.*

"I look beyond;
Flowers are not,
Nor tinted leaves.
On the sea beach
A solitary cottage stands
In the waning light
Of an autumn eve."
(Anon)

Ecology and conservation

Pesticides

The publication of Rachel Carson's *Silent Spring* in 1962 alerted the public to the problems caused by the widespread use of pesticides, particularly the long-lived organochlorines such as DDT. Over 25 years later, we seem to have forgotten her vital message and our gardens have become even more of a chemical battleground. In fact, home owners have been found to use more pesticides per hectare than farmers!

Recently, research in the US has suggested that regular spraying of homes and gardens with pesticides is linked to the development of acute leukemia, and pesticides containing the active ingredient oxydemeton-methyl may result in birth defects.

Many pesticides can be stored in body fat and can in this way accumulate to toxic levels. The effects of long-term, low-level exposure to pesticides is not yet known but according to poison-control centre reports, children under the age of five are involved in 70% of all reported pesticide-related incidents. And over half those who die from pesticide-related causes are children. Although testing of these products is now more stringent, they are usually carried out only on animals – a process that, apart from being morally objectionable, does not guarantee their safety for humans.

Action These problems, together with the rising costs of agricultural chemicals, gave birth to an alternative approach to pest control for farmers – Integrated Pest Management (IPM). The aim is to reduce the use of chemical pesticides by combining them with other nonchemical methods, such as resistant plants, crop rotation, and biological controls (including insect traps and natural predators to keep the pest population down to manageable levels). But by using chemicals at all, this approach is not suitable for organic growers, who rely on biological controls alone.

Flies and tiny wasps are examples of parasites that live within the body of insects and caterpillars and either kill their hosts or eat their larvae. Lady birds, hover flies, dragon flies, and spiders are predators that prey on a wide range of insect pests. Sticky or oily boards in greenhouses and hessian (burlap) around fruit trees trap many pests. Birds and poultry are also very effective predators of snails, slugs, and beetles, as are toads and hedgehogs. Ashes, soot, lime, and sawdust around plants act as barriers; upturned pots with straw or paper attract earwigs; and nets prevent birds reaching ripening fruit. Aromatic plants – garlic, onions, marigolds, and tansy – repel some insects and these plants can be made into natural sprays.

The success of these methods depends on you knowing exactly what is happening in your garden and then learning who the real enemies are and how to combat them. Biological controls take longer to work, so you must be patient and be prepared to tolerate a small amount of initial pest damage. Grow a wide variety of plants and mix them in the same bed to ensure a diversity of predators. As a general rule, select resistant plant varieties and make the soil rich in organic compost to suppress soil pests and diseases. It is best to time your plantings to avoid seasonal infestations. But if needs be, use weak vegetable oil and soap solution sprays or low-toxic derris and pyrethrum powder sparingly (except where there are fish).

Water

Lawns and flower and vegetable beds are considerable users of water, especially if you use a hose and sprinkler system. Water consumption is much higher in affluent areas because gardens are more common and larger. In fact, in the dry US and Australian climates, well-watered gardens can use up to 80% of a household's daily water expenditure. This water is usually from drinking supplies, and is, therefore, inappropriate for watering lawns, cleaning cars, and hosing down concrete driveways and paths.

Action Reduce the size of your lawn and introduce native, water-conserving groundcover plants and trees. Use watering cans instead of a hose. Collect rainwater and use it for the garden, greenhouse, and car. In dry areas, use shade trees, creepers, and courtyards to provide shelter from the sun. Plant local moisture-retaining vegetation. Use recycled "greywater".

Lead

Some gardens near heavily used roads may have soil containing high levels of lead and other pollutants.

Action Ask your local environmental health department to test the soil or vegetables grown in it. Remove and replace contaminated soil in vegetable and flower beds with a deep layer of organic topsoil.

Bonfires

A smoky bonfire pollutes the air and can annoy neighbours. You may also be breaking the law. Rubber and plastic cause toxic fumes.

Action Compost as much garden rubbish as possible. Take woody cuttings and other noncompost rubbish to an official dumping site or ask your local authority to collect it. Don't use plastic bags, since they are not biodegradable. Use cardboard boxes or strong paper or hessian (burlap) sacks instead. If you do have a fire, burn only dry material and choose a dry and mild windy day to disperse the smoke.

Noise

Garden machines such as power mowers, hedgetrimmers, chainsaws, and DIY tools are very noisy and disturb the neighbourhood, especially at weekends.

Action Use hand tools whenever possible. By reducing the lawn size and establishing a natural landscape, you will need to do less cutting, and what there is will be manageable with hand mowers and hand clippers.

Epilogue

The inspiration for this book came from many people and sources around the world. It has been a voyage of discovery into the often uncharted territories of ecology, health, and spirit of the home. Of course, many others have ventured forth before, but most have tended to follow only one of these paths. And this, it seems, is where the main problem lies. An ecologist or energy conservationist will produce an "eco-home"; a medical practitioner or allergy expert, a "healthy home"; and those who advocate sacred architecture and healing environments, a "spiritual home". But a natural home must, like the concept of Gaia, be rounded and whole and embody all three – the "eco-home", the "healthy home" and the "spiritual home". But it is this combination that is not easy to find in modern houses and apartments. It is to older houses that one has often to turn to find their unconscious presence.

The more our homes have come to be designed and built by specialists, the more they tend to reflect certain imbalances. Although architects and designers are trained to assemble information and then synthesize it into the design of a building, the stumbling block, at present, is that critical information is missing – the new information and criteria about ecology and health so vital to all our futures.

The world has changed a great deal during the time this book has been in production and the pace of awareness and action is quickening, especially among the general public. The environmental crisis has deepened and worries about the effects of chemical and other pollution on personal health have increased. It is easy to become despondent or apathetic and feel that it is hopeless to even try to do anything. Quite to the contrary, however, what is surprising is the determination of those who now see these problems to confront them and to bring about change. They all seem to share the same sense of urgency.

As soon as you become involved, you know time is short. It is not a matter of taking action by the year 2000 – you have to start today. There are some optimistic signs and the gatherings of world government representatives are now beginning to bring action. The banning of harmful CFCs, albeit not immediate enough, is a hopeful example. The global warming is being taken seriously at last and tough measures to control greenhouse gases must be imminent. These decisions will have repercussions on our daily lives and on our homes. The only really effective way, however, will be if concerted action happens on all fronts and involves everyone.

And everyone can help in many simple ways in their lifestyles and around the home. You don't have to give up everything you like and your home can still be comfortable. In fact, it will be even more so. It will be healthier for you and it will do less harm to the environment. You will begin to feel more satisfaction and know that, at last, you are doing something positive.

You don't have to change everything, or do it all at once – make changes gradually and, above all, enjoy the process. Make it creative, involve others, share your ideas, join a campaigning organization, and support "green" issues, locally and internationally, at every possible opportunity.

This book, like any book, can only be a beginning, but if it helps to start you on the path toward a healthier lifestyle and one that is more caring of the environment, it will have served a good purpose, and you will already have taken the first steps toward making a natural home.

Note to reader: Making a natural home is still something new. We would be interested to hear any comments or suggestions you may have on this book, your personal experiences in adapting your home or building a new one to make it more natural, and any suppliers of natural products you have found helpful. Please write to the address below and, if in the UK, enclose a stamped, self-addressed envelope if you need a reply:

The Natural House Book
Gaia Books Ltd
66 Charlotte Street
London W1P 1LR

APPENDICES

CHARTS

Sustainable timber

To conserve tropical forests use both indigenous woods and timber from managed plantations round the world. As this chart shows, there is an extensive variety of hardwood and softwood trees available not under threat. Softwood doors and window frames are just as serviceable as those made from a tropical hardwood such as mahogany. For strength and durability, consider using native hardwood species such as beech and oak.

Terms used below refer to the time taken for timber to decay when in contact with the ground. Perishable: less than 5 years; Non-durable: 5-10 years; Durable: 15-25 years; Very durable: resistant for more than 25 years.

Hardwoods

Alder
Straight, fine grain, and even texture. Light red to orange brown. Seasons well, very water resistant. Comparative lightness, softness, and ease of working makes this a suitable wood for brooms and brush backs, toys, and general turnery. Also used for plywood. Perishable. Native to UK and northern Europe.

Apple
Dense, heavy wood with fine texture. Turns and finishes well. Dries slowly with a marked tendency to distort. Native to UK and Europe. Perishable.

Ash, American
The sapwood is almost white with a tough, coarse texture. Used for tool handles, spades, and caravan frames.

Ash, European
White to light brown in colour, turning temporarily pink when freshly cut. Straight grained and coarse textured, ash is exceptionally strong with good bending properties. Stains and polishes well. Used widely for sports goods, tool handles, cabinet work, and chairs. Boat oars, tillers, and canoe frames are also made from this tough wood. Perishable.

Aspen
Greyish white or pale brown in colour with a fine, even texture. Used extensively for veneers, boxes, crates, and the interior parts of furniture. Widely used in North America for the manufacture of wood pulp and paper, and for plywood and chipboard. Native to Europe and North America.

Beech
Whitish to very pale brown, darkening on exposure to a slightly reddish brown. Knot free with flecked grain pattern giving a uniform and attractive finish. One of the strongest European timbers with exceptional bending and turning properties. Used in larger quantities in the UK than any other hardwood, mainly to make furniture such as chairs and desks; also veneers, doors, and block flooring. Not recommended for exterior use. Perishable. Native to Europe.

Birch
White to light brown in colour with a fine texture. Widely used as plywood. Solid birch mainly used in furniture for upholstery, framing; in doors; turnery. Perishable. European native.

Blue gum, Australian
The blue gum Eucalyptus is exceptionally fast growing. Well established in California by the late 19th century. Has about 50% more strength than white oak but needs to dry very slowly to prevent splitting. Used for construction and, to a limited extent, boatbuilding.

Elm
Brown, attractive wood which has good working and bending properties. Dutch elm is 40% tougher than English but has been decimated by disease. Very resistant to splitting due to cross grain, and highly water resistant. Used in the furniture industry for cabinet work, chairs, settee frames, and the seats of windsor chairs. Widely used for coffins and in boat building. White elm has great bending properties and is also used for flooring. European native. Non-durable.

Hickory
Brown or reddish-brown with a rather coarse texture. Exceptionally tough and shock resistant. Used for tool handles and sports goods. In the US it is used for vehicle building where ash would be used in the UK. Native to North America.

Lime
Uniform white or pinkish-yellow colour, turning pale brown on exposure. Straight grained with a fine texture, this soft wood is easy to machine and good for carving, turnery, furniture, and parts of musical instruments.

Maple
Creamy white with a reddish tinge. Some trees have a fine-figured wavy grain known as "bird's eye" maple. Strong and resistant to wear, it is very suitable for furniture making, worktops, and panelling. An excellent flooring timber that wears smoothly. Non-durable. Native to Europe and North America. In Australia, Queensland Maple (silkwood) has similar uses.

Oak
Yellowish-brown with very distinct broad rays, giving a beautiful "silver-grain" effect. Gallic acid present in oak corrodes ironwork and other metals that come into contact with it in damp conditions. One of the most widely used hardwoods for construction, furniture, panelling, and high-quality interior joinery for stairs, parquet floors, and boat building. Its strength, durability, and impermeability make it suitable for exterior use in window sills, fascias, doors, and fencing. White oak is stronger than American red, which grows faster but is less suitable for exterior use and more susceptible to pests. Resistant to weather, fungi, and insects. Good alternative to mahogany or teak for dining room furniture. Durable. Native to Europe, North America. Australian silky oak is similar to American red and stains and polishes well.

Pear
Pinkish-brown in colour with a fine, even texture. Used for musical instruments, carving, and veneers, with excellent turning properties for fruit bowls and so on. Easily stained and polished. European native.

Poplar

Light in colour, varying from white, greyish, or pale brown to reddish and with a woolly grain. Natural moisture may result in patchy staining. A lightweight timber that is very tough for its weight and less liable to splinter than softwoods. Used for matches, shelving, interior joinery, turnery, and plywood manufacture. Non-durable. European native.

Sycamore

White or yellowish white with a natural lustre. Some wood has a curly grain and is traditionally used for violin backs. Good for staining and polishing and is used for furniture, domestic utensils, brush handles, veneers. Perishable.

Walnut, American

Rich, dark brown deepening with age. Grain is usually straight but can be wavy and the texture is coarse. Widely employed as a decorative veneer in high-quality furniture. Seasons well.

Walnut, European

Variable in colour with a greyish-brown background marked with irregular dark streaks. Grain is naturally wavy. Excellent for staining and polishing. Used for furniture, veneers, and turned bowls.

Walnut, Australian

Light or pinkish brown to dark brown, with vari-coloured markings. Grain is interlocked and wavy, producing a striped effect. Difficult to work. Used for superior decorative work and plywood.

Whitewood, American

Sapwood is almost white in colour with a fine and even texture. Used in carpentry, furniture, and boat building. Good quality, soft, and easily worked. Often used for kitchen furniture. Extensively used for plywood manufacture in the US. Non-durable. North American native.

Softwoods

Cedar, western red

Reddish brown weathering to silver grey. Very durable and resistant to fungi and rodent attack. Easy and light to work. Used for construction, exterior cladding, roof shingles, and venetian blinds. Red cedar was used extensively in Australia until it became scarce in the early part of this century.

Fir, Douglas

Pink to light reddish-brown Straight grained with a tendency to wavy or spiral grain. Difficult to work but strong and available in long lengths and large sections. Stains but does not paint well. UK and western American native.

Hemlock, western

Pale brown with distinct growth rings; usually straight grained and fairly even textured. Stains and paints well but not durable when subject to alternating wet and dry conditions. Used in construction and general joinery, panelling, furniture, and flooring. Western American native.

Larch

Reddish brown heartwood and yellowish white sapwood. Straight grained, very durable, tough, and strong. Used for planking, heavy construction, poles, fencing, gates, flooring, furniture, windows, and interior and exterior doors. Harder than pine, very resinous and difficult to stain or varnish. Difficult to plane and splinters easily. European native.

Pine

Many varieties are available including pitch pine, red pine, and yellow pine. Used for joinery, construction, furniture, panelling, windows, and interior and exterior doors. Exterior cladding. Good durable timber, easy to work. Rich in resin. Must be sealed before being stained or treated. Good alternative to teak and mahogany shelving, bowls, and chopping boards in the kitchen. Europe and North and South American native.

Spruce

White to pink and mostly straight grained. Stains, paints, and varnishes well. Used for construction timbers, roofbeams, cladding, floors, carpentry, planking, joinery. Resistant to weather and fungi, and insects. UK and North American native.

Yew

Orange-brown heartwood and white sapwood with attractive grain. Used for furniture, especially for bedrooms, interior joinery. Strong, hard, and durable.

Note:

Naturally occurring resins in pine, spruce, fir, and other coniferous woods are a potential irritant to the highly sensitive. Acceptable if sealed.

Threatened tropical hardwoods*

There is a strong lobby against imported rainforest timbers, especially those from Malaysia where destruction of the forest has become a worldwide political issue. Those listed here are in widespread use. Always check the country of origin of imported timber before buying. Avoid tropical timber unless produced on managed plantations.

Afrormosia
Ebony

Gaboon/Okoume
Iroko
Jelutong
Kapur
Kempas
Keruing
Mahogany (from Africa, Brazil, Central America, Cuba, Jamica, Spain)
Meranti/Lauan
Merbau
Padauk
Ramin
Rosewood/Jacaranda
Sapele
Teak
Utile

Softwoods

Overuse of softwoods is becoming a problem. Redwood (sequoia) is a decay-resistant timber valued for construction. Buy only from managed sources. Some cedar and cypress species are also depleted.

*FOE Good Wood Guide

Fabrics, grasses, and canes

This chart provides information for those with allergies or sensitivities to pesticides and other chemicals by giving details on current practices of treating natural fibres. It also provides information on the conservation status of reed, rattan, and bamboo.

Natural fabrics

Treatment of natural materials: growing and processing

Cotton growers are heavy users of pesticides and fertilizers. The seed is treated with fungicides and the plant is vulnerable to attack from a large variety of pests. Increased resistance of insects to general-purpose pesticides has awakened further interest in biological controls. In parts of India, pheromones are used to control the breeding of cotton boll moths. Yet this same country's cotton growers use DDT – one of the hazardous organochlorine group of pesticides largely banned in the US. Pesticide manufacturers who trade worldwide are, however, reluctant to invest in such controls since they are species-specific and may be appropriate only for crops in one particular region or country. Linen is also sprayed with pesticides, but to a much lesser degree since its growing cycle is shorter than that of cotton. Wool and silk are not derived from plants so the pesticide problem does not arise.

Once harvested, cotton is bleached, treated, and dyed. The same applies to linen, which traditionally used to be left out in the fields to bleach naturally by exposure to the direct action of sunlight, rain, and dew. This process has now been replaced by chemical bleaching. Not all treatments, however, are potentially harmful. "Sanforized" cotton is preshrunk and "mercerized" cotton is treated with a nontoxic solution to improve strength and colour-fastness. "Easy care" and "crease resistant" cotton and linen, however, have

been treated with a cross-linking chemical – usually formaldehyde resin. Correctly applied, the easy-care properties will remain for the life of the fabric. Sensitive individuals are well advised to avoid such finishes if fabric is likely to come into contact with the skin. Not all fabric treated with formaldehyde resin is, however, labelled "easy-care", "crease-resistant" or "non-iron". At the point of sale, it is almost impossible to tell if a finish has been applied. Silk, too, may be lightly treated with formaldehyde to prevent water spotting but hand washing in soapy water can often remove the finish.

Chemical dyes for cotton, linen, wool, and silk or the mordant used to fix the colour may be toxic to certain individuals. If you cannot find material in its raw state, choose natural or light-coloured fabrics. Rich or brightly coloured materials that bleed strongly when washed will be absorbed more easily through your skin. Vegetable-dyed material is available, but is more likely to have been already made up into furnishings or garments rather than sold in lengths. Avoid "weighted silk", which is treated with salts of tin and lead to make it heavier.

In the US it is possible to buy 100% organically grown cotton bed linen – futons, pillows, quilts – although in 1988 there was only a single supplier. Organic cotton is not yet available in the UK. Unbleached cotton and linen are, however, available, so you can make up your own furnishing materials, curtains, and clothes. Colour

them with vegetable dyes if you wish. An easier option is to buy pure cotton and linen, or cotton flannel, sheets, and pillowcases, that do not have easy-care finishes, although they can be relatively expensive.

The manufacturing process of wool uses few chemicals, except at the scouring stage to remove grease. Wool is naturally elastic, so easy-care finishes are unnecessary. But most wool is mothproofed before sale. Untreated wool can, however, be bought direct from suppliers and many craft stores and specialist suppliers sell unbleached or vegetable-dyed rugs, knitwear, and other wool products. Chemical-free wool futons, mattresses, and underblankets are available in the US. To add colour to your home, look out for beautiful pure-wool rugs, known as Dobag, from northwestern Turkey. Made by village co-operatives who have rediscovered the old processes and plants used before the advent of synthetics, all the rugs have been dyed with plants such as chamomile, walnut, and madder root.

Natural fabrics and fire retardants

Cotton, linen, and other plant-based fibres begin to char at relatively low temperatures – 150°C (300°F). If the temperature rises above this level, they flare up and blaze. For this reason, hospital bedding and babies' and children's nightwear is treated with a flame-resistant finish. In the UK, a melamine formaldehyde compound is one of the chemicals used. Such treatment may leave "free"

fomaldehyde or other chemical residues on the fabric and expose young children to skin irritations. Nightwear for older children and adults will carry a fire warning if it has not been treated with a flame retardant. In the US and Canada the law requires that all mattresses and futons are treated with a fire retardant. In the UK, impending legislation requires that all new furniture sold in stores, including mattresses and bedbase fillings, must have either a covering fabric that resists a stringent test with a match flame, or a fire-retardant interlining fabric between cover and filling. From March 1993, these same rules will apply to all second-hand furniture.

Other types of fibre burn at much higher temperatures than those that are plant based. Protein-based wool, silk, and leather are a safer bet: they begin to smoulder and char, but not flame, at about 130°C (266°F). Synthetic fibres and polyurethane foam, on the other hand, melt first, then burn, while giving off choking, toxic fumes. Wool is naturally flame resistant due to the presence of water and the protein keratin. When alight, it is slow to smoulder and gives off little heat. In the US, wool mattresses and futons are exempt from fire regulations, or you can buy untreated bedding with a doctor's prescription. In the UK, if you do not want to sleep on a treated mattress or futon cover, buy bedding with a flame-retardant interlining. You can then cover your bedding with a naturally flame-proof fleece underblanket.

Rattan, bamboo, and reed

Hazards

○ Most fabrics, except wool and silk, will contain a certain amount of pesticide residue. Organophosphate and organochlorine varieties are absorbed through skin contact.
○ Virtually all fabric has been bleached before it is sold.
○ Most wool is cleaned or "scoured" with chemicals and mothproofed before the knitting or weaving process.
○ Many cottons are given "easy-care" or "non-crease" finishes by fixing chemicals known as "cross-linking agents" to the fabric.
○ Synthetics are often mixed in with natural fabrics. Poly-cotton is a mixture of polyester and cotton, and polyester has been treated with formaldehyde resin.
○ Chemical dyes and fixatives (mordants) may contain toxins, such as benzidene.

Suggestions

○ Soak all textiles in hot water with baking soda, vinegar, or borax before use to reduce pesticide residues. Wash thoroughly.
○ To avoid bleaching, buy "grey" unbleached fabric direct from spinners and weavers. Bleach the fabric naturally in sunlight.
○ Avoid fabrics with "easy-care" and "non-crease" finishes. These labels mean that the fabric has a permanent formaldehyde finish. This binds to the material: washing will not remove it.
○ Check labels carefully when buying natural materials and choose those with recognized marks, such as the woolmark, to avoid buying synthetic mixtures by mistake.
○ If you want coloured fabrics, look for those that have been dyed with pure vegetable dyes and nonchemical fixatives.

Rattan

Used for: cane furniture, basketware, mats, pots, ropes.
Most of the 600 species of rattan palms are native to the tropical rainforests of South East Asia. Rattan harvesting has given rise to a large industry employing many people. There is, however, a serious shortage of raw rattan cane on the world market. This is in part due to an export ban by Indonesia, which produces 80% of the world's harvest, but fundamentally because of over exploitation and rainforest clearing in countries such as Thailand and the Philippines where rattan was once plentiful. The overharvesting of rattan in these countries has made them totally dependent on imports.

Since virtually all rattan grows wild, pesticides are not usually employed. The crop is, however, fumigated with sulphur to prepare it for export and to protect it against deterioration while in transit.

The only way to stave off the destruction of wild rattan is the establishment of managed plantations. Work at an experimental plantation in Sabah has shown that rattan is a promising crop. But the value of rattan as a raw material means that it is difficult to protect in reserves and national parks. A total boycott on rattan, however, would have a disastrous effect on the millions of people who depend on the rattan industry for their livelihood, or to supplement a meagre income. A partial boycott would effectively reduce the market incentive to fund badly needed research into rattan cultivation. Try to buy cultivated rattan if you can find it. Ethical traders exist who supply rattan products produced under equitable conditions.

Bamboo

Used for: furniture, cases, baskets, screens, cooking utensils, rafts, bridges, houses, scaffolding, ski-sticks, pole-vaults, aeroplane wings, bicycle frames, pipes, beer.
You can make practically anything from bamboo: it is light but exceptionally strong, and flexible when heated. Most bamboo is found in China yet India is now the main commercial exporter. Since it is a persistent and particularly fast-growing plant there is little concern over its preservation, except where bamboo groves are being cleared to make way for agricultural crops. Bamboo is useful for reforesting and for controlling soil erosion.

Pesticides are not widely used in bamboo cultivation since infestations can be controlled simply by cutting out infected stems. Boring insects do, nevertheless, attack the crop once it has been cut and it is at this stage that most bamboo is treated. In small-scale production, soaking in water to reduce starch and sugar discourages insects but makes the stems brittle and may stain them. Rangoon oil, a type of thick petroleum, is widely used as a preservative, but large-scale growers believe that the most effective treatment for pests is a solution of boiled DDT and coconut oil. This mixture is applied to the outside of the canes but it is not yet known how permanent this toxic coating is. One precaution for the healthy home is to seal the bamboo with natural varnish, shellac, or even paint.

Look out for products made out of cultivated bamboo to avoid localized overharvesting and the endangering of wild life.

Reeds

Used for: roofing – sod, grass and thatch; woven artefacts such as mats, baskets, ornaments, and chair seats. Some are used for fillers and also to make brooms and brushes.
Reeds, grasses, and other non-woody plants have been used all over the world as a substitute for timber and stone. Every country has its own varieties, though some trade in the more uncommon or most useful types does take place. Holland provides much of the reed now used for thatch, while seagrass is imported from China and Taiwan.

Grasses for the home are collected from the wild as well as being a byproduct of cultivation. True grasses grow from the base, so with minimal management they easily survive mowing. Some of the plants used, however, are not true grasses, such as saw sedge and seagrass. These have to be more carefully managed to avoid overharvesting.

The most pressing source of danger for grasses is the general threat to their habitats. The reclamation of wetlands for agriculture deprives water reeds of their environment. The fertilizers leached into the water where others grow, reduce the quality of the reed. Desertification in Africa has also affected the supply of wild grass normally used for thatch.

Pesticide treatments and finishes used on grass products are minimal. Cultivated varieties may be treated with pesticides but many grasses are cut from wild sources. After harvesting they are dried and therefore not particularly prone to pest attack, though excessive wetting may encourage moulds. Some products, such as coloured baskets, may contain synthetic dyes.

Natural paints, varnishes, and finishes

Before deciding to introduce solid colour or finishes extensively into your home, consider leaving some surfaces untreated. White or coloured plaster, for example, needs no further treatment and good quality wood can be left alone to allow the grain to deepen. Natural materials are healthy and have their own special beauty: further embellishment may well be unnecessary.

Paints and varnishes checklist
○ Watch out for the lead content of paints, primers, and varnishes. Lead was traditionally used as a drying agent by paint manufacturers. Although it is now being phased out, it has not been totally excluded, only considerably reduced – to 0·25% in the UK, for example.
○ Study labels closely and avoid those products that have no information at all or list the most chemicals. Some chemicals are now acknowledged to be sufficiently dangerous for authorities to require the phrase "may cause cancer" to be shown on the label.
○ Conventional synthetic wood varnishes contain 40-50% solvents; nitro-cellulose varieties contain 70% solvents. Suspension paints generally have only a small proportion of solvents – around 2%.
○ Shellac, a pure resin used as a varnish, seals up to 80% of the fumes emitted by chemically treated building materials, such as particle board and plywood.
○ Be critical, even in the choice of natural paints and varnishes. Study labels closely and choose those products that list the ingredients most fully.

Making your own paint
One way of avoiding the potential health hazards of synthetic oil-based and emulsion paints is to make your own. By doing this you can experiment with colour and achieve unique and beautiful finishes. Distemper has been used for centuries on interior walls: add pigments to produce subtle tones. Transparent colour washes or glazes can be applied over a pale basecoat or straight on to plaster. For distempers and washes you will need, first of all, to make some hot size glue.

Hot size glue: soak 1 cup of size (available from artists' suppliers) in 1 litre (2 pints) water overnight. Heat in a bain-marie ready for use and add a drop of carbolic or boric acid to stop it turning rancid. For *colour washes* put 1 part artists' pigment into a bowl, add 1 part hot size glue and 5 parts water. Mix. For 5 litres (1 gallon) *distemper* mix 20 kilos (44lb) whiting (chalk) in a 5-litre (1-gallon) bucket of water, leave overnight and pour off excess water. Stir in hot size glue. For coloured distemper, add a paste of ½ kilo (1lb) tinting pigment mixed with water. (These recipes are taken from Kevin McCloud's article in *Country Living* magazine, August 1988.)

Natural paints
Natural resin organic paints contain none of the fungicides, plastics, or other chemical derivatives always present in synthetic paint. These can be personally and environmentally hazardous. Instead, natural paints allow you and your house to breathe. They are based on plant oils, particularly linseed, plant resins, and natural ingredients, such as chalk, india rubber, indigo, and pure aromatic oils.

Wall paint
Organic emulsion wall paint is easy to apply by brush or roller and has good covering qualities. It is usually available in white and has a semi-gloss finish. You then add natural toning pigments to create your own colour. There is also an inexpensive chalk-based off-white paint. It is like an improved whitewash and can be sponged but not washed. Other water-based indoor paints, such as traditional distemper or those thinned with milk casein, are also free from synthetic ingredients. Casein wall paint can be washed.

Oil paint
Organic oil-based gloss paint can be used on wood, stone, and metal surfaces both indoors and outdoors. Surfaces must first be primed. Durable and easy to apply using a brush or roller, the paint comes in a variety of colours produced by added earth pigments. It is purposely slow drying to maintain surface elasticity. An organic masonry paint is also available for exterior stone and plaster. Or you can use a lime-based whitewash and add colour by mixing in pure plant pigments.

Shellac and varnishes
Traditional varnishes are based on natural resins from tropical trees, plus linseed oil and thinners. The finest resins are called copals. Shellac and manila are other pure resins with excellent sealing qualities. Unfortunately, natural resins and varnishes have largely been superseded by synthetic products with potentially allergenic ingredients, such as solvents.

Organic paint suppliers, however, have produced a translucent wood protection that contains natural tree and plant oils, herb extracts, and lead-free drying agents. Known as "lazur", this varnish is microporous, which means that it allows the wood to breathe while preventing water penetration. Synthetic varnish simply traps its chemical vapours in the wood to be released when the surface becomes worn. For exterior use, the varnish must be tinted with natural nonfading pigments to protect the wood from the sun's UV rays. Windows, doors, porches, and garden furniture can all be finished and protected in this way.

Because no chemicals are used in its manufacture, lazur does not emit fumes. It is pleasantly scented and biodegradable.

Natural treatments

Preservatives

Most commercial wood treatments, especially for exterior wood, contain toxic arsenics or creosote. Acceptable, natural alternatives include a borax wood impregnation treatment that protects wood against fungus and insects. Pulverized borax salt particles lodge in the wood, preventing insect eggs from hatching. A wood-pitch impregnation made from resin-oil and beechwood distillate is also available for outdoor wood protection. Water resistant yet allowing the wood to breathe, this natural impregnation can be used on greenhouses, cold frames, garden furniture, and other architectural woodwork in constant contact with moisture. It does not harm plant growth.

Sealants and primers

The majority of wood sealants are synthetic preparations based on polyurethane and can be allergenic. For interior and exterior woodwork, cork, and clay try natural resin-oil primers. Their deep penetrating action enhances grains and patterns as well as giving lasting protection. Resin and oil finishes are another nontoxic alternative. These are water resistant, give a soft sheen, and are suitable even for surfaces on which food is prepared, such as chopping boards and worktops. Floors and furniture also benefit from this natural finish, which can be tinted with natural stains and pigments.

Stains and pigments

Stains and pigments derived only from vegetable and mineral sources, dispersed in natural binders, are available from organic paint suppliers. They offer both rich and subtle colours for inside and outside the home without harming the environment. Pigments sold by suppliers of artists' materials are mostly metal oxides from minerals that are dug out of the ground and washed. Others, however, are produced chemically to give a wider range of colour. Check with your supplier first to ensure that you buy only pigments from mineral or vegetable sources.

Water-based stains and toning pigments can be added to natural resin and water-based paints to achieve a wide variety of subtle pastel tones. For a particularly beautiful finish for walls, cover a white or pale-coloured basecoat with a transparent glaze made from diluted natural plant pigments, or use the colourwash recipe. Experiment with different colours and layering techniques: use two or three colours successively in thin washes for a subtle effect, or intensify the colour by applying several layers of the same shade. This system of painting has tremendous design potential.

Interior wood stains made from plant extracts will give warm tones to interior woodwork while bringing out the grain. Surfaces can then be treated with protective resin-oil, natural varnish, shellac, or wax to preserve colour and shine.

Thinners

Turpentine substitute or white spirit is the synthetic replacement for pure turpentine. This natural thinner and cleaner is distilled from a resinous oil derived from balsa wood and can be bought from builders' merchants and artists' suppliers.

Natural paint manufacturers have also produced their own thinner, derived from citrus peels. Similar to lemon oil but not as thick, it is free from any pesticides used to treat the fruit trees due to the relatively low temperature of the extraction process. It contains no petrochemicals and has a shorter drying time than white spirit, turpentine substitute, and natural turpentine. So, those with sensitivities to the turpentine substitutes, or even to turpentine itself, may be able to tolerate this natural alternative – if not immediately, then certainly after a comparatively short time.

Wax

Pure beeswax produces a soft sheen on all kinds of interior wood and gives a pleasant scent to your home. It feeds and protects all wood surfaces – new, old, and antique – while bringing out the natural beauty of the grain. Commercial furniture waxes made from beeswax and pure turpentine are widely available. They are suitable for sealed or unsealed wood.

Natural paint suppliers produce a mixture of beeswax and plant waxes that gives a durable, water-resistant finish and is pleasantly scented. It is particularly suitable for floors. Liquid beeswax is another natural treatment for wood, cork, stone, and clay. When used to treat wood floors, both these types of wax, solid and liquid, produce a semiconducting surface that has antistatic properties. Synthetic carpets, on the other hand, insulate and produce static, while metal surfaces result in too much electrical discharge. Unlike both these extremes the semiconducting surface produced by natural wax harmonizes with the electrostatic balance of our own bodies. By using wax on your floors you can improve the climate of your rooms.

Household cleaners

Washing powders

Personal hazards
Bleaching agents irritate the skin while enzymes may cause allergic reactions. Skin and breathing problems can result, further exacerbated by the residue that lingers on bedding and clothing.

Environmental hazards
Phosphates in detergents overfertilize algae, which multiply, rot, and clog up water. Oxygen supplies for fish and other plant life are then severely reduced resulting in suffocation.

Alternatives
Use phosphate-free, biodegradable products that are non polluting and nonirritating. Leading brand (see Resources p. 275) contains coconut and palm-oil-based cleaners, citrus oil, and dirt removers made from cotton and wool pulp. Being bleach and enzyme free, it is suitable for hand or machine washing. Biodegradable wool wash liquid and a fabric conditioner based on natural fatty acids, lemon oil and water, are also available. Pre soak heavily soiled articles in borax solution: 1 tbsp to 4·5 litres (1 gallon) of water. Borax deodorizes as well as removes stains. Try adding 1 tsp of white vinegar or baking soda per machine load to freshen and remove odours. For hand washing use plain, unperfumed soap flakes or make soft soap: dissolve 2 cups grated bar soap in 4·5 litres (1 gallon) of hot water: simmer 10 min, cool.

Washing-up liquid

Personal hazards
Detergent, dye, and artificial fragrance can irritate, dry out, and cause chapping of the skin. Toxic if swallowed.

Environmental hazards
Washing-up liquids contain water-polluting phosphates that destroy fish and plant life and require lengthy and complex procedures for their breakdown.

Alternatives
Phosphate-free products do not contain irritating petrochemical agents or synthetic colours. Leading brand (see Resources p. 275) has a coconut oil and milk whey cleanser, sea salt, plus chamomile and calendula extracts that soften and condition the hands as well as promoting the healing of small cuts and scratches. Citrus oils give a pleasant lemon scent. Or use plain liquid soap and add fresh lemon juice to cut grease.

Bleaches and scouring powders

Personal hazards
Chlorine compounds, such as sodium hypochlorite, found in most bleaches, give off toxic fumes that are highly irritating to eyes, nose, and throat, and can damage lungs. Bleach burns the skin and is toxic if swallowed. Some scouring powders contain ammonia: never mix these with bleach or toilet-bowl cleaners – this releases deadly chloramine gases.

Environmental hazards
Bleach and ammonia pollute water and destroy beneficial bacteria that break down sewage. They also cause serious damage to septic tanks.

Alternatives
Biodegradable cleaners are available for sinks, tiles, baths, and toilets. Leading brand of general-purpose surface cleaner (see Resources p. 275) contains coconut and palm oil soap, chalk, sea salt, and chamomile and calendula extracts to make an effective yet nonabrasive cleaner. A baking soda and water paste or borax sprinkled on a damp cloth are both efficient scouring powders for baths, sinks, tiles, and work-tops. A leading toilet cleaner contains acetic rather than strong hydrochloric acid plus pine, lemon, eucalyptus and lavender oils, which are naturally disinfectant. Pouring vinegar down the toilet, leaving overnight, and then brushing well, or brushing with baking soda, are gentle but highly efficient cleaners and disinfectants.

Floor and furniture polish

Personal hazards
Toxic chemicals, such as phenol, in polish produce skin rashes and may cause convulsions if swallowed. Nitrobenzene, another ingredient, can cause skin discoloration and vomiting. Once applied, residues continue to give off fumes.

Environmental hazards
In aerosol form, spray polish discharges particles of chemical solvents into the atmosphere. Propellants may contain ozone-damaging CFCs.

Alternatives
Buy pure beeswax polishes or melt 57g (2oz) beeswax, 140ml (5fl oz) real turpentine, 2 tbsp linseed oil, and 2 tsp cedar oil over simmering water. This will clean and care for wooden furniture as well as scenting the atmosphere. Or mix 3 parts olive oil with 1 part white vinegar; 2 parts vegetable oil with 1 part lemon juice; or use plain mayonnaise: the smell quickly dissipates. Apply with a soft cloth. For oak: boil 1 litre (2 pints) beer with 1 tbsp sugar and 2 tbsp beeswax. Cool, wipe on to wood, and allow to dry. Polish with a chamois cloth. To renovate leather furniture, mix 1 cup vinegar with 1 cup linseed oil and apply.

Metal polishes

Personal hazards
Ingredients such as ammonia and sulphuric acid burn the skin and emit toxic fumes. These plus unknown petroleum distillates are highly irritant, corrosive, and poisonous.

Environmental hazards
Chemical fumes from metal polishes pollute indoor air and, if emptied down the drain, the water supply.

Alternatives
Clean cutlery by laying a sheet of aluminium foil in a pan; cover with 5-7·5cm (2-3in) of water, then add 1 tsp salt and 1 tsp baking soda. Bring to the boil and then add cutlery, ensuring it is submerged. Boil for 2-3 min, remove, rinse, and dry. For silver jewellery, shred enough foil to fill half a glass jar, add 1 tbsp salt and top up with water. Drop in small items for 2-3 min, then rinse and dry. Keep jar covered. For brass and copper, make a paste of lemon juice and salt, or clean with a lemon wedge dipped in baking soda. Hot white vinegar and salt or hot tomato juice also cleans brass and copper effectively.

Air fresheners

Personal hazards
Most air fresheners contain naphthalene, phenol, and other toxic chemicals, which combine with the artificial perfume to produce respiratory and eye problems, headaches, and nausea.

Environmental hazards
Chemical particles in air fresheners pollute rather than freshen indoor air. Propellants in aerosols may contain harmful CFCs.

Alternatives
Buy or make your own pot pourri from fragrant dried flowers, such as lavender, rose, carnation, and chamomile. Tip into a bowl and add a few drops of a complementary essential oil, such as lavender. Your favourite essential oils can also be burned in incensors and vaporizers: sandalwood is relaxing, lemon and pine are refreshing. Bunches of flowers and pots of home-grown herbs are excellent ways of sweetening indoor air or simply add cloves and cinnamon to simmering water. An opened box of baking soda placed in the refrigerator will absorb smells and deodorize the inside.

Personal cleansers

Personal hazards
Soap can upset the skin's natural acid balance, leaving it vulnerable to germs and chemical toxins. Deodorants destroy beneficial, protective skin flora. Infections and irritations can result. Antiperspirants that use zinc or aluminium salts to block up sweat ducts prevent toxins from being excreted. Colours and preservatives in shampoo irritate skin and eyes.

Environmental hazards
Aerosol deodorants and antiperspirants may contain CFCs. Many soaps and shampoos are tested via insertion into the eyes of live rabbits. Acid effluents released when manufacturing the titanium dioxide pigments used in toothpaste acidify rivers and seas.

Alternatives
The many fragrant herbal soaps and shampoos on the market will cleanse the hair and skin, restoring their natural acid balance. The plant oils in herbal cleansers are gentle and nourishing. Choose biodegradable products with minimum packaging which have not been tested on animals (see Resources p. 275). An infusion of rosemary is excellent for dark hair; of chamomile for light. Make your own deodorant from dried and powered orange peel, lemon peel, and orris root. Pat on like talc. Or use plain baking soda, which minimizes odour and absorbs wetness. For teeth, use bleach- and detergent-free herbal toothpastes from health food stores, or make your own using 1 tbsp arrowroot, 1 tsp fine sea salt, ½ tsp bicarbonate of soda and 10 drops peppermint oil.

Insect repellants

Personal hazards
Fly sprays release airborne poisons that are then inhaled and which may contaminate food. Diethyl toluamide, found in commercial insect repellants, can eat through plastic and is highly irritating to the skin and respiratory tract.

Environmental hazards
Insecticides not only destroy pests but also upset the natural balance by eliminating other beneficial insect predators that feed on the pests. Their chemical constituents can be passed on in food to cause serious digestive problems. Aerosol repellants may contain CFCs.

Alternatives
Repel flies by hanging up bunches of cloves or filling vases with deterrent herbs, such as tansy' rue, and penny royal. Or grow basil, rosemary, and thyme, which are also good repellants. Make your own fly papers by boiling equal parts of sugar, corn syrup, and water together: spread on brown paper. Plant mint outside the house to keep out ants, or sprinkle dried chilli or paprika round doors and skirting boards. Walnut leaves – 6 handfuls to 500ml (1 pint) of water boiled for 20-30 min are another excellent ant deterrant. Aphid infestation can be treated herbally with pure derris or pyrethrum powder, or spray plants with soft soap: a nontoxic mixture of vegetable oils and potash that smothers pests without harming plants.

Household waste

Reuse of nontoxic waste

○ It has been estimated that 80% of rubbish could be reused in the same form or processed to make a new product.

○ Recycling reduces the need for unattractive landfill sites. These are becoming scarcer in small countries such as the UK.

○ Nonrenewable resources are used much more economically and efficiently if we recycle and reuse rather than throw away.

○ Recycling encourages us to protect our local environment and, by extension, conserve resources worldwide.

○ Properly managed waste can generate income. It can also provide energy for heat and electricity.

What you can do

○ Create less waste in the first place by buying only what you need.

○ Reuse and mend whenever possible. Avoid using things that cannot be recycled.

○ When disposal is necessary, recycle as much material as possible.

○ Avoid plastics. Due to the extensive variety of chemical compositions that require separate treatment, plastics are very difficult to sort and recycle.

○ When shopping, reuse plastic carrier bags if you already have them. Do not use fresh ones. Ask for paper carriers or better still take your own basket.

○ Avoid nonreturnable and plastic bottles; buy glass instead, which can be recycled. Facilities for recycling plastic bottles are not generally available.

○ Avoid overpackaged goods such as prepacked vegetables on polystyrene trays covered in clingfilm, which cannot be recycled. Refuse plastic bags and buy in bulk: this means less packaging, less waste, and less damage to the environment.

○ Campaign for local recycling schemes and lobby manufacturers to aid recycling by labelling their containers and plastic packaging.

○ If you have a garden, turn kitchen waste into compost and improve the productivity of your soil.

Recycling in the home

Recycling facilities differ widely according to where you live. If no facilities exist for recycling glass, cans, and plastic, campaign for them to be provided by your local authority.

Glass

Glass can be recycled over and over again without any deterioration in quality. It is cheaper than new glass and a more efficient use of natural resources. Buy refillable or returnable bottles, like the UK milk bottle, when you can. Nonreturnable bottles and jars can be deposited in your nearest bottle bank. Wash them first and remove tops and caps. Sort into clear and coloured glass. If no bottle bank exists, suggest it to your local authority. Campaign for banks to be sited in convenient places such as supermarket car parks and shopping malls.

Cans

Cans made from tin-plated steel (eg beer cans) can be melted down and processed but the metal produced is not of particularly good quality. Aluminium is easier to recycle and much more valuable. Most soft drinks are sold in aluminium cans, which can be recycled to produce new, high-quality aluminium. Can manufacturers are considering having standard symbols on cans to tell the consumer their composition. Campaigning for the introduction of these symbols and can recycling facilities would reduce waste and be less of a drain on mineral resources. Collection points do exist for aluminium cans. In the US, deposits are reclaimed when cans are recycled. Rinse cans and squash them, ready for recycling. Aluminium foil (eg food containers and milk bottle and yoghurt carton tops) is also accepted by some charities. Recycle larger metal items by taking them to scrap metal merchants: they will buy iron, steel, copper, tin, lead, and zinc.

Paper

Buying recycled paper, from toilet rolls to writing pads, helps to reduce the massive number of trees cut down each year to satisfy the demands for paper and board. Recycled toilet paper does not contain bleach so it is more biodegradable than bleached and coloured varieties. Save newspapers, cards, and junk mail, and tie them in bundles ready for collection and recycling. If there is no collection in your area, take paper to your local recycling centre or waste paper merchant. Don't throw away magazines: save and donate them to health centres, hospitals, and homes for the elderly. White computer paper is particularly valuable to waste paper merchants since it is usually only lightly inked.

Plastic

Specialist recycling facilities are necessary for plastic since there are more than 50 types in use that may need different treatment. Experimental bottle banks have been set up to take the large polyethelene terephthalate (PET) plastic bottles that usually contain soft drinks and mineral water. Some countries have banned plastic bottles altogether. All plastic is highly combustible but not biodegradable. Never burn plastic foam or rubber in an open fire. Recycling plastic, because of the specialist classification necessary, is also expensive. Cut down on the amount of plastic in your home by choosing glass bottles and jars. Refuse plastic bags and carrier bags. Avoid plastic-packaged goods and plastic food wrapping. Use greaseproof paper or cellophane – a natural plant product that is biodegradabe.

Organic matter
If you have a garden, vegetable peelings and uncooked left-over food, even eggshells and bones, provide valuable nutrients for your garden. In Germany city dwellers have separate green dustbins for organic waste, which is then taken away for use as garden or farm compost.

Textiles and clothes
Charity shops, jumble sales, and textile merchants will accept clothes and fabrics. Some wool and cotton garments can be unravelled and the yarn reused.

Building materials
Reuse second-hand bricks, stone, tiles, timber beams, weatherboard, shingles, and solid doors rather than buy new ones. Some towns have recycling centres for older materials.

Hazardous waste
The availability of hazardous waste collection services is mixed. Some areas are very advanced with a home collection service and centres already set up. In other areas, no provision is made for the domestic consumer: services are aimed only at industrial users. Campaign for a hazardous waste collection in your area and contact pressure groups, such as Friends of the Earth or Greenpeace, as well as government agencies.

Virtually every household that uses synthetic goods made from petrochemicals produces harmful or hazardous waste. Pouring bleach, scouring powder, metal polish, or paint thinner down the sink or drain, for example, contributes to the contamination of our drinking water.

Use the information in this chart to identify safer ways to dispose of hazardous household waste. Refer also to the chart on pages 266-7 for natural household products that will not damage your home or the environment.

Checklist
○ Use natural, nontoxic household products whenever possible.
○ If you have no option, try to buy products that contain only very small quantities of toxic chemicals. Use them very sparingly and avoid "concentrated" varieties.
○ Do not throw away partially used containers and keep substances in the original container with lids tightly secured until they can be safely disposed of.
○ Never pour gasoline, motor oil, or engine cleaning fluid down the drain.
○ Stop buying household products in aerosol containers, or buy only non-CFC brands. Use up contents and throw aerosols away only when empty: the contents explode when incinerated and discharge chemical gases into the air.
○ Campaign for a hazardous waste collection service in your community. Commercial contractors may agree to collect only large quantities of waste. Organize a joint collection with friends and neighbours.

Disposal of hazardous waste

Furniture, floor, and metal polish; oil paints and paint stripper; wood stains and preservative:
Do not dispose of these substances. Store them safely and take them to a hazardous waste collection centre, if one exists. If not, campaign for one to be set up.

Ammonia-based cleaners; chlorine bleach; disinfectants; flea spray; moth balls; oven cleaners:
Do not discard or pour them down the drain. Use contents fully and then dispose of them with household waste. If you cannot use up the contents fully, store them until a hazardous waste collection can be made.

Used car oil, transmission fluid, batteries:
Take them to a service station or reclamation centre for recycling.

Water-based paint:
Air-dry water-based paint until the contents solidify and then dispose of the container with other household waste.

Thinners and turpentine:
Keep these substances in a tightly closed jar and allow the contaminants to settle out. Strain the thinner through muslin or fine-mesh gauze. Reuse the liquid. Let the remaining deposit solidify and then dispose of them as above.
(Hazardous waste disposal information reproduced from US Environmental Hazards Management Institute guidelines.)

Rating your home

Health hazard checklist

This checklist itemizes the hazards you are most likely to find around your home and garden. Use the list as a guide to check hazards in each area and room of your house. Then you will be able to identify those parts where action is most needed.

Building structure
Formaldehyde in: fibreboard, particle board, plywood.
Radon gas via: air, water, some building materials.
Insulation materials: UFFI in cavity walls.
Asbestos around: pipes, boilers, furnaces; in roof and floor tiles; fireproofing boards.
Toxic timber treatment: roof and floor timbers.

Basement
Asbestos fireproofing and insulation.
Boilers: coal, gas, wood, oil.
DIY materials: cleaners, oil, paints, thinners.
Radon gas from sub-soil.

Garage (attached)
Exhaust fumes.
DIY materials.
Antifreeze.
Aerosol sprays.
Brake fluid.
Oil and gasoline.
Paints.

Kitchen
Gas stoves (with pilot lights).
Microwave ovens.
Cooker without extractor hood.
Fluorescent lights (old).
Particle-board units, worktops, shelves.
Petrochemical-based paints and varnishes.
PVC flooring.
Polluted tap water.
Spring water in plastic bottles.
Pesticides in foods.
Cookware: aluminium or non-stick.
Paper products.
Plastics in: bottles, cups, food packaging, glasses, light fittings, plates.
Household cleaners: aerosols,

air fresheners, ammonia bleach, chlorinated scouring powder, detergents, dishwashing liquid, disinfectants, drain cleaners, fabric cleaners, oven cleaners, polishes, metal polishes, stain repellants.

Living room
Gas fire.
Open fireplace.
Paraffin/kerosene heater.
Wood or coal stove.
Wallpaper and paste with fungicides, insecticides.
Petrochemical-based paints and varnishes.
Plastic equipment and fittings.
Synthetic wall-to-wall carpet.
Polyurethane foam in upholstery.
Television.
Formaldehyde in: decorative panelling, foam carpet backing or underlay, foam padding in furniture, non-iron chair/sofa covers, particle-board furniture, shelving.
Toxic household cleansers: aerosols, air fresheners, carpet and upholstery shampoo, furniture and floor polish.

Home office
Personal computers and word processors.
Photocopying machines.
Rubber cement, fixatives, and glues.
Typewriter correction fluid.

Bedroom
Petrochemical-based paints and varnishes.
Synthetic wall-to-wall carpets.
Metal bed frames.

Sprung mattresses.
Electric blankets, alarm clocks, radios.
Formaldehyde in: easy-care sheets and pillowcases, foam mattresses, foam pillows, particle-board fitted units, polyester-filled mattresses, quilts, pillows, duvets.
Fire retardants in: bedding, nightwear, mattresses, quilts, duvets.
Permanent-press clothing.
Mothballs.
Aerosol sprays.
Cosmetics.

Nursery and children's bedrooms
High-voltage overhead power cables near to house.
Power sockets and cables near bed.
Leaded paints.
Petrochemical-based paints and varnishes.
Painted wood.
Vinyl wallpapers.
Formaldehyde in: easy-care sheets, polyester-filled mattresses, quilts.
Fireproofed sleepwear.
Metal toys.
Plastics in: waterproof pants, nappies/diapers, undersheets, toys.
Bleached paper nappies/diapers.

Bathroom
Petrochemical-based paints and varnishes.
Fungicides in paints.
Vinyl wallpaper.
Poor ventilation.
Mould.
PVC flooring.
Plastics in: basin, bath, shower curtains.
Radon gas from water.
Shower head (not cleaned).
Medicine cabinet – unlocked.

Personal cleansers: aerosol deodorants, hair sprays, perfumes.
Synthetic soaps and shampoos.
Household cleansers: air fresheners, bleach, disinfectant, scouring powder.

Garden
Traffic fumes.
Lead in soil.
Bonfires.
Timber preservatives, creosote.
Insect repellants.
Pesticides.
Fertilizers.
Aerosol sprays.
Power tools.

Energy and water

To find out how much energy and water your household consumes, fill in the charts below. Then check with your local energy and water conservation offices to find out if your consumption is too high.

Energy

Look at your energy bills for the last year or two and record the following quarterly and total amounts:

	units consumed					
	spring	summer	autumn	winter	totals	cost
Gas (therms/cu ft)						
Electricity (Kwh)						
Coal (kilos/cwt)						
Oil (litres/gals)						
Other ( )						
					total cost	

In cold and temperate climates you will almost certainly find that peak consumption occurs in the winter heating quarter. In hot climates you will use as much, or more, on cooling your house during the summer quarter. It is during these peak months that you can make the greatest energy and cost savings. Space heating and cooling account for most energy consumption, followed by cooking, lighting, electrical appliances, and water heating. With simple energy conservation measures – draughtproofing, insulation, and using hot water and electricity economically – you can save up to half of your consumption.

Check if your home has the following:

☐ Draughtproofing on windows and doors
☐ Loft insulation
☐ Hot water tank insulation
☐ Foil behind radiators on outside walls
☐ Thermostats – house and hot water tank
☐ Wall insulation
☐ Ground floor insulation
☐ Double/secondary glazing

If not, start now to incorporate these in your home. You can also consider other measures:

☐ Heat/cool rooms for shorter periods
☐ Adjust thermostats (slightly lower for heating and higher for cooling)
☐ Replace an old boiler with a more efficient model
☐ Install individual room/radiator thermostats
☐ Add a sunspace to collect solar heat
☐ Increase shelter or shade to outside of house

Then check electrical appliances. Do you have a:

☐ Refrigerator
☐ Freezer
☐ Washing machine
☐ Dishwasher
☐ Clothes dryer
☐ Electric cooker
☐ Microwave oven
☐ Electric kettle
☐ TV
☐ Video
☐ Stereo
☐ Blender
☐ Mixer
☐ Others: list

You may use all of these, and more. Old appliances generally use more energy than newer ones. Try to replace them with energy-efficient models and use economy settings whenever possible.

Water

If you have a water meter fitted to your incoming supply, you will find it easier to record your consumption, both quarterly and annually. Keep detailed records, and notice where the consumption peaks occur. Ask your water supply authority or company to calculate whether your consumption is above average. If you have a garden, you will use most in the summer months, especially if you use a hose or sprinklers. If you do not have a meter, consider having one fitted now. Do you:

☐ Use a hose to water the garden
☐ Use a hose to clean the car or driveway
☐ Use lawn sprinklers
☐ Take baths rather than showers
☐ Use a washing machine for small loads
☐ Use a dishwasher (or use it for small loads)

If so, you are using unnecessary amounts of water. See pp. 92–5, 252, and 257 for ways to use less. The toilet is the main offender. See pp. 92–5 and 228 for alternatives.

Indoor air pollution

Although standards exist for the maximum permitted levels of certain (but by no means all) pollutants in air, these standards vary widely from country to country. Just as important as the level of a contaminate measured, however, is your exposure to this level. The US standards distinguish between average exposures over a year and continuous and even hourly exposures. Radon gas is now recognized to be one of the most hazardous contaminates and is linked with an increased risk of lung cancer. The UK government has recently accepted the recommendation of the National Radiological Protection Board that action should be taken to reduce levels in existing dwellings where the effective dose equivalent exceeds 20 millisieverts (mSv) per annum. New dwellings in areas with high levels of radon are to be built to a design standard of 5 mSv per annum. These doses are equivalent to annual average radon concentration in the air (measured in becquerels per cubic metre) of 400 Bq/m^3 for existing dwellings and 100 Bq/m^3 for new homes – far higher than the maximum levels recommended in the chart below by the World Health Organization (WHO) and the American Society of Heating, Refrigeration and Air-Conditioning Engineers (ASHRAE) (see pp. 100-1 for remedies).

Current recommended maximum contaminant levels *(mg³ unless specified)*

Pollutant	WHO (1)	HSE (2)	ASHRAE (3)
Passive smoking (respirable particulates)	0.15	(–)	(–)
Nitrogen dioxide	0.32	5 0	0.100 (av time 1 year)
Carbon monoxide	30.00	55.0	40.00 (1 hour)
Carbon dioxide	12,000.00	9000.0	4500.000 (continuous)
Formaldehyde	0.12	2.5	0.120 (continuous)
Sulphur dioxide	1.35	5.0	0.080 (1 year)
Ozone	0.15	0.2	0.100
Particulates	(–)	5.0	0.75 (1 year) 0.260 (24 hours)
Asbestos (fibres/m³)	10^5	2×10^5	(–)
Radon (Bq/m³)	70	(–)	37 (1 year)

(–) means figures not available

1 World Health Organization, *Indoor Air Pollutants: Exposure and Health Effects.* Report on WHO meeting, Copenhagen, June 1982.

2 Health and Safety Executive, London, *Occupational Exposure Limits,* 1985, Guidance Note EH 40/85.

3 American Society of Heating, Refrigeration and Air-Conditioning Engineers, *Ventilation for Acceptable Indoor Air Quality*, Standard 62-1981.

Source of chart: *Changes in Building Design, Use and Ventilation* by DP Gregory in a paper given at the 1987 Workshop on Indoor Air Quality at the UK National Society for Clean Air.

Resources

Planning changes to your home or designing a new one can be both exciting and challenging. It can also be confusing and frustrating. If you want your home to be a healthier and more conserving environment, the demands on your time and energy increase. The key to success, however, is to remember that the most important element in this process is *you*, and that it is your needs that must control the process. Start by researching the type of environment you want your home to be. Look closely at the materials you want to use and those you want to avoid. Think about the order of the work needed – perhaps improving your lighting and heating should take priority over, for example, purifying your air and water supply. Design, layout, and colour are also important in making your home feel more supportive and comfortable. Be realistic in assessing your own abilities to undertake the work yourself. If you don't feel completely confident, use a professional architect or interior designer who understands your requirements. Whereas solar-design and energy conservation practices are becoming more widespread, the field of healthy housing is relatively new, except in all but a few countries. Few architects and builders have the necessary specialized knowledge. And solar building, ironically, often uses unhealthy and unconserving materials. So, in view of the added complexity of healthy and ecological criteria, using professional people will greatly simplify the process of building a new house or undertaking large-scale adaptions. Because of the relative newness of many of the areas of concern, you will have to look for architects, designers, and contractors who are willing to work in new ways with different materials. Suppliers of healthy, ecologically sound materials can be found, and professionals with specialist knowledge of working with older traditional materials, and using traditional methods do exist. You may even be lucky enough to find local builders who are prepared to use past skills and take care and delight in their work. The extra time, money, and effort involved in selecting the right team will certainly be repaid with many years of healthy, conserving, and happy living.

LIFE SYSTEMS

Air

Ionizers

London Ionizer Centre
65 Endell Street
London WC2H 9AJ

Mountain Breeze
Peel House
Peel Road
Skelmersdale
Lancs WN8 9PT

Ionizers, humidifiers, dehumidifiers, purifiers

Air Improvement Centre Ltd
23 Denbeigh Street
London SW1V 1HF

Select Air
Becketts Wharf
Lower Teddington Road
Hampton Wick
Kingston
Surrey KT1 4ER

Air filter and ventilation systems

Greenwood Airvac Ventilation
Ltd
PO Box 3
Brookside Industrial Estate
Rustington
Littlehampton
W Sussex BN16 3EH

Passivent
Willan Building Services Ltd
2 Brooklands Road
Sale
Cheshire M33 3SS

Extractor fans

Aidelle
Lancaster Road
High Wycombe
Bucks HP12 3QP

Scent

Neals Yard Remedies
5 Golden Cross Walk
Cornmarket Street
Oxford OX1 3EU

Suffolk Herbs
Sawyers Farm
Little Cornard
Sudbury
Suffolk CO10 0NY

Heating and energy conservation

Practical Alternatives
Victoria House
Bridge Street
Rhayader
Powys LD6 5AG

Low Energy Supply Systems
84 Colston Street
Bristol BS1 5BB

Filsol Ltd
Ponthenri Industrial Estate
Ponthenri
Dyfed SA15 5RA
(solar water heaters)

Water

Filters and purifiers

Brita (UK) Ltd
Ashley Road
Walton on Thames
Surrey KT12 1HG
(filter jugs)

Aquastream
Scandinavian Direct Ltd
Aries House
East Grinstead
W Sussex RH19 3UG
(silver-treated filter)

Express Health Ltd
3rd Floor
344 Kensington High Street
London W14 8NS
(purification systems)

General Ecology (UK) Ltd
Green Dragon House
64-70 High Street
Croydon CR0 9XN

Water savers for cisterns

Cistermiser Ltd
Unit 1 Woodley Park Estate
59-69 Reading Road
Woodley
Reading RG5 3AN

Water softeners

Europlan Water Ltd
Kingsville House
345 Eastern Avenue
Gants Hill
Ilford
Essex IG2 6NJ

Sunbury Softeners Ltd
97 French Street
Sunbury-on-Thames
Middx TW16 5BR

Water meters

Mary Water Metres
37C St Mary's Road
London SE15 2EA

Water sculptures

John Wilkes ARCA
Flow Research Group
Emerson College
Forest Row
Sussex RH18 5JX

Light and colour

Full-spectrum lighting

Truelite SML
Unit 4
Wye Trading Estate
London Road
High Wycombe
Bucks HP11 1LH

UV-emission-free lights

Sungro-Lite Ltd
118 Chatsworth Road
Willesden Green
London NW2 5QU

Energy-saving lights

Marlin Lighting Ltd
Feltham
Middx TW13 6DR

Mole-Richardson
Ladbroke Hall
Barlby Road
London W10 5HH

Wotan Lamps Ltd
1 Gresham Way
Durnsford Road
London SW19 8HU

Robert Lord
Colour for Buildings Ltd
18 Michael Fiords
Forest Row
E Sussex RH18 5BH
(colour consultants)

Sound

New World Cassettes
Paradise Farm
Weshall
Halesworth
Suffolk IP19 8BR

MATERIALS

Stone

Bath & Portland Stone Ltd
Moor Park House
Moor Green
Corsham
Wilts SN13 9SE

CED
728 London Road
West Thurrock
Grays
Essex

Heritage Stone Ltd
Heritage Way
Corby
Northants NN17 1XW

Plaster
(lime plaster, gypsum)

British Gypsum
Westfield
360 Singlewell Road
Gravesend
Kent DA11 7RY

H J Chard
Feeder Road
Bristol
Avon
(lime-based products)

Glass

Pilkington Glass Ltd
Prescot Road
St Helens
Merseyside
(Kappafloat low-emissivity glass)

Hand-made bricks

Bulmer Brick & Tile
Bulmer
Nr Sudbury
Suffolk

Mid-Essex Trading Company
Montrose Road
Dukes Park Industrial Estate
Chelmsford
Essex

Clay and terra-cotta tiles

Fired Earth
Twyford Mill
Oxford Road
Adderbury
Oxon OX17 3HP

E Parkinson
British Railway Sidings
Page Green Road
London N15

Terra-cotta ridge tiles, finials, chimney pots

Red Bank
Measham
Burton-on-Trent
Staffs

Roofing slate

Burlington Slate
Cavendish House
Kirkby-in-Furness
Cumbria LA17 7UN

Penrhyn Quarries Ltd
Bethesda
Nr Bangor
Gwynedd LL57 4YG

"Green Roofs"
Erisco Ltd
Broughton House
Broughton Road
Ipswich
Suffolk IP1 3QS

Timber

For sustainably managed timber and local suppliers consult The Good Wood Guide from:
Friends of the Earth
26-8 Underwood Street
London N1 7JQ

Log Building Manufacturers
Old Rayne
Insch
Aberdeenshire
AB5 6RX

Moss & Co
Dimes Place
104 King Street
London W6

Furniture from recycled timber

Atelier Furniture
Glenholm
George Street
Nailsworth
Glos GL6 0AG

The Parnham Trust
Parnham House
Beaminster
Dorset DT8 3NA

Japanese kit houses

Southern Pine Marketing
Council
101 Wigmore Street
London W1H 9AB

Cedar roof shingles

John Brash (Timber Treatment) Ltd
The Old Shipyard
Gainsborough
Lincs DN21 1NG

Cork tiles

Wicanders GB Ltd
Stoner House
Kilnmead
Crawley
W Sussex RH10 2BG

Recycled building materials

London Architectural Salvage
& Supply Company
Mark Street
off Paul Street
London EC2

Bamboo, cane, rattan, wicker, basketwork

Mail order from Third World sources

OXFAM
272 Banbury Road
Oxford OX2 7DZ

Traidcraft
Kingsway
Gateshead
Tyne & Wear NE11 0NE

Fabrics

Bed and household linen

Celeriac
Whitley Willow Mills
Lepton
Huddersfield HD8 0NH
(cotton blankets)

Limericks
Limerick House
117 Victoria Avenue
Southend-on-Sea
Essex SS2 6EL
(mail order: 100% cotton, linen, flannelette sheets etc, unbleached cotton sheeting, cellular blankets, wool-filled pillows)

Peter Reed Textiles
Springfield Mill
Churchill Way
Lomeshaye
Nelson
Lancs BB9 6BT
(100% cotton bed linen; will supply name of local stockist)

Natural fabrics for home furnishing

Laura Ashley
Braywick Road
Maidenhead
Berks SL6 1DW
(head office)

Liberty & Co
Regent Street
London W1

Naturally dyed fabrics

Contact:
The Crafts Council
12 Waterloo Place
London SW1Y 4AU

David Black
96 Portland Road
London W11 4LN
(Dobag Turkish carpets)

Natural fibre clothes
(by mail order)

Asdir Ltd
PO Box 306
Sharnbrook
Beds MK44 1TQ

Denny Andrews
Clock House Workshop
Coleshill
Nr Swindon
Wilts SN6 7PT

Natural Fibres
2 Springfield Lane
Smeeton Westerby
Leicester LE8 0QW

Traidcraft
Kingsway
Gateshead
Tyne & Wear NE11 0NE

Untreated and vegetable-dyed woollens

Black Sheep
9 Penfold Street
Aylsham
Norfolk NR11 6ET

The Sheep Shop
54 Neal Street
London WC2

Natural paint

Saffron Building & Design Ltd
16 Church Street
Saffron Walden
Essex CB10 1JW
(importer of Auro organic paint from W Germany)

Crown Berger
PO Box 37
Crown House
Hollins Road
Darwen
Lancs BB3 0BG
(ammonia and formaldehyde-free acrylic eggshell)

Pigments

Brodie & Middleton
68 Drury Lane
London WC2B 5SP

SPACES

Living spaces

Back-care furniture

Alternative Sitting
PO Box 42
Abingdon
Oxon OX14 2EH

The Back Shop
24 New Cavendish Street
London W1

The Back Store
330 King Street
London W6 ORR

Balans Chairs
Lecton House
Lake Street
Leighton Buzzard
Beds LU7 8RX

Design for Good Use
21 Lyndhurst Road
London NW3 5NX
(owner is a teacher of the Alexamder Technique)

Back supports and cushions

Putnams
Back Care Systems
133 Goswell Road
Islington
London EC1V 7JT

Floor coverings

Futon Company
82/3 Tottenham Court Road
London W1P 9HD
(Japanese tatami mats)

Quarry tiles
(see Clay and terra-cotta tiles)

Crucial Trading
PO Box 689
London W2 4BX
(sea grass flooring and mats)

Home office

Recycled paper

Conservation Papers
228 London Road
Reading
Berks RG6 1AH

Earthwrite Co-operative
Unit 1b, Carlisle House
Carlisle Street East
Sheffield S4 7QN

Paperback Ltd
8-16 Coronet Street
London N1 6HD

Sleeping spaces

Beds and bedding

Dunlopillo
Pannal
Harrogate
N Yorks HG3 1JL
(aerated latex mattresses for allergy sufferers and Carefoam DX: combustion-modified foam)

Full Moon Futons
20 Bulmershe Road
Reading
Berks RG1 5RJ

Futon Company
82/3 Tottenham Court Road
London W1P 9HD
(futons and furniture, catalogue available)

German Bedding Centre
138 Marylebone Road
London NW1
(100% down quilts plus nontoxic cleaning/re-covering service)

Hope Mill
112 Pollard Street
Manchester
(mattresses and pillows for allergy sufferers)

Woolrest New Zealand Ltd
101 Kew Road
Richmond-upon-Thames
Surrey
TW9 2PN
(100% fleece underblankets)

Kitchen spaces

Cookware and utensils

Habitat Designs Ltd
Hithercroft Road
Wallingford
Oxon OX10 9EU
(head office)

David Mellor
4 Sloane Square
London SW1 8EE
(mail order available)

Bathing spaces

Showers, saunas, whirlpools and deep-soaking tubs

Jacuzzi Whirlpool Bath & Spa Centre
157-8 Sloane Street
London SW1X 9BT

Mantaleda Bathrooms
6-10 Progress Row
Leeming Bar Industrial Estate
North Allerton
N Yorks DL7 9DH
(deep-soaking tubs)

Nordic Saunas Ltd
Fairview Estate
Holland Road
Oxted
Surrey RH8 9BZ

Salamander
PO Box 111
Bromham
Bedford MK43 8TG
(pumped shower massage systems)

Triton PLC
Triton House
Weddington Industrial Estate
Nuneaton
Warwicks CV10 0AG
(mains shower systems)

Compost Toilets
Swedal Leisure (UK) Ltd
PO Box 14
Egham
Surrey TW20 0QP

Health spaces

Marsh Couch
3 Panxworth Road
Hemel Hempstead
Herts HP3 9HQ
(massage tables)

Putnams
Back Care Systems
133 Goswell Road
Islington
London EC1V 7JT
(exercise and yoga mats)

United Health Promotions Ltd
The Old Rectory
Lyneham
Wilts
(UV-transmitting glazing)

Greenspaces

Classical Conservatories
Gardenvase Ltd
Unit 16C
Chalwyn Industrial Estate
St Clements Road
Poole
Dorset BH15 3PE

British Earthworm Technology
Harding Way
St Ives
Cambridge PC17 4WR

Household cleansers

ECOVER products from:
Full Moon
Charlton Court Farm
Mouse Lane
Steyning
W Sussex BN4 3DF
(and selected stores)

The Little Green Shop
8 St George's Place
Brighton BN1 4GB

Henry Flack
PO Box 78
Beckenham
Kent BR3 4BL
(beeswax polish)

Personal cleansers

(natural and cruelty-free products)

Body Shop International
Hawthorn Road
Wick
Littlehampton
W Sussex BN17 7LR

Creighton Products
Water Lane
Storrington
Pulborough
Sussex

Weleda (UK) Ltd
Heanor Road
Ilkeston
Derbyshire DE7 8DR

ORGANIZATIONS
General

Federation of Master Builders
33 John Street
London WC1 2BB

National House Building
Council
58 Portland Place
London W1N 4BU

Royal Institute of British
Architects
66 Portland Place
London W1N 4AP

Building materials

Brick Development
Association Ltd
Woodside House
Winkfield
Windsor
Berks SL4 2DX

The Building Centre
26 Store Street
London WC1

Building Research Establishment
Garston
Watford
Herts WD2 7JR

Cork Industry Federation
c/o Mrs J Iliffe
62 Leavesden Road
Weybridge
Surrey KT13 9BX

Swedish-Finnish Timber
Council
21 Carolgate
Retford
Notts DN22 6PZ

Timber Research & Development
Association
Stocking Lane
Hughenden Valley
High Wycombe
Bucks HP14 4ND

Energy

Association for the
Conservation of Energy
9 Sherlock Mews
London W1M 3RH

British Wind Energy
Association
4 Hamilton Place
London W1V 0BQ

Centre for
Alternative Technology
Llwyngwern Quarry
Machynlleth
Powys SY20 9AZ

Energy Efficiency Service
Department of the Environment
Room 312 Thames House South
Millbank
London SW1P 3QJ

Energy and Environment Unit
Open University
Milton Keynes MK7 6AA

Energy Inform Ltd
5 Charlotte Square
Newcastle Upon Tyne
NE1 4XF

Energy matters

Energy Research Group
Open University
Walton Hall
Milton Keynes MK7 6AA

International Solar
Energy Society UK
Kings College London
Atkins Building South (128)
Campden Hill Road
London W8 7AH

Solar Energy Unit
University College
Newport Road
Cardiff CF2 1TA

Solar Trade Association Ltd
Brackenhurst
Greenham Common South
Newbury
Berks RG15 8HH

Warmer Campaign
83 Mount Ephraim
Tunbridge Wells
Kent TN4 8BS
(energy from waste)

Environmental/ecological

Association for Ecological
Design
PO Box 27
S-233 00
Svedala
Sweden

Campaign for Lead Free Air
(CLEAR)
3 Endsleigh Street
London WC1H 0DD

Centre for Urban Ecology
(BSCUE)
c/o The Birmingham Settlement
318 Summer Lane
Birmingham B19 3RL

Ecology Building Society
18 Station Road
Cross Hills
Keighley
W Yorks BD20 7EH

Friends of the Earth
26-28 Underwood Street
London N1 7UJ

The Green Party
10 Station Parade
Balham High Road
London SW12 9AZ

Greenpeace UK
30-31 Islington Green
London N1 8XE

Henry Doubleday Research
Association
National Centre for Organic
Gardening
Ryton-on-Dunsmore
Coventry CV8 3LG

Institute of Environmental
Health Officers
Chadwick House
48 Rushworth Street
London SE1 0QT

Institute of Water Pollution
Control
Lenson House
Maidstone
Kent ME16 8JH

London Ecology Centre
45 Shelton Street
London WC2H 9HJ

National Society for Clean Air
136 North Street
Brighton BN1 1RG

Permaculture Association
8 Hunters Moon
Dartington
Totnes
Devon TQ9 6JT

Soil Association
86 Coulston Street
Bristol BS1 5BB

SustainAbility Ltd
1 Cambridge Road
London SW13 0PE

Women's Environmental Network
287 City Road
London EC1V 1LA

World Wildlife Fund for Nature
Panda House
Weyside Park
Godalming
Surrey GU7 1XR

Recycling

Aluminium Can Recycling
Association
Suite 308
I-Mex House
52 Blucher Street
Birmingham B1 1QU

The Can Makers
36 Grosvenor Gardens
London SW1W 0ED

Community Furniture Network
Highbank
Halton Street
Hyde
Cheshire SK14 2NY

Glass Manufacturers
Association
19 Portland Place
London W1N 4BH

London Waste Regulatory
Authority
(see below)

Packaging Council
c/o INKPEN
College House
Great Peter Street
London SW1

Recycling Advisory Unit
Warren Spring Laboratory
Department of Trade and
Industry
Gunnels Wood Road
Stevenage
Herts SG1 2BX

Warmer Campaign
(see above)

Environmental medicine

Dr Jean Monro
Allergy and Environmental
Medicine Hospital
Breakspear Hospital
Abbots Langley
Herts WD5 0PU

and

The Lister Hospital
Chelsea Bridge Road
London SW1W 8RH

Health and safety

British Society of Dowsers
Sycamore Cottage
Tamley Lane
Hastingleigh
Ashford
Kent

British Safety Council
62-64 Chancellors Road
London W6 9RS

Consumers' Association
2 Marylebone Road
London NW1 4DX

Consumer Safety Unit
Dept of Trade & Industry
Room 306
10/8 Victoria Street
London SW1H 0NQ

Dulwich Health Society
130 Gypsy Hill
London SE19 1PL
(research into harmful earth
rays)

Health & Safety Executive
Bayards House
1 Chepstow Place
London W2 4TF

Hygeia College of Colour
Therapy
Brook House
Avening
Tetbury
Glos GL8 8NS

London Hazard Centre
3rd Floor, Headland House
308 Grays Inn Road
London WC1X 8DS

London Waste Regulatory
Authority
Hazardous Waste Unit
Room N4B
The County Hall
London SE1 7PB
(will collect small quantities
of asbestos and household
chemicals. Outside London,
check with your local authority)

National Back Pain
Association
31-33 Teddington Park Road
Teddington
Middx TW11 0AB

National Radiological
Protection Board
Chilton
Didcot
Oxon OX11 8RQ
(advice on radon)

Noise Abatement Society
PO Box 8
Bromley
Kent BR2 0UH

Society of Teachers of the
Alexander Technique
10 London House
266 Fulham Road
London SW10 9EL

Union of Construction and
Allied Trades Technicians
177 Abbeville Road
London SW4
(publicized hazards of wood
preservatives)

Magazines

Earth Matters
Friends of the Earth
26-28 Underwood Street
London N1 7JQ

Econews
(see Green Party above)

Here's Health
Victory House
Leicester Place
London WC2H 7NB

Kindred Spirit
PO Box 29
Warminster
Wilts BAS12 9YD

Resurgence
Ford House
Hartland
Bideford
Devon

Architects and consultants

David Austin
Dodges Farm
Plaw Hatch Lane
Sharpthorpe
Sussex RH19 4JG
(Rudolph Steiner
architectural projects)

Peter Ayley
13 Canynge Road
Bristol BS8 3JZ

Busch Masheder Associates
16 Church Street
Saffron Walden
Essex CB10 1JW

Keith Critchlow
Royal College of Art
London SW7
(sacred architecture)

Christopher Day
Pen-Y-Lyn
Brynberian
Crymych
Dyfed SA41 3TL
(healing buildings)

Fielden Clegg Design
1 Canton Place
London Road
Bath BA1 6AA
(sunspace and greenspace
design)

Gaia Associates Ltd
115 Lower Baggot Street
Dublin 2
Eire

Gaia Environments Ltd
Umbrella Studios
12 Trundle Street
London SE1 1QT

Keystone Architects and
Designers Cooperative
52 Gladsmuir Road
London N19 3JU

The Arthur Quarmby
Partnership
83 Fitzwilliam Street
Huddersfield HD1 5LG
(earth-covered buildings)

Baubiologie

Institute of Building Biology
16 Church Street
Saffron Walden
Essex CB10 1JW

Dr Anton Schneider
Institut für Baubiologie und
Ökologie
Holzham 25
D-8201 Neubeuern
W Germany

Glossary/bibliography

Although every effort has been made to define terms and expand initials where they occur for the first time in the text, you might find the following list of acronyms a helpful reminder of some you might not be familiar with.

ac alternating current

ASHRAE American Society of Heating, Refrigeration and Air-conditioning Engineers

ATO Alternative Trading Organization

CFC Chlorofluorocarbons

CHP Combined Heat and Power

dc direct current

DDT Dichlorodiphenyltrichloroethane

EEC European Economic Community

ELF Extremely Low Frequency EMF

EMF Electromagnetic Field

EPA Environmental Protection Agency

HRV Heat Recovery Ventilator

HSE Health and Safety Executive

IPM Integrated Pest Management

IR Infrared

IT Intermediate Technology

MDF Medium Density Fibreboard

Micro-CHP See CHP

NASA National Aeronautics and Space Administration

PCB Polychlorinated Biphenyls

PCP Pentachlorophenol

PET Polyethylene Terephthalate

PP Polypropylene

PVC Polyvinyl Chloride

REM Rapid Eye Movement

RSJ Rolled Steel Joist

SAD Seasonal Affective Disorder

SOC Synthetic Organic Compound

UFFI Urea-Formaldehyde Foam Insulation

UV Ultraviolet

UV -A
UV-B Types of Ultraviolet
UV-C

VDU Visual Display Unit

VOC Volatile Organic Compound

WHO World Health Organization

Further reading

There are many aspects of environmental concern this book has only been able to touch on briefly. If you wish to consult additional sources of information then you might find some of the following titles of interest.

Alexander, Christopher, *A Pattern Language*, Oxford University Press, New York, 1977 and *The Timeless Way of Building*, Oxford University Press, New York, 1979

Baggs, Dr Sydney A, Baggs Joan C, Baggs David W, *Australian Earth-Covered Building*, New South Wales University Press, New South Wales, 1985

Banham, Reyner, *Well-tempered Environment*, Architectural Press, London, 1969

Berglund, Magnus, *Stone, Log and Earth Houses*, The Taunton Press, Connecticut, 1986

Boericke, Art and Shapiro, Barry, *Handmade Houses*, Idea Books International, London, 1975

Brown, R J, *The English Country Cottage*, Hamlyn, London, 1984

Christensen, Karen, *Home Ecology*, Arlington Books, London, 1989

Clegg, Peter and Watkins, Derry, *Sunspaces*, Garden Way Publishing, Vermont, 1987

Clifton-Taylor, Alec, *The Pattern of English Building*, Faber and Faber, London, 1987

Concern Inc (ed), *Drinking Water – A Community Action Guide*, Washington DC, 1986

Conran, Terence, *New House Book*, Conran Octopus, London, 1985

Curwell, S R and March, C G, *Hazardous Building Materials*, Spon, London, 1986

Dadd, Debra Lynn, *Non-toxic & Natural* Jeremy P Tarcher, Los Angeles, 1984

Dadd, Debra Lynn, *The Non-toxic Home* Jeremy P Tarcher, Los Angeles, 1986

Downing, Dr Damien, *Day Light Robbery*, Arrow Books, London, 1988

Dutton, E P, *Interior Design with Feng Shui*, New York, 1983

East West Journal, "Creating the Nontoxic and Natural Home", Brookline MA, March 1987

Elkington, John and Hailes, Julia, *The Green Consumer Guide*, Victor Gollancz, London, 1988

Elkington, John, Burke, Tom, and Hailes, Julia, *Green Pages*, Macdonald Optima, London, 1988

Fitch, James Marston, *American Building – The Environmental Forces That Shape It*, Schocken Books, New York, 1972

Friends of the Earth International, *A Hard Wood Story*, London, 1987

Friends of the Earth UK, *The Good Wood Guide*, London 1988

Foley, Mary Mix, *The American Home*, Harper & Row, New York, 1980

Good, Clint and Dadd, Debra Lynn, *Healthful Houses*, Guaranty Press, Maryland, 1988

Golos, Natalie and Goblitz, Frances Golos, *Coping With Your Allergies*, Simon & Schuster, New York, 1986

Greenfield, Ellen J, *House Dangerous*, Vintage Books, New York, 1987

Grilli, Peter and Levy, Dana, *Furo – The Japanese Bath*, Kodansha International, 1985 (distributed by Harper & Row, New York and London)

Guidoni, Enrico, *Primitive Architecture*, Faber and Faber, London, 1987

Huxley, Anthony, *Green Inheritance*, Collins, London, 1984 and Doubleday, New York, 1984

Hylton, William H, *Build Your Harvest Kitchen*, Rodale Press, Pennsylvania, 1980

Jacobs, Herbert and Katherine, *Building with Frank Lloyd Wright*, Chronical Books, San Francisco, 1978

Kern, Ken, *The Owner Built Home*, Charles Scribner's Sons, New York, 1975

Langdon, Philip, *American Houses*, Stewart, Tabori & Chang, New York, 1987

Lewith, Dr G T and Kenyon, Dr J N, *Clinical Ecology*, Thorsons, Northampton, 1985

Lidell, Lucinda, *The Book of Massage*, Ebury Press, London, 1984 and Simon & Schuster, New York, 1984

Lobell, John, *The Little Green Book*, Shambhala, Colorado, 1981

London Hazard Centre, *Toxic Treatments*, London, 1988

Lovelock, J E, *Gaia – A New Look at Life on Earth*, OUP, Oxford and New York, 1979 and *The Ages of Gaia*, OUP, 1988 (W W Norton & Co, New York)

Mabey, Richard (consult ed), *The Complete New Herbal*, Elm Tree, London, 1988 and as, *The New Age Herbal*, Viking Press, New York, 1988

McKay, W B, *Building Construction*, Vols 1-3, Longmans, 1944 (metric edition 1978)

Mather, Christine, Woods, Sharon, *Santa Fe Style*, Rizzoli, New York, 1986

Morse, Edward S, *Japanese Homes and Their Surroundings*, Charles E Tuttle Co, Vermont, 1986

Myers, Norman (gen ed), *The Gaia Atlas of Planet Management*, Pan Books, London, 1985 and Doubleday, New York, 1984

Murck, Alfreda and Fong, Wen, *The Chinese Garden Court*, The Metropolitan Museum of Art, New York, 1985

National Society for Clean Air, *Indoor Air Quality*, Brighton, UK, 1987

New York State Power Lines Project, *Biological Effects of Power Line Fields*, New York, 1987

Oliver, Paul, *Dwellings – The House across the World*, Phaidon Press, Oxford, 1987

Ott, John, *Health and Light*, Pocket Books, New York, 1982 and *Health, Radiation and You*, Devin-Adair, New York, 1985

Pennick, Nigel, *Earth Harmony*, Century, London, 1987

Porritt, Jonathon, *Seeing Green*, Blackwell, 1984 and *The Coming of the Greens*, Collins, London, 1988

Register, Richard, *Ecocity Berkeley*, North Atlantic Books, California, 1987

Rich, Dr R and Smith, Keith, *Earth Garden Building Book*, Viking O'Neil, Victoria, Australia, 1988

Rousseau, David, Rea, W J, and Enwright, Jean, *Your Home, Your Health, and Well-Being*, Cloudburst Press, Hartley & Marks, Vancouver, 1988

Rybezynski, Witold, *Home*, Penguin, New York, 1986

Samuels, Mike and Bennett, Hal Zina, *Well Body, Well Earth*, Sierra Club Books, San Francisco, 1983

Sardinsky, Robert and Klusmire, Jon, *Resource-Efficient Housing Guide*, Rocky Mountain Institute, Colorado, 1987-88 edition

Schneider, Dr Anton, *Working Papers in Building Biology*, Institute of Building Biology, Essex and *Schriftenreihe "Gesundes Wohnen"*, Institut fur Baubiologie & Oekologie, West Germany, 1986.

Schwartz, W and Schwartz, D, *Breaking Through*, Green Books, Devon, 1987

Seike, Kiyoshi, Masanobu, Kudo, and Engel, David H, *A Japanese Touch For Your Garden*, Kodansha International, 1987 (distributed by Harper and Row, New York and London)

Shelter Publications, *Shelter*, Bolinas, California, 1973 (distributed by Random House, New York and London)

Sivananda Yoga Centre, *The Book of Yoga*, Ebury Press, London 1983 and Simon and Schuster, New York 1983

Smith, Dr Cyril, *Electro-Magnetic Man*, Dent, London, 1989

Smith, Ralph Lee, *Smart House*, GP Publishing, Maryland, 1988

Stanway, Dr Andrew (gen ed), *The Natural Family Doctor*, Century, London, 1987 and Simon and Schuster, New York, 1987

Starr, Gary, *The Solar Electric Home*, Integral Publishing, California, 1987

Stulz, Ronald, Mukerji Kiran, *Appropriate Building Materials*, Intermediate Technology Publications, Dorset, 1988

Taylor, John S, *Commonsense Architecture*, W W Norton, New York, 1983

Todd, Nancy Jack, Todd, John, *Bioshelters, Ocean Arks, City Farming*, Sierra Club Books, San Francisco, 1984

United Nations Environment Programme, *Radiation – Doses, Effects, Risks*, United Nations Publications, 1986

Venolia, Carol, *Healing Environments*, Celestial Arts, California, 1988

Watson, Donald, *Designing and Building a Solar Home*, Garden Way Publishing, Vermont, revised ed 1985

Wells, Malcolm, *Gentle Architecture*, McGraw-Hill, New York, 1982

World Commission on Environment and Development, *Energy 2000*, Zed Books, London and New Jersey, 1987 and *Our Common Future*, Oxford University Press, Oxford and New York, 1987

Yagi, Koji, *A Japanese Touch For Your Home*, Kodansha International, distributed by Harper and Row, New York and London, 1987

Zamm, Alfred V and Gannon, Robert, *Why Your House May Endanger Your Health*, Simon & Schuster, New York, 1980

Index

Acknowledgements

Author's acknowledgements

This book has been a co-operative team effort and has drawn on the knowledge, experience, and skills of many people in many places. First, I would like to give my warm and grateful thanks to all the team at Gaia Books, in particular to Jonathan Hilton for his patient and expert editorial input and project management. My thanks also to Lizzie Boyd for her editorial work, her enthusiasm, and her research, involving the translation of information from many disparate sources; to Bridget Morley and Patrick Nugent who created the brilliant design concepts; to the artists, in particular Keith Banks; and to Shona Wood for researching the stunning photographs. Also many thanks to the rest of the Gaia team: Anna Kruger for her thorough research and resources listing; Eva Webster for her invaluable editorial assistance and index; Helen Banbury for her translations of German source material; and to the production team – Susan Walby, Lesley Gilbert, and Penny Cowdry. And, of course, to Joss, for being, as always, the great inspiration behind us all.

I would also like to give my warmest thanks to all those who brought their knowledge and specialist experience to the project: in particular to Sydney Baggs in Australia and Debra Lynn Dadd in the US for commenting on the manuscript and for their support and encouragement. In England, thanks to Jean Monro, Hartwin Busch, and Michael Schimmelschmidt for reading certain chapters and their helpful advice on environmental medicine and Baubiologie; Jane Fielding for her advice on posture and furniture; and to Arthur Quarmby, David Elliott, John Wilkes, Peter Ayley, Chris Day, and Hildegard Pickels, and to Helmut Zeihe who introduced me to Baubiologie.

Also a special thanks for the contributions and help from many people, including Paul Leech in Ireland; Floyd Stein, Hamish Stewart, Anne Orum, and Ulla Flack in Denmark; Peter Schmid and Jon Kristinsson in the Netherlands; Anton Schneider, Gernot Minke, Alessandro Vasella, Kiran Mukerji, and Rex Raab in West Germany; Chris Butters and Bjorn Berge in Norway; Fritz Fuchs and Erik Asmussen in Sweden; Francis Séguinel, Bernard Arditti, and Jean-Luc Thomas in France; Sim van der Ryn, Carol Venolia, Clint Good, Richard Register, Lawrence Schechter, and Nanci Lewis in the USA.

Publisher's acknowledgements

Gaia Books would like to thank the following individuals and organizations for their help in the production of this book: John Elkington, Malcolm Wells, John Archer, Richard Freudenberger, Heidi Catlin, Cass Pearson, and Wolfgang Mezger. Thanks also to Friends of the Earth, Greenpeace, World Wide Fund for Nature, The Green Party, Centre for Alternative Technology, Wales, London Hazard Centre, Open University, Urban Centre for Alternative Technology, Bristol, National Society for Clean Air, in the UK; New Alchemy Institute, Rocky Mountain Institute, Space Biospheres, Ventures, The Masters Corporation, National Wildlife Federation, Ecology Center, Berkeley, University of Arizona, West Virginia University (HIRAC), in the US; Ecology House, Canada; The Association for Ecological Design, Sweden; Arbeids-gruppen HUS, Norway; CRATerre, France.

Many individuals and companies kindly provided examples of natural materials or goods manufactured from them. In particular, Gaia Books would like to thank the photographic stylist Jean Banks for gathering the reference for the Materials chapter, and also: Townsends, London NW8; Ormonde Oriental Antiques, Ormonde Gallery, London W11; Martin Gibbons, The Palm Centre, London SW8; Civil Engineering Development, Grays, Essex; This and That Gift Shop, London W11; Peter Hillman at the Vauxhall College of Building, London SW3; Royal Botanic Gardens, Kew, Surrey; Stuart Duncan at Moss & Co., London W6; Bath and Portland Stone, Corsham, Wilts; Red Bank, Burton-on-Trent, Staffs., Risky Business Antiques, London NW8; Mid-Essex Trading Company, Chelmsford, Essex; Brodie & Middleton, London WC2; Cornelisen, London WC1; Carolyn Warrender, London SW1; Frank Romany, London NW1; Conran Shop, London; and Karen Rowe, Middle Aston, Oxford, for the African slates.

Illustration credits

Gaia Books would like to thank the following artists for their contributions to this book.

Keith Banks: pp. 182-3; 198-9; 204-5; 214-15; 226-7; 232-3; 238-9; 246-7; 248-9; 252-3. **Dick Bonson:** pp. 47; 59; 132-3; 136-7; 141; 144-5; 196-7. **Chris Forsey:** pp. 29; 52-3; 56-7; 68-9; 123. **Sally Launder:** pp. 24-5; 72-3; 79; 82-3; 90-1; 92-3; 94-5; 100-1; 134; 138; 142; 148; 149; 150; 152; 153; 156; 157; 158; 160; 162; 166; 200-1; 209; 225; 228; 237; 241; 244; 245. **Sheilagh Noble:** pp. 74; 76; 77; 84-5; 88-9; 96-7; 108-9; 110-11; 112-13; 155; 116-17; 118-19; 121; 176-7; 180-1; 184-5; 188-9. **Ann Savage:** pp. 16-17; 21; 28; 32-3; 66; 222; 256.
Drawing p. 41 by David Pearson.

Sources and references

The extremely diverse nature of the information contained in this book and the numerous disciplines outlined, lead the author and researchers to a large number of published sources and references. Gaia Books would like to express its gratitude to all those consulted and, in particular, to those listed below.

p. 25 Diagrams of energy flows through house adapted from Berge, Bjørn, *De Siste Syke Hus*, Universitetsforlaget, Oslo, 1988 **p. 45** Graph adapted from Samuels, Mike; Bennett, Hal Zina, *Well Body, Well Earth*, Sierra Books, San Francisco, 1983 **p. 66** Comfort zone diagram adapted from Olgyay, V, *Design with Climate*, Princeton University Press, 1963 **pp. 94-5** Casa del Agua, Tuscon, Arizona. Water and Energy Demonstration Project of University of Arizona **pp. 109-10** Sound diagram adapted from *Environment and Services*, Mitchell's Building Construction Series, Batsford, London **p. 116** Orientation diagram adapted from Rousseau, *et al, Your Home, Your Health and Well-Being*, Hartley and Marks, Vancouver, 1988 **p. 128** Energy production table, Dr Anton Schneider, Course Unit 8 Institut fur Baubiologie und Oekologie, W. Germany, 1986 **p. 132** Drawing of New York brownstone adapted from Foley, Mary Mix, *The American Home*, Harper & Row, 1980 **p. 145** Making earth bricks drawn from a photograph in Oliver, Paul, *Dwellings – The House Across the World*, Phaidon, 1987 **p. 177** Dragon and tiger illustration adapted from Skinner, Stephen, *The Living Earth Manual of Feng Shui*, Routledge, London, 1982 **p. 177** Chinese house adapted from Rossbach, Sarah, *Feng Shui*, E P Dutton, 1983 **p. 184** Text examples of focal points – from Pennick, Nigel, *Earth Harmony*, Century, 1987 **p. 185** Window seat and balcony redrawn from photographs in Alexander, Christopher, *et al, A Pattern Language*, Oxford University Press, New York, 1977 **p. 201** EMF diagram adapted from Berg, Bjørn, *Syke Hus*, Universitetsforlaget, Oslo, 1983 **p. 228** Compost toilet and p. 244 greenhouse window adapted from Olkowski, Helga and Bill, *et al, The Integral Urban House*, Sierra Books, San Francisco, 1979 **p. 237** Ba Duan Jin diagram adapted from Reid, Howard, *The Way of Harmony*, Unwin Hyman and Fireside, 1988 **p. 246** Solar greenhouse redrawn from photograph in Clegg, Peter and Watkins, Derry, *Sunspaces*, Garden Way Publishing, Vermont, 1987

Photographic credits

(Key: b = bottom; t = top; c = centre; r = right; l = left)

Peter Ayley p. 39 (designer). **Sydney Baggs** p. 30 (architect). **Jean-Paul Bonhommet** pp. 130; 202b. **Bonytt** pp. 6-7 (Gaia Architects); 31tl (Gaia Architects); 38; 67t; 75t; 170bc; 171. **Guy Bouchet** pp. 123; 211. **Karen Bussolini** pp. 70br (T. Whitcomb & Inglehart – architects); 223 (Nelson Denny – designer); 250-1 (Dennis Davey – architect). **Camera Press** pp. 27br; 99; 115t; 187br; 203; 207; 218bl; 219bl; 242b; 251. **Philip Dowell** pp. 134; 138; 142; 150; 153; 163; 167. **Elizabeth Whiting Associates** pp. 43; 62 (Karl Dietrich Buhler – photographer); 63 (Karl Dietrich Buhler); 147 (Tim Street Porter); 155 (Tim Street Porter); 175 (Karl Dietrich Buhler); 179b (Tom Leighton); 187tr (Neil Lorimer); 190; 191 (Tom Leighton); 195 (Tim Street Porter); 210t (Karl Dietrich Buhler); 210bl. (Spike Powell – photographer); 218tl (Spike Powell); 230 (Rodney Hyett – photographer); 231t (Andreas von Einsiedel – photographer) 231bl (Rodney Hyett); 243 (Karl Dietrich Buhler); 255 (Rodney Hyett). **Ezra Stoller** p.23 (photographer; Frank Lloyd Wright – architect) © Esto. **Hutchison Library** pp. 10-11 (Andre Singer – photographer); 14b (J G Fuller – photographer); 18; 19tr; 127 (Michael McIntyre – photographer); 131tl (Sara Ellis – photographer); 146tl; 146bl; 178 (Timothy Beddow – photographer). **Dennis Krukowski** pp. 179tr (Mazurca – designer); 202tr (Mazurca – designer). **Paul Leech** p. 31tr (architect). **Kai Lohman** p. 15 (architect; Maja Kujara – photographer). **Mary Evans Picture Library** p. 42. **Michael Boys Syndication** pp. 187tl; 194bl (John Stefanidis – designer). **Gernot Minke** p. 26; 75br (architect). **Jack Parsons** pp. 2 (Charles Johnson – architect); 34-5 (Charles Johnson – architect); 147 (Charles Johnson – architect); 174bl (Frank Lloyd Wright – architect); 186; front cover (US and UK editions). **David Pearson** pp. 22b; 79; 86-7 (Frank Lloyd Wright – architect). **Robert Perron** pp. 22t; 67b (Swentzel – architect); 70-1tr (Barber/Moore – architects); 71br (C/S Architects); 126bc; 187bl; 218-19tc (Turner Brooks, Architect); 219br (Cooley House); front cover (Australian edition). **Undine Prohl** p. 87 (Antoine Predock – architect). **Arthur Quarmby** p. 61 (architect). **Robert Harding Picture Library** p. 131b (James Green – photographer). **Fritz von der Schulenburg** p. 155b. **Francois Séguinel** p. 27 (architect). **South American Pictures** (Marion and Tony Morrison) pp. 154-5. **Floyd Stein** p. 27bl (Morten Kjaergaard – photographer). **Susan Griggs Agency** p. 254 (Adam Woolfitt – photographer). **John Wilkes** p. 86b (designer). **Henry Wilson** pp. 19br; 39br.

Addendum

Timber

Ecological Trading Company plc
659 Newark Road
Lincoln LN6 8SA

Milland Fine Timber Ltd
The Working Tree
Milland
Nr Liphook
Hants GU30 7JS

Natural Paint

Auro Organic Paints Supplies Ltd
Unit 1, Goldstones Farm
Ashdon
Saffron Walden
Essex CB10 2LZ

Nutshell Natural Paints
Newtake
Staverton
Devon TQ9 6PE

Environmental Paints Ltd
11 Dunscar Industrial Estate
Blackburn Road
Egerton
Bolton BL7 9PQ

Thermal Insulation

Excel Industries Ltd
13 Rassau Industrial Estate
Ebbw Vale
Gwent NP3 5SD
(cellulose fibre)

High-Performance Windows

Swedish Window Company Ltd
Milbank
The Air Field
Earls Colne
Colchester
Essex CO6 2NS

Natural Floor Coverings

Crucial Trading Ltd
77 Westbourne Park Road
London W2 5QH

Sleeping Places

Alphabeds
8 Foscote Mews
London W9 2HH

Electromagnetic Shielding Devices

Natural Theraputics
25 New Road
Spalding
Lincolnshire PE11 1DQ

Furniture

The Chartwell Design Co
Brook Lane
Plaxtol
Nr Sevenoaks
Kent TN15 0QR

Greenspaces

Camphill Water
CVT Ltd
Oaklands Park
Newnham-on-Severn
Gloucestershire GL14 1EF
(reedbed sewage treatment systems)

Chase Organics (GB) Ltd
Coombelands Lane
Addlestone
Weybridge
Surrey KT15 1HY
(organic gardening supplier)

Good Gardener's Association
Arkley Manor
Barnet
Herts

London Ecology Unit
Bedford House
125 Camden High Street
London NW1 7JR

Permaculture Association
(Britain)
P.O. Box 1
Buckfastleigh
Devon TQ11 0LH

Environmental building/ ecological design organizations

Association of Environment
Conscious Building
Windlake House
The Pump Field
Coaley
Gloucestershire GL11 5DX

British Earth Sheltering
Association
The Caer Llan Berm House
Lydart
Nr. Monmouth
Gwent NP5 3JJ

Ecological Design Association
20 High St
Stroud
Gloucestershire GL5 1AS
(Founded by the author)

Scottish Ecological Design
Association
c/o Royal Institute of
Architects in Scotland
15 Rutland Square, Edinburgh
EH1 2BE

(The above organizations hold lists of member architects, designers, builders and craftspeople specializing in environmental and healthy building)

BIBLIOGRAPHY

Bower, John, *The Healthy House*, Stuart Lyle, New York, 1989

Broome, John & Richardson, Brian, *The Self-build Handbook*, Green Books, 1992

Day, Christopher, *Building with the Heart*, Green Books, 1988

Day, Christopher, *Places of the Soul*, Aquarian Press, Thorsons, 1990

Dudley, Nigel & Strickland, Sue, *G is for ecoGarden*, Gaia Books, 1991

Fathy, Hassan, *Natural Energy and Vernacular Architecture*, University of Chicago Press, 1986

Girardet, Herbert, *The Gaia Atlas of Cities*, Gaia Books, 1993

Harper, Peter, *The Natural Garden Book*, Gaia Books, 1994

Hartland, Edward, *Eco-Renovation*, Green Books, 1993

Johnston, Jacklyn & Newton, John, *Building Green*, London Ecology Unit, 1993

Kruger, Anna, *H is for ecoHome*, Gaia Books, 1991

Lynn-Dadd, Debra, *Non-toxic, Natural & Earthwise*, Jeremy Tarcher, Los Angeles, 1990

Vale, Brenda and Robert, *Green Architecture*, Thames & Hudson, 1991

Wells, Malcolm & Wood, Charles, *Building your Natural House*, Van Nostrand, New York, 1993